GEOGRAPHIES OF AN IMPERIAL POWER

JEREMY BLACK

GEOGRAPHIES OF AN IMPERIAL POWER

THE BRITISH WORLD, 1688–1815

INDIANA UNIVERSITY PRESS

This book is a publication of

Indiana University Press
Office of Scholarly Publishing
Herman B Wells Library 350
1320 East 10th Street
Bloomington, Indiana 47405 USA

iupress.indiana.edu

© 2018 by Jeremy Black

All rights reserved

No part of this book may be reproduced or utilized in any form or by any means, electronic or mechanical, including photocopying and recording, or by any information storage and retrieval system, without permission in writing from the publisher.

The paper used in this publication meets the minimum requirements of the American National Standard for Information Sciences—Permanence of Paper for Printed Library Materials, ANSI Z39.48–1992.

Manufactured in the United States of America

Cataloging information is available from the Library of Congress.

ISBN 978-0-253-03157-0 (cloth)
ISBN 978-0-253-03158-7 (paperback)
ISBN 978-0-253-03159-4 (ebook)

1 2 3 4 5   23 22 21 20 19 18

For David Starkey

CONTENTS

Preface   ix
List of Abbreviations   xvii

1. Accumulating Knowledge   1
2. The Spatial Matrix of Military and Political Power   43
3. Territorialization and the Mapping of Authority   77
4. The Public Sphere   99
5. The Debate on Tourism, Religion, and Culture   152
6. Responding to Novelty   169
7. Responding to the Transoceanic World   190
8. Responding to Coal and Commerce   226
9. Geographies in Retrospect   245
10. Conclusions   264

Selected Further Reading   277
Index   281

PREFACE

GEOGRAPHY, POWER, WORLD—each is a potent word. What they represented were closely related in the eighteenth century and should be linked in order to offer an account of key developments then. These developments, moreover, are still relevant today, as modern states struggle to understand the contemporary world and to reconcile ideologies, interests, and geopolitics in a world that is globalized. Similarly, as the eighteenth-century world had to adjust to its own possibilities and tensions of globalization, albeit a very different globalization to that of the twenty-first century. Interest in eighteenth-century Britain in developments across the world reflected an awareness of the globalization of that period, and an attempt to adapt to, and mold, this world was central to the geographical awareness of the period. Furthermore, as both experience and perception, geography in the eighteenth century meant even more than it does today, as subsequent technologies of travel that have helped overcome distance, both in reality and in symbolic terms, notably air travel, were still in the future and an aspect of fantasy. In practice, however, geography and geopolitics remain highly significant today, and there has been a recent revival in writing about geopolitics.[1]

This book will probe power in the eighteenth-century British world, its understanding and use, by looking at the spatial character and understanding of this power and of the related power relationships. To adopt a useful modern distinction, this will be done both for hard power, in the shape of the forces of the state, notably the world's strongest navy, Britain's Royal Navy, and soft power, for example, information and perception as monitored in the coverage of foreign states by the British press. Again, Britain is the key state for soft power as the rapidly growing London press was the most dynamic and most free in the world. It was only rivaled by the Dutch, but, outside Europe, the British press was greater in scope than that of the Dutch. Partly as a result, the London press drew on an unrivaled international network of news that comprehended the trans-Atlantic world as well as Europe.

There are also aspects of spatial power that, while important, are harder to classify. In domestic terms, these range from the enclosure of fields, and associated changes in land use and ownership, to the dynamic character of English cultural influence in the British Isles. The latter was different to the hard power, of military force, that established and maintained the cohesion of the British Isles, but cultural, economic, political, and social influences were all significant in cementing and enhancing this cohesion.

We will be looking at a range of approaches and topics, including strategic culture and the geography of government on the one hand, and the public context of geographical understanding and concerns on the other, with attention devoted in particular to maps and the press. How was the world presented in these, and other, contexts and formats? A society's mental geography is linked to its cultural and national identities. A focus will be on the understanding and use of geographical knowledge and on its transformation into power; and the emphasis will be on the political usage of information, with politics understood in a broad fashion. Of course, contrary to some theoretical reflection, not all knowledge was/is political or can best be presented in that fashion. However, this book will emphasize that dimension, thereby offering a political reading of the Enlightenment period and project, or, rather, projects.

Moreover, the Enlightenment will be presented as dynamic in that the eighteenth-century world, as known by the West, was expanding, indeed continuously and self-consciously expanding, with knowledge in particular being acquired about the Pacific and North America. As discussed in chapter 1, this is the age of Banks, Cook, Mackenzie, Vancouver, and many others. New Western settlements, notably by the British in Australia in

1788, expand the area that was, and is, subject to interest and concern by contemporaries. In Britain, which became the major maritime global economic power in this period, and maintained that position despite a series of challenges, geography offered a form of science as a tool for understanding and controlling the world, and for shaping the processes of discovering and using new information.

The service of the state also encouraged an interest in geography. There was an important and persistent relationship between this interest and the development of ideas about imperial expansion, as with the circle centering on Herman Moll (ca. 1654–1732), a German-born London mapmaker discussed in chapter 1.[2] Alongside the concern with the wider world will come one with the British Isles as a geographical space. This will bring up both the contemporary view of geography and the realities of geographical relationships. Moreover, this issue invites discussion as how best to assess these relationships at this scale and, notably, the questions of agency and assessment at the regional level. Indeed, regionalism, and the problems it poses, emerge as a significant issue in this book and especially so in chapter 9.

The book will be organized as follows, while, at the same time accepting that because not all the book may be read, it will be necessary for each of the chapters to stand on its own. In addition, there is no necessary organization of the chapters in terms of their order or the intellectual approach. That is not simply some postmodernist point that draws attention to the role of the author and/or the reader. Instead, it is appropriate to underline the extent to which there is no necessary sequence in the discussion, while, in addition, different disciplines come into play in the book. To put the standard academic approach first is to emphasize definitions and to stress intellectual strategies. However, to put a cultural studies approach first is to consider how geographical information was used and to appreciate the ad hoc nature of much of the use of geography. In choosing the topics for individual chapters, and in researching and writing the latter, I have deliberately chosen to handle more than one topic per chapter, as well as to range widely in the treatment of the topics. This approach is designed to capture the simultaneity of circumstance and experiences facing contemporaries, which is an element that can be readily lost if a rigid classification and firm typology are adopted in the coverage. The theme of geography and power plays out both internationally and in terms of the domestic resonances of geographical knowledge.

Chapter 1 focuses on the accumulation of knowledge and covers the quest for geographical information as an aspect of statecraft and of public identity, both within the state and with regard to foreign states. Empirical information was a key theme in eighteenth-century thought and can be seen in the eager assimilation of material from explorers. Geography will be assessed as an aspect of the information society, including with reference to maps.

Chapter 2, on the spatial matrix of military power, considers how spatial issues were assessed and addressed in this context and relates this to mapping and to the nature of strategy. For example, there was greater British spatial knowledge of, and concern about, Scotland in response to the Jacobite risings of 1715 and 1745. Moreover, the naval drive for information on currents and coastlines was in large part in order to enhance operational and tactical possibilities. Similarly, the search for longitude was an aspect of understanding the world but also very much of using it for maritime and naval advantage. The close relationship between the military and geography was particularly pronounced in the case of the navy but was also present for the army and notably for the ordnance. Spatial factors were linked to strategy and as a military and a political practice.

Chapter 3, on territorialization and the mapping of authority, assesses frontiers, maps, and the understanding of international power as a territorial concept. The role of maps in asserting authority and demonstrating power will be considered, as will be clashes with other powers' views of territory. Competing cartographies, notably in North America, provided a knowledge-based means to compete, and one that could take note of the latest information. Moreover, the politics of geography was amply displayed.

Chapter 4, on the public sphere, assesses the world as an object of public consideration. It offers a case study of the press and how the press provided accounts of the outside world and thereby shaped it. The sources used, and the volume and character of press comment, are discussed, as are the questions of how far the press was political and how much background information was included. The quality of the understanding offered will also be considered. For Britain, there is also discussion of spatial power with specific reference to landed estates and to London. As a result, the chapter encompasses stately homes and their grounds, enclosure, and the divisions of London life.

Chapter 5, on the debate on tourism, considers a particular issue in the public sphere—namely, the cultural impact of the engagement with the outside world by means of tourism abroad. The social configurations of the politics of geography emerge clearly when considering the debate on tourism. Cosmopolitanism and xenophobia are seen as in tension.

Chapter 6, on responding to novelty, uses, as its point of departure, a case study of the British press response to Russia's rise as an important instance of a new geography of awareness and concern. In this case, great-power issues in Baltic power politics were linked to the perception of a new order in Russia. There was no clear division between domestic and international dimensions in this consideration. More generally, the spatial dimensions of the rethinking of European power relationships will be the focus of this chapter. What did Europe mean, and how did the boundaries of "barbarism" alter? Edward Gibbon's response to the rise of Russia will be contrasted with that of the press. Another branch of novelty will be the alleged "barbarism" in Western Europe seen with the French Revolution. Edmund Burke's views will be presented as offering a new geography of concern and threat, but one that was very much contested.

Chapter 7, on responding to the transoceanic world, covers a range of aspects of this response, notably coverage especially, and of, North America, specifically the War of Independence (1775–83). The creation of a new geography of commitment and concern is a theme. There was also rising interest in India where Britain was a major power after Robert Clive's victory over the Nawab of Bengal at Plassey in 1757 and, more particularly, by the mid-1790s. The need was for mapping and other aspects of knowledge in order to embrace hinterlands and continental interiors, as well as coastal littorals. Knowledge, geographical and other, was both push and pull: push from a greater understanding of the world, and pull in terms of a demand for more information and a need to conceptualize it in terms of existing views. The extent to which India posed issues for British culture, notably religion, will be considered.

Chapter 8 considers the geography of coal, literally a fuel of power, discusses the power brought by its calorific value and use, and assesses the related changes in industrial geography. This approach provides opportunities to assess key elements of the broader economic transformation, notably improvements in communications and the economic significance of consumerism. The geography of Britain was being changed by the construction of turnpikes and canals which compressed time and space and allowed easier movement of fuel (coal), raw materials, manufactured goods, and people. Easier movement allowed more men and women to observe the regional differences in environment, economic activity, and lifestyles within Britain.

Chapter 9 considers later approaches to the historical geography of the period reaching to the present. This chapter offers an understanding of the extent to which no account can be definitive. There is particular discussion of the unit of analysis.

Chapter 10, the conclusions, will focus on the reality of dynamic concerns and of there being no sense of stability. As a result, there was continual demand for news and the accompanying pressure for analysis and classification. Geography both recorded new data, often exotic or surprising, and sought to shape it.[3]

Geography as description and response, prescription and power, reality and perception all emerge in this study. In that, geography is an aspect of the current interest in borders and in their relationship to identity formation. However, there was no clear-cut relationship. Indeed, geographical views and works could respond passively or critically to attempts to adapt and change existing boundaries and to the more general tensions involved in interactions, notably creolization—for example, in "cis-Atlantic history."[4] Looking back, the modern understanding on boundaries can be valuable, but it can involve a somewhat disorienting reading of eighteenth-century geographical assumptions.

More generally, ordering reality, then and now, had a number of contexts and purposes. It was linked to state-building and nationalism in a dynamic fashion but also to alternative narratives and analyses. While Anglocentric and Eurocentric perspectives tended to shape the prevailing perceptions of the world and the geographical and anthropological perspectives used to engage with them, there were both varied and contrary views.

I have benefited from work over many decades on the geographies of the period, notably in cartographic and newspaper forms and with reference to the logics of war and international relations. I would like to thank those who have given me opportunities to develop ideas, including by means of invitations to speak at the British Library, the Guildhall in London, the Institute of Historical Research in London, Harvard, the College of William and Mary, the Royal Albert Memorial Museum in Exeter, the French Revolution seminar at the Sorbonne, the annual conference of the Blue Badge Guides, and in Bampton, Bridport, Bristol, Ciudad Rodrigo, Edinburgh, Liskeard, Malvern, Newton Abbot, Okehampton, Ross-on-Wye, Salamanca, Shrewsbury, Sidmouth, Stockport, Torbay, Totnes, and Trowbridge, and by having the opportunity to write and present a BBC documentary on the Industrial Revolution. I also benefited from teaching a Maps and History course at Exeter. I would like to thank John Weston-Underwood for giving access to his family papers.

This book takes me back to school days when I found Geography A level as rewarding as its History counterpart. I have always been committed to historical geography, a subject currently "owned" by historical geographers. I feel that there is room for a greater contribution by historians.

I would like to thank Jonathan Barry, Tony Claydon, Jean-Paul Forster, John Gascoigne, Perry Gauci, Bill Gibson, Roger Kain, Neil York, and three anonymous readers for their most helpful comments on an earlier draft. They are not responsible for errors or opinions in this book. I have also benefited from advice on particular points from Brian Blouet, Colin Haydon, and Bob Higham. Jennika Baines has proved a most helpful editor, and I thank Carol McGillivray for her help as an exemplary copy editor. The book is dedicated to David Starkey, a friend of many years and a major and thoughtful interpreter of the nation's history.

Notes

1. H. Sicherman, "The Revival of Geopolitics," *Intercollegiate Review* (spring 2002): 16–23.

2. D. Reinhartz, *The Cartographer and the Literati: Herman Moll and His Intellectual Circle* (Lewiston, NY, 1997); D. N. Livingstone and C. W. J. Withers, eds., *Geography and Enlightenment* (Chicago, 1999).

3. B. Schmidt, *Inventing Exoticism: Geography, Globalism, and Europe's Early Modern World* (Philadelphia, 2015).

4. J. Smolenski, *Friends and Strangers: The Making of a Creole Culture in Colonial Pennsylvania* (Philadelphia, 2010).

ABBREVIATIONS

Add	Additional Manuscripts
AE	Paris, Ministère des Relations Extérieures
Ang	Angleterre
BB	Bland Burges papers
BJECS	*British Journal for Eighteenth-Century Studies*
BL	London, British Library, Department of Manuscripts
Bod.	Oxford, Bodleian Library
Cobbett	W. Cobbett, ed., *Cobbett's Parliamentary History of England . . . 1066 to . . . 1803* (36 vols., London, 1806–20)
CP	Correspondance Politique
CRO	County Record Office
Eg	Egerton Manuscripts
Farmington	Farmington, Connecticut, Lewis Walpole Library
FO	Foreign Office papers
NA	London, National Archives
SP	State Papers

GEOGRAPHIES OF AN IMPERIAL POWER

1

Accumulating Knowledge

"THOSE PARTS OF the Earth which were anciently known, have their coasts engraven (as usually) with the shade falling outwards whereas the parts anciently unknown have their coasts shaded inwards." The potential of geography, understood as the depiction of the world, was ably captured at the outset of the century by Edward Wells (1667–1727), an Oxford academic, in the first map of his *New Set of Maps Both of Ancient and Present Geography* (1700). Dedicated to Princess Anne's young son and would-be successor, William, Duke of Gloucester, who, in fact, was to die the following year, these maps had pedagogic purposes. The full title of the book made these purposes clear: "the most remarkable differences of ancient and present geography may be quickly discerned by a bare inspection or comparing of correspondent maps; which seems to be the most natural and easy method to teach young students." Wells revealed contemporary knowledge as far more extensive. Indeed, as he proclaimed with the first map, an entire hemisphere was "unknown to the Ancients" unless America was their Atlantis. Even so, the Ancients could not map it.

The struggle of the Ancients and Moderns was one in which geography, or, rather geographical knowledge, was very much on the side of the latter.[1] Moreover, in an analog of other contemporary Ancient/Modern debates, debates in which Britain took part in a wider discussion,[2] the celebration of the Modern was linked to the culture of Protestant northern Europe and, more particularly, to the new British state, and the related Anglicanization of Classical and Hebraic traditions and forms.[3] The Moderns benefited from the emphasis on incremental fact gathering and thus the constant novelty of the new. As a result, the contrast between Ancient and Modern knowledge became much wider, and more striking, with time.

In consequence, geographical knowledge of the Ancient world was increasingly distinguished with specific texts and maps for those of the Bible and the Classics.[4] This was an important instance of the growing differentiation, or segregation, of geography and history, as also, for example, of the Royal Society and the Society of Antiquaries; although, in each case, it is important not to adopt too schematic an approach. Indeed, at the same time, works continued to place both together, as in Alexander Adam's *A Summary of Geography and History, Both Ancient and Modern* (1794) and William Pinnock's *A Comprehensive Grammar of Modern Geography and History* (1828).

It is necessary not to read back from modern definitions of either history or geography.[5] In the case of geography, it is particularly important not to read back from modern academic concerns and definitions, not least because there were no Regius Professors of Geography at Cambridge and Oxford, as was the case with history. Instead, geography in effect was understood by contemporaries as a gazetteer, in the form of a guide to places and their locations and characters, one that was essentially organized by country. As such, geography offered an account that was at once both mathematical and descriptive, notably topographical. This was very different to later approaches, and the latter can be applied with value, but that does not mean that eighteenth-century accounts were therefore deficient. Indeed, a positive reevaluation has been offered from the perspective of historical geography.[6]

Gazetteers enjoyed both popularity and longevity. *The General Gazetteer or Compendious Geographical Dictionary*, a work of 1762, published in a number of versions by the prolific miscellaneous writer Richard Brookes, appeared in its fifteenth edition in 1819, although in practice, there were more editions if the versions are all included. As an example of the nonspecialized nature of publications, Brookes produced similar works on natural history and medicine and also translated a French history of China. Thomas Salmon defined the field at the start of his *New Geographical and Historical Grammar* (1749): "By Geography is understood a description of the surface of the natural terraqueous globe, consisting of earth and water, which is represented by the artificial globe."[7] By 1770, this work had reached its eleventh edition, and by 1785 its eighteenth. Alongside this description of geography, and what can be garnered from books that include geography in the title, there are the varied uses of geography understood as spatial awareness.

Wells's works were popular and indicated strong contemporary interest in geography. His *Treatise of Ancient and Present Geography, Together with a Set of Maps*, first published in 1701, appeared in a fifth edition in 1738, and his *Historical Geography of the New Testament . . . Adorned with Maps* (1708), in a third in 1718. So also with the response to Wells's older contemporary Herman Moll (ca. 1654–1732). They operated in different milieux, and it was instructive that Wells, a clergyman, was from 1702 a holder of rural rectories. Moreover, he wrote on ecclesiastical and Classical matters, and his geographical studies were aspects of these.[8]

In contrast, Moll was very much a London-based cosmopolitan figure, like indeed George I (r. 1714–27) and George II (r. 1727–60). Moll, Geographer to the King, was a key figure in the spread of geographical information. His activities revealed the entrepreneurial nature of London publishing and also the way in which London served as a clearinghouse for information and as a forcing house for new projects. The scale of the city and its openness to talent were both important in these respects. Thus, Moll knew Dampier, Defoe, Hooke, Locke, and Swift. *The World Described*, a folio atlas by Moll, proved especially significant. At least eight London editions appeared, as well as two Dublin ones.

Moll's geographies were an attempt to define, as well as to satisfy, a field. The lengthy titles provided the prospectus but also placed geography as a complete guide, and one that encompassed history as well as exploration. There were parallels with Wells, notably with his *Atlas Geographus: or, a compleat System of Geography, Ancient and Modern* (1711) as well as with John Senex's *A New General Atlas: Geographical and Historical* (1721). Moll's publications included *A System of Geography, or a New and Accurate Description of the Earth in all its Empires, Kingdoms and States. Illustrated with History and Topography, and Maps of every Country. Fairly Engraven on Copper, according to the latest Discoveries and Corrections, by Herman Moll. To which are added Alphabetical Indexes of the Names, Ancient as well as Modern, of all the Places mentioned in the Work. And a General Index of Remarkable Things* (1701).

As an instance of his engagement with British expansion, specifically in the Caribbean, came a *View of the Coasts, Countries, and Islands within the limits of the South Sea Company. Containing an Account of the Discoveries, Settlements, Progress and Present State; together with the Bays, Ports, Harbours, Rivers, etc.* (1711).[9] Moll's map of the Caribbean marked in Spanish trade routes and thus threw light for the public on the options for British naval action. At the same time, as with other maps, but not always with printed discussion, there was no hint of the role of disease. In practice, disease was greatly to affect British amphibious operations in the Caribbean, notably against Cartagena in 1741. Maps and figures of British operations there—for example, of the base the British temporarily established in Guantánamo Bay in Cuba in 1741—did not make reference to disease.

The role and, therefore, place of geography was made both dynamic and significant by increased knowledge of the world and by an awareness, indeed conviction, that this increase would continue. The third edition of Moll's *The Compleat Geographer* (1709) emphasized its use of recently appearing travelers' accounts and included a list of the travelers used.[10]

Moreover, this process in geography, one of observation, description, dissemination, and comprehension, that went back to the fifteenth century, and in many respects earlier, could serve as a universal prototype for knowledge. Exploration, generally presented as discovery, provided a rhetoric that was applied to the search for truth in the natural world, as well as to personal relationships, the understanding of self, and changes in human society. The last provided a way to locate and explain the past, underlining the relationship between geography and history. Some episodes proved of particular interest—for example, the development and diffusion of the printing press. The incremental nature of enhanced geographical knowledge looked toward the empirical nature of scientific advances (and what was held to be the empirical nature) and vice versa.[11] The theme of new discoveries in the accounts of voyages of exploration encouraged a call for new discoveries on the part of experimental philosophers. These discoveries crucially were, it was argued, to be grasped and validated through experience, and to be disseminated through print.

In short, knowledge was not to be referential to the past, as on the pattern of theology or law, but to be focused on the new. The past therefore was to be understood in part as a sequence of such new knowledge, rather than as a source and site of fundamental authority. In turn, the flood of new information, or, rather, of reports or rumors of information, created pressures for comprehension and analysis.[12] In both description and analysis, measurement was to help inform practice and for geographers and others.[13] Geography, therefore, as a developing, in part new, subject was a potent force of change in eighteenth-century society and one that both benefited from, but also underpinned, a strong respect for "new" empirical knowledge, compared to more traditional forms. This prospectus provided a challenge (implicit or explicit) to the older learned professions. Indeed, geography thereby was an aspect of the development of a "creative class," one primarily located in urban society, scientific culture, and a degree of secularism.[14] Geography can be seen as sharing in many aspects of the development of science, not least in the contingent nature of organizations.[15] Like most British science, geography in Britain was essentially a collaborative, public enterprise.[16] A key element intellectually was the claim to system, and this was seen in titles as in *A New Moral System of Geography, Containing an Account of the Different Nations Ancient and Modern: Their Situation and Climate—their Rise and Fall—their Customs and Manners* (3rd ed., 1792).

Turning to another aspect of modern analysis, knowledge as power, and as a means to power, is a major and established theme in the scholarly literature in a number of subjects, and the power of place is an aspect of this discussion, not least as this power can be seen as "produced."[17] More particularly, geography has been frequently linked by modern scholars to imperialism and to the construction of national identities.[18] At times, these themes can be seriously overworked and can, in part, underplay the extent of autonomy in the pursuit and use of knowledge, in short the specific issues involved in individual branches of knowledge and, linked to this, the extent to which both issues and branches were not just about power. This can be seen, for example, in John Green's *The Construction of Maps and Globes* (1717) which included an appendix "wherein the present state of geography is considered. Being a seasonable enquiry into maps, books of geography and travel. Intermixed with some necessary cautions, helps, and directions for future map-makers, geographers, and travellers." A prolific "Grub Street" writer, Green referred to this inquiry being an "unprecedented" attempt, and continued: "The abuses of negligent and unskillful geographers, had long since made something of this kind necessary, in order to put a stop to those spurious maps and incorrect books which were daily published by them, and continued more and more to involve geography in error and contempt. . . . The best accounts of travellers are not free from errors; their many irreconcilable differences perplex and mislead us, and much of countries remain undiscovered."[19]

Nevertheless, there is also a fundamental basis for the approach focused on knowledge and power. As this book will show, the quest for geographical information was an important and dynamic aspect of statecraft and of public identity, and both in Britain and with reference to foreign states. The meaning, sources, and means of this aspect varied, but one key element was the significance, alongside systematization, of empiricism in eighteenth-century thought. This is a parallel with the position as far as the accumulation, understanding, and use of historical knowledge were concerned. Knowledge was there to be acquired but not by means of magic or prophetical means. The pursuit of knowledge through rational exploration, and its subsequent assimilation and dissemination, proved particularly important in the Western world. Moreover, this work was to be publicly presented and, thus, to be verified or queried in the public sphere. For Edmund Burke in 1777, it appeared appropriate to use the map as the image of knowledge, one appropriate for both historical and geographical knowledge. He wrote to William Robertson about the latter's just-published *History of America*: "now the Great Map of Mankind is unrolled at once; and there is no state or gradation of barbarism, and no mode of refinement which we have not at the same instant under our view. The very different civility of Europe and China; the barbarism of Persia and Abyssinia. The erratic manners of Tartary and of Arabia. The savage state of North America and of New Zealand."[20]

Such information, and notably for Western powers, was not that of a static world, but, rather, of one that was changing rapidly and significantly, and was seen in this light by contemporaries. This change was not least due to interaction with the environment,[21] but also to the information produced by exploration and the assumptions confirmed by it.

EXPLORATION

It may appear obvious to make a move now to discuss exploration during the century, but there are some issues with such a move. Focusing on exploration tends to become a positivist, progressive account of activity and results, one that appears a quasi-immutable process of improvement, as well as being an account of white men. Moreover, precisely because there is a lot of information on the topic, it is easy to devote much space to it, and, in contrast, to devote less to other aspects of the accumulation of knowledge, or to make exploration serve to establish a general model or rule for the latter. As far as geographical information was concerned, exploration was certainly newsworthy, but it was not the sole source of such information.

There was also the question of what exploration excited attention. Dramatic voyages were favored by the public (not sailors), not least because, aside from the drama, fortitude, and heroism involved, and the ease with which voyages could be linked and compared in order to provide a narrative of progress, much of the news was readily present in London, and especially because so many of the voyages were of naval vessels. In contrast, there was a marked tendency to underplay the significance of exploration across the land frontiers of British colonies.

The nature of the British world was such that it was best placed to serve as the basis for exploration. This was a reflection of Britain's oceanic position on the edge of Europe, its extensive maritime activity, its unprecedented naval strength, and the location and extent of Britain's colonies already at the start of the eighteenth century. The record of exploration by other states, particularly France, Spain, the Netherlands, Russia, and Portugal, indicated that Britain was very much not alone in these factors or consequences. Nevertheless, there was a particular energy to British exploration, one that was encouraged by a governmental position that was both supportive and relatively permissive. The latter was notably so as a consequence of partly successful moves against the monopolistic commercial position of the chartered companies after the "Glorious Revolution" of 1688–89, especially the Royal African Company. These companies had been associated with the government of James II and with earlier royal privileges.[22]

The years of and after the Glorious Revolution were in effect the beginning of the eighteenth century. Similarly, Britain, which, after William III's conquest of Ireland in 1690–92, did not have land borders in Europe, was the leading naval power from the early 1690s when it replaced France, the navy of which was heavily defeated by an Anglo-Dutch fleet at Barfleur–La Hougue in 1692. The role of contingent factors was repeatedly significant and notably success in war. This did not only involve victories over France and Spain, important as they were. There were also the contingent consequences of such victories. They included the decisions made by governments, British and foreign, notably the French focus on the army in the 1690s and 1700s rather than on rebuilding the navy,[23] as well as the ability of the British state to suppress and block foreign-supported opposition in the British Isles and, therefore, to ensure that the maritime resources of the latter were united in support of one goal. Naval victory over the French meant that the latter could not sustain intervention in Ireland, a situation that was to recur in the late 1790s and, even more, early 1800s.

The years after the Glorious Revolution were also important to British exploration. At the close of the seventeenth century and in the early years of the eighteenth, both the astronomer Edmund Halley and the explorer William Dampier published their findings, and each enjoyed much attention. Dampier published a highly successful *New Voyage Round the World* (1697), *A Discourse of Winds* (1699), and *Voyage to New Holland* [Australia] *in the Year 1699* (two parts: 1703, 1709).[24] Navigational information was offered alongside more specific material on particular locations. Halley produced his chart of trade winds in 1689, the first scientific astronomical tables in 1693, and his "General Chart" of compass variations in 1701. Each was a significant tool for navigators and was seen in that light, and their combined importance was even more valuable. Halley's "General Chart," a chart of terrestrial magnetism, was designed to enable navigators to establish the variation between true north and magnetic north (to which compass needles point), and thus to calculate longitude accurately. This was a major aid to navigation. Halley had employed logbooks to offer a scientific account of the atmosphere's global circulation in a piece published in the *Translations of the Royal Society* in 1686.[25]

The years 1698–1701 were a time of peace for Britain between the Nine Years' War, which ended in 1697, and the War of Spanish Succession, in which Britain joined in 1702, and such years offered particular opportunities. However, the process of investigation and exposition continued in wartime. Indeed, that was a key aspect of Britain's maritime power. More generally, this process continued as far as the linkage of the maritime world with astronomy was concerned. Halley's interest in the transit of Venus looked toward James Cook's first voyage to the Pacific in 1769–71 and the attempt then to provide observations from around the world.

There was also interest in marine currents and an attempt to present it to the general public, making craft knowledge relevant for nonspecialists. Thus, in 1768, Benjamin Franklin published a chart showing the Gulf Stream, knowledge of which he had gained from seamen. An understanding of the Gulf Stream was commercially as well as intellectually significant, notably in terms of assisting navigation across the North Atlantic.

In Britain, as elsewhere in oceanic Europe, there was an accretional character to exploration, as knowledge of particular locations or conditions—for example, of ocean currents—then served as an aid and prompt to fresh exploration, consideration, and speculation. Moreover, as with new historical knowledge, the culture of print and its relationship with disseminating scientific work encouraged this process. This was especially so due to the significance of information on, and for, navigation, whether scientific or specific. The British readily disseminated knowledge of their own explorations and were also able to draw on what was available in print about exploration by other Western powers. In contrast, there was scant public knowledge in Russia of the distant voyages in the North Pacific of Vitus Bering, after whom the Bering Strait is named. In addition, the diffusion of news about Spanish exploration was limited, while most Catholic missionaries in the Americas did not provide accounts that were published.

Investigation and exposition occurred on a variety of scales. In the eighteenth century, travel narratives, a well-established genre, became increasingly common. These narratives were an aspect of the more general use of itineraries as a way to express the overcoming, experience, and recording of distance. In many respects, itineraries were more potent than maps as an account of experience, and they were certainly better suited to the religious and psychological dimensions of travel, that of the individual soul or spirit, and, subsequently, the particular sensibility. As Daniel Defoe, Laurence Sterne, Tobias Smollett, and others demonstrated, the form was capable of many literary uses. Their use of itineraries underlined satirical purposes, and these could be deployed for both real and fantastic journeys. Most of these were in real time, but it was also possible to offer travel narratives located in the past or the future.

Moreover, itineraries easily lent themselves to the exploratory narrative of guidebooks. As Defoe showed for Britain, in his readily-accessible *A Tour through the Whole Island of Great Britain* (1724–26), this geography provided the opportunity not only for the inherent interest of travel but also for offering an exemplary, politicized account, one that was very much to a purpose. The publication of the *Tour* reflected widespread interest in the nature of the country and was related to the translation by Edmund Gibson of William Camden's *Britannia* (1586) that was published in two editions in 1695 and 1722. Defoe noted the dynamism of cities, writing: "The fate of things gives a new face to things, produces changes in low life, and innumerable incidents; plants and supplants families, raises and sinks towns, removes manufactures and trades; great towns decay and small towns rise; new towns, new palaces, new seats are built every day; great rivers and good harbours dry up, and grow useless; again new ports are opened, brooks are made rivers, small rivers navigable, ports and harbours are made where none were before, and the like."[26] That Defoe's work attained classic status, and was clearly intended to do so, is instructive. He indicated a need to focus on Britain at a time when the elite was concentrating on the Grand Tour abroad and was more able to do so because Britain was at peace. There was a parallel with the emphasis on English culture in the 1720s, notably with the success of John Gay's vernacular *The Beggar's Opera* (1728), which was a deliberate counterpoint to the Italian opera that was then popular in the circles of the royal court and the social elite. Furthermore, Defoe anticipated the interest in travel within Britain that was to be seen in the last three decades of the century, although writers and painters then very much focused on landscape, and not human society, and lacked Defoe's commitment to the developing economy and to the vitality of trade and towns; he was particularly impressed by Liverpool, which was also praised in the anonymous *Tour through Ireland*.[27]

A simplistic account would suggest that during the eighteenth century, itineraries were replaced by maps, with a comparable moving of an understanding of reality from an unpredictable to a more predictable template, or, at least, from one type of predictability to another. As with the Newtonian view of matter and the cosmos, this template left less direct role for divine intervention. And yet, such an interpretation underplays the continued potency of religious and spiritual understandings of experience, quests, and places. In addition, the role of the narrator in itineraries, more especially travel narratives, captured the extent to which there was a crossover between fact and fiction, as well as observation and comment.[28] This approach proved especially attractive.

So also with letters, which were frequently a version of itineraries as they recorded journeys: there was no need to write letters if people had face-to-face contact, which was the normal form of interaction. Letters recorded the journeys of real people,[29] directly or indirectly, as well as of their fictional counterparts (to a degree far greater than in modern novels), and each category offered geographies that helped shape itineraries and responses for others. Letters, like itineraries, both fictional and factual, provided opportunities for the psychological response that narrative offered.

For Britain, an important group of travel narratives were very much located in a distant maritime world. Significant ones included, and this selection is for a brief period and for one particular area, Lionel Wafer's *A New Voyage and Description of the Isthmus of Panama* (1699), William Funnell's *A Voyage Round the World* (1707), Edward Cooke's *A Voyage to the South Sea and Round the World* (1712), and Woodes Rogers's *A Cruising Voyage Round the World* (1712). The context of most narratives was autobiographical, but an overlapping of fact and fiction was seen in the sources used in Defoe's novel *Robinson Crusoe* (1719), which was based on the marooning of the privateer Alexander Selkirk on the island of Juan Fernández in 1704–9, and in Jonathan Swift's imaginative fantasy novel *Gulliver's Travels* (1726) in which Gulliver traveled to Lilliput, which was located in the South Pacific. Fictional histories were also in evidence, including fictitious genealogies that testified to the significance of respectability and continuity.[30] Travel narratives helped clarify routes to the Pacific and, linked with this, to establish a sense of the Pacific as an ocean open to profitable British penetration and one that could be seized from the real and imagined grasp of Spain, although it is important not to adopt too instrumental an account.

The travel narratives provided a sense of the proximity of the Pacific. They focused on the period of the narrator in distant waters, and not that of the long and tedious time taken to get there and the difficulties of the voyage. As a consequence, a misleading sense of the ease of access was created, rather like the topological mapping in the classic London Underground map, devised in 1931 by Harry Beck and used from 1933, a map that consistently and deliberately underrates the distance between the inner city and the outer suburbs. To a great extent, the Pacific was "imaginatively grasped" before a presence there was practical, and certainly a presence that was more than transient and that was readily reportable. Yet, the earlier history of exploration showed that this process had more generally been the case. Moreover, this foreshortening of the experience of the wider world fulfilled the wishes and interest of the readers, as well as satisfying the need to supplement existing accounts.

To a degree, there was, moreover, a depoliticization of the space involved, as the need for Britain to consider Spanish responses was downplayed. This process was also seen with exploration elsewhere. The Spanish government sought to block attempts to enter the Pacific from around South America. In 1749, it objected to British plans for an expedition to the Pacific and the establishment of a base on the Falkland Islands that would support further voyages in southern latitudes. An unwillingness to anger Spain at a time of improved Anglo-Spanish relations after the Anglo-Spanish War of Jenkins' Ear (1739–48) and the broader War of the Austrian Succession with France (for Britain, 1743–48) ensured a change in policy. The openness on show on the part of the British government when George Anson entered the Pacific during the period of Anglo-Spanish conflict, and achieved naval success that was made highly conspicuous, was no longer present in 1749. As was usual during peacetime, diplomacy trumped naval power, and this shaped the space for exploration as for other activity. The chronology of "new geography" was therefore shaped by international politics.

The competition between different geographical axes, and involving the competing interest groups involved, were shown in the contemporary British interest in discovering a navigable Northwest Passage to the Pacific around the north of North America. Such a route would link to the British presence already in the region and would not face the issues of distance (and therefore time and supplies) and of Spanish opposition involved in sailing to the Pacific round South America. The North Pacific was unknown to the British and therefore an area of apparent opportunity. Several efforts were made from the already-existing British bases on Hudson Bay, a major center of the fur trade and one that ensured a local presence that could support expeditions. Such incrementalism was important to most exploration. In 1741, the Admiralty sent the *Discovery* and the *Furnace* to Hudson Bay under Christopher Middleton. The following year, he sailed farther north along the west coast of the bay than any previous European explorer, which was always the basis for comparison and for exploration more generally. However, Middleton could not find the entrance to a passage, and the naming of Repulse Bay testified to his frustration. In 1746–47, William Moor, who was dispatched by the Northwest Committee organized by Arthur Dobbs, a critic of the Hudson's Bay Company, also failed. One lasting consequence was a scattering of the names of British ministers along the coasts of the bay, as with Chesterfield Inlet and Wager Bay after a secretary of state and a first lord of the Admiralty, respectively. In 1748, the Hudson's Bay Company commissioned a map of North America. This map, however, contained many errors. It showed Compaignes Land, a nonexistent island in the North Pacific that stretched from near Kamchatka to near North America, depicted California as an island, and presented America as joined to Greenland. The lack of knowledge of the North Pacific was particularly apparent, in part because the news of Russian exploration was not adequately disseminated. This lack was to have changed greatly by the end of the century, in large part due to British explorers, notably Cook and Vancouver.

The naval situation as far as both Atlantic and Pacific were concerned did not alter until after the Seven Years' War (1756–63). The crushing of the French navy in late 1759 in European waters, with separate fleets heavily defeated by the British at Lagos (Portugal, not Nigeria) and Quiberon Bay (France), created new opportunities for British maritime activity. This was the case both in these waters and further afield. The opportunities were underlined by bad postwar relations with France and Spain. The capture of Manila from Spain by an expedition sent from the British base at Madras (Chennai) in 1762 increased British interest in the Pacific and offered a new point of access to it. Although Manila was returned under the subsequent peace treaty, the widespread sense that British maritime dominance should be used became an important factor in encouraging exploration of the Pacific and in probing how it could be used.

Geography was very much an aspect of the pursuit and use of power. Exploration owed something to scientific interest but was also driven by the widespread sense that the British maritime position would be challenged in the future and that any such war would focus even more on colonial and maritime rivalry than the Seven Years' War had done. This was indeed to be the case as French participation in 1778–83 (and Spanish in 1779–83) in the War of the American Independence showed.

There was also strong public interest in Pacific exploration after the Seven Years' War. Explorers were the celebrities of their day. This interest encouraged, and was sustained by, publications, such as Alexander Dalrymple's *Account of the Discoveries Made in the South Pacific Ocean* (1767) and, more successfully, his *Historical Collection of the Several Voyages in the South Pacific Ocean* (1770–71).[31] A copy of the first was taken on Cook's first voyage. In 1787, Jacob Edwards, a Norwich bookseller, described "Travels" as among the contents of his circulating library.[32]

The pace of exploration increased in the 1760s with peace accompanied by continued international competition between Britain and both France and Spain and by periodic war panics, notably in 1770. Entering the Pacific in 1767, Samuel Wallis "discovered" many Pacific islands, including Tahiti, which he called King George the Third's Island. Philip Carteret, another naval officer, "discovered" and named many other islands in 1767 including Pitcairn. In 1781, George III also had Uranus, the new planet discovered by William Herschel, initially named after him as Georgium Sidus, a reference to Virgil's *Georgics* that claimed immortality for George: exploration and naming took many forms.

Fame, however, was to be more the fate of James Cook, not least because he sailed to the Pacific on three occasions, but also because, with his death, he fulfilled the desire for a new heroism. This desire was a characteristic of British activity. In 1769, Cook was sent to Tahiti on the *Endeavour* in order to observe Venus's transit across the sun. This was part of a collaborative international observation, but Cook also had secret orders to search for the Southern Continent that had been believed since Greek speculations in Antiquity to balance Eurasia. He conducted the first circuit and charting of New Zealand and the charting of the east coast of Australia. Here, in 1770, Cook landed in Botany Bay, the first European to land on the east coast, and claimed the territory for George III. Thus, knowledge and expansion were linked. George had made a large personal contribution of £4,000 to the Royal Society toward the costs of this voyage.[33] Following up earlier Portuguese and Dutch exploration of western and northern Australia, Cook had both limited the possible scope of the Southern Continent, by showing that it did not extend farther eastwards and had advanced British territorial interests. On his return to London, George granted Cook an hour-long audience, and Cook presented the king with a hei-tiki, or Maori stone embodying the spirits of ancestors, that he had been given in New Zealand in 1769.

On his second voyage, in 1772–75, Cook's repeated efforts to find the "Southern Continent," efforts that included the first passage of the Antarctic Circle, failed. However, knowledge of the southern Pacific and southern Atlantic was greatly increased. On his third voyage (1776–79), Cook sailed, in 1778, to a new farthest north—70°44′ N at Icy Cape, Alaska—and proved that pack ice blocked any possible Northwest Passage, while he "discovered" Christmas Island and Hawai'i, being killed in a skirmish on the latter.[34] This captured the need that contemporaries had for honorable death, a need more generally seen in battle, as with James Wolfe (1759), Horatio Nelson (1805), and John Moore (1809), each of which were deaths overseas. These and other deaths provided a new pantheon of bravery, providentialism, imperial destiny, and Christian self-sacrifice, one that superseded that from Antiquity. Other than for those trained in the Classics, heroes from Antiquity no longer appeared so relevant. Engravings took these new exemplars into many households.

Cook reflected the extent to which it was possible to acquire important additional information without any transformation in the relevant technology. This illustrated the accretional capability of what might be seen as a technological ancien régime. Such a terminology is ahistorical in that it employs terms not used at the time but also captures the extent to which it is necessary to avoid any perception that appreciable change only occurs as a consequence of a revolutionary transformation in capabilities. Instead, it was the capacity of traditional society to adapt that proved impressive. Looked at differently, Britain, from 1688, represented such a revolutionary transformation, albeit a very different one to France from 1789.

Attracting much contemporary attention, and making geography, at least new geography, news, oceanic voyages were recounted in a number of media. These included the pocket globes produced by John Newton which presented information in a very different and easier-to-handle format to that of the large library globes that his firm also produced. There was also extensive reporting in the press, as well as praise from Edward Gibbon in his great history: "The five great voyages, successively undertaken by the command of his present Majesty, were inspired by the pure and generous love of science and of mankind." Such praise fixed Cook in an account of the history of Western civilization, one in which modern Britain played a central role. Wesley thought some of Cook's descriptions "things absolutely incredible."[35]

Cook's reputation was not restricted to Britain. His voyages attracted interest across the West, and this interest was highly sympathetic. There was an understanding of exploration as a civilizational process. Georg Forster, who took part in Cook's second voyage, published an account, *Reise um die Welt* (1778), that made Forster a celebrity in Germany, and, as a result, he had an audience with Emperor Joseph II in 1784.[36]

Presented as heroic,[37] Cook's voyages owed much to technical developments, especially John Harrison's invention of an accurate chronometer to measure longitude (itself a heroic story), as well as to an ability to keep crews and ships at sea for long periods[38] and to government support. The formidable task of searching for a reliable and predictable method for determining longitude at sea revealed the capacity to organize scientific inquiry. Parliament established a Board of Longitude in 1714 and offered a substantial reward, but the problem long proved intractable. However, in 1761–62, Harrison, a clockmaker, devised a chronometer, the timekeeping of which was so accurate that on a return journey from Jamaica, the ship carrying it found its distance run erred by only eighteen miles on the anticipated position. Such calculations depended on the precise measurement of local time in relation to the time at the Greenwich Meridian, a fixed location in Britain. Harrison had much trouble in getting his chronometers accepted because the Royal Society believed in astronomical tables as the solution to the problems of longitude. Thus, as so often with information and its assessment, there was a tension over intellectual authority and, notably, a contrast between experience and its understanding. There were also improvements in the methods for finding latitude more precisely.

At one level, there was a persistent drive for information from the Seven Years' War (1756–63) on. For example, in 1764–81, George Gauld charted the waters of the Gulf of Mexico in response to instructions from the Admiralty. It wished to consolidate the recent acquisition of Florida from Spain as part of the peace settlement at the end of the Seven Years' War: at that stage,

Florida extended on the Gulf Coast as far as the Mississippi. It was therefore necessary to understand all the inlets on the coasts of what are now Florida, Alabama, Mississippi, and eastern Louisiana. The charting was important also to Caribbean trade and to an appreciation of the interplay of currents, tides, winds, islands, and navigable routes. The Admiralty also provided two ships to Constantine Phipps in his failed attempt in 1773 to sail toward the North Pole in search of a more direct passage from Britain to the East Indies. This attempt, made in peacetime when there were ships free for use, disproved the thesis that the sea did not freeze because of its salt content.

However, at ministerial levels, there was also a picture of significant, but episodic, interest.[39] In particular, the Pacific was not consistently at the center of government concern. Instead, naval issues focused on capability in "known waters," especially in Europe, the Caribbean, and off India. It is not easy to map government interest, but there are criteria that can be offered, notably the location of warships. The resulting pattern can be variously interpreted. While the number of warships in the Indian and, even more, Pacific Oceans remained relatively small, it still became a factor from the 1750s. Looked at differently, the Royal Navy came to play a regional role, especially from 1756–57, taking over the reliance simply on the Bombay Marine, which was the navy of the East India Company. This more direct commitment represented a major change for British power and arose from the stronger governmental engagement with India and from the conflicts that stemmed from confrontation with France. The struggle with France entailed wide-ranging operations, as with the interest in the Red Sea in response to the French invasion of Egypt in 1798.

British voyages to the Pacific benefited from the better technology for long-distance navigation. In particular, the number of bigger ships increased, while there were significant improvements in navigation, hull design, and rigging. Changes in sail plans made ships easier to handle, enhanced their performance, and required less manpower. The copper sheathing of ships' wooden bottoms, in order to resist burrowing worms, which were a particular problem in tropical waters, improved both durability and speed. Such changes were a reminder of the significance of incremental developments within a fixed technology, that of wooden ships driven by wind power. Moreover, the information available for voyages increased greatly despite there being a largely fixed technology with the exception of the chronometer. This technology was also seen in methods used, notably for assessing the depth of water.

Thanks to frequent voyages, particularly, but not only, to the Pacific, information was accumulated and previous reports tested. This accumulation was of direct value. Arthur Phillip used Cook's chart when he sailed into Botany Bay in Australia in 1788, an episode, the first Western settlement in Australia, to be acted out in 1791 in "a pantomime exhibition" in Birmingham's New Street theater. By then, despite important activity by French and Spanish voyagers in the Pacific, it was the British who were clearly the most active. This position became more apparent as a result of the dislocation of the French overseas empire after the two powers went to war in 1793. The Spanish, Dutch, and Portuguese empires were to follow into wartime dislocation and loss.

Already, however, the British were in the ascendant. In the waters of the Southwest Pacific, they added to their empire, Lord Howe Island (1788), the Chatham Islands (1791), and Pitt Island (1791). This process was linked to the accumulation of information and to the presentation of an imperial narrative. Captain William Bligh made intelligible charts of Fiji, the Banks group, and Aitutaki in the Cooks, and also provided a narrative of his long voyage in an open boat after many of the crew of the *Bounty* mutinied. This was a narrative of Pacific drama, endurance, and navigation that greatly engaged public interest. Captain Lever "discovered" the Kermadecs and Penrhyn Island, and Captains Gilbert and Marshall the islands that still bear their names. Indeed, the naming of many Pacific islands reflected the voyages of these years. The voyage home of the crew of the shipwrecked *Sirius* in 1791 on a Dutch merchantman led to the publication in 1794 of a nautical chart of Port Hunter (now known as Balanawang) on Duke of York Island, located between New Britain and New Ireland. The chart was accompanied by a view of the ship firing on native canoes, which was the version of a watercolor painted by midshipman George Raper.

Commander George Vancouver was the key figure in the 1790s. Sent to the Pacific in 1791 in order to carry out survey work and to secure Britain's possession of the Nootka Sound coastline on what is now Vancouver Island in the face of Spanish claims and expansionism that had nearly led to war in 1790, Vancouver explored part of the coast of New Zealand, "discovered" the Chatham Islands, and charted the Snares, as well as thoroughly surveying the Pacific coastline of modern Canada and Alaska in 1792–94, both confirming and overturning some of Cook's results. His expedition brought a range of information, from confirmation that there was no water passage between the Atlantic and the Pacific south of the Arctic, to items of Native American life as well as a large number of plants. Vancouver used dead reckoning, lunar observation, and chronometers to calculate longitudes.[40]

In a process of cumulative knowledge, expeditions continued to reiterate or qualify data gained from earlier explorations, brought information that aided navigation, and, thereby, directly made the empire more efficient. George Bass and Mathew Flinders circumnavigated Tasmania in 1798–99, establishing that it was an island, and therefore that ships sailing to Sydney from around the Cape of Good Hope (in modern South Africa) did not need to round Tasmania, but, instead, could go through Bass Strait. This was a shortening of the possible distance that was a contrast to the situation of sailing round Sri Lanka if en route to, or from, the Bay of Bengal. The route round the Cape of Good Hope was easier than that via Cape Horn at the southern end of South America.

There was also considerable public interest in overland expeditions. This was especially so of James Bruce's "discovery" of the source of the Blue Nile in 1770, Alexander Mackenzie's overland crossing of North America from the Atlantic to the Pacific in 1792–93, and Mungo Park's "discovery" of the direction of the River Niger in 1796. As with aspects of exploration elsewhere, it is unhelpful to think of the century as a unit, as it was its latter decades that were crucial and different, in the ambition and intensity of activity, to the early decades. This contrast can also be seen with public attention.

Although foreign sources of information on Africa were also used by the press,[41] Bruce's tour of Ethiopia in 1768–73 helped to increase British interest in the interior of Africa as a whole. His *Travels into Abyssinia* (1790) were excerpted in newspapers that year, for example in *Ayre's Sunday London Gazette* and in the *Sheffield Advertiser* of May 7. A landowner, Bruce was fired by intellectual curiosity, rather than by hope for economic advantage. He had already shown great interest in the non-European world, including consideration of a career in India, studying Arabic, acting as British consul at Algiers, and traveling in North Africa, Syria, and Egypt.

These activities serve as a reminder of the range of interest and commitment that was possible. Bruce wanted to gain fame by discovering the source of the River Nile. Plunged into the complex and violent world of Ethiopian politics, he was able to reach the springs of the Blue Nile in 1770. Despite his claims, however, Bruce had not "discovered" the source of the Nile, a totemic goal for exploration, but rather "rediscovered" that of its largest tributary, the Blue Nile. This source had been reached by the Portuguese Jesuit Pedro Páez in 1618, a fact Bruce challenged unreasonably. Fame was a key motivator and one that was very directly communicated in print.

The very process of contention about Bruce's "discoveries," which was much reported, helped increase interest in African exploration, contributing to an identity that was different to that of Pacific exploration. William Browne, another traveler with independent means, was encouraged by reading Bruce and the first report of the African Association. Having studied Arabic in Egypt, he was thwarted in his goal of visiting Ethiopia, instead traveling to Darfur (in the west of modern Sudan), becoming, in 1793, the first European to do so. Like others intending to impress contemporaries and posterity, Browne published his travel account. His *Travels in Africa, Egypt and Syria* (1800) were unusual because he compared the customs of the people he visited favorably with those of Europe. This was a verdict that was not fashionable for this area or period, although one that matched an earlier approach to the Pacific.

In 1788, organizational coherence was provided when Sir Joseph Banks, the influential and ever-active president of the Royal Society, and, again, a member of the landed elite, played a major role in founding the Association for Promoting the Discovery of the Interior Parts of Africa, or African Association. This was a society of British scientists and scholars that actively sponsored exploration. The association began by seeking to use the trans-Saharan trade routes to send explorers into the African interior and was also interested in trying to penetrate the interior from the River Gambia. Britain had a territorial presence on the coast due to its prominent role in the slave trade and its competition with France, the second most important slave trader. Daniel Houghton, an ex-army officer, who had served at Gorée on the Gambian coast, went further beyond the River Senegal into the interior than previous European travelers. However, his efforts to open a trade route were unsuccessful, and he was robbed and died in 1791, well short of his goal, Timbuktu. Many other explorers died, and their deaths could be presented in an exemplary fashion in order to dramatize and eulogize the process of discovery, and, in particular, to strengthen a religious theme.

In 1795–97, the association supported Mungo Park's first journey to West Africa in which he investigated the River Gambia and reached the River Niger at Segu, showing that it flowed eastward. Like other explorers, notably in North America, but also in the Pacific and elsewhere, Park had native assistants who tend to be forgotten, in his case six Africans. Publication was a key point. Park's *Travels in the Interior Districts of Africa* (1799) was a great success, going through three editions that year, and also focused international attention on British activity, with French and German editions appearing in 1800. The interest in Africa was linked to the rapidly rising and highly contentious debate about abolishing the slave trade.

The range as well as intensity of British exploration increased in the late eighteenth century. This was seen in Tibet where, by the late eighteenth century, the European contacts were British and not, as earlier in the century, Jesuits based in China. Instead, exploration in Tibet was an aspect of the military-commercial presence of the East India Company. George Bogle and Alexander Hamilton were sent from India in 1774 in an attempt to establish relations, with Samuel Turner following in 1783. Moreover, William Kirkpatrick led an embassy to Katmandu (in Nepal) in 1798, while, in 1799, Michael Symes led one to Myanmar. Many overland expeditions were impressive steps, but there was not the information to match that of coastlines, and this contrast was reflected in the mapping of the period.[42]

REPORTING DISCOVERY

Exploration was important in providing new material for edifying display in Britain, both by private individuals and by public bodies, most obviously the British Museum which successfully set out to offer a programmatic account of knowledge and one in no way restricted to the British Isles.[43] A different collection was assembled by Ashton Lever (1729–88), a Lancashire country gentleman and omnivorous collector, who, in 1774, moved his collection, which he called the Holophusikon, to London where he rented Leicester House and charged admission. Jefferson was a visitor in 1786. In 1783, the trustees of the British Museum declined to buy it and the collection was eventually dispersed by auction in 1806. It included objects from Cook's expeditions, a stuffed elephant, and lots of shells, fossils, stuffed birds, and non-Western clothes and weapons.[44] Such displays were an important instance of the more general relationship of science and empire[45] and of the dissemination of information through public presentation.

Books, magazines, and newspapers were important to the spread of information to the reading public.[46] For example, in the case of the Red Sea, Jean de la Roque's account, published in Paris in 1715, appeared in London in 1726 as *A Voyage to Arabia the Happy, by the Eastern Ocean and the Streights of the Red Sea*, which appeared again in 1732 and 1742. A condensed English translation of Carsten Niebuhr's travels to Yemen in 1762–63, travels in part motivated by a wish to understand the world of the Bible,[47] appeared in Edinburgh in 1792 under the title *Travels through Arabia, and Other Countries in the East*. There were also the journeys of British travelers, notably Alexander Hamilton's *A New Account of the East Indies* (1727), and Eyles Irwin's *A Series of Adventures in the Course of a Voyage Up the Red Sea* (1780) as well as a much extended third edition in 1787 that covered his 1780 journey overland from Aleppo to Basra. Born in Calcutta, Irwin was an example of the widening circle of personal histories that made up the British world. In 1806, the *Gentleman's Magazine* carried the account of a voyage to the Red Sea in 1795.[48] On December 4, 1791, the first number of the *Observer*, a London weekly newspaper that has continued to the present, advertised on its front page the publication, on the following day, of the first of a projected sixty-part *New Universal Traveller. A full and accurate Abridgement of all the latest, most authentic, and most interesting Voyages and Travels, Whether English, French, or German . . . The First Volume contains M. Vaillant's celebrated Travels through Africa*.

Alongside an awareness of increased knowledge and expanding power, it is appropriate to focus on the difficulties that faced attempts to do either, as well as on reasons, explicit and implicit, practical and political, that discouraged the very effort. Notable among the latter were power-political and cultural factors encouraging an emphasis on Europe. As far as the expansion of power was concerned, choice of direction was a continual feature, so that there was the geography of alternatives—for example, the Caribbean or North America, and the Americas or India.[49] Opportunities were linked to this. Thus, the British were able to operate in South Asia rather than South America. Moreover, American independence lessened the options for the British in North America and largely directed them to what became Canada.

EXPERIENCING TRAVEL

To move to the situation in Britain is to place transoceanic exploration in a number of contexts including knowledge of it at home but also the very different experience of the bulk of the population. Newspapers and maps offer two excellent means through which to consider exploration, the accumulation of information, and other aspects of geographical perception. Maps were more separate from newspapers than in the present day, notably because the latter carried very few illustrations, a situation that did not change during the century. Maps, instead, were usually freestanding, including the "dissected maps" or "Beaumont maps" used as jigsaws to teach geography, or part of books or magazines.

There were other links between maps and publications. Some writers—for example, William Guthrie, author of the highly successful and much reprinted *New Geographical, Historical and Commercial Grammar* (1770)—also made maps. Indeed, in one respect, newspapers, maps, and books were aspects of an entrepreneurial world in which writers such as Guthrie produced works in a variety of mediums and covering a range of topics, including reporting Parliament for the *Gentleman's Magazine* and writing popular histories. Thus, they were aspects of what is something classified as "Grub Street."[50] Geography lent itself to this as it was possible, as it was necessary, to assemble books with relative ease, pulling in information on new "discoveries." That was also true of contemporary historians and "miscellaneous writers"—for example, James Ralph and Richard Rolt—some of whom, notably Oliver Goldsmith, have retained considerable fame.

This, however, is both an overly limited definition and account of geographical writing and also one that fails to engage with the range of geographies at play in recording, defining, and challenging spatial experience and the spatial imagination. This range is not one that is covered solely, or even mainly, by different types of geographical writing. For much of the population, the experience of travel and the outside world, but not necessarily the imagination, was very limited. There were many, who were fit, who essentially lived a life constrained by the limits of the local market town or fair.

Yet, that limitation did not necessarily capture the extent of their spatial imagination. There were tales about the wider world that were retold, and thus part of family and communal memories. There was also the world as repeated through the church. In addition, market towns were both the destination of strangers and often the base of printers who produced newspapers alongside much ephemera, including material for local elections, as well as more substantial works, such as local histories.

Many of the poor, furthermore, traveled far more widely, generally for work. This highly varied category included recruits for the army, navy, and the merchant marine; those droving animals; would-be servants seeking employment; other servants accompanying masters; and so on. In 1799, Patrick Colquhoun referred to the "inconceivable" number of those "who with their families, find their way to the Metropolis, from the most remote quarters of Great Britain and Ireland."[51] These travels generally left far less of a record than those of the more affluent, a point clear from the limited sources for servants' views on the Grand Tour. Nevertheless, in a numerical sense, these travels were more significant and many were very far flung.[52] In addition, part of the facilities for travel existed for this varied group.

However, compared to the poor, the more affluent were those who in particular experienced an expanding world, at least as assessed in terms of travel itself and of the description and consideration of travel. In the latter case, geography as consumerism was, and is, an important aspect of the story, with consumerism especially present through publications. Geography as consumerism, however, can also be overplayed, and, as with so many so-called revolutions, that of a consumer revolution in eighteenth-century Britain requires qualification when employed as either description or explanation, or both.

THE INFORMATION SOCIETY

The publication of reports of exploration was a particularly notable aspect of the information society that, in Britain, was a conspicuous feature of the period. This provision of information was both an aspect of a growing concern with the need for self-consciously instructed decision making that can be seen from the late seventeenth century, and also of the view that appropriate behavior required knowledge, as well as intelligence, and that "breeding" was incomplete without them. Indeed, the reconceptualization, in the eighteenth century, of both social status and of appropriate behavior for men and women was important to the quest for geographical knowledge, as to much else, including its historical and scientific counterparts. Being "polite" in part involved not being foolish, and that state and practice required knowledge. Geography was a form of genteel as well as utilitarian knowledge, one that was comparable to the natural sciences. This interest was covered in publications and lectures.

The appeal of these types of material and activities was underlined by the extent to which they were seen in the provinces and not solely in London and the other major cities. Thus, in Devizes in 1774, appeared *A Concise System of Geography: wherein the first principles of the science are laid down in a plain and easy manner, suited to the capacities of youth*. Furthermore, publications and lectures could be combined and for a full range of pedagogic purposes and audiences. Examples included Benjamin Martin's *A Course of Lectures in Natural and Experimental Philosophy, Geography and Astronomy* (1743), which was published in Reading; Robert Davidson's *The Elements of Geography, Short and Plain. Designed as an easy introduction to the system of geography in verse* (1787); Dominique de St. Quentin's *A Complete System of the Commercial Geography of England; laid down in a plain and concise manner, for the use of schools. With a map of England* (1794); and Henry St. John's *Elements of Geography, expressly designed for the use of schools* (1799). Benjamin Martin defined geography as "The Theory of the Earth, and Use of the Terrestrial Globe, explain'd," an approach that very much aligned it as an aspect of the science he covered. In his preface, he noted that "Knowledge is now become a fashionable thing." This was even truer by the end of the century, although it was pedagogic and utilitarian purposes that were emphasized then, rather than fashion.

A focus on geography, however, could be criticized, and notably in the early decades of the century. Thus, in June 1724, the *Universal Journal* printed a letter from a country reader attacking a neighboring landlord, the young Mr. Novel—in other words, a stereotype. This "errant coxcomb" ignored his steward's accounts, in order to read newspapers, and indulged in incessant political speculation: "beginning with the Persian rebels, makes the tour of the whole world, settles treaties, unhinges governments, and reforms our state." In Persia (Iran), the Safavid Empire was overthrown in 1722 by Afghan rebels, and instability there continued to be a major theme in the press until Nadir Shah rose to power in the 1730s. In 1730, the pro-government *Weekly Journal: or, The British Gazetteer*, in its issue of April 4, attacked the opposition press for stirring up popular concern about alleged repairs to the French port of Dunkirk, a process "calculated for the shattered remains of Sacheverel's Mob, to furnish them with chat for settling the Nation over gin and pots of ale."

Linked to a focus on an inappropriate concern with political geography, a lack or failure of knowledge could be satirized and made to appear absurd, as by Henry Fielding in his play *Rape upon Rape or the Coffee-House Politician* (1730). In this lively play, "Politic," a London tradesman, is so concerned about press reports of international developments that he neglects threats to his daughter's virtue. His first soliloquy is devoted to the Turks: "I cannot rest for these preparations of the Turks.... Should the Turkish galleys once find a passage through the Straits [of Gibraltar], who can tell the consequence?" (I, iii). He returned to his concern in the following scene, and again in the next act (II, xi):

> I dread and abhor the Turks. I wish we do not feel them before we are aware ... what can be the reason of all the warlike preparation, which all our newspapers have informed us of? ... Is the design against Germany? Is the design against Italy?—Suppose we should see Turkish galleys in the Channel? We may feel them yes, we may feel them, yes, we may feel them in the midst of our security. Troy was taken in its sleep, and so may we ... should the Turks come among us, what would become of our daughters then? ... and our religion, and our liberty? ... Give us leave only to show you how it is possible for the Grand Signor [the Turkish ruler] to find an ingress into Europe. Suppose, Sir, this spot I stand on to be Turkey—then here is Hungary—very well—here is France, and here is England—granted—then we will suppose he had possession of Hungary—what then remains but to conquer France, before we find him at our own coast ... this is not all the danger.... He can come by sea to us.

While resonant of past fears, and also satire, this account noted the attention paid to the press reporting of foreign news. At the same time, the satire was directed not just at the ludicrous nature of Politic's reasoning and the hysteria to which it could give rise but also to the dated nature of the fears. The Turks had been decisively defeated outside Vienna in 1683 and, again, outside Belgrade in 1716 and 1717. In the Austro-Turkish wars of 1683–99 and 1716–18, wars well covered in the British press, the Turks, despite a rally in 1690, had made major territorial losses, culminating with eastern Hungary, Belgrade, northern Serbia, and Little Wallachia (southwestern Romania) in 1718. There had been Turkish successes elsewhere, notably defeating Peter the Great of Russia at the River Pruth in 1711 and conquering the Morea (Peloponnese) from Venice in 1715, and also Turkish advances, especially the unsuccessful attempt to take Corfu from the Venetians in 1716. However, failure was the overwhelming theme. The idea of the Turks advancing through Hungary, as in 1529 and 1683, was ridiculous, and between Hungary and France there was the Empire (Germany).

Although the seventeenth century had seen raids on the south coast of England by "Barbary pirates" (North African privateers), the idea of the Turks coming by sea was also absurd. While still a regional naval power in the eastern Mediterranean and the Black and Red Seas, the Turks lacked the capacity for long-range naval operations they had already showed in the Indian Ocean in the sixteenth century. Nor did they display a capacity to match that of Russia in the early eighteenth century in creating an effective new navy. Even within the Mediterranean, the Turks no longer had the capacity shown in the sixteenth or even, in the conquest of the Venetian colony of Crete, the seventeenth centuries, and their use of their navy in 1715–17 was essentially limited to Greek waters.

In contrast, Britain and France now had a significant naval presence in the Mediterranean. The British had displayed this in the 1700s, 1710s, and 1720s, notably against Spain in 1718, and it was anchored by their control of Gibraltar and Minorca from 1704 and 1708, respectively. Thus, "Politic" was highly unpolitic, and his lack of an understanding of political geography, geopolitics, and military capability made him foolish. An interest in the hypothetical was referred to by John Walter, in the first issue of the *Daily Universal Register* (the forerunner of the *Times*) on January 1, 1785, when he commented on readers interested in "political speculations about the measures that the different courts in Europe might probably adopt." Then, indeed, there were many speculations, as there also were at the governmental level.

Ignorance was a charge thrown out against rival newspapers, as by the *Post Man and the Historical Account* of February 8, 1718, which employed the information that Messina and Palermo, the major cities in Sicily, were "above 160 miles distant," in order to criticize an opponent's claim about journey times. Sicily was to the fore in news that year due to a Spanish invasion. The *Weekly Medley* of December 6, 1718, explained that it was giving an account of Norway which Charles XII of Sweden had just invaded, so that its readers should be "free from puzzle and perplexity which news writers, who know nothing of the place themselves, and write they know not what, might be apt to throw them into, at every turn." The *Corn-Cutter's Journal* of October 23, 1733, printed a letter from "T" in Rochester, a provincial town, who claimed that the press made nothing of writing about "Princes and towns that never had an existence, especially when they get into Poland and Muscovy; and we have lately observed some of them make mention of Alsace and the Breisgau [in modern Baden-Württemberg], which are known to be large countries, as if they had supposed them single towns."

The critical approach could also be aimed at higher ranks, as in the preface to the English edition of Robert Davidson, an edition published by Wilkins, a major London publisher. Davidson himself was an American, and the London edition of 1787 was a reprint of his *Geography epitomised; or, a tour round the world: being a short but comprehensive description of the terraqueous globe: attempted in verse* (Philadelphia, 1784): "That most accomplished man, James Hervey, assured me that after he entered into Holy Orders, being one day at dinner with a number of gentlemen, the city Jerusalem was mentioned; he was so ignorant of geography, as not to know in what quarter of the world it stood: he was so vexed and ashamed at his own ignorance and his tutor's negligence, that he went immediately and bought a book of maps, and studied geography." This led Davidson to a reflection on Hervey's Oxford education.[53] Such a reflection was justified given the limited teaching of geography in the universities.

Geographical satire was clearly displayed in the novel *Humphry Clinker* (1771), in which the Tory journalist Tobias Smollett made the need for cartographic information apparent. This need provided a way to mock Thomas, Duke of Newcastle, a leading British Whig minister from 1724 to 1756 and 1757 to 1762, and generally one of the two leading ministers of that period, with reference to the situation at the beginning of the Seven Years' War (1756–63):

> this poor half-witted creature told me, in a great fright, that thirty thousand French had marched from Acadie [Nova Scotia] to Cape Breton—"Where did they find transports? (said I)" "Transports! (cried he) I tell you they marched by land"—"By land to the island of Cape Breton?" "What! is Cape Breton an island?" "Certainly." "Ha! are you sure of that?" "When I pointed it out in the map, he examined it earnestly with this spectacles; then, taking me in his arms, "My dear C—! (cried he) you always bring us good news—Egad! I'll go directly, and tell the king [George II] that Cape Breton is an island."

In practice, there is no information on how far, and how, Newcastle read maps. Indeed, at the individual level, such information is rare for this period. As a secretary of state from 1724 to 1754, Newcastle would have had ready access to the resources of the British foreign service. He also had the ability to reflect on international relations, as in 1762 in defense of wartime intervention: "the recalling our troops from Germany, and abandoning the continent entirely would now render the House of Bourbon [France and Spain] absolute master of all Europe, enable them to obliged every neutral power to submit.... We should be reduced to that miserable condition of defending ourselves at home, with our wooden walls, our militia, or perhaps our own troops, excluded from all commerce abroad, and all connection with the other powers of Europe."[54]

Maps certainly played a role in strategic discussion and planning. This was seen clearly in 1712, during the negotiations over ending the War of the Spanish Succession, when Torcy, the experienced French foreign minister, urged his British counterpart, Bolingbroke, to look at a map in order to see the strategic threat posed by the Alpine demands of Victor Amadeus II of Savoy-Piedmont.[55] During the Dutch crisis of 1787, a map played a role in the advice offered the British Cabinet, then led by William Pitt the Younger, the first lord of the Treasury. The advice was offered in person on May 23 by Charles, 3rd Duke of Richmond, the master-general of the ordnance (artillery), the sponsor of the Ordnance Survey, and Sir James Harris, the experienced British envoy in The Hague. Richmond "talked of military operations—called for a map of Germany—traced the marches from Cassel and Hanover, to Holland, and also from Givet to Maastricht." The former would be the route followed by troops from Hesse-Cassel and Hanover if sent, in accordance with British wishes, to help the Orangists, the latter that anticipated for the French were they to intervene on the side of the rival Patriots. The following day, Harris saw Pitt, who "sent for a map of Holland; made me show him the situation of the [United] Provinces [the Netherlands]." A map would also demonstrate the contrast between the distance allied Prussian troops would have to travel from their Rhineland bases at Cleves and Wesel, in order to mount an invasion of the Netherlands, with the greater distance which France's forces would have to take from Givet in order to intervene on behalf of its Dutch protégés, the Patriots. This advice was designed to encourage British support for action on behalf of the Orangists by illustrating its viability. In the event, the British lent naval backing, the Prussians successfully invaded, and French preparations did not result in action.[56]

In 1792, George III used a map to follow the Prussian invasion of France, an invasion finally checked by a larger French army at Valmy. Earlier that month, James Bland Burges, under-secretary of state in the Foreign Office, informed his brother-in-law, "I have not forgot your commission respecting the new map of France, but my endeavours to procure one for you have been unsuccessful, as I am assured by Faden, who is omniscient in all matters relating to geography, that there is not one to be met with in London."[57]

There was a separate assumption that diplomats, experienced gentlemen as a group, would be knowledgeable and would work to be more so. In 1751, Joseph Yorke, a British diplomat, pressed the need to appoint individuals "knowing in the geography of America and the West Indies" as commissioners to negotiate frontier disputes with France.[58] An anonymous article published in the *Centinel*, a London newspaper, on September 27, 1757, called for the establishment of a political academy for the formation of statesmen to prevent the British from being duped in negotiations. The academy was to include "a Geographical School; in which our young students in politics should be instructed in the knowledge of the globe and maps." Indeed, in 1762, a map was joined to the instructions of John, 4th Duke of Bedford, the British negotiator in Paris and a former secretary of state from 1748 to 1751, to help him negotiate the Mississippi boundary of the new British possessions.[59] That year, however, Walter Titley, the veteran British envoy in Copenhagen, found it difficult to obtain a map to clarify the developing international crisis over Holstein. He did not emerge as cartographically sophisticated,[60] but the issue was a complex one and the mapping of it not easy.

Alongside the mockery directed at the inappropriate quest for information or the flawed use of it, instructed opinion, whether as a gentleman for leisure or as a gentleman taking part in informed decision making, was regarded as important, and geography was part of this process. The significance of geography was evident in the widespread ownership of geographical works and of globes.

Maps, moreover, very much emphasized new information. The *New Map of South America* published in 1794 by Robert Wilkinson of London, continued in its title *Drawn from the Latest Discoveries*. Such titles stressed both novelty and accuracy and added a sensational character. More generally, novelty was a key aspect of the process of validating information and making it interesting. Gentlemen were to be informed of this new information. The very extent and pace of geographical novelty, however, created problems of inclusion, depiction, and accuracy. In terms of what it showed, the perception of space offered by a map was very different to that of personal experience, not least as a map provided an apparent fixity and objectivity.

In 1781, the "advertisement" for General Henry Lloyd's *Continuation of the History of the Late War in Germany, between the King of Prussia, and the Empress of Germany and her Allies* noted:

> In order to elucidate in one view the particular reflections and descriptions contained in this work, as well as in military history in general, a map on a large scale is now engraving, that will comprehend the countries between the Meridian of Paris and that of Petersburg [St. Petersburg], and from the latitude of the last mentioned place, to that of Constantinople [Istanbul]; on which will be traced the natural lines of operation, leading from the frontiers of the respective countries; as also the lines on which the respective armies did really act in the several campaigns during the war we describe, which will enable the reader to see and judge of the propriety of their operations. This map will be given to purchasers of the work.

Separate to the knowledge to be deployed by the "genteel" and to help readers, knowledge focused on utility as well as politeness: on channels to navigate, harbors to use as ports, lands to cultivate, and so on. For example, oceanic voyages identified resources that could be exploited. Thus, Cook reported on the availability of flax, seals, sea otters, timber, and whales.

Fur traders and whalers followed, and notably along the Pacific seaboard of North America.

Alongside official reports, the public discussion of the wider world focused on usefulness. For example, the *St. James's Chronicle*, a leading London newspaper, in its issue of July 24, 1766, printed a letter, dated Mobile, February 21, that was from Thomas Miller, who was trying to develop a plantation, to John Ellis, a linen merchant and naturalist who was king's agent for West Florida and later Dominica. Having stressed the quantity of wood available, he continued: "Those swamps appear to me to be good lands, capable of producing either rice, hemp, flax, indigo, or cotton; indeed, indigo and cotton I have seen succeed in them very well. The whole face of the country is covered with grass of so good a kind that cattle fat to good beef on it . . . the woods abound with deer, turkeys, quails, rabbits, etc. . . . I never saw a place so full of fine fish as this Bay of Mobile."

Travel and publication at every level spread knowledge of different environments. The focus was very much on contrasts, not least because it was newsworthy, as well as offering opportunities. For example, based on his travels in 1712–25, Mark Catesby's *The Natural History of Carolina, Florida, and the Bahama Islands* (1731), a work George III was to buy a copy of in 1768, underlined differences to the flora and fauna of Europe. In turn, such information could be passed on through magazines, newspapers, and engravings. Thus, the *Darlington Pamphlet* (in fact a newspaper) of July 10, 1772, provided "A Description of the Animal Flower, from the Rev. Mr. Hughes's Natural History of Barbadoes," itself published in 1750.

There was strong interest in unusual plants and in particular in expanding the range grown in Britain. Diplomats were instructed to secure them, George, 7th Earl of Kinnoull, envoy in Constantinople, being sent a list in 1730 of seeds required "for the improvement of our kitchen-gardening."[61] Thomas, Duke of Newcastle, then secretary of state for the Southern Department, was very interested in gardening, and under his supervision, members of the Greening family brought the gardens at his principal seat, Claremont in Surrey, to an eighteenth-century standard of excellence. Newcastle was personally committed to increasing the range of plants available in the Claremont fruit and vegetable gardens. In 1735, he instructed Robert Trevor at The Hague to obtain apricot plants.[62] Two years earlier, James, 2nd Lord Tyrawly, envoy at Lisbon, had been asked to send beans and onion seeds. He sent the beans, "a young corral tree," and some tomatoes:

> I don't know that I have any other vegetable worth sending you, except tomatoes, which is a large round fruit, as big as a small orange (of which I believe you have none in England) it is not to be eaten, by itself, yet comes within your rule, of having nothing but belly timber, for if your cook scalds them first in hot water, four, or five of them, or more, or less according as you like the last, or without scalding, put them whole into your soup, provided that it stands afterwards, time enough to mitoner, it will as we think here, much mend your soup, by giving it a far more agreeable tartness, than sorrel, or any other herb; it grows up to a tall shrub with many leaves the fruit, being when ripe, as red as a cherry.[63]

Prior to 1734, only 300 American species had been introduced into British gardens, but by 1770, another 320 were introduced, in part due to the plants and seeds sent by John Bartram (1699–1770), a Philadelphia farmer interested in botany who became an agent for British collectors. Plants he sent over included the Franklin tree and the witch hazel. Bartram indeed received George III's favor.

Foreign plants and animals in Britain were frequently reported in the press, as with the *London Chronicle* of April 8, 1762:

> **Extract of a letter from Cumberland, March 22**
>
> A wild animal has very much amused the people between Cockermouth and Whitehaven, in this county, all the winter. At first it was chased by the hunters for a fox with a white tail; then for a wolf brought over sea, and here set at liberty. And to such a height was the people's curiosity raised by it, that some hundreds assembled on set days, with their several packs of hounds (which here abound to the destruction of game, and encouragement of idleness) to hunt this terrible wolf; but very few of the dogs would hunt it, and those few afraid to approach it; so that the creature yet ranges the country, and is now reported to be a wild dog from Sweden, which lives upon mice, frogs, etc. It is of a dun colour, and seems white at a distance; has rough shaggy hair, and long tail; about 20 inches high, short legs, and thick body. If any of your correspondents have seen such an animal in Sweden, or elsewhere, we should be glad if they would satisfy our curiosity, in giving some public account of it, and whether we may expect any harm from it to the sheep and lambs.

Australasia offered far more difference. An artist accompanied Dampier's voyage of 1699–1700, and his drawings were published in Dampier's *Voyage to New Holland*. More information came back as a result of Cook's voyages, which returned with sketches, dried specimens, and skins, for example of a kangaroo. Drawings and paintings recorded the situation.[64] Thus, the gentleman-botanist Joseph Banks took two artists with him on Cook's first voyage. Banks also collected plants on expeditions to Newfoundland and, in 1772, Iceland, as well as succeeding George III's favorite, John, 3rd Earl of Bute, in 1772, as director of the new Royal Botanical Gardens at Kew. Drawing on the global presence of British power and trade and seeing plant classification as a means to imperial benefit, Banks helped to make Kew a center for botanical research based on holdings from around the world and on information derived from a far-flung system of correspondence. Although the attempt by the Spanish crown in the sixteenth century to make scientific use of its American conquests[65] anticipated some aspects of this activity, the scale and ambition were now very different. Kew represented not only a means, at once enlightened and self-interested, to imperial benefit but also an expression of long-standing Judaic-Christian ideas about the ability of humanity to use God's gift of control over nature in order to produce a better world and the obligation to do so. This was an ideology of "improvement" that spanned any divide between the religious and the secular.

The active president of the Royal Society from 1778 to 1820, Banks established both the idea of the scientist as heroic explorer and statesman, and the Royal Society as a key source and means of state policy and on the world scale. British imperial activity was presented and understood as a means to further scientific progress, while the latter was to benefit empire. For example, in order to reduce tea imports from China, Banks suggested its cultivation in India. This indeed, happened, in what was intended, and became, a major instance of imperial activity linked to environmental changes. With his role in establishing the Royal Institution, Banks also helped popularize science. Banks was also interested in the popularization of science and technology.[66]

Travelers' narratives publicized different issues across the full range of human activity and thought, including questions about the causes of human diversity, of God's providential plan, and of the progress and condition of civilization. At the same time, this process was scarcely value-free, as it reflected assumptions about scientific and historical classification. As part of the mix of ideas and information, translations spread knowledge of truth and fiction. For example, John Trusler's twenty-volume *The Habitable*

World Described (1788–97) included P. S. Pallas's *Travels into Siberia and Tartary*, an English version of *Reise durch verschiedene Provinzen des Russischen Reichs* (1771–76). In 1766, *Voyages and Travels in the Levant*, the first English edition of the travels of Frederick Hasselquist, was published in London. Translations were mostly from Western European languages.

Alongside bias, there could also be error and indeed straightforward deception. In 1703, George Psalmanazar arrived in London, claiming to be a native of Formosa (Taiwan). He published *An Historical and Geographical Description of Formosa* (1704), in which he wrote of commonplace cannibalism. Psalmanazar, who had also invented a Formosan language, which he was asked to teach to missionaries, was discredited in 1708.

WEATHER

Geographical knowledge took many forms, and information was diffused accordingly. There was also an assumption that gentlemen would be fluent in these forms. Most of the discussion focuses on human geography, but physical geography, particularly in the shape of the weather, was significant. In this case, as in others, it is easy to suggest a clash between past and future methods and assumptions, notably demands for information being now addressed by drawing on the barometer. It is, however, overly facile to adopt this distinction, although, nevertheless, this element was indeed important, not least as throwing light on how a sense, as well as reality, of change were readily apparent to contemporaries. Providential accounts of the weather offered echoes of the past. In 1701, a "Humble Adorer of God in His Word and Works" wrote *Stars and Planets the Best Barometers and Truest Interpreters of All Airy Vicissitudes. With Some Brief Rules for Knowledge of the Weather at All Times*. Two years later, came Richard Chapman, vicar of Cheshunt, and the publication of his sermon *The Necessity of Repentance Asserted: In Order to Avert Those Judgments Which the Present War, and Strange Unseasonableness of the Weather at Present, Seem to Threaten This Nation With*. The terrible storm of November 26–27, 1703, led to much discussion of the moral dimension, but attempts, linked to this, to restrict the freedom of the stage, and thus limit immorality, were fruitless.[67]

Underlining the diversity of modes of explanation seen in the discussion of floods,[68] the barometer was different to the items above and to the almanac. It might not discover apparent purpose in the weather, as Chapman did, but the barometer clearly suggested less dramatic processes and causes. In 1700, Gustavus Parker published *An Account of a Portable Barometer, with Reasons and Rules for the Use of It* and *A New Account of the Alterations of the Wind and Weather by the Discoveries of a Portable Barometer*. Indicating the varied nature of the culture of print, with its many forms, these were issues of a serial broadsheet which Parker published under the general title of *Baroscopical Discourses, or The Monthly Weather Paper*, which was still appearing in 1711. This broadsheet offered information on likely wind directions and predicted the weather conditions for the forthcoming month.

Significantly, Parker's publication extended to an explanation of how the weather operated, why wind directions were so variable, and why predictions sometimes proved inaccurate. The last reflected an awareness of the dynamic nature of the weather and a willingness to engage explicitly with the limitations of this particular approach to analysis. Moreover, controversy played a role in discussion of the weather, and this controversy spilled into print. In 1700, John Parker, a noted maker of mathematical instruments and barometers, set out, using his own research with the barometer, to contest Gustavus Parker's work.[69]

Separately, the measurement of temperature by means of thermometers developed, with various scales employed, and again as an aspect of ready record and of scientific rationalism. The use of such equipment was linked with, but separate to, the more general accumulation of information, notably in the shape of Royal Navy logbooks, the oldest of which date from the 1670s. The requirement on all principal officers to keep them was established on a more formal basis by the Naval Instructions of 1731: "He is, from the time of his going on board, to keep a journal . . . and be careful to note therein all occurrences, vis place where the ship is at noon, changes of wind and weather . . . remarks on unknown places; and, in general, every circumstance that concerns the ship . . . he is to send a copy of his journal for the said time, to the Secretary of the Admiralty." The emphasis on the duty to return data is instructive. Wind direction, which could be based on the compass, was important for navigation, notably procedures, known as "dead reckoning," that were discussed in texts on navigation[70] and were also taught by example. Navigation records were valuable in providing information for future operations. Standardization rapidly became part of the record-keeping process with a conventional layout of logbooks. From the 1780s, preprinted sheets on which to write logbook accounts were available.[71] Another form of classification—that of Luke Howard in his *On the Modifications of Clouds* (1803)—established and named three major categories of clouds: cumulus (heap), stratus (layer), and circus (rainy).

Meanwhile, knowledge was displayed and enjoyed with the furnishing of houses with clocklike cased barometers. These were an aspect of geography as furniture also seen with the display of globes and maps. With barometers, it was physical geography that became an aspect of "taste."[72] This was a part of a more general use of geographical information in order to assert and display social and intellectual status. This usage was important to the development and social configuration of the subject. As such, geography matched science, including astronomy which was much discussed in the press.[73]

GEOLOGY

So also with the vogue for geology in the closing decades of the century. James Hutton (1726–97) was particularly important, while John Playfair (1748–1819) made his work readable for a wider audience, notably with his *Illustrations of the Huttonian Theory of the Earth* (1802). This vogue was linked to an interest in the workings of Providence, in history, in the underpinning of physical geography, and in tourism within the British Isles. Far from subjects such as geology being separate, they were joined in a sense of appropriate knowledge. As with other branches of knowledge, print played a key role in the dissemination of information and in contention over its analysis. This contention owed much to the implications of geology for the biblical account of Creation and the earth, and therefore for the authority of the Bible itself. Geology indeed posed a fundamental question to the Bible historically, just as astronomy had earlier offered a spatial challenge.[74]

If the situation across time was crucial to geology, and fossils were a topic of long-standing interest,[75] the gathering and depiction of the information also had a strong spatial characteristic. Thus, geology suggested a new physical geography and history for Britain, which, indeed, was depicted in William Smith's *Delineation of the Strata of England and Wales with Part of Scotland* (1815).[76] Geological mapping was developed for utilitarian reasons, and this was linked to the evolution of minerology, an evolution that was related to a dynamic expansion of accessible and useful knowledge.[77] Geology became an element in the new domestic tourism that gathered pace at the close of the century, not least with an interest in fossils. Illustrations were to be significant to geology, both to public interest and to intellectual changes, with Charles Babbage in the 1820s and 1830s developing techniques of printing diagrams and tables in order to provide uniform proofs of the effects of geological phenomena and therefore to help make the subject more scientific.[78]

POPULATION AND INFORMATION

Although highly important for its relationship with religious interpretations of time, as a utilitarian tool and as a metaphor, geology was not the prime suggestion of transformative change. Instead, it was industrial development and geopolitical strength that represented dramatic changes. In addition, although less dramatic, the human context for the geography of Britain was far from static: the dynamism of a rapidly growing economy and an expanding transoceanic presence was matched by a major increase in the population. After a century of limited growth, if not stagnation, population growth rates shot up, leading to a rise in the population of England and Wales from, in millions, 5.18 (1695), 5.51 (1711), 5.59 (1731), 6.20 (1751), and 6.97 (1771) to 8.21 (1791), with the growth rate being highest in 1781–91 at 0.83 percent per annum. The Scottish population rose from 1.26 million in 1757 to 1.6 million in 1801. In short, the situation prefigured the current rapid growth in the global population.

This growing population established new spatial patterns within Britain, enhanced demands for goods, and provided more demand for information about the world. This demand helped to finance both new transport links and entrepreneurial publishing, which, generally, sought "to reconcile cheapness with utility."[79] The accessibility of geographical information helped meet this latter need. Its capacity to be, at once, educational, utilitarian, and an aspect of politeness, was highly significant, but all of those factors had to be argued and defined.

Notes

1. J. M. Levine, *The Battle of the Books: History and Literature in the Augustan Age* (Ithaca, NY, 1991).
2. L. Dutens, *An Inquiry into the Origin of the Discoveries attributed to the Moderns* (London, 1769); edition of a French original of 1766.
3. H. D. Weinbrot, *Britannia's Issue: The Issue of British Literature from Dryden to Ossian* (Cambridge, 1993).
4. Bowles's *Geographia Classica* (London, 1784); W. A. Koelsch, *Geography and the Classical World: Unearthing Historical Geography's Forgotten Past* (London, 2012).
5. J. Black, "Ideology, History, Xenophobia and the World of Print in Eighteenth-Century England," in J. Black and J. Gregory, eds., *Culture, Politics and Society in Britain, 1660–1800* (Manchester, 1991), 184–216; L. Cormack, "'Good Fences Make Good Neighbors.' Geography as Self-Definition in Early Modern England," *ISIS* 82 (1991): 639–61.
6. R. Mayhew, "The Character of English Geography, c. 1660–1800: A Textual Approach," *Journal of Historical Geography* 24 (1998): 388–93; *Enlightenment Geography: The Political Languages of British Geography, 1650–1850* (Basingstoke, 2000); and "The effacement of early modern geography (c. 1600–1850): a historiographical essay," *Progress in Human Geography* 25 (2001): 383–401. For earlier, critical views, see, e.g., A. Downes, "The Bibliographic Dinosaurs of Georgian Geography, 1714–1830," *Geographical Journal* 137 (1971): 379–87.
7. T. Salmon, *A New Geographical and Historical Grammar* (London, 1749), 1.
8. R. A. Butlin, "Ideological Context and the Reconstruction of Biblical Landscapes in the Seventeenth and Early Eighteenth Centuries: Dr. Edward Wells and the Historical Geography of the Holy Land," in A. R. H. Baker and G. Bigger, eds., *Ideology and Landscape in Historical Perspective* (Cambridge, 1992), 31–62.
9. G. Hutchinson, "Herman Moll's View of the South Sea Company," *Journal for Maritime Research* 6 (2004): 87–112.
10. On Moll, A. Zukas, "The Cartography of Herman Moll and European Views of Muslim South Asia, 1700–1730," *Journal of World History* 25 (2014): 311–39.
11. M. Bowen, *Empiricism and Geographical Thought: From Francis Bacon to Alexander von Humboldt* (Cambridge, 1981).
12. R. Mayhew, "Geography, Print Culture and the Renaissance: 'The Road Less Travelled By,'" *History of European Ideas* 27 (2001): 366.
13. C. W. J. Withers, "Reporting, Mapping, Trusting. Making Geographical Knowledge in the Late Seventeenth Century," *Isis* 90 (1999): 521.
14. I. Inkster, *Scientific Culture and Urbanisation in Industrialising Britain* (Aldershot, 1997); P. Elliott, "The Origins of the 'Creative Class': Provincial Urban Society, Scientific Culture and Socio-Political Marginality in Britain in the Eighteenth and Nineteenth Centuries," *Social History* 28 (2003): 361–87.
15. B. T. Moran, ed., *Patronage and Institutions: Science, Technology and Medicine at the European Court, 1500–1750* (Woodbridge, 1991).
16. M. B. Hall, *Promoting Experimental Learning: Experiment and the Royal Society, 1660–1727* (Cambridge, 1991).
17. D. Hayden, *The Power of Place: Urban Landscapes as Public History* (Cambridge, MA, 1995), 21.
18. D. G. Burnett, *Masters of All They Surveyed: Exploration, Geography and a British El Dorado* (Chicago, 2000); D. W. Clayton, *Islands of Truth: The Imperial Fashioning of Vancouver Island* (Vancouver, 2000); F. Driver, *Geography Militant: Cultures of Exploration*

and Empire (Oxford, 2001); C. W. J. Withers, *Geography, Science and National Identity: Scotland since 1520* (Cambridge, 2001).

19. J. Green, *The Construction of Maps and Globes* (London, 1717), Dedication: 2.

20. Burke to Robertson, June 9, 1777, *The Correspondence of Edmund Burke*, edited by T. W. Copeland et al. (10 vols., Cambridge, 1958-78), III, 351.

21. J. F. Richards, *The Unending Frontier: An Environmental History of the Early Modern World* (Berkeley, 2003).

22. A. M. Carlos and J. B. Kruse, "The Decline of the Royal African Company: Fringe Firms and the Role of the Charter," *Economic History Review*, 2nd ser., 49 (1996): 291-313.

23. G. Symcox, *The Crisis of French Naval Power, 1688-1697* (The Hague, 1974).

24. G. Norris, ed., *The Buccaneer Explorer: William Dampier's Voyages* (London, 1994).

25. E. Halley, "An Historical Account of the Trade Winds and Monsoons, observable in the Seas between and near the Tropics, with an attempt to assign the physical cause of the said winds," *Philosophical Translations of the Royal Society* 16 (1686): 153-68.

26. P. Rogers, "Defoe as Plagiarist: Camden's *Britannia* and *A Tour thro' the Whole Island of Great Britain*," *Philological Quarterly* 52 (1973): 771-74, and "Defoe at Work: The Making of *A Tour thro' Great Britain*, Volume 1," *Bulletin of the New York Public Library* (summer 1975): 431-50.

27. Anon., *A Tour through Ireland* (Dublin, 1746), 33.

28. E. Zimmerman, *Swift's Narrative Satires: Author and Authority* (Ithaca, NY, 1984).

29. For example, B. Mitchell and H. Penrose, eds., *Letters from Bath 1766-67 by the Rev. John Penrose* (Gloucester, 1983).

30. D. Gore, "A Mild Deception," *Journal of the Wiltshire Family History Society* 65 (1997): 15-18.

31. N. Rennie, *Far-Fetched Facts: The Literature of Travel and the Idea of the South Seas* (Oxford, 1995).

32. T. Fawcett, "Eighteenth-Century Norfolk Booksellers: A Survey and Register," *Transactions of the Cambridge Bibliographical Society* 6 (1972): 9.

33. H. B. Carter, "The Royal Society and the Voyage of HMS *Endeavour* 1768-71," *Notes and Records of the Royal Society of London* 49 (1995): 245-46.

34. N. Thomas, *Discoveries: The Voyages of Captain Cook* (London, 2004); G. Williams, ed., *Captain Cook: Explorations and Reassessments* (Woodbridge, 2004).

35. Edward Gibbon, *The History of the Decline and Fall of the Roman Empire*, edited by J. B. Bury (7 vols., London, 1897-1901), IV, 168-69; *The Journal of the Rev. John Wesley*, edited by N. Cumock (8 vols., London, 1909-16), VI, 7.

36. J.-M. Lacroix, "La perception des voyages de Cook dans le Pacifique, à travers les magazines anglais," *Trema* 9 (1984): 103-18; R. J. King, "The Call of the South Seas: Georg Forster and the Expeditions to the Pacific of Lapérouse, Mulovsky and Malaspina," *Georg-Forster-Studien* 13 (2008): 149-50.

37. G. Quilley, "Introduction: Mapping the Art of Travel and Exploration," *Journal of Historical Geography* 43 (2014): 6.

38. F. E. Cuppage, *James Cook and the Conquest of Scurvy* (Westport, CT, 1994).

39. D. Mackay, "British Interest in the Southern Oceans, 1782-1794," *New Zealand Journal of History* 3 (1969): 124-42.

40. R. Fisher and H. Johnston, *From Maps to Metaphors: The Pacific World of George Vancouver* (Vancouver, 1993).

41. *Bristol Journal*, April 19, 1777, for French sources. See also *London Chronicle*, January 26, 1779.

42. F. Fernandez-Armesto, ed., *Edward Gibbon's Atlas of the World* (London, 1991), 14.

43. K. Sloan, ed., *Enlightenment: Discovering the World in the Eighteenth Century* (London, 2003).

44. G. Shaws, *Museum Leverianum* (London, 1792).

45. J. Delbourgo and N. Dew, *Science and Empire in the Atlantic World* (Abingdon, 2008).

46. For a theoretical approach, J. S. Duncan and D. Gregory, eds., *Writes of Passage: Reading Travel Writing* (London, 1999).

47. J. Sheehan, *The Enlightenment Bible: Translation, Scholarship, Culture* (Princeton, NJ, 2005).

48. J. H. Thomas, "The Sea Captain, the Nawab and the Pilgrimage: A Maritime Yarn Examined," *Archives* 35 (2010): 38, 43.

49. P. Mapp, *The Elusive West and the Contest for Empire, 1713-1763* (Chapel Hill, NC, 2011).

50. P. Rogers, *Grub Street: Studies in a Subculture* (London, 1972).

51. P. Colquhoun, *The State of Indigence and the Situation of the Casual Poor in the Metropolis, Explained* (London, 1799), 5.

52. L. Colley, *Captives: Britain, Empire, and the World 1600-1850* (London, 2002).

53. Davidson, *Geography*, 4-5. Hervey (1714-58), the son of a vicar, was first educated at the grammar school in Northampton. At Oxford, he was influenced by the Methodists

54. Newcastle to Joseph Yorke, envoy in The Hague, January 8, 1762, BL. Add. 32933 fols. 113-14.

55. Torcy to Bolingbroke, July 28, 1712, NA. SP. 78/154.

56. 3rd Earl of Malmesbury, ed., *Diaries and Correspondence of James Harris, First Earl of Malmesbury* (4 vols., London, 1844), II, 304-6.

57. William, Lord Grenville, Foreign Secretary, to George III, September 25, George to Grenville, September 26, 1792, BL. Add. 58857 fols. 37, 39; Burges to Lewis Montolieu, September 15, 1792, Bod. Bland Burges 48, vol. 127.

58. Yorke to his father, Lord Chancellor Hardwicke, August 27, 1749, BL. Add. 35355 fol. 103.

59. Z. E. Rashed, *The Peace of Paris 1763* (Liverpool, 1951), 166 and map opposite 254.

60. Titley to Edward Weston, Under-Secretary at the Northern Department, March 2, 9, 27, 1762, Farmington, Lewis Walpole Library, Weston papers, vol. 5; P. Barber and J. Black, "Maps and the Complexities of Eighteenth-Century Europe's Territorial Divisions: Holstein in 1762," *Archives* 22 (1995): 79-82. For the maps of the period, R. Hansen, "Die Nordgrenze Deutschland sim Lauf der Geschichte," *Grenzfriedensefte* Nr. 1/90: 25-27.

61. Kinnoull to Charles Delafaye, Under-Secretary, August 19, 1730, NA. SP. 97/26.

62. Trevor to Andrew Stone, Newcastle's confidant, December 23, 1735, NA. SP. 84/581 fol. 400.

63. Tyrawly to Delafaye, June 12, 15 (quote), August 10, 1735, NA. SP. 89/37 fols. 238, 248, 256.

64. G. Quilley and J. Bonehill, eds., *William Hodges 1744-1797: The Art of Exploration* (New Haven, CT, 2004); H. Guest, *Empire, Barbarism, and Civilisation: Captain Cook, William Hodges, and the Return to the Pacific* (Cambridge, 2007).

65. A. Barrera-Osorio, *Experiencing Nature: The Spanish American Empire and the Early Scientific Revolution* (Austin, TX, 2006).

66. J. Gascoigne, *Joseph Banks and the English Enlightenment. Useful Knowledge and Polite Culture* (Cambridge, 1995); R. Drayton, *Nature's Government: Science, Imperial Britain, and the "Improvement" of the World* (New Haven, CT, 2000).

67. E. L. Avery, "The Great Storm of 1703," *Research Studies* 29 (1961): 38–49.

68. J. E. Morgan, "Understanding Flooding in Early Modern England," *Journal of Historical Geography* 50 (2015): 37–50.

69. E. G. R. Taylor, *The Mathematical Practitioners of Tudor and Stuart England* (London, 1954), 414; "Reflections upon the New Account of the Alteration of Wind and Weather," BL. 537.1.23(3).

70. J. Robertson, *The Elements of Navigation* (5th ed., London, 1986).

71. D. Wheeler, "Archives and Climatic Change: How Old Documents Offer a Key to Understanding the World's Weather," *Archives* 31 (2006): 121–23.

72. J. Golinski, *British Weather and the Climate of Enlightenment* (Chicago, 2007).

73. *Leeds Mercury*, December 26, 1775.

74. M. J. S. Rudwick, *Bursting the Limits of Time: The Reconstruction of Geohistory in the Age of Revolution* (Chicago, 2005).

75. R. Rappaport, "Hooke on Earthquakes: Lectures, Strategy and Audience," *British Journal for the History of Science* 19 (1986): 129–46.

76. S. Winchester, *The Map That Changed the World* (London, 2001); K. Cook, "From False Starts to Firm Beginnings: Early Colour Printing of Geological Maps," *Imago Mundi* 47 (1995): 155–72; M. J. S. Rudwick, "A Visual Language for Geology, 1760–1840," *History of Science* 14 (1976): 149–95.

77. B. Dolan, "Pedagogy through Print: James Sowerby, John Mawe and the Problem of Colour in Early Nineteenth-Century Natural History Illustration," *British Journal of the History of Science* 31 (1998): 275–304.

78. B. Dolan, "Representing Novelty: Charles Babbage, Charles Lyell, and Experiments in Early Victorian Geology," *History of Science* 36 (1998): 321.

79. Preface to translation of D'Anville's *Compendium of Ancient Geography* (London, 1791), ii.

2

The Spatial Matrix of Military and Political Power

POTENT IDEAS OF national power and imperial growth were related to the presentation or, sometimes, study of geography. This was long-standing. A sense of English maritime destiny had been developed and pressed forward during the long reign of Elizabeth I of England (1558–1603) by a number of writers and in publications including John Dee's *General and Rare Memorials Pertaining to the Perfect Act of Navigation* (1577) and Richard Hakluyt's *Principal Navigations, Voyages, Traffiques, and Discoveries of the English Nation* (1598–1600), writers who enjoyed much influential patronage and publications that collectively offered much geographical information.[1] This theme, which presented national interest in terms of transoceanic endeavor, notably at the expense of the (Catholic) Spanish Empire, continued into, and throughout, the eighteenth century, being regarded then as the British national destiny.

Indeed, there were many references then back to Elizabeth's reign, not least from opposition newspapers in the 1720s and 1730s complaining about a lack of governmental firmness toward Spain and pressing for transoceanic conquests. This was an aspect of the time-space conflation in which political geography was positioned. This conflation rose to a height in 1738–39 and contributed to the outbreak of the War of Jenkins Ear in 1739, although the key elements were very much those of the present in the shape of the political and military moves by both British and Spanish governments.

Historians are affected by similar conflations. For the eighteenth century, the understanding of the Enlightenment as, at least in part, a product and an aspect of the highly competitive European international relations of the period has become increasingly important in academic circles. This is particularly so as attention has shifted from the French *philosophes*, some of whom criticized the French state, for long the focus of scholarly attention, and, instead, has become more diffused. Increasingly, attention has focused on the state-directed Enlightenment projects and not only of the German and Italian states. These projects, often referred to as Enlightened despotism, reflected, in part, the need to prepare for the frequent conflicts of the period—in short, strengthening the state and nation for competition, if not war. This historiographical situation, at once a shift and a tension in approach, is highly relevant to geography, however geography is understood, whether as a branch of the Enlightenment or as a less coherent activity and, indeed, set of assumptions.[2]

So also for Britain. The tendency in treating Britain was for long to suggest that it did not experience in the eighteenth century anything that was akin to the Enlightenment, or certainly in England as opposed to Scotland where an Enlightenment was long perceived. From the 1990s, and notably due to the work of the late Roy Porter,[3] that approach has been replaced by one that emphasizes an English Enlightenment. That is generally presented in terms of peaceful practices and structures, such as scientific lectures and freemasonry, libraries and subscription concerts, spas and assembly rooms, and there has been particular interest in female intellectual activity.

At the same time, this was a period of frequent warfare and imperial expansion, and notably so for Britain, which was at war in 1689–97, 1702–13, 1718–20, 1739–48, 1754–63, 1775–83, 1793–1802, and 1803–15. That standard list reflects conflicts with other European powers and with American colonists but is misleading as it can be greatly expanded if attention is also devoted to conflict with non-Western powers and people, particularly in India and also with Native Americans. Britain was at war for longer than most other European states and very much more so than the United Provinces, Sweden, Denmark, and Portugal. The varied and overlapping spatial matrices, both of military power and of the discussion and understanding of this power, therefore deserve attention.

Geography here becomes a matter in large part of geopolitics and of strategy, but before the terms *geopolitics* and *strategy* were used. Therefore, insofar as a discussion in formal terms is to be expected, the sources available are tenuous. That, however, does not make the subject unimportant or unapproachable. Moreover, even when sources are few, misleading, or nonexistent[4]—for example, for the impact of the physical environment, especially slope profiles, drainage, and soil quality, on agriculture—that does not mean that the subject is unimportant or that there are no relevant sources. In that case, the very physical environment serves as evidence for the spatial perceptions and activities of the age, not least with the settlement patterns and rental values of the period, and with the content and organization of the land use. Settlement patterns and fixed boundaries leave plentiful evidence that survives to the present.[5]

GEOPOLITICS

Irrespective of the lack of formal discussion of geopolitics—a word coined by the Swedish political scientist Rudolph Kjellan (1864–1922)—and strategy in those terms in this period, there was also a very finely calibrated spatial consideration of these issues.[6] In particular, discussions over international relations and wartime strategy played a major role in politics, whether ministerial, parliamentary, press, or popular, and the issues were readily graspable. Furthermore, this was far more so than is so often (although not invariably) the case in a modern world where, instead, socioeconomic issues are to the fore and where, for the United States and Britain, conflicts can be referred to as "wars of choice," even though they were not necessarily thought of as such at the time.

In the eighteenth century, as today, contemporary geopolitical considerations related to areas of concern[7] and to the question of where to operate militarily and diplomatically in order to achieve goals. Thus, both policy and implementation were at stake. This was not least because of the important concept of the balance of power and the view that it encompassed states with which Britain had tensions, such as France, as well as states that possibly offered more direct balancing relations. The former could also entail states at a distance, such as Russia in the 1720s, and, therefore, knowledge about them was required.

Moreover, this situation was dynamic as a result both of changes in British politics and, indeed capabilities, and of the real and apparent actions of foreign states. Notions of threat and deterrence were part of the military balance and of the related geopolitics. The location of military units and their preparedness then became part of the equation. The measure of the geography of power extended to include the preparedness of the navy,[8] which included the degree of certainty over the supply of the all-important naval stores, notably timber, iron, hemp, and pitch. Reports and rumors over the state of French and Spanish naval preparedness were particularly significant for British political geography. This significance, however, confronted serious problems in assessing the situation, not least due to major limitations in the nature of surveillance.

The naval situation also encouraged a determination to chart waters and, more generally, to understand the operational context and tactical character of warfare at sea. The cartographic dimension is considered later in the chapter. It should be understood as a key aspect of British geopolitics, one directly involving the crucial elements of naval strength and security.

The complex interrelationships of political and military power were debated, or, at least, asserted, with contention over the very value of the concept of the balance of power, as well as its application. The balance provided an apparently coherent and readily measurable notion of force in international relations, one that lent itself to mechanistic interpretations that were similar in character to Newtonian physics. However, the implementation of these ideas was difficult and contentious. As a result, political geography was very much a matter of perception as well as of realism and was highly politicized accordingly. The very porosity of the term and the flexibility of interpretation helped to make the balance of power particularly useful for contention but less so for analysis. This was not simply a matter of vocabulary but also of a more fundamental problem with the balance of power and thus with the political geography of the period. This was namely whether the balance was descriptive of processes that naturally happened, notably an automatic balancing of would-be hegemonic powers, or, alternatively, primarily, prescriptive, in the sense of arguing that such processes should, and must, happen, as in "to take a part for preserving the balance of Europe."[9] As is often the case today, a zero-sum approach played a major part in contemporary views: "All Greatness is comparative; whatever contributes to the aggrandizement of one power does necessarily tend to the diminution of another."[10] The tension between the descriptive and prescriptive approaches remained central to discussion of the balance throughout the period, and therefore of geopolitics. More generally, there was a tension between the descriptive and the prescriptive character of politics.

Linked to the balance of power, the mental equipment of the period, more specifically the belief in mechanistic, rather than organic, theories of states and the state system, encouraged an approach to international relations that was instrumentalist: by means of adopting a specific policy, there would be assured outcomes. This approach reflected a confidence, born of the mathematization of experience in an age in thrall to Newtonian physics, that rational calculation could be applied to understand and solve problems. Such an approach, however, had to confront the unwillingness of foreign powers to conform to such calculation, as well as the more general unknowable character of developments.

The public politics of British geopolitics were significant because the ministers and officials who directed Britain's responses to geopolitical issues were not in some fashion separate from this politics. Indeed, the opposite was the case. To an extent that is far greater than in modern Britain, there was scant sense that government was separate to the political process. As an aspect of this, senior bureaucrats were both "placemen," appointed for political reasons, and were frequently Members of Parliament (MPs) as well. This situation has the advantage for historians that they might leave sources in the sphere of public politics, notably parliamentary speeches.

Much about geopolitics related primarily to politics, and not so much to geography. Physical geography attracted little attention in this regard, except insofar as factors of closeness and distance, those of locational geography, were concerned. Moreover, there could be discussion about the practicalities of invasion plans and therefore the feasibility of invasion. Most of this discussion focused on naval strength, as with consideration in 1726 about the vulnerability to British naval action of any Austrian-backed Jacobite invasion from Ostend, then in the Austrian Netherlands (Belgium). Nevertheless, there was also frequent assessment of the probable impact of winds and distance on any invasion attempt.

The political character of geopolitics was notably apparent with the emphasis on the particular concern of the Hanoverian dynasty with its native electorate in modern Germany. In this instance, because of strong and persistent criticism of the Hanoverian succession from 1714 to the late 1750s and/or of particular kings, geopolitics was intensely political in that links with the Continent were to be defended or to be criticized, at least in part accordingly. This aspect was very apparent in the discussion under George I (r. 1714–27) over the fate of Bremen and Verden, Swedish territories acquired by Hanover. The linkage between this outcome and the dispatch of British warships to the Baltic in order to exert pressure, in practice a close but concealed linkage, attracted exposition and controversy in Parliament, pamphlets, and the press. The Hanoverian relationship was central to Britain's commitment to Europe as it created a composite polity, that of Britain-Hanover, at one level.[11] Moreover, the political geography of the Continent could not readily be considered in Britain without being aware of this commitment and its contentious quality. Thus, to write of the German states and, in particular, of their constitutions, histories, and geographies, was not value-free. By extension, such writing could be seen as commentary on Hanover, and about Continental interventionism, and, indeed, was often designed accordingly.

So also with the confessional (religious) geopolitics bound up in ideas of anti-Catholicism and, as a related but separate issue, of "the Protestant interest." This geopolitics was not lessened by the general move toward Europe in place of Christendom.[12] Confessional geopolitics again ensured a geopolitics in which the emphasis was on the politics involved, while the geography was essentially an expression of this politics. London, however, was not the center of Protestantism, as Rome, both classical and modern, had been/was of religions. The geographical discussion of confessional geopolitics was wide ranging. One important instance related to Grand Tour literature and to discussion about the Grand Tour, on which see chapter 5.

The issue also underlines the number of geographies on offer because British Catholics did not share this geopolitics. Indeed, many sent their children to be educated in Catholic schools on the Continent, a presence that continued thereafter with entry into nunneries and seminaries. There were occasional press reports about the extent of this education, as in the critical reports in the *St. James's Chronicle* of May 13 and 15, 1766. In the latter, there was a call to end the free movement of people in and out of the kingdom on the grounds that it helped "popery." There was, moreover, intermarriage with Catholic families on the Continent. These links were also very important in Ireland, not least because, in 1751, Pope Benedict XIV decreed that diocesan priests could be ordained only after they had agreed to go to a Continental seminary to study theology.[13]

Correspondingly, Protestant views of the "Protestant interest," and of the merits accordingly of military and diplomatic intervention abroad, varied greatly.[14] They did so at least in part in accordance with confessional politics in Britain: supporters of the Church of England were sometimes less keen on Continental Protestants than were Nonconformists, although the church raised large sums for Protestants in Poland and Savoy-Piedmont. Religion cut across nationalism as well as lending support to what, in practice, were rival British nationalisms.[15] Again, educational links played a role, as with Scots (and others including William Pitt the Elder) going to study in the universities of the Dutch Republic, which was Calvinist like Scotland.

Each category of Protestants included a broad range of interest and values. For example, the correspondence of William Wake, archbishop of Canterbury from 1716 to 1737, revealed a degree of Church of England interest in, and commitment to, the position of Continental Protestants that was greater than that generally shown in the second half of the century. The same was even more the case for Wake's interest in Gallican Catholics opposed to papal authority, and in the possibility of a reunion of the Catholic Church and the Church of England. This offered a religious geography that was very different to the conventional one.[16]

The theme of Britain as involved in a struggle against the sinister, even "hellish,"[17] forces of international Catholicism, forces with a wide-ranging scope and a universal intention, continued to be expressed, not least in press reports of Catholic persecution abroad.[18] This was an aspect of the extent to which the "Glorious Revolution" appeared less as the terminus of a century of political, constitutional, and religious dispute, dissension and polemic, and international threat than as another stage in the process. To contemporaries, the tensions that were explicit in the Revolution Settlement were but part of the wider disorder, both British and foreign, in political society and culture. Commentators saw not so much the rise of political stability, the British Empire, Whig consensus, and a polite and commercial people, as flux, uncertainty, disorder, and division.[19]

Concern about international Catholicism became more potent at times of Franco-Austrian understanding or apparent understanding. On February 13, 1759, John Watson, an Anglican curate, informed the readers of *The Union Journal: or, Halifax Advertiser* that Louis XV of France had attacked Britain in the Seven Years' War (1756–63) as the first stage to subject the powers of the earth. There was a crucial moral dimension to the struggle:

"how unjustly the rights of Englishmen have been attacked by a cruel and ambitious enemy."

BRITISHNESS

Britishness was a strong strand in the political geography of the state and of the related spatial system of power. In a tremendous display of military power, republican forces, notably under the command of Oliver Cromwell, had, in 1649–52, followed up their earlier victories in the First (1642–46) and Second (1648) Civil Wars by conquering both Scotland, a success that had eluded many English monarchs, and Ireland, as well as the remaining English Royalist bases in the Channel Islands, the Isles of Scilly, and the Isle of Man, and Royalist areas in the New World. Thereafter, there was not to be a lasting difference in military-political control between England, Scotland, and Ireland until the British state lost most of Ireland in 1922 at the close of the Irish War of Independence. Short-term variations in allegiance—between England and Ireland in 1689–91 or England and Scotland in the winter of 1745–46—were unstable and, despite discussion of possible separate destinies, were seen as such on both sides. There was an assumption that those in control of one would try to gain control over the other. The events of 1660 (the successful invasion of England by General George Monck, the military commander in Scotland) and of 1689–91 (the conquest of the British Isles by William III) encouraged this well-founded assumption.

Thus, irrespective of their precise constitutional relationship and of the understanding of it, England, Ireland, and Scotland had become an interconnected unit in the geography of military power. This was a response both to the need to adapt to the new state formed in 1707 by the Act of Union of England and Scotland and to the specific, but acute, threat from Jacobitism from 1689. This threat was significant as late as the large-scale French invasion scheme of 1759. More specific needs were created by real and apparent challenges to the Revolution Settlements of 1688–1707, dates chosen in order to include the Act of Union in the Revolution Settlement.

In particular, the Forty-Five, the large-scale Jacobite uprising in 1745–46, inspired fear and hatred of the Scots, Philip, 4th Earl of Chesterfield, writing to a fellow office-holder: "that damned beggarly rebellious people provoke me."[20] The rapid Jacobite advance south, through Scotland and into England as far as Derby in the Midlands, which was entered on December 4, 1745, posed the danger that the Jacobites might press on to London as their leader, Charles Edward Stuart, "Bonnie Prince Charlie," wanted. This immediate threat obliged ministers and commentators to grasp a new geography of Britain, that of an invaded state, and an apparently successfully invaded state. This Jacobite advance represented an inversion of the natural order as far as they were concerned, not least because the invasions of England in 1660 by General George Monck and, even more, 1688 by William III of Orange were presented as in some ways restorations of the proper political order and therefore not, as they really were, military invasions. Such assumptions were highly significant for political geography. A reluctance to understand these as invasions of England was important in the consideration of English vulnerability. The reluctance reflected the dominance of legitimacy in the discussion of political geography.

In a more subtle form of military geography, the Jacobite advance south in 1745 revealed the partly inconsequential nature of fortifications mostly left over from an earlier era of warfare, and, linked to this, the extent to which the country was only poorly defended. There were fortified positions that affected the campaign, notably Carlisle, Edinburgh, and Newcastle. The last, where there was a large force to protect the crossing of the River Tyne, as well as the possibility of shipping in reinforcements, ensured that the Jacobite advance south did not occur along the east coast. Instead, it was launched farther west, via Carlisle. Despite fortifications, both Carlisle and, earlier, Edinburgh fell to the Jacobites. Moreover, there was no resistance to their advance in most of the towns they entered. On the western route into England, these included, south of Carlisle, which had resisted, successively Preston, Manchester, and Derby, none of which was fortified or contained garrisons. As a consequence, rivers, such as the Ribble and the Trent, on which Preston and Derby respectively sat, were crossed with ease and the capacity to use them for the defense was lost. The invasion underlined the significance of river-crossing points, namely bridges, which, indeed, had been very important in the unsuccessful Scottish invasions of 1648, 1651, and 1715, which were defeated at Preston, Worcester, and Preston, respectively. These places provided, as John Adams suggested when he visited Worcester in 1786, part of a political geography of the country, a geography, however, that was highly contentious.[21]

Britain as a unit was not, as in the Civil War of 1642–46, one in which advances were contested but, instead, apparently wide open. The contrast was, in practice, less clear cut, in either case, but a different military geography and, notably, a geography of vulnerability, was revealed. The vulnerability shown in 1745 encouraged later invasion concerns, especially about the prospect of French invasions in 1756, 1759, and 1779, as well as fortifications in the Scottish Highlands, especially the large Fort George near Inverness,[22] a fortress that, in practice, did not hear shots fired in anger. In 1745, however, Charles Edward did not press on from Derby toward London, as he indeed wished, because the Highland chiefs, partly swayed by inaccurate intelligence about the moves of the regular army, refused to march on. On December 6, 1745, as a result, the Jacobites retreated north, beginning the process that led to their total defeat at Culloden the following April.

Mapping played a role in the response to the Jacobite threat. As with naval charts, a key element in the military use of mapping was provided by its institutional framework. The Board of Ordnance was responsible for artillery and engineering, including the provision of maps. The reorganization of the Ordnance that followed the 1715–16 Jacobite Rising led to the establishment of a body of twenty-eight engineers as well as an increase in mapping.[23] This mapping was to be important to the attempt to provide a military infrastructure to hold down the Scottish Highlands.[24] Aside from fortifications, the engineers produced road maps that were designed to provide strategic and operational information to help military planning and moves.[25] Mapmaking reflected both need and a perception of weakness. There was certainly a shortage of maps, one that General Hawley regretted during the Forty-Five.[26]

The military survey by William Roy of the Royal Engineers between 1747 and 1759 was therefore a valuable addition. Six surveying parties were employed, and the survey was the basis for a map. Survey and map were designed to help in the British military response to any future rebellion and to assist in the process of the governmental reorganization of the Highlands. This was a key aspect of a longer term extension of central control that included roadbuilding and the establishment and improvement of fortified positions, notably the still-impressive Fort George. The survey covered roads as well as terrain, but the mapmaking instruments available, and the speed of the survey, posed problems of accuracy. The survey itself was unpublished until used in 1805 as the basis for a map by the noted entrepreneurial mapmaker Aaron Arrowsmith. This represented a relationship between military mapping and private entrepreneurship that was less close than that for maritime charts where there was the incentive of the market for merchants.

In the aftermath of the Forty-Five, traditional patterns of Highland politics and society—notably heritable jurisdictions and the basis they offered for clannish resistance to the state—were changed by government action, creating a new geography of power. Thomas Sherlock, the influential bishop of Salisbury, warned that laws on these jurisdictions had been passed before: "but never executed, and perhaps the main thing to be provided for is we secure an execution of the *King's* laws in the country; which is at present under the absolute *will* of the lairds."[27]

Sherlock was well connected, his correspondence offering a form of linkage that itself had political and spatial dimensions. Mapping the correspondence of leading figures is an approach that has not been adopted. For individual bishops, it was one that tended to focus on London and their diocese, which was a parallel to that of major landowners on London and their estates. Thus, bishops and major landowners lived in two worlds and so had two mental maps: their London lives and their dioceses or estates. This must have affected their thinking.

As a related factor, it is possible to use correspondence to note the travels of such figures. For example, for Sir Robert Walpole, there was a focus on the London area but also journeys to his Norfolk seat at Houghton where he held an important annual politico-social meeting. Conversely, Walpole never went abroad, or to Scotland, Wales, and Ireland. For Thomas, Duke of Newcastle, it was London and his properties in the South-East. Although a secretary of state from 1724, he did not go abroad until 1748 and did not visit Scotland, Wales, and Ireland. The travels of George I and George II contrasted greatly with those of Walpole, as Hanover posed a jurisdictional demand different to that simply of visiting their estates. In contrast, George III never visited Hanover. He saw more of Britain than his two predecessors, although only of southern England: George III traveled no farther north than Worcester, which he visited in 1788. Like George I and George II, he never visited Ireland, Scotland, or Wales.

Although the process varied in its effectiveness, much of Scottish society was increasingly pulled toward England from 1691 and, even more, 1707 and 1746. This was least the case with Scottish religion and law, where national distinctiveness was legally established, but far more the case with national politics and business. Indeed, Scottish lobbying increasingly focused on London, where, after the union of the kingdoms in 1707, a union that entailed one of the Parliaments of Edinburgh and Westminster, Scotland had 45 out of the 558 MPs. The absentee kingship seen with the Union of the Crowns in 1603 was matched, with the 1707 union, by the abolition of the Scottish Privy Council. Trade and capital flows between England and Scotland increased, as did the movement of ideas. Talented Scots increasingly chose to make their reputations in London.

At the regional level, the change in Scotland was particularly clear in the Highlands and Islands, a largely Gaelic-speaking clan society that had threatened the Scottish Lowlands even more than control from London. The replacement of the clan system was linked to the impact of an agrarian commercialism that led to emigration as well as to increased recruitment into the army.[28] The Augmentation Returns suggested that, in midcentury, the Highlands and North-East were not yet experiencing the population growth seen elsewhere in Scotland. Contemporary readers were provided with more information on the Highlands, whether John Campbell's *Full and Particular Description of the Highlands of Scotland* (1752) or the later products of the travels of Johnson and Boswell.[29]

Ireland, in contrast, maintained a separate Parliament and government, but the control of London was hardwired into this system. A different political geography had been glimpsed in 1689 when James II's Parliament in Dublin had rejected much of the authority of the Westminster Parliament. This path had, however, been blocked as a result of William III's successful invasion of 1690.

Wales did not have a comparable constitutional trajectory, but it was widely seen in England as wild and lawless. In addition, there was a linguistic difference between England and Wales, while North Wales was a Jacobite enclave. The remoteness of much of Wales meant that redress from the rule of local gentry was well-nigh impossible, so that the poor were in their hands. Even Lewis Morris, who held a royal warrant to exploit the lead mines in north Cardiganshire, was unable to carry out his work without troops to guard his mines and workers.[30]

Jacobitism, and the strategic threat posed by an independent Scotland and Ireland, pushed together those politicians in the three kingdoms who were opposed to it. In the early eighteenth century, there was some support for union with England among Irish Protestants, but it was unsuccessful. The preservation of a Parliament in Dublin enabled Ireland's Protestant politicians to retain a measure of importance and independence, although it was very much separated from the bulk of the Irish population. This was seen with the definition offered in the title to the call by the Irish writer Samuel Madden for an improvement of society: *Reflections and Resolutions proper for the Gentlemen of Ireland, as to their conduct for the service of their country, as landlords, as masters of Families, as Protestants, as descended from British ancestors, as country gentlemen and farmers, as justices of the peace, as merchants, as members of Parliament* (Dublin, 1738). Moreover, legislation in Westminster, the result of strong and persistent protectionist lobbying by English interests, hindered Irish exports, particularly to English and colonial markets.[31] This legislation sustained a boundary in the economic geography of Britain, with Ireland thus separated in a way that was not captured on maps. There was particular opposition in England to Irish wool and cloth exports.[32] In addition, the granting of Irish lands and pensions to favored courtiers exacerbated the problem of absentee landowners and revenue holders, with a consequent drain of money out of Ireland, much to the fury of Jonathan Swift.[33] This situation also was not captured in maps.

The inclusion of Ireland in maps and descriptions of Britain was notable, but there was an awareness of difference between Ireland and the rest of Britain. This difference included maps that indicated the security issue. Thus, in Herman Moll's atlas *The World Described* (1720), the "New Map of Ireland" that was included depicted the places containing barracks, which was not necessary for England. In addition, an inset map demonstrating Ireland's relationship to Britain and to northwest Europe, including the French naval base at Brest and the Spanish one at "the Groyne" (the archaic name for Corunna), both demonstrated the risk of invasion and threw light on the Anglo-Spanish conflict of 1718–20, a conflict that included a Spanish invasion of Scotland in 1719.[34]

The situation, or, rather, varied situations, of Ireland was a prime instance of the extent to which Britain involved both cohesion and also a range of political arrangements that created in effect zones of authority.

These were not mapped out but, however, created a sense of spatiality in assumptions. This was a dynamic and controversial situation. In practice, Britishness was, in some respects, a product of English triumphalism and providentialism and, in part, a vehicle for it. Conceptions of Englishness, not least of the notion of a chosen Protestant nation, and of a law-abiding society, were translated into Britishness[35] and were then employed to find others deficient; and this despite differences in the Established Church and legal system on the British scale.

Many Welsh, Irish, and Scots sought to benefit from the range of links with England. For the Scots, the Union of 1707 brought access to a greatly expanded network of patronage. They came to play a major role in the expansion of empire, not least through disproportionate service in the army and in the East India Company, but also through the development of specific economic links.[36] Protestantism (whatever the quarrels between Protestants), war with France, and the benefits of empire together helped to create a British nationhood, one that developed alongside the still-strong senses of English, Scottish, Irish, and Welsh identity.[37]

History is affected by the shifting patterns of present concerns and opinions. This is not only a case of academic priorities and methods but also of modern-day politics. As a consequence, there can be an emphasis on cooperation or, conversely, on coercion when looking at past power relationships. For example, the English dimension of Britishness was highlighted by Scottish separatists from the late twentieth century. They presented the creation and sustaining of Britain as resting in large part on historic military conquest and political corruption and underplayed the vitality and strong appeal of England as a model for Scotland in the eighteenth century. This approach has implications for the analysis of the understanding of spatial relations in the period.

Aside from this point, the geography of power needs to be seen in a complex fashion, one that had a variety of meanings. In part, indeed, the skill of the concept of Britishness rested on its ability to draw on assessments of Englishness but not to associate them too closely with England. Alongside Britishness, there were still vigorous senses of local, provincial, and national identities, which were expressed in a variety of forms, including custom and lore. An example from Wales, notably its remoter parts, was "petty marriage," the custom of an engaged couple living together until such time as a clergyman could legally marry them. This coexistence was an aspect of the compromise, cooperation, and symbiosis that, in addition to coercion, were aspects of the geography of power. This combination makes it complex to analyze and, indeed, map the situation.

For example, hostility to Jacobitism linked the Irish, Scottish, and Welsh political establishments and social elites, as remodeled from 1689, to London. This hostility was also the case within England. In part, it drew on the detailed configuration of politics seen both with the legacy of the civil wars of the 1640s and early 1650s (across the different parts of Britain) and with the related (but separate) strong impact of confessionalism and notably of anti-Catholicism. The legacy of these civil wars was important to political localism, as with Whiggery in Taunton as a continuance of 1640s' Parliamentarianism and a bitter Royalist siege then during the Civil War. This continuance drew on the Nonconformist tradition in Taunton.

On the British scale, shared interests, histories, and ideologies among England, Wales, Ireland, and Scotland, or aspects thereof, produced pressure for cooperation that was distinct from the conventional social aspirations of elite coherence and leadership that eased the path of management. These interests gave a substance to a Britishness defined in terms of the defense of the Revolution Settlement. Yet again, this represented the joining of geographical and historical themes. "Sharing" took a number of forms. For example, both the Protestant and the Catholic churches in Ireland disliked the use of Gaelic, the native language, while the use of print, which was almost monopolized by the English speakers of Ireland, joined the literate, whatever their church, in a common culture.[38] This is a past situation that many today do not find welcome when hearing accounts of this part.

Aside from particular readings of the placing of English, Irish, Scottish, and Welsh history, there was, and still is, a general failure to devote sufficient attention to regional history within any of these units and, more particularly, in England.[39] In part, this failure reflected the lack of a strong modern political consciousness of regional history or of an institutional context for advancing one. The extent to which the eighteenth-century world understood a strong regional stance is unclear, and notably within England, as opposed to the more pronounced Highland/Lowland divide in Scotland, or the divide around the Welsh language in Wales. Regional links and networks in England can be noted, as in the circulation networks of provincial papers, on which see chapter 4. Moreover, there are some valuable discussions of urban political culture, particularly in Bristol and Norwich.[40] Yet, confessional divisions within England were not identified with regional character. There were disproportionately more Catholics—for example, in Lancashire, Sussex, and Essex—but not so as to produce a sectarian geography, other than on the local scale, where such a geography was generally highly significant. So also with Nonconformists in particular areas. There is no equivalent for the eighteenth century to the recent academic coverage of the country at the county level for the mid-seventeenth century and particularly for the background to the Civil War of 1642–46. This aspect of geography by omission, omission in the sense of a lack of current attention, is notable. How far it matches a deliberate lack of attention in the past is open to discussion. That the Tories and Whigs were both national parties is significant. They had particular areas of strength but not so as to produce a stark regional divide. There were Tories and Whigs across the country, even though Tories, for example, were strongest in county seats in the West Country.

THE POLITICS OF PLACE

In turn, political links and divisions affected the reading of the world abroad as part of a broader pattern of the politics of place, a politics that reflected the significance of spatial factors.[41] In particular, foreign policy was closely bound up with notions of geographic significance. Security and economic factors were the major issues at stake and were frequently presented in a highly partisan fashion. For example, the Tory ministry that negotiated a settlement with France in the Peace of Utrecht of 1713, ending British participation in the War of the Spanish Succession, was committed, in part in reaction to Whig interventionism on the Continent in the 1700s, to a policy of commercial growth and transoceanic expansion. Looking back to attitudes and policies during the War of the Spanish Succession, there was also Tory political interest in the Pacific and in the lands round the estuary of the River Plate. However, those ideas lacked the military, economic, and logistical practicability of power projection and commercial penetration that was needed to develop the greater Caribbean, as key British interests more plausibly sought. Indeed, the Philippines and the Plate were marginal to the main thrust to the Spanish New World. In contrast, the Whigs, who came to power anew in 1714, lacked the Tory commitment to transoceanic possibilities. They focused, instead, in accordance with the wishes of George I (r. 1714–27), on European power politics and on trade rather than territorial expansion. The significance of trade to the Spanish New World in the Caribbean region was reflected in its being covered in maps, especially one by Moll, on which see chapter 1.

The political agenda shifted from the late 1730s in a more transoceanic direction, and the geography of state ambition changed with it, albeit in a more hesitant fashion. The latter led to press and parliamentary attacks on the supposed weakness of the Walpole government and notably in not pushing forward claims and interests against Spain in the Caribbean. These attacks by Tories and opposition Whigs alike related politics within Britain to the wider world of international conflict. Thus, in the run-up to the Yorkshire by-election of January 1742, the *York Courant*, the leading newspaper in the region, carried a letter on October 20, 1741, from "J.S." of Leeds attacking one of the candidates, Cholmley Turner, for having voted for ministerial measures, including the Convention of the Pardo, an unsuccessful attempt in 1738–39 to settle differences with Spain. A week later, friends of Turner replied, claiming (correctly) that the opposition was using the convention as a cant phrase. The dispute reflected the extent to which the political public were offered international issues in a partisan fashion, issues, however, that assumed a knowledge of geography. This was true throughout the century, and, in some respects, more significantly so than during the last century, and, notably, the early years of the twenty-first century.

LONDON

The political reading of geography and the geographical reading of politics each took a number of forms. The most common was that of a different perception of particular places. As a subject, London was the most striking in Britain and certainly until the cult for landscape, late in the century, led to a marked shift in preference, from urban elegance to sublime landscape. This change was both to affect the mental geography of Britain and also to provide the background for a harsher view of the city as a physical environment, a harsher view that comprehended London in the nineteenth century although it drew more heavily on the industrial cities of northern England.

Throughout the eighteenth century, London was presented by some as a site of liberty, trade, and progress. Indeed, its rebuilding after the devastating Great Fire of 1666 was a consciously modern project with philosophical ideas underlying those of architecture, engineering, and social organization.[42] Others viewed London in terms of moral, political, and economic disorder and dissolution, an approach that went back to the classical treatment of Rome. Urban living served, as so often, to delineate, if not define, issues and alignments. Whigs tended to take the former view, looking favorably on London and urban life and, more especially, treating them as progress and as the cause of progress. In contrast, Tories focused more on London as a problem and as the cause of problems, although their tone could vary. Thus, *The Rape of the Lock* (two versions, 1712, 1714), a witty satire by the Tory Alexander Pope, was set in London polite society. It offered criticism, but not fury, and was directed against social mores rather than at London itself.

Yet, there is a need for care in taking a clear party line on values and their geographical placing, whether domestic or in terms of foreign policy, a point true of many facets of activity—for example, garden design. For example, Joseph Yorke, a well-connected member of the "Old Corps" Whig establishment, criticized London in 1763 and pressed the need for its physical restraint: "Don't you think that the overgrown size of our metropolis is one great cause of the frivolousness, idleness and debauchery of our times. I have often wondered that the legislature has not long since laboured to put bounds to its increase, for it is really too big for the good observance of the law or the gospel."[43]

Alongside grand perceptions of the overall significance of London came, as with other regions, localities and places, the more detailed local geography of reality and perception within London. At the most detailed urban level, the physical creation of British cities in this period (although not of new cities in the overseas empire) was an evolutionary, piecemeal process, with much development taking place out of existing housing types and traditional layouts. The surviving evidence on London housing improves from the eighteenth century,[44] as also for other towns.[45] And, like today, maintaining, changing, and upgrading the structure of houses made them perfectly suited to a society of consumption geared toward continual renewal and replacement. As in modern cities, this was a process that reflected and sustained social distinctions, both within and between communities. Gradual, but important, shifts in the social character of districts could, over time, become easily discernible.

The nature of these distinctions might also be seen in open spaces, the definition and placing of which altered as cities expanded. In London, squares such as Hanover Square, laid out between 1717 and 1719, were a key element in the development of the West End. They tended to be public, rather than private, arenas until the 1720s. Then the emphasis came to be on exclusivity: open spaces were enclosed, laid out as gardens, and restricted to residents. This Georgian gentrification helped to further, or at least redefine, a process of social exclusion, both very locally and within London,[46] being contrasted with the less polite worlds of East London, Southwark, and Covent Garden.[47]

Social exclusion was not the sole theme. There was also inclusion. Pleasure gardens and assembly rooms, like "politeness" itself, served to further the ideal of a free, but yet ordered, city, one in which people mixed in an orderly fashion. As a result, these contrived spaces helped both to challenge the belief that linked circulation of luxury commodities with social dislocation and to tame the fears and concerns surrounding the commercial expansion of the metropolis.[48]

MAPS AND MILITARY POWER

To move from the perception of London to issues of military power is a big leap, although, in 1780, there was a bridge in the shape of the Gordon Riots, a major challenge to public order arising from anti-Catholic riots. This episode led to the deployment of troops in London, and their location and patrols was recorded on a map that was clearly used for planning.[49] This put London temporarily alongside the earlier mapping of Highland Scotland and the response to Ireland, notably in the 1700s and 1790s. The use of troops served to underline the role of force in politics.

This role was also seen in the precautions made against the linked challenges of radicalism and invasion in the 1790s, including suppressing opposition newspapers and building barracks and, in particular, in the response to the naval mutinies of 1797 at the Nore and Spithead. The interactions of military power and geography were readily apparent for both sea and land, the naval and the military. Indeed, this dual character was important to the development of geographical knowledge and to its reach into the British state and society.

Land warfare required a strong spatial awareness. At the tactical level, that of battles, it demanded the understanding, indeed the detailed understanding, of the relationships between place and terrain, notably height, slopes, and water features, especially rivers and marshy ground. Each of these was, and is, significant for the tasks set for military units and for their relative effectiveness in discharging them. At the operational level, that of campaigns, the conduct of war necessitated an understanding of routes and of the relationships between place and terrain over the area of campaign. These were necessary for there to be effective planning, both about advances and concerning supplies. At the strategic level, there were the needs for geopolitical information, such that challenges and opportunities could be grasped and priorities determined. All of these levels involved the equations of force and space, and each required maps, maps to present, maps to understand, and maps to convince.

For most of history, and still to this day, the relevant maps have overwhelmingly been mental maps, the understanding of place in the mind's eye. These were ready means to help consideration and exposition. For example, the plan of an ambush or a fort might be drawn with a stick, a finger in the dirt, or in powdered sand, might be sketched in the air or described with words. At the same time, war, and notably as conducted by Western powers, developed paper-based mapping from the early-modern period.

Maps became very much more significant in diplomacy and warfare with the eighteenth century as part of the development both of a new form of military professionalism and of the public discussion of politics. Encouraging the map culture, there was a general downgrading of theory in favor of facts, not least as the notion of applied knowledge acquired definition and prestige, especially as received wisdom was increasingly superseded by new information. Linked to this, there was a more explicit process of planning. Scientific methods entailed not only the concern of generals with artillery and sieges but also the use of scientific knowledge at the operational level, with the need to plan foraging and marches requiring detailed information. Logistical skills were important to the staff planning that was at an increased premium.

The establishment of accurate values for longitude, and the diffusion of the new method, one of the major British practical and organizational achievements of the century (see chapter 1), ensured that it became possible to locate most places accurately. In turn, the development of accurate and standard means of measuring distances made it easier for mapmakers to understand, assess, and reconcile the work of their predecessors. Maps also became more predictable as mapping conventions developed. Even at the end of the seventeenth century, there was no standard alignment of maps, which was an aspect of a more general lack of standardization and, even, precision. However, in the following century, the convention of placing north at the top was established.

Mapping was at the scientific end of geography and increasingly appeared so as the decorative dimension was downplayed.[50] Like other aspects of the science of the period, it represented an infinitely extendable attempt to understand natural forces and to encode them in laws that did not rest for their authority on a culturally specific priesthood or foundation myth. The map as a presentation and metaphor of space was part of the Newtonian downplaying of uncertainty; but it also faced the problems of its use in a more malleable public politics. An increased awareness of cartographic distinctiveness and change encouraged the idea that maps could, and thereby should, improve and respond to new and more accurate information. The correct relative location of features was expected, as was appropriate proportionality, and keeping to scale. In addition, aside from specific improvements in mapping techniques and concepts, maps were increasingly created for general reference, a process that enhanced their use.

The military were the major source for mapping across much of Europe. The long-standing surveying and charting facilities and interests of Western armies and navies varied greatly but proved very important in the eighteenth century. In terms of scale, comprehensiveness, and accuracy, the surveys then were in a different class to those a century earlier. Britain was not at the fore in Europe but was far more significant for mapping outside Europe. Drawing on the cartographic traditions of their varied possessions, especially Italy and the Austrian Netherlands (modern Belgium), the Austrians were especially prominent in this mapping in Europe, in their far-flung possessions of Sicily, Lombardy, Austria, Bohemia, Hungary, and the Austrian Netherlands.

Conflict encouraged both supply and demand: military mapping and the commercial production of maps. Thus, James Bruce (1669–1735), the son of a Scot who had settled in Russia, produced a map of the Azov region to help Peter the Great's 1696 siege of Azov. In 1758, during the Seven Years' War, Lord George Sackville, who was in command of British forces in Germany, had written to Robert, 4th Earl of Holdernessse, a British secretary of state, who had traveled as a diplomat, "You will see Cappenburgh in the map."[51] As Lord George Germain, Sackville was to be in charge of British strategy during the War of American Independence.

In North America, forces had to traverse vast distances, often through wild, inhospitable terrain, making the British vulnerable to enemy tactics of *petite guerre*, by which small, highly mobile detachments carried out fleeting attacks and ambushes on the flanks of their larger adversary. Commanders therefore required maps that both gave an account of routes and terrain suitable for planning and that conveyed very practical knowledge that would allow their forces to move quickly without being overexposed to enemy action. Commanders ordered the preparation of reconnaissance maps and route maps. The former involved the rapid production of information, and the resulting maps were generally crude. For example, in February 1775, just months before the Battle of Bunker Hill, General Thomas Gage, the British commander, dispatched two amateur surveyors to reconnoiter the countryside around Boston, which was the key British garrison point and the center of political contention.[52]

Route maps, which were of more particular significance, were usually executed by professional military surveyors. While they may have incorporated intelligence gleaned from reconnaissance maps, these maps laid out specific routes for the army to take, often also drawing on information from (sometimes already-existing) topographical surveys conducted under scientific conditions. This mapping was frequently undertaken with specific reference to an intended itinerary, which considered daily progress and the most appropriate sites for encampments and resupply of the force. As a result, an accurate and formal detailing of distances and features of the landscape was crucial.

War in North America in 1743–48, 1754–63, and 1775–83 encouraged the appearance of more maps of that continent, at least insofar as known by Europeans, and these were widely publicized. Thus, new maps of North

America were announced in the issues of a London newspaper, the *Daily Advertiser*, on August 3, September 5, and September 10, 1755, as large-scale conflict between Britain and France began there in 1755.

Although they could be rejected as any sort of juridical proof of sovereignty,[53] maps also played a role in supporting the discussion of policy and notably in differences between Britain and France over the North American interior.[54] John Clevland, Secretary to the Admiralty, had a copy of a series of tracts of 1755–56 that dealt with North America, tracts supported by maps. One of the tracts was Lewis Evans's *Geographical, Historical, Political, Philosophical, and Mechanical Essays. The first containing an Analysis of a General Map of the Middle British Colonies in America and of the country of the confederate Indians* (London and Philadelphia, 1755). It was used by General Edward Braddock who advanced into the interior in 1755, only to be successfully ambushed by French and native forces close to his intended destination, the French base of Fort Duquesne, near modern Pittsburgh.

The accuracy of maps were contested and with reason. This was a matter of disputes between British and French maps. Indeed, in 1786, the issue of a ban on the copying of foreign maps arose in France as it was felt that they would confirm foreign views of territorial limits.[55] There were also disputes concerning the British maps. Criticism of Evans's map led in 1756 to the publication of a second essay by Evans. In turn, Ellis Huske's *The Present State of North America* (1755) backed the cartographer John Mitchell in his pro-British *Map of the British and French Dominions in North America* (1755). Public interest can be gauged from the fact that two editions of Huske appeared in Boston in 1755 and two in London. The accuracy of Mitchell's map was challenged by Thomas Jefferys in his *Explanation for the New Map of Nova Scotia . . . with the adjacent parts of New England and Canada* (1755).[56]

The press could play a role in the debate, including making political remarks about the use of maps. Thus, *Old England*, a leading opposition newspaper, in its issue of February 24, 1750, reported, "The French have, for some years past, been meditating encroachments upon us; and therefore their geographers have calculated maps for their purpose, whereby they have greatly enlarged their own, and in proportion lessened our boundaries there; which our mapmakers, and some of them in royal pay too, have as stupidly followed without a meaning, as the French have meaningly contrived them. I make no doubt, that the descriptions of our own copying geographers will be produced and insisted upon against us."

The difficulties of mapping owed much to the problems of using local knowledge in the mapping of the interior. The diversity of Native American languages, the hostile relations between different Native American peoples, and the absence of a central government requiring the locals to assist with the survey made accurate mapping too difficult. Also contributing to failure were the different conceptions of maps and geographical knowledge by Native Americans and Europeans. The latter, dedicated to abstract, Cartesian lines on nature, counterpointed the Native American focus on the most practical routes between geographic landmarks without concern for compass directions.[57]

In turn, the capture of Québec from France in 1759, which was correctly seen at the time as a great triumph, led to the production and sale in Britain of more maps on North America. Moreover, *A Universal Geographical Dictionary; or, Grand Gazetteer* (1759) was, the title-page proclaimed, "Illustrated by a general map of the world, particular ones of the different quarters, and of the seat of war in Germany." The maps included one of the Battle of Zorndorf the previous year, a major battle between Prussian and Russian forces. Also in 1759, a map of the British campaign against Fort Niagara was published. In 1759, the *Grand Magazine of Magazines, or Universal Register: Comprising all that is Curious, Useful, or Entertaining* published a map of the island of Gorée, a French slaving station in West Africa recently captured by the British. That year also saw the publication of *A Universal Geographical Dictionary; or Grand Gazetteer . . . Illustrated by A General Map of the World, particular ones of the different quarters, and of the Seat of War in Germany*. Readers of the *London Magazine* who wished to follow the course of the war of 1760–61 in North America between the Cherokees and British and colonial forces could turn to *A New Map of the Cherokee Nation . . . engraved from an Indian draught by Thomas Kitchin* in early 1760. In 1762, a map of the successful British siege of Havana was published. Maps in magazines, which had begun in the *Gentleman's Magazine* in 1739, made cartography more accessible. By 1754, the magazine had included forty-nine engraved maps, which, from 1748, focused on North America.[58]

Military concerns led to some impressive mapping, as in William Brasier's 1759 plan for an attack on the French base at Ticonderoga.[59] In

October 1760, Lieutenant-Colonel James Montresor wrote to General Jeffrey Amherst, the British commander in chief in North America, a master of planned, methodical campaigning and the orchestrator of the final conquest of New France (the French-ruled parts of modern Canada) in 1760:

> I think it my duty to acquaint your Excellency that I have got in great forwardness a general map of that part of North America which has been the seat of war wherein is distinguished the roads that have been made by the troops, the navigation of its rivers, its carrying places, the new forts and posts constructed, the several hospitals, barracks and buildings for the soldiers, the marches of the army, the places where have been engagements, attacks, sieges and camps, interspersed with useful remarks. The most part laid down by actual surveys with geographical and military observations made in that country from the year 1754 to 1760. As this map will show at one view what has been done in that country, I hope that it will be very acceptable, as well to the ministry as to the military, as your Excellency's march from Albany to Montreal, and Brigadier-General Murray's from Quebec is only wanting to complete it.

Montresor sought information on the details of these successful advances.[60] Amherst himself collected maps. Montresor's career showed the significance of British imperial conflict and expansion for mapping. His father, James Montresor, a Huguenot (French Protestant), had served in the British army, eventually as lieutenant-governor of Fort William in Scotland, an important base in containing any possible Jacobite rising, although it failed to do so in 1745–46. The James Montresor (1702–76) quoted here served in the army before becoming a practitioner-engineer, gaining a reputation as a draughtsman. Having been in the garrisons at Gibraltar and Minorca, he became chief engineer at Gibraltar in 1747. From 1747 to 1752, Montresor produced twenty-six plans of various parts of Gibraltar's defense works, with sections of the fortress and barracks of Gibraltar and of the nearby Spanish lines and forts. In 1753, he produced a plan of the fortifications. Montresor became chief engineer of the Braddock expedition in 1755. After its disastrous defeat by a French–Native American force, Montresor prepared plans and projects, surveying and mapping part of Lake Champlain, a key area of operations for the advance north on French Canada, an area where the British finally succeeded after initial failure. Becoming director of the Royal Engineers in 1758, Montresor played a leading role in operations until 1760.

Montresor's eldest son, John, a lieutenant, was himself wounded on Braddock's expedition in 1755. In 1758, he became a practitioner-engineer, before constructing a chain of redoubts near Niagara in 1764 and producing linked plans. Montresor was appointed chief engineer in America in 1775 and constructed the defense lines near Philadelphia in 1777–78 after it was captured by William Howe following the British victory at Brandywine. From this stage of his career, Montresor produced plans of Boston, New York, and the Battle of Bunker Hill in 1775, on which see chapter 7.

Engineering officers continued to produce first-rate topographical maps recording battles and positions. Thus, Alexander Taylor, a captain in the Royal Engineers, produced a map of Vinegar Hill, in County Wexford, showing the battlefield where British forces crushed the Irish rising of 1798. This map was then printed.

MARITIME MAPPING

The naval dimension to mapping was especially significant, as the mission and location of ships essentially depended on an understanding of the waters in which they could, should, and would operate. One testimony to the value of maps was provided by the many attempts to restrict their availability. These attempts underlay the extent to which non-Western governments did not publish much material. This tendency was not restricted to non-Western powers. In particular, the Spanish government which, like others, had sought to keep secret information about its discoveries from the outset, came to focus on trying to keep other Europeans out of the Pacific, which it regarded as a monopoly, and on restricting information about the ocean. However, in 1680, a band of English buccaneers under Bartholomew Sharp crossed the Isthmus of Darien from the Atlantic to the Pacific not far from the present Panama Canal. Using a Spanish ship they had seized off Panama, they attacked Spanish shipping before returning to England in 1682. The band included Basil Ringrose, who both wrote a journal of the expedition that was published in 1685 and compiled a substantial "waggoner"—the term then used for a description in the form of sailing directions—to much of the coast he sailed along, as well as to some parts he never visited. This description stemmed from the *derrotero* or set of official manuscript sailing directions, illustrated by a large number of coastal charts, that Sharp seized from a captured Spanish ship in 1681 and that he presented to Charles II in order to win royal favor. Such atlases had been regarded by the Spaniards as too confidential to go into print, which therefore limited their circulation and meant that the standardization, for good or ill, offered by print did not occur.[61]

The sense of mapping as a vital aid to national defense was seen in England in 1681 when the government appointed a naval officer, Captain Greenville Collins (ca. 1634–94), commander of the eight-gun yacht HMS *Merlin*, "to make a survey of the sea coasts of the kingdom by measuring all the sea coasts with a chain and taking all the bearings of all the headlands with their exact latitudes." Collins had extensive experience of navigation, including on a failed attempt to reach Japan by a northeast passage north of Asia, an attempt that was wrecked off the island of Novaya Zemlya. He had also served in the Mediterranean against Algerine privateers (pirates to the English), who were a major and conspicuous threat to trade, and Collins drew maps on his mission. Collins lobbied for an improved survey of Britain's coast, not least to rectify mistakes, to provide a centralized system for collecting and disseminating improved maps, and to give himself something to do. The survey, which lasted seven years, faced many problems due to the speed with which it was accomplished, the limited manpower available, and the lack of an available comprehensive land survey of the coastline as the basis for a marine survey. More generally, maritime mapping is in part dependent on its land counterpart, both practically in fixing the coastline and what is on it, and functionally in terms of the linking to amphibious operations.

Collins published his results in *Great Britain's Coasting Pilot*, which contained sailing directions, tide tables, coastal views, and charts, thus offering a codification of information that often hitherto had been a matter of the local "secret" knowledge of pilots. The complete work was first published in 1693. Collins was allowed to style himself hydrographer in ordinary to the king from 1683. The survey was reprinted frequently in the eighteenth century. The interest in such mapping was utilitarian in an economic sense, as well as military and political. In 1670, Charles II ordered the Council of Plantations "to procure maps or charts of all ... our plantations abroad, together with the maps ... of their respective ports, forts, bays and rivers," in short to prepare a cartographic record of empire.

Eventually running to four books encompassing the known globe, numerous editions of *The English Pilot* were published throughout the eighteenth century. Although many of the maps were derivatives of earlier Dutch charts, the work proved enormously popular, not least due to the charts' accompaniment with sailing directions written in English. English knowledge of foreign languages was limited. The *English Pilot* was a direct and ultimately successful challenge to Dutch hegemony over the sea chart market, a market crucial for mariners.

An instance of the ownership of maritime maps is shown by the copy of Defoe's *Atlas Maritimus and Commercialis; or, a General View of the World* (1728) that belonged to John Clevland. A commissioner of the Royal Navy from 1743 to 1746, he became Joint Secretary to the Admiralty from 1746 and sole Secretary from 1751 until his death in 1763. This *Atlas Maritimus* included a coasting pilot for mariners with fine charts of most trading areas of the world.

Governments developed important collections of maps. In France, where cartography was in part linked to the state, the naval ministry established its *Dépôt des Cartes* in 1720 (well before most states), but did not use its power as an official agency to implement a kind of standardization of maps.[62] Britain did not match this agency, although George III developed a cartographic archive probably unrivaled by any other contemporary crowned head and also organized a survey of Hanover.[63]

The production of accurate maps was necessary because most of the world's waters were uncharted. In his *The Construction of Maps and Globes* (1717), John Green noted the repeated errors of existing geographers and observed of Europe: "Tis observable, that not only the sea coasts, in two several maps of the same parts commonly differ strangely from each other; but also rarely ever any agree in that respect with the sea charts," which was not surprising due to the problems of establishing longitude. There was a widespread lack of standardization in measurements, notably of a standard of length. This helped make it complicated, for Britain as for other powers, to compare maps of the same part of the earth. This situation caused major problems for blockading ships, and the blockade of French ports was a key role for the British navy. It was necessary in order to protect Britain from invasion, notably a recurrence of the sort of invasion attempted in 1588 (the Spanish Armada) and, very differently, experienced in 1688.

These problems were accentuated by difficulties in establishing location at sea and the related problem of timekeeping. The difficulty of establishing a location in part rested on a lack of knowledge of the exact time and thus of a reliable measurement of traveled distance. Thus, in 1708, when a French squadron carrying the so-called James VIII and III, the Jacobite pretender to the crowns of Scotland and England, succeeded in avoiding the British blockading squadron off Dunkirk in the mist, reaching Scottish waters before its pursuers, the initial landfall was made not at the mouth of the Firth of Forth but, as a result of error, one hundred miles farther north. As a consequence, the French lost the initiative, British pursuing warships came up, and the French returned to Dunkirk, their only port on the North Sea. James was not landed, and the projected invasion did not occur.[64] Nevertheless, the plan underlined the degree to which, for Britain, the price of liberty was eternal vigilance, at least as measured by the availability of a strong and well-directed navy, a navy that lessened the need to rely on "Protestant winds," although big Spanish and French invasion fleets were thus dispersed in 1719 and 1744, respectively.

As a different instance of the difficulties of fixing position, George Anson of the Royal Navy, on his way round South America from the Atlantic, nearly ran aground on the island of Tierra del Fuego: dead reckoning had put his position more than three hundred miles out to sea. He pressed on to enter the Pacific, seize a Spanish treasure ship in 1743, and sail round the world, a triumph of navigation and resolve and one that helped provide the heroic tales that was important to the national self-image as a naval power.

As a result of the difficulties of mounting blockades, the British navy made major efforts to produce accurate charts of the waters off France and Spain, although blockading ships still ran aground. This owed something to the difficulties of keeping away from the coast when being driven toward it by the wind, a situation that did not change until the onset of steam-powered warships in the nineteenth century, although this onset itself posed problems as the wheels and, later, screws of steam power at sea were vulnerable to damage in shallow waters. During the French Revolutionary and Napoleonic Wars (1793–1815 for Britain), the Royal Navy lost more ships as a result of running aground than due to enemy action. Indeed, navies as a rule lost ships to navigational hazards unless they were confined to port. Inshore waters, notably on entry and exit from ports, were of greater danger for warships and merchantmen, and where they could, the British mapped coastal waters. When they attacked Copenhagen in 1801, the British used

Dutch maps but, on their withdrawal, charted nearby waters, especially the Belt, which provided more information that was available for subsequent successful British naval deployments, notably in 1807 and 1854–56, against Denmark and Russia, respectively.

More problems were encountered in mounting operations far from home waters. When, in 1791, the British government came close to war with Russia in the Ochakov Crisis, it discovered that it had no charts for the Black Sea and had to turn for information to their Dutch ally who, characteristically, had more information. Indeed, the lack of knowledge left the British unclear whether the fortress of Ochakov, the crucial issue in the negotiations, really controlled the entrance to the River Dnieper, as was claimed in order to demonstrate its strategic importance to Russia and Turkey. Ochakov is, in fact, on the northern shore of the Dneprovskiy Liman, a nearly landlocked section of the Black Sea into which the estuaries of both the Bug and the Dnieper open. Ochakov is situated at the narrow strait that forms the seaward entrance of this section or bay, but the British lacked adequate maps and coastal charts to show this.[65]

These were not the sole deficiencies the British faced. In 1805, HMS *Victory*, Nelson's flagship, had to rely on a French chart that was forty years old in order to navigate in the western Mediterranean. At the same time, during the War of American Independence (1775–83), the French, including the navy, in order to make up for their lack of knowledge and access to the North American shoreline, relied for their operations in and off North America on the availability of British printed maps sold through the map trade.[66] This was an approach to information very different to that of Spain.

The sources of initiative for mapping varied, including, in the case of Britain, the Royal Navy, colonial governments, and private individuals. The net effect was one of major improvement. For example, successive surveys of the Carolina coast led to improved maps, especially the coverage of the coast in Edward Moseley's detailed map of 1733, although, by then, piracy, a target of British action in the 1710s and 1720s, had been brought under control. Most notably, having conquered New France from France in 1757–60, the British surveyed Canadian Atlantic waters. The most prominent surveyor, the Swiss-born Joseph Frederick Wallet Des Barres, who had been trained at the Royal Military College, Woolwich, was ordered by the Admiralty to survey the coasts of Nova Scotia and Cape Breton Island, which, having been conquered, had been acquired from France under the Treaty of Utrecht (1713) and the Peace of Paris (1763), respectively. In 1777, the first edition of an atlas of his navigational charts, the *Atlantic Neptune*, was published for sale. This was an impressive attempt to provide a systematic charting of North American waters and ultimately comprised 115 charts and maps.[67]

Alexander Dalrymple, official hydrographer to the East India Company in 1779, also became Hydrographer to the Admiralty in 1795. The Order in Council instructed Dalrymple "to take charge of such plans and charts as are now or may hereafter be deposited in this office belonging to the Public, and to be charged with the duty of selecting and compiling all the existing information as may appear to be requisite for the purpose of improving the Navigation, and for the guidance and direction of the commanders of Your Majesty's ships." This process might appear overdue but reflected the awareness of the need to accumulate and apply information and around the world. War required such information, but it also helped remold political geography and thus increase public interest in such geography and underline its significance for education and publications. In 1799, Henry St. John Bullen, a clerical schoolmaster in Bury St. Edmunds, began his *Elements of Geography, Expressly Designed for the Use of Schools* by writing, "At a time when such astonishing naval and military expeditions are taking place, and all the countries of the world seem to be necessarily forming one general system of communication with each other; and while Europe in particular is in many places undergoing a total change in her territorial names and possessions, it appears to be highly necessary that Modern Geography should form a part, and that not an inconsiderable one, of a liberal education."[68]

Notes

1. R. A. Beddard, "The Sources of Anthony Wood's Life of Nicholas Hill," *Archives* 29 (2004): 7; R. Fox, ed., *Thomas Harriot and His World: Mathematics, Exploration, and Natural Philosophy in Early Modern England* (Farnham, UK, 2012).

2. C. W. J. Withers, *Placing the Enlightenment: Thinking Geographically about the Age of Reason* (Chicago, 2007).

3. R. Porter, *Enlightenment: Britain and the Creation of the Modern World* (London, 2000).

4. P. D. A. Harvey, "The Documents of Landscape History: Snares and Delusions," *Landscape History* 13 (1991): 47–52.

5. T. Williamson, *Environment, Society, and Landscape in Early Medieval England* (Woodbridge, UK, 2013) is very insightful on regionality, but he is avowedly a geographical determinist and underplays the human role.

6. J. Black, *Geopolitics and the Quest for Dominance* (Bloomington, IN, 2016); J. Black, *Plotting Power: Strategy in the Eighteenth Century* (Bloomington, IN, 2017).

7. D. A. Baugh, "Withdrawing from Europe: Anglo-French Maritime Geopolitics, 1750–1800," *International History Review* 20 (1998): 1–32.

8. B. Pool, *Navy Board Contracts, 1660–1832* (London, 1966).

9. Horatio Walpole to Harrington, October 19, 1734, NA. SP. 84/333.

10. Anon., *The History of the Succession to the Countries of Juliers and Berg* (London, 1738), 129–30.

11. N. Harding, *Hanover and the British Empire, 1700–1837* (Woodbridge, UK, 2007).

12. P. Burke, "Did Europe Exist before 1700?" *History of European Ideas* 1 (1980): 26–27.

13. I. Murphy, *The Diocese of Killaloe in the Eighteenth Century* (Blackrock, Ireland, 1991).

14. L. H. Boles, *The Huguenots, the Protestant Interest, and War of the Spanish Succession, 1702–1714* (New York, 1997); T. Claydon, *Europe and the Making of England 1660–1760* (Cambridge, 2007).

15. T. Claydon and I. McBride, eds., *Protestantism and National Identity. Britain and Ireland c. 1650–c. 1850* (Cambridge, 1998).

16. N. Sykes, *William Wake: Archbishop of Canterbury, 1657–1737* (Cambridge, 1957). See also W. R. Ward, *The Protestant Evangelical Awakening* (Cambridge, 1992).

17. *Weekly Medley*, June 28, 1729.

18. *Derby Mercury*, May 25, 1732.

19. M. Schohorn, *Defoe's Politics. Parliament, Power, Kingship, and "Robinson Crusoe"* (Cambridge, 1991).

20. Chesterfield to John, Earl Gower, November 11, 1745, NA. PRO. 30/29/1/11 fol. 295.

21. There had been Jacobite contributions from northern England as well, notably in 1715. John Adams, *The Works of John Adams, Second President of the United States: With a Life of the Author, Notes and Illustrations, by his Grandson Charles Francis Adams*, 10 vols., vol. 3 (Boston, 1851).

22. William, 2nd Earl of Albemarle, Commander-in-Chief in Scotland, to Thomas, Duke of Newcastle, Secretary of State for the Southern Department, October 15, 1746, C. S. Terry, ed., *Albemarle Papers* (Aberdeen, 1902), I, 289–900.

23. D. W. Marshall, "Military Maps of the Eighteenth Century and the Tower of London Drawing Room," *Imago Mundi* 32 (1980): 21.

24. C. J. Anderson, "State Imperatives: Military Mapping in Scotland, 1689–1770," *Scottish Geographical Journal* 125, no. 1 (2009): 4–24.

25. Edinburgh, National Library of Scotland, Department of Manuscripts, MS. 1646Z 02/39a.

26. C. Tabraham, "The Military Context of the Military Survey," in *The Great Map: The Military Survey of Scotland, 1747–55, by William Roy* (Edinburgh, 2007), 35; Y. O'Donaghue, *William Roy, 1726–1790: Pioneer of the Ordnance Survey* (London, 1997).

27. Sherlock to Edward Weston, May 25, 1746, Farmington, Lewis Walpole Library, Weston papers, vol. 3.

28. T. M. Devine, *Clanship to Crofters' War: The Social Transformation of the Scottish Highlands* (Manchester, 1994); F. Ramsay, ed., *The Day Book of Daniel Campbell of Shawfield 1767 with Relevant Papers Concerning the Estate of Islay* (Aberdeen, 1991).

29. P. Rogers, ed., *Johnson and Boswell in Scotland: A Journey to the Hebrides* (New Haven, CT, 1993); C. W. J. Withers, *Geography, Science, and National Identity: Scotland since 1520* (Cambridge, 2001).

30. B. Phillips, *Peterwell: The History of a Mansion and Its Infamous Squire* (Llandyssul, Wales, 1983).

31. *British Journal*, January 27, 1750.

32. Edward Tenison to Alan, Viscount Midleton, May 27, 1726, Guildford, Surrey Record Office, Brodrick Mss. 1248/7 fol. 29; *Bristol Journal*, January 20, 1750.

33. J. Kelly, "James Kelly and the Irish Economy in the 1720s," *Eighteenth-Century Ireland* 6 (1991): 7–36.

34. J. E. Crowley, "Herman Moll's *The World Described* 1720: Mapping Britain's Global and Imperial Interests," *Imago Mundi* 68 (2001): 19.

35. J. C. D. Clark, "Protestantism, Nationalism, and National Identity, 1660–1832," *Historical Journal* 43 (2000): 274–75.

36. R. C. Nash, "Irish Atlantic Trade in the Seventeenth and Eighteenth Centuries," *William and Mary Quarterly*, 3rd ser., 62 (1985): 329–56.

37. L. Colley, *Britons: Forging the Nation 1707-1837*, 2nd ed. (New Haven, CT, 2009).

38. T. C. Barnard, "Protestants and the Irish Language, c. 1675–1725," *Journal of Ecclesiastical History* 44 (1993): 271–72.

39. For valuable approaches, C. Eastbrook, *Urbane and Rustic England: Cultural Ties and Social Spheres in the Provinces, 1660–1780* (Manchester, 1999); H. French, *The Middle Sort of People in Provincial England, 1620–1750* (Oxford, 2007).

40. N. Rogers, *Whigs and Cities: Popular Politics in the Age of Walpole and Pitt* (Oxford, 1989); K. Wilson, *The Sense of the People: Politics, Culture, and Imperialism in England, 1715–1785* (Cambridge, 1995).

41. P. Stock, ed., *The Uses of Space in Early Modern History* (New York, 2015).

42. L. Hollis, *The Phoenix, St. Paul's Cathedral, and the Men who Made Modern London* (London, 2008).

43. BL. Add. 58213 fol. 216.

44. C. Thom, *Researching London's Houses* (London, 2005); I. Watson, "The 'Place in the Sun' A2A Index to Insurance Policy Registers at Guildhall Library," *Archives* 31 (2006): 18–34. E. McKellar, *Landscapes of London: The City, the Country and the Suburbs, 1660–1840* (New Haven, CT, 2013); E. Tierney, "'Dirty, Rotten Sheds': Exploring the Ephemeral City in Early Modern London," *Eighteenth-Century Studies* 50 (2017): 231–52.

45. J. H. Thomas, "Devices in the Eighteenth Century: The Evidence from Fire Insurance Records," *Archives* 30 (2005): 75–89.

46. H. W. Lawrence, "The Greening of the Squares of London: Transformation of Urban Landscapes and Ideals," *Annals of the Association of American Geographers* 83 (1993): 90–118.

47. V. Gatrell, *The First Bohemians: Life and Art in London's Golden Age* (London, 2013).

48. J. Conlin, "Vauxhall on the Boulevard: Pleasure Gardens in London and Paris, 1764–1784," *Urban History* 35 (2008): 24–47, esp. 46.

49. Maps of London during the Gordon Riots, BL. Add. 15533 fols 39–51. From a collection of mainly manuscript water color plans of military encampments in Britain from 1763 to 1783 prepared by General George Morrison, the quartermaster general, for presentation to George III. He kept these volumes for himself and another set is in the King's Military Collection, a subset of George III's General Atlas in the Royal Library. Some of the plans of military precautions in 1780 were manuscript ones, others annotated printed maps.

50. M. S. Pedley, *Bel et Utile: The Work of the Robert De Vaugondy Family of Mapmakers* (Tring, UK, 1992).

51. Sackville to Holdernesse, October 1, 1758, BL. Eg. 3444 fol. 75. This is a reference to Cloppenburg in Lower Saxony. With thanks for a map of Bohemia where campaigning then focused, George Cressener, Minister at Cologne, to Onslow Burrish, envoy in Munich, April 9, 1757, NA. SP. 110/6.

52. J. C. Hosmer, *The Narrative of Gage's Spies, March 1775* (Boston, 1912), 9–11.

53. M. S. Pedley, "Map Wars: The Role of Maps in the Nova Scotia/Acadia Boundary Disputes of 1750," *Imago Mundi* 50 (1998): 103.

54. Mirepoix, French envoy in London, to Rouillé, French Foreign Minister, January 16, March 8, 1755, AE. CP. Ang. 438 fols 18, 261; Joseph Yorke to Holdernesse, February 21, 1755, BL. Eg. 3446 fol. 42; Bonnac, French envoy in The Hague, to Rouillé, February 21, 1755, AE. CP. Hollande 488 fols 106–7; Bussy, French envoy in Hanover, to Rouillé, July 29, 1755, AE. CP. Brunswick-Hanovre 52 fol. 22; A. Reese, *Europäische Hegemonie und France d'outre-mer. Koloniale Fragen in der französischen Aussenpolitik 1700–1763* (Stuttgart, 1988), 274–310.

55. *Daily Universal Register*, August 11, 1786.

56. M. H. Edney, "John Mitchell's Map of North America (1755): A Study of the Use and Publication of Official Maps in Eighteenth-Century Britain," *Imago Mundi* 60 (2008): 63–85; E. Berkeley and D. S. Berkeley, *Dr. John Mitchell: The Man who Made the Map of North America* (Chapel Hill, NC, 1974).

57. G. M. Lewis, "First Nations Mapmaking in the Great Lakes Region in Intercultural Contexts: A Historical Review," *Michigan Historical Review* 30 (2004): 1–34; P. W. Mapp, *The Elusive West and the Contest for Empire, 1713–1763* (Chapel Hill, NC, 2011).

58. E. A. Reitan, "Expanding Horizons: Maps in the *Gentleman's Magazine*, 1731–1754," *Imago Mundi* 37 (1985): 54–62 and "Popular Cartography and British Imperialism: 'The Gentleman's Magazine,' 1739–1763," *Journal of Newspaper and Periodical History* 2, no. 3 (1986): 2–13; B. Harris, "'American Idols': Empire, War, and the Middling Ranks in Mid-Eighteenth-Century Britain," *Past and Present* 150 (February 1996): 124–25.

59. Library of Congress, G3804. T5526 1759.B7.

60. Montresor to Amherst, October 18, 1760, NA. War Office, 34/83 fols 120–21.

61. D. Howse and N. J. W. Thrower, *A Buccaneer's Atlas. Basil Ringrose's South Sea Waggoner* (Berkeley, CA, 1992).

62. J. W. Konvitz, *Cartography in France, 1660–1848: Science, Engineering, and Statecraft* (Chicago, 1987).

63. I have benefited from discussing George III's role with Peter Barber.

64. J. Gibson, *Playing the Scottish Card. The Franco-Jacobite Invasion of 1708* (Edinburgh, 1988).

65. William, Lord Auckland, envoy in The Hague, to William Lord Grenville, government business manager in the House of Lords, January 29, 1791, BL. Add. 58919 fol. 33; Auckland to James Bland Burges, Under-Secretary in the Foreign Office, March 1, 9, 1791, Bod. BB, vol 30 fols 129, 133.

66. M. S. Pedley, *The Commerce of Cartography: Making and Marketing Maps in Eighteenth-Century France and England* (Chicago, 2005).

67. G. N. D. Evans, *Uncommon Obdurate: The Several Public Careers of J. F. W. Des Barres* (Peabody, MA, 1969). I have benefited from reading forthcoming work by Alex Johnson.

68. H. Bullen, *Elements of Geography* (London, 1799), vii.

3

Territorialization and the Mapping of Authority

MAPPING AND MAPS

The ability to understand, interpret, and discuss spatial issues rose with the development of geography, both as an intellectual subject and as a sphere of publishing. As introduced in the last chapter, maps were an aspect of these geographies, more especially geography, as part of the world of publishing, offering a new ideal of science as a tool for understanding and controlling nature. Carto-literacy in Britain had increased and altered from the sixteenth century with the production of greater numbers of printed maps and atlases.[1] Moreover, the changes coming from new discoveries and, more particularly, the awareness that there would be more, created a sense that knowledge was dynamic.

In his play *Twelfth Night* (1602), William Shakespeare had the duped Malvolio "smile his face into more lines than is in the new map with the augmentation [addition] of the Indies" (III, ii). That map contained more information than its predecessors, and Shakespeare's London audience was expected to appreciate the fact, although not to comment on his mistake in this play in putting Bohemia (most of the Czech Republic) on the coast: it is far from it. The notion of the map as a revelation of personality or mood was, as in the case of Malvolio, a well-established literary conceit. This conceit threw light on the value of maps, or at least on their standard image as mirrors of reality, or, failing that, would-be, or should-be, mirrors.

Visual appeal was a crucial factor in the popularity of maps, and thus their commercial appeal, but it was far from being the sole one. Maps, indeed, were a key element in the spatial politics of the period. They were a tool in policy, a means in the discussion of policy, and a part of the widening public engagement with the outside world. The last was captured in the educational dimension, as in John Clegg's *Elements of Geography, or an easy introduction to the uses of the globes and maps; consisting of a concise treatise on the Astronomical Part of Geography* (1795). This book included geographical questions on each of the maps and blank maps as part of the exercise, with the answers printed separately. To deal with the course, Clegg assumed that each pupil was provided with a globe. More generally, the importance of maps threw attention onto their quality. In particular, there were questions about the accuracy of maps, and this situation looked toward modern interest in the way in which they were made and understood.

Alongside the intellectual and, to a degree, social hierarchies involved in cartography and its conceptualization,[2] entrepreneurial activity was crucial to mapping and especially so in Britain and the United Provinces (Dutch state, modern Netherlands). Such activity both reflected the role of government and, yet, was also separate to it and not centrally controlled. As a result, ideas of direction and of some, in effect, geographical master plan directing cartography, are inappropriate. In France, map production benefited from the centralized, institutional support and training provided by a number of government institutions. In Britain, in contrast, surveying continued to be a privately funded activity, a situation that remained the case until the civilian use of the Ordnance Survey maps became important in the mid-nineteenth century. This had consequences for the context of map making and for the contents of maps.

As a result of entrepreneurship and, therefore, private funding, British map publishers could be heavily reliant on foreign maps for information. The Dutch, in particular, dominated the map trade at the outset of the period and, notably, the mapping of the seas and coastlines of the world. Although the English map trade in the late seventeenth century was modest in comparison to that of the Dutch, shops, such as that of Philip Lea in London in the 1690s, carried a considerable stock. In 1709, Reverend John Crakanthorp, who held the rural living of Fowlmere, south of Cambridge, went to London where he purchased not only spectacles, religious tracts, and a new gown but also a map of Europe and one of Flanders where British troops were then fighting the French in the War of the Spanish Succession.³

Because the gathering and compiling of data were the most expensive aspects in the production of printed maps, copying them (and thus using already-prepared data) was a sensible investment, irrespective of the intellectual value of the procedure. Furthermore, potential profitability encouraged imitators, plagiarists, and copyists. Alongside these limitations arising from the nature of the entrepreneurship and the limited investment necessary, there was an extensive map culture in which interest in new exploration and participation in war encouraged their purchase and, thus, production. Moreover, in Britain, maps were more affordable, compared to other commodities, than they were in France. As a result, printed maps were not a luxury item for those who were able, for example, to purchase brandy. A map was not quite as cheap in Britain as a measure of brandy, which was a luxury import, but it was no more expensive than a novel.⁴ However, the last itself serves as a reminder of the changing nature of comparisons, as novels are now paperbacks that are cheap and readily disposable. This was not the case in the eighteenth century.

Cost was not the sole element. From the perception of modern critics of the objectives and accuracy of cartography, there was a considerable degree of national and class self-interest in eighteenth-century mapping, as of its modern successor. That criticism offers an important approach. The focus, however, here is primarily on the perspectives and views of the period on mapping, and on what these entailed for the awareness of spatial issues. Advertisements and notices make it clear that accuracy was regarded as possible, as well as desirable and marketable. Moreover, although there was a broader political bias, notably toward national perspectives and the authority of the state, that bias did not preclude value and values in mapping.

The appearance of maps and therefore of geographical information were frequently linked to specific political circumstances. Wars greatly encouraged public interest in maps, and entrepreneurial publishers responded. Thus, the Huguenot (French Protestant) exile Abel Boyer, a major figure in journalism, published, in London in 1701, *The Draughts of the Most Remarkable Fortified Towns of Europe . . . with a geographical description of the said places. And the history of sieges they have sustained.* This was a moment in international tension that was propitious for entrepreneurs, as the wide-ranging and lengthy War of the Spanish Succession (1701–14, Britain involved 1702–13) was beginning. Three years later, seven engraved folding maps, five by Robert Morden, appeared in *A Description of all the Seats of the Present Wars of Europe, in the Netherlands, Germany, Hungary, Italy, Spain and Portugal. Being a particular survey of all these countries; setting forth the situation and distances of their provinces, cities, towns, villages, etc. With Historical Remarks... With an Exact Delineation of the March of the Germans... the French... our Forces.* Published by John Nicholson, this was a necessary adjunct to understanding the Blenheim campaign which, in 1704, entailed the march of British troops under John, 1st Duke of Marlborough, to Danube, the farthest deployment of a British army hitherto in the wars with Louis XIV. Knowledge of victories, and thanksgiving services for them, fueled an appetite to see where they were on maps.

The war also led to freestanding maps, such as *A True and Exact Map of the Seat of War in Brabant and Flanders with the Enemies Lines in their Just Dimensions* (1705). In this detailed map, the moves of Anglo-Dutch-German forces commanded by Marlborough, and of their French opponents, could be charted. This map was followed by the issue, by John Harris, of *A New Map of Europe Done from the most Accurate Observations communicated by the Royal Societies at London and Paris Illustrated with Plans and Views of the Battles, Sieges and other Advantages Obtained by her Majesty's Forces and those of Her Allies over the French*. Insets in this map included plans of the battles of Blenheim (1704) and Ramillies (1706), both key victories for Marlborough.[5]

There was a danger that the French would invade Ireland where they had sent troops in 1689 during the previous war. In 1708, the year in which the French, in fact, launched an abortive invasion of Scotland, an invasion in part thwarted by poor navigation, Henry Pratt's wall map of Ireland was advertised in London as at sale for a guinea (£1.05). This was a map that would have helped ministers and civilians alike to follow any fighting that broke out there. Roads and barracks were depicted, while the map was flanked by town plans that made clear citadels and walls—for example, at Kinsale. Moreover, that of Drogheda included a plan of the nearby Battle of the Boyne. Fought in 1690, this was the decisive engagement in which William III defeated James II, pressing on to capture Dublin.

In many cases, it was clear why particular maps appeared. In 1727, the second edition of Jacques Ozanam's *A Treatise of Fortification* was published in London, with the addition of *A New and Exact Plan of Gibraltar with all its Fortifications* by Herman Moll, the latter plan made topical by the Spanish siege that year. Moreover, the publication of this edition as a whole was a response to the more general international crisis of 1725–27. In this crisis, a large-scale war appeared probable in 1726–27 and, in particular, a full war between Britain and Spain.

As with the later pulse of geographical activity and reimagination after the Seven Years' War (1756–63), the War of the Spanish Succession was followed by a similar process, in large part because of British success in the conflict, combined with the more far-flung colonial and commercial interests stemming from the war and from the Peace of Utrecht (1713). Utrecht recognized the British wartime conquests of Gibraltar, Minorca, and Nova Scotia and also saw Britain gain limited, but significant, commercial access to the Spanish Empire in the Caribbean.

The structure of Moll's *The World Described* reflected this engagement in the post-Utrecht world, with Britain at the center of the atlas and Britain's global position a theme. At the same time, successive editions indicated concern about power politics in particular areas. Thus, the edition that appeared in about 1730–32 included a map of northern Italy at a time when the fate of the duchies of Parma and Tuscany was highly contentious. The edition of 1740–42 included second maps of the Baltic and the Rhineland, respectively: the former was pertinent for the Russo-Swedish War of 1741–43 and the latter for the outbreak of the War of the Austrian Succession in 1740 and, more particularly, for the movement of French troops across the Rhine in 1741. In the map of Scotland, castles and roads were shown.[6]

Moll was far from alone in producing maps to inform the public during crises. Thus, in 1740, the *Gentleman's Magazine* produced a map of James Oglethorpe's unsuccessful attack on St. Augustine, the major Spanish position in Florida. The Forty-Five led not only to mapping for the government but also for the public. In January 1746, a map of roads in the Highlands was published. Although a defeat, the Battle of Falkirk led to a map, but the decisive victory of Culloden was more important. The Battle of Falkirk was also rapidly commemorated in a map showing the general area that included a plan of that battle and of the battle at Culloden later that year. Thirty maps of Culloden appeared in 1746.⁷ Advertisements stressed the veracity of particular maps.⁸

The relationship between war and knowledge was repeatedly seen with cartography. Reviewing Lewis Evans's *Analysis of a General Map of the Middle British Colonies in America* in the *Literary Magazine* of October 15, 1756, Samuel Johnson wrote that "the last war between the Russians and the Turks [1736–39] made geographers acquainted with the situation and extent of many countries little known before," a reference to the lands on the northern shore of the Black Sea: the khanate of the Crimea, a Turkish vassal state, attracted few visitors and there were no reliable maps of it.

The use of maps to follow wars, both in the eighteenth century and thereafter, was an aspect of a general map culture, with rising map consumption being focused on particular interests. This focus involved not only conflicts in which one's own country was a participant but also others. Maps were part of the news explosion. Cartography served as an aspect of government applying knowledge and as a means to understand the news. It was doing so in a West in which the provision of news was becoming more central and the presentation of news more clearly scientific and rational, rather than providential and impressionistic.

Maps were significant for governments as they represented a way to fix boundaries and notably with reference either to natural features or to the graticule of latitude and longitude. Maps were cited as boundaries in treaties between the British North American colonies and native tribes, such as that of 1765 with the Lower Creeks over the Florida borderland.⁹ The mapping of the frontiers between colonies within individual imperial systems thickened the knowledge grid and, as a related process, made mapping and European control increasingly normative. Thus, a survey of 1728 which established the boundary between Virginia and North Carolina greatly increased knowledge of the back country of both that was distant from the ocean. William Byrd's account throws light on the difficulties of carrying out a survey for this boundary in terrain such as the Great Dismal Swamp. The Pennsylvania-Maryland boundary was surveyed in 1763–67.¹⁰

This process was in part a matter of aggrandizement, as with the *New Map of Georgia* by Emmanuel Bowen, "Geographer to His Majesty," that accompanied the description of Georgia included in John Harris's multivolumed work, *Navigantium atque Itinerantium Bibliotheca*, or *A Complete*

Collection of Voyages and Travels (1748). By extending the name *Georgia* on the map from west of the Mississippi to the Savannah River, Bowen reflected the expansive limits in Georgia's original charter. The text of this charter was included in the Harris piece on Georgia. According to the charter, Georgia's limits extended from the headwaters of the Savannah and Altamaha rivers "Westward in Direct Lines to the South Seas," the Pacific Ocean. Georgia's southern boundary was the Altamaha. Bowen showed a branch of that river reaching the sea between Cumberland and Amelia islands, which was far south of its true course. Placing the Altamaha farther south in this fashion was in Britain's favor in defining the frontier with Spanish Florida. Reflecting such an assertion was difficult because few accurate surveys were then in existence. In 1763, with Florida now British, Georgia's southern limit was indeed extended from the Altamaha to the St. Mary's River, which finds its way to the sea between Cumberland and Amelia.

As with much else, the pace of mapping increased after the Seven Years' War. In India, most notably, mapping served to help Britain understand its recent conquests there, as well as to legitimate the British presence which had expanded greatly in the 1750s and early 1760s. Already, published maps had recorded British victories, such as the capture of the Maratha privateering base at Gheriah on the west coast in 1756 and Robert Clive's victory at Plassey in Bengal in 1757. In 1754, the commander in chief of the Madras army, a British force in India, was informed by his superiors that "the map of the country which you have will show you the distance and situation," as far as his general instructions were concerned.[11]

Systematic British surveying and mapping of India followed the appointment of James Rennell (1742–1830), in 1767, as the first surveyor-general of the Bengal Presidency, a post he held until 1777. Rennell had served in the Royal Navy in India from 1760, transferring to the East India Company after the end of the Seven Years' War in 1763. He first charted the Palk Strait and Pamban Channel between India and Sri Lanka (for long called Ceylon by the British), the shoals of which were a major challenge to ships seeking to sail round India en route to or from Calcutta and/or Madras (rather than also having to sail round Sri Lanka).

Then, Rennell transferred his attentions to land. After its major territorial gains in midcentury, the company was in dire need of a reasonably accurate survey of India so that it could estimate the potential revenue from its acquisitions and plan how best to defend them from attack. Rennell began to survey Bengal in 1765, the year a settlement with the Mughal emperor brought an end to a major war, measuring distances and directions along the major roads in order to produce "route surveys" of the entire presidency of Bengal. This project was accompanied by the measurement of the latitude and longitude of major points. Although he was badly injured when he was ambushed on the frontier of Bhutan in 1766, Rennell remained in the field as a surveyor until 1771. His general map of Bengal and Bihar, sent to Britain in 1774, was based on no fewer than five hundred original surveys. Some parts of Bengal were only surveyed in 1776, but the large number of maps produced by Rennell was to be the basis of his *Bengal Atlas* (1780). Rennell's work was used by Gibbon. Samuel Showers did similar work farther west. Both men have been seen as owing much to the support for mapping by Robert Orme in his *Essay on the Art of War* (1765), a work by a former official of the East India Company who became its historiographer.[12]

Having returned to London, Rennell became a commercial cartographer. He went on to map all of India in 1782, followed, in 1788, by *A New Map of Hindoostan* and by a revised map in 1793. These maps reflected both public demand in Britain and the response to the growing amount of information about India available to the British as their activity and power there increased. Indeed, in 1782, the French foreign minister complained to the British envoy about British expansionism in India, adding, with regard to Britain, a reference to an established organic image of power: "our arms were grown too long for our body."[13] However, there were major gaps both in British imperial power and in cartographic coverage, especially for western and central India. Formal trigonometrical surveys followed the mapping by Rennell and his contemporaries. Thus, in 1800, William Lambton began the triangulation of India.

In India, the East India Company's administration was already a significant patron of local cartography. Its interests were reflected in the nature of the survey undertaken or the map created. Thus urban maps developed from plans that reflected a military engineering perspective, that of defense, to ones concerned with effective urban planning and improvement. The first known British map of Calcutta was published in 1742. Subsequently, a survey of the city was initiated by the Commissioners of Police and was carried out by Lieutenant-Colonel Mark Wood, the chief engineer. Officially aimed at the "convenience of the health of the said settlement," this map was published in 1792. It showed the Old Fort, now a customs house, as the nucleus of the urban settlement, with the extensive new star-shaped Fort William set within a massive cleared area, known as the Maidan, to the south of the town. The map distinguished between areas inhabited by "Europeans" and by "Natives."

The surveying of British colonies readily displayed social and economic landscapes. The utilitarian origins of the plans ensured that a premium was placed on accuracy of representation and measurement. And successfully so. Tests for Jamaica of point-to-point distance measures for a number of examples suggest a range of error of less than 2 percent for the gross dimensions of plantations. Planters there wanted precise information for land use management. Fields planted with major export crops were plotted more carefully than areas of woodland or than land planted with provision crops in what were known as "Negro grounds." Thus, as more generally with mapping, a blanket assessment of accuracy is inappropriate.[14] The social context was clear. In about 1745, Michael Hay, a surveyor on behalf of Edward Trelawny, governor of Jamaica, produced a cadastral map of Kingston, Jamaica. Each property lot in the map was identified with a number that corresponded to its owner, while the upper sides of the map showed prominent homes.

Aside from maps of existing colonies, mapping rapidly followed conquest.[15] For example, John Barrow, private secretary to Lord Macartney, governor of Cape Colony, which the British had conquered from the Dutch in 1795, was instructed by the governor to gather topographic knowledge so that he could draw up a map, which he did in 1801. This helped the British when they reconquered the colony in 1806 after having returned it under the Peace of Amiens of 1802.

NAMING AND APPROPRIATION

Mapping was linked to naming. In both practical and symbolic terms, maps served as assertions and communicators of proprietal and territorial rights and in a long-standing, often adversarial, process.[16] Conversely, maps also had "silences": peoples who were ignored or marginalized. This process can be regarded in two very different ways. On the one hand, naming was an aspect of appropriation, one that owed much to the process by which colonies (and states) were creations or essays in the structuring of space by power. This was very much an approach taken from the 1960s on, and notably by J. B. (Brian) Harley.[17] On the other hand, the modern theory of knowledge construction offers only limited guidance to the processes and problems of map creation, not least the exigencies and compromises that always characterize the collection of data and the decision of what should be mapped and how best to do so. Therefore, although political and social issues were indeed involved, both directly and in contextual terms, solely to politicize these processes of choice and compromise is to simplify a complex situation. Practical issues also played a role. At the same time, how these issues were, and are, addressed is scarcely value-free.

Accepting this, the cartographic process was at the center of a construction and representation of knowledge that was very important to the extension of British power.[18] For example, from 1764 to 1775, the Board of Trade sponsored a scientific and systematic mapping program, the General Survey of British North America, commencing with the territories recently acquired: Canada from France and Florida from Spain. Especially in such "new" territories, or new to the British, maps of sufficient scale, detail, and accuracy were of critical importance to administrators when deciding where to locate towns, infrastructure, and defense works, and how precisely to demarcate landholding boundaries. Moreover, these colonies were reimagined and relocated, as they were now to be understood and presented as part of British North America.

As part of the General Survey, Samuel Holland mapped Île Saint-Jean (Prince Edward Island), from which the native population of French settlers had been expelled following its conquest by the British from France in 1758. Holland's map (1765) subdivided the island into sixty-seven lots, which were given away by lottery in 1767. It would be better known if it had been a map of part of the United States. Holland's map, which was subsequently published by William Faden, a major London map publisher, showed the island divided into counties, parishes, lots, and coastal harbors, with an inset map indicating the island's position. A supplementary map, displaying new settlements and roads, followed in 1798. Holland saw himself as a man of science and hoped that his work would bring benefit to the empire. James Cook, who had played a role in the successful operation against Québec in 1759, learned some of his cartographic techniques from Holland and later used them in mapping Newfoundland.

At the same time, such a progressivist account can be misleadingly congratulatory. Major problems remained in map coverage. For example, concerned about territorial boundaries between a part of Massachusetts (modern Maine) and Canada, John Adams, America's first envoy in London and a perceptive diplomat, complained in 1786 about the difficulties of finding on maps the rivers running into the Bay of Passamaquoddy, adding, "It is astonishing that to this hour, no man can produce a map of all the Bay's harbours, islands, and rivers in that neighbourhood, that can be depended on."[19] Yet, as a reminder of the often ambiguous nature of evidence, it is significant that Adams found this problem "astonishing."

The process of naming is readily apparent from maps. For example, Dampier's voyage in 1700 led to the naming of islands such as New Britain, New Ireland, New Hanover, and Rooke Island, as well as of features such as Cape St. George, Cape Orford, Cape King William, Cape Anne, St. George's Channel, and Montagu Harbor. Thus, the royal family, and key naval figures such as Orford and Rooke, were imprinted on the map, and therefore for posterity, as loyalty was affirmed by the explorer. Philip Carteret "discovered" Osnaburg, Duke of Gloucester, and Queen Charlotte islands—each named after a member of the royal family—as well as Gower's, Simpson's, Carteret's, Hardy's, Wallis's, and Leigh's islands, and those of Sandwich, Byron, New Hanover, the Duke of Portland, and the Admiralty. Cook's additions included the Hervey Islands and Palmerston Atoll. Again, key official and aristocratic families were thus commemorated, notably if linked to the Royal Navy, as with Sandwich.

Naming was also seen with places on land, notably forts and new settlements. Royal names, and variants thereon, played a key role, notably George, Frederick, William, Cumberland, York, Caroline, and Charlotte, and the less specific King's and Queen's town or county. Thus, there were Georgetown, Charlottesville, Prince William County, Fort William, and so on. The range was great. Annapolis Royal reflects the conquest of Nova

Scotia from France under Queen Anne. References to Hanover, Brunswick, and Guelph were a result of the Hanoverian accession. Prominent generals were also celebrated, not only Cumberland but also Marlborough, Wolfe, and Amherst. Royal ministers and colonial proprietors were recorded. British place names were also translated to the colonies. In this process, British names replaced French, Dutch, and Spanish ones, as well as native non-European names.

LANDOWNERSHIP AND AGRICULTURE

The global dimension was not the sole one for territorialization or for a visual culture that included maps.[20] The same process was seen within Britain, not least in order to arbitrate disputes over landownership. The unreliable nature of land demarcation encouraged disputes as did the conflicting memories of witnesses to it.[21] Mapping played a role, as in a major legal case, in the Court of Exchequer in 1705–8, between Thomas, 1st Marquis of Wharton, and Reginald Marriott over the lead mines on Grinton Moor in Swaledale, Yorkshire. Two maps of the contested area were made by two different surveyors, one for each party. The surviving map, the oldest dated map of the area in question, broke new ground in that it enshrined traditional knowledge that had previously been handed down orally through the generations but that was not easy to reconstruct other than in such a legal session. The map was ordered by the court and was shown to members of the jury at a viewing of the disputed ground two weeks before the London trial.[22] A leading Whig, Wharton was an important political figure, but, in this case, he had to accept the need to yield to the arbitration of the law courts and their reliance on information. In 1702, Wharton had lost the case in the Queen's Bench, but he then launched successive appeals with the case lasting into the 1710s.

Maps played a key role later in the eighteenth century in the enclosure of agricultural land. This led to the local mapping of much of the country[23] and to the linked development and dissemination of surveying skills and methods. These were long-standing, as surveying had become more significant from the sixteenth century, again a period of large-scale enclosure. There was relatively little opposition to the enclosure of the eighteenth century, in large part because the landed elite were thoroughly behind the process, but also because, in contrast to the sixteenth century, the opposition by the nonelite rural population was weaker: there was no equivalent to Kett's Rising in Norfolk in 1549. At the local level, enclosure, a process that involved valuation and valuers as well as surveying, was frequently linked to changes in naming, not least of field names, local terrain features, and roads. This naming reflected alterations in layout as well as in land use and agricultural practices. There was a linear aesthetic of form and function that corresponded with the usefulness of enclosure.

The relationship between economic development and sociological theories of change was not to the fore when the specifics of what would later be termed the agricultural revolution were assessed by contemporaries. This interpretation largely came later, with the argument that the rural labor force was proletarianized as a consequence of the enclosure of common lands,[24] a process supposedly extended to opening up "a deep wound in rural popular practices of socialisation and in the very modes of governing territory."[25] Whatever the social politics at the time and in hindsight, enclosure certainly confirmed and underlined aspects of local and regional geography.[26]

In doing so, the relationship with political power in the shape of social control varied. These variations were both regional and local. In Northumberland, for example, formal enclosure methods were only used in particularly complex, or contentious, situations,[27] an instance of the degree to which the causes of such enclosure varied regionally.[28] The degree to which there was a consensual character to enclosure is far from clear. The chronological element brought in another element of power, notably the relationship between enclosure and the need to raise food production in wartime. This was a relationship that had to be grasped by entrepreneurs.

So also with the possibilities of benefiting from Continental demand for grain (corn) in wartime by means of grain exports. These created a regional geography in the shape of those parts of the country that took part in such exports, notably East Anglia and Sussex. That, in turn, had political consequences. Sussex and East Anglia were centers of Whig landed interests, notably of the Dukes of Newcastle and Richmond in Sussex and of Sir Robert Walpole, Viscount Townshend, and the Duke of Grafton in East Anglia. What might seem an agricultural interest in effect was a number of different and sometimes competing interests. The latter was notably so in terms of competition between Irish and non-Irish producers.

The agricultural geography repays attention, not least because it could be somewhat obscure in this public discussion of the economy. This profitability of animal-rearing encouraged the open-field arable farmers and landowners on the heavy English Midlands soils of Leicestershire, Northamptonshire, and Warwickshire—greatly affected by falling prices and rents in the 1720s—to switch to it, and this change reflected the ability, psychologically and practically, to response to market opportunities. So also in East Anglia, where advances in agricultural productivity were not solely a matter of new crops that may, in the shift from hay, have been linked to climatic trends[29] but reflected more fundamental change: there were important improvements to the soil, especially in marling and underdraining. By altering the chemical and physical structure of the soil, these improvements aided its productivity.

Local circumstances played a major role in the agricultural mix, a mix that was important to regional variations. These variations fed through into public discussion. For example, a pamphlet of 1731 highlighted the problems of wool production, especially in the West Country. The full title of the pamphlet indicated the linkage between the productive economy and the hierarchies of agrarian society and of metropolitan-provincial life: *The West-Country Farmer, or, a Fair Representation of the Decay of Trade, and Badness of the Times: in a letter of complaint from a tenant in the country, to his landlord in London*. The details of sales outlets provide an insight into an aspect of the political geography of the period. These details offer an insight into how provincial opinion could be articulated for, unlike most pamphlets, this one was not published in London. Instead, it was sold by the printer in Taunton, as well as in Bristol, Exeter, Gloucester, Sherborne, and Tiverton and by those who distributed the *Gloucester Journal* around its circulation area, which, itself, was extensive.

The region is not the sole area for analysis. Alongside regional agricultural differences, there were more specific local ones. The evidence of agricultural depression in the early eighteenth century varied by estate, with fewer problems, for example, on the Beaumont, Coke, and Leveson-Gower estates. East Anglia, the center of agricultural improvement, and the sphere of such iconic names as "Turnip Townshend" (Charles, 2nd Viscount Townshend) and (Thomas) Coke of Holkham (who became Earl of Leicester in 1744), was scarcely immune from these difficulties, which encouraged pressure for greater productivity. Joseph Windham Ashe, a Norfolk landowner, received commiserations in 1739 on having "a farm to let now, when everything is so low, and a prospect of the prices of grain falling yet now." As a reminder that Members of Parliament were affected by such pressures, Windham Ashe was a government supporter.[30]

Alongside regional differences,[31] there were national trends. In particular, the continued growth and integration of the market economy was a product of improved transport links and the rise in population and, therefore, demand—a demand these links could address. As the national market developed, so the relative importance of local consumption declined; regional variations in price became less pronounced.

Elite power remained a key facet. It was reflected in the concentration of landownership, in electoral politics, and in the role of local figures in the administration and operation of the Land Tax.[32] The use of the Strict Settlement, a legal provision ensuring inalienable possession, helped protect estates from dispersal due to the weaknesses of individual members of families. Moreover, the political and religious antagonisms of the fifteenth to seventeenth century were less intense, which ensured a degree of cohesion.[33]

SURVEYING

Land surveying, like map-making skills, increased during the century, both aspects of the technology and material culture of geography. A longstanding practice,[34] land surveyors were numerous, and cadastral maps (showing the extent, value, and ownership for taxation purposes) were produced in large numbers. Yet again, distance could be overcome. Landowners could give a sense of place to reports from distant estates. Thus, in 1739–42, Wadham College, Oxford, had five maps made of its Essex estates. Similarly, William Brasier mapped properties belonging to New College, Oxford. Estate maps enhanced status and were commissioned to help in the development of an estate, as well as to settle disputes and to record property when it changed hands or was to be let.

Surveyors developed appropriate conventions in the way they recorded information, so that estate maps from different areas could be compared. Whereas the estate map of Cotehele in Cornwall that probably dates from the 1550s lacked a sense of scale and is, in part, diagrammatic, in contrast the maps of Cotehele produced in 1731 and 1784 were more reliable as to scale and distance. This was also true more generally, for example of the estate map of 1699 for Baddesley Clinton, the Stourton map of 1725, and George Ingham's 1764 survey map of Kedleston in Derbyshire. Both works of art and as useful information, surveys were retained even though their contents could date. Thus, in 1725, the steward of the royal manor of Hitchin, itself a major market town, had a copy made of the survey carried out in 1676 by an earlier steward. This covered the boundaries and customs of the manor, as well as the holdings of tenants and the endowments for local charities.[35] The detail could be great. Charles, 2nd Earl of Radnor, owner of the stately home at Lanhydrock, commissioned Joel Gascoyne's *Land Atlas* of 1694–99, a masterpiece of the estate surveyor's work. It depicts more than forty thousand acres of his Cornish estates in color on 258 parchment maps. Gascoyne also produced the Stowe Atlas for the Grenville family showing their extensive estates, as well, with Cornwall in 1699, as the first large-scale map of any county, one that included parish boundaries.[36] The Duchy of Cornwall pursued systematic estates mapping from the 1770s. As guides to the localities, estate survey maps were often to be supplemented by enclosure and tithe maps. Between 1755 and 1760, John Rocque surveyed the extensive Irish estates of the Earl of Kildare, producing what became eight volumes of maps.[37] Such information, its forms and its milieus, were different to the doings of local agricultural improvement societies and the reporting of them or other methods in the press.[38]

Although the Land Surveyor's Club, the forerunner of the Institute of Chartered Surveyors, was not founded until 1834, guides to surveying appeared much earlier, including William Leybourne's *The Compleat Surveyor* in 1685. In *The Duty of a Steward to his Land* (1727), Edward Laurence claimed, "As a steward should know the quantity and quality of every parcel of land occupied by the several tenants, so likewise he should have a map of the whole drawn out in the most perfect method; which may show . . . the true figure of every parcel . . . so nearly that he may detect any tenant from alienating the least parcel of any land form his lord."[39]

Estate mapping was less used by some landowners than others,[40] a point that directs attention to different courses to modernization and the symbolization accordingly. Nevertheless, such mapping became more common, accurate, and practical from midcentury. Moreover, like entrepreneurial county mapping, it remained significant until the Ordnance Survey in the nineteenth century, by making large-scale maps readily available, changed the situation.

Land surveying, which involved many individuals,[41] was also carried out by nonspecialists as part of their role in the community. Thus, Jeffrey Whitaker (1703–75), the owner of a Baptist school in Wiltshire, farmed, drafted legal documents, assessed property for taxation, and carried out surveying.[42] Thomas Boutflower (1732–75), a former naval purser who had drawn naïve sketch maps of the Falklands (over which Britain came near to war with Spain in 1770), in 1774 produced the first manuscript map of Ottery St. Mary in Devon, a year before a plan was produced based on a survey book.[43] The clergy tended to be a repository of cartographic knowledge in their parishes.

Aside from estate maps, there were new initiatives in the publication of printed county maps in the mid-eighteenth century. Hitherto, the Elizabethan maps had been reprinted with scant alteration, due to the absence of new fieldwork. Written in the late sixteenth century, an edition of Richard Carew's *Survey of Cornwall* was published in 1769 and another in 1811.[44] However, new surveys of entire counties were undertaken in the eighteenth century, and maps were produced on detailed scales: one or more inches to the mile. The first of the county maps appeared in 1699—that of Cornwall by Joel Gascoyne—but by 1750, only eight counties had been mapped at one inch to a mile or larger. The work from 1759 was in part encouraged by prizes of £100 awarded by the Society for the Encouragement of Arts, Manufactures, and Commerce, one of the major "improving" bodies of the period, for an "accurate, actual survey of any county." Published in 1765, Benjamin Donn's one-inch map of Devon was the first winner of these prizes. The son of a schoolmaster, Donn was an able surveyor.[45]

By 1775, nearly half of the English counties had been surveyed at one inch to a mile or larger. Essex was surveyed by John Chapman and Peter André in 1772–74, and the resulting map was published in 1777. Produced at a scale of two inches to the mile, the map contained a range of detail lacking in earlier maps, including watermills and windmills, as well as the double gallows on Barking Level. As was often the case, the names of the owners of seats appeared where appropriate. The map was published in twenty-six sheets, each measuring twenty-three by nineteen inches. A set of sheets could be bought for £1 15d 0d (£1.75 currently) if hand colored, £1 5d 0d (£1.25) if plain, or £2 12s 6d (£2.62½) if bound into a leather-backed book. A countywide index map was included. It helped the purchaser identify the particular sheet of interest. The map included a list of the 224 subscribers who had supported the project. The map was reprinted in 1785 and 1833. The role of accumulated experience, a frequent factor, was shown with Chapman, who had worked with Rocque's widow in London and had been involved in the publication of county maps of Durham, Nottinghamshire, and Staffordshire, while André, who was of Huguenot descent, had been involved in that of Surrey. In 1793, John Lindley published his *Memoir of a Map of the County of Surrey; From a Survey made in the Years 1789 and 1790*. There was also an interest in earlier county maps.

Mapping extended to areas outside the traditional county structure. Peter Fannin, master of the *Adventurer*, one of the ships on Cook's first expedition, then set up a school on the Isle of Man where he taught navigation. In 1789, he published his *Correct Plan of the Isle of Man*, which offered a better account of the topography of the island than earlier maps, as well as the first indication of the island's roads and the first town plan of Douglas, the major town on the island, although the coastline was less accurate than in Mackenzie's maritime survey of 1775. This contrast underlined the difficulties of reconciling mapping on land and at sea.

There was only limited mapping of smaller towns, unless they were dominated by a single large landowner and therefore, in effect, part of the estate. Thus, the surveys that survive are valuable—for example, that of St. Ives, Huntingdonshire, in 1728 by Edward Pettis, a middling tradesman and Land Tax assessor. Pettis produced a map and survey and also used them to record other information.[46] Offering very different information but also reflecting interest in towns and the wish for precise representation, topographical views were popular. Most focused on individual towns, as with those of Swansea in 1791–92 by Thomas Rothwell.[47] There were also major works that covered many towns, as in *Buck's Antiquities* (1774), which offered a series of accurate town prospects of England and Wales, mostly made between 1728 and 1753. In this work, London was reproduced in five plates. In these maps, there was no attempt to omit the poor or to idealize rural life.[48] Painters trained as topographers, such as Edward Dayes, Paul

Sandby, and John Robert Cozsens, were influential in the development of landscape painting.

Alongside surveying, there were other forms of information. There was an ad hoc use of questionnaires prior to the first national census, that of 1801. For example, between 1747 and 1756, Jeremiah Milles, dean of Exeter, sent a questionnaire to all the Devon parishes. This was intended as a background for a gazetteer or history that was never in fact produced. The questions included farming practices, such as the usual value of arable, meadow, and pasture per acre. However, the answers were limited, with replies only from 57 percent of the county's parishes.[49] County agricultural societies provided valuable material in the second half of the century.

Maps depicting agricultural production, as opposed to organization in the shape of estates and enclosure, were in short supply. Thomas Milne's *Land Use Plan of London and Environs* (1800), a carefully color-coded map, marked a critical milestone in the advent of this new cartographic genre.[50] Land use as a concept was another aspect of land control. The politics were different but the concept similar.

CONCLUSION

At times, the signs of authority and power are clear, but the nature of authority frequently has to be assumed from the surviving evidence. This is particularly so for how territorial control operated. Indeed, much of the work on electoral interests over the last quarter century has emphasized the extent to which the sway of the elite was conditional and often, although not always, contested. Tenants and other dependents did not necessarily conform to the views of the landowners and landlords. The sway of the elite within parliamentary boroughs, although important,[51] was also conditional. This conditionality cannot be readily mapped. Any emphasis on negotiation, as a means of maintaining social mores and structures and of handling disputes,[52] suggests a density of political space as a key element.[53]

Because of the difficulties of mapping social negotiation, there has frequently been an emphasis in recent decades on the response to control, notably in the form of riots and crime. This emphasis is different in character but similar in impact to that of the stress on consumers, rather than producers, in economic developments, and on the public, as well as the state, in the operation of the law. The net effect is to underline the complex relationship between authority and power and the extent to which many had ownership in the operation of the latter.

Notes

1. N. J. W. Thrower, ed., *The Compleat Plattmaker: Essays on Chart, Map, and Globe Making in England in the Seventeenth and Eighteenth Centuries* (Berkeley, CA, 1978).

2. M. Edney, "Mathematical Cosmography and the Social Ideology of British Cartography, 1780–1820," *Imago Mundi* 46 (1994): 101–16.

3. P. Brassley, A. Lambert, and P. Saunders, eds., *Accounts of the Reverend John Crakanthorp of Fowlmere 1682–1710* (Cambridge, 1988).

4. M. S. Pedley, *The Commerce of Cartography: Making and Marketing Maps in Eighteenth-Century France and England* (Chicago, 2005).

5. For the situation in the 1690s, R. B. van Luijk, "Maps of Battles, Battle of Maps: News Cartography of the Battle at Neerwiinden, Flanders, 1693," *Imago Mundi* 60 (2008): 211–20.

6. J. E. Crowley, "Herman Moll's *The World Described* 1720: Mapping Britain's Global and Imperial Interests," *Imago Mundi* 68 (2001): 16–34.

7. R. C. Woosnam-Savage, "'To Gather an Image Whole': Some Early Maps and Plans of the Battle of Culloden," in T. Pollard, ed., *Culloden: The History and Archaeology of the Last Clan Battle* (Barnsley, UK, 2012): 163.

8. *General Advertiser*, May 17, 1746.

9. L. De Vorsey Jr., *The Indian Boundary in the Southern Colonies, 1763–1775* (Chapel Hill, NC, 1966).

10. M. B. Pritchard and H. G. Taliaferro, *Degrees of Latitude. Mapping Colonial America* (Williamsburg, VA, 2002).

11. Presidency at Fort St. George (Madras) to Colonel John Adlercron, December 20, 1754, BL. Eg. 3488 fol. 30.

12. M. H. Edney, "British Military Education, Mapmaking, and Military 'Map-Mindedness' in the Later Enlightenment," *Cartographic Journal* 31 (1994): 14; F. Fernández-Armesto, *Edward Gibbon's Atlas of the World* (London, 1991), 85.

13. Thomas Grenville to Charles James Fox, Foreign Secretary, May 10, 1782, NA. FO. 27/2 fol. 61.

14. B. W. Higman, *Jamaica Surveyed. Plantation Maps and Plans of the Eighteenth and Nineteenth Centuries*, 2nd ed. (Kingston, 2001).

15. Re Mysore, M. Edney, "The Patronage of Science and the Creation of Imperial Space: The British Mapping of India, 1799–1843," *Cartographica* 30 (1993): 62.

16. B. Schmidt, "Mapping an Empire: Cartographic and Colonial Rivalry in Seventeenth-Century Dutch and English North America," *William and Mary Quarterly*, 3rd ser., 64 (1997): 549–78, esp. 575.

17. J. B. Harley, "Deconstructing the Map," *Cartographica* 26 (1989): 1–20; J. B. Harley and P. Laxton, *The New Nature of Maps: Essays in the History of Cartography* (Baltimore, 2001); B. Klein, *Maps and the Writing of Space in Early Modern England and Ireland* (Basingstoke, UK, 2001).

18. J. R. Akerman, ed., *The Imperial Map: Cartography and the Mastery of Empire* (Chicago, 2009); J. G. Reid, "The Conquest of 'Nova Scotia': Cartographic Imperialism and the Echoes of a Scottish Past," in N. C. Landsman, ed., *Nation and Province in the First British Empire: Scotland and the Americas, 1600–1800* (Cranbury, NJ, 2001), 39–59.

19. Adams to James Bowdoin, June 2, 1786, in G. Lint et al., eds., *The Adams Papers. Papers of John Adams*, vol. 18 (Cambridge, MA, 2016), 329.

20. J. Crowley, *Imperial Landscapes: Britain's Global Visual Culture, 1745–1820* (New Haven, CT, 2011).

21. N. Cusworth, "A Tithe Case in Sheviock after the Restoration," *Journal of the Royal Institution of Cornwall* (2003): 39–53.

22. T. Gates, ed., *"The Great Trial": A Swaledale Lead Mining Dispute in the Court of Exchequer, 1705–1708* (Woodbridge, UK, 2011).

23. D. Hall, "Enclosures in Northamptonshire," *Northamptonshire Past and Present* 9 (1997–98): 350–67.

24. R. A. Butlin, *The Transformation of Rural England c. 1580–1800: A Study in Historical Geography* (Oxford, 1982).

25. A. Sevilla-Buitrago, "Territory and the Governmentalisation of Social Reproduction: Parliamentary Enclosure and Spatial Rationalities in the Transition from Feudalism to Capitalism," *Journal of Historical Geography* 38 (2012): 219.

26. T. Williamson, *The Transformation of Rural England—Farming and the Landscape 1700–1870* (Exeter, UK, 2002).

27. R. O'Donnell, "Conflict, Agreement, and Landscape Change: Methods of Enclosure of the Northern English Countryside," *Journal of Historical Geography* 44 (2014): 119.

28. Ibid., 120.

29. M. Overton, "Weather and Agricultural Change in England, 1660–1739," *Agricultural History* 63 (1989): 77–88.

30. J. V. Beckett, "Regional Variation and the Agricultural Depression," *Economic History Review*, 2nd ser., 35 (1982): 35–51; St. Clair to Windham Ashe, February 12, 1739, Norwich, Norfolk CRO., Ketton-Cremer Mss. WKC 6/24 401X.

31. E. Kerridge, *The Common Fields of England* (Manchester, 1992); C. Phythian-Adams, ed., *Societies, Cultures, and Kinship, 1580–1850: Cultural Provinces and English Local History* (Leicester, UK, 1993); M. Kowaleski, *Local Markets and Regional Trade in Medieval Exeter* (Cambridge, 1995).

32. M. Turner and D. Mills, eds., *Land and Property: The English Land Tax 1692–1832* (Gloucester, UK, 1986); R. Davey, *East Sussex Land Tax 1785* (Lewes, UK, 1991); D. Ginter, *A Measure of Wealth. The English Land Tax in Historical Analysis* (London, 1992).

33. B. English, *The Great Landowners of East Yorkshire 1530–1910* (London, 1992).

34. M. Netzloff, ed., *John Norden's "The Surveyor's Dialogue," 1618: A Critical Edition* (Farnham, UK, 2010).

35. B. Howlett, ed., *Survey of the Royal Manor of Hitchin 1676* (Hitchin, UK, 2000).

36. J. Gascoyne, *A Map of the County of Cornwall, 1699* (Exeter, UK, 1991).

37. H. Cobbe, "Four Manuscript Maps Recently Acquired by the British Museum," *Journal of the Society of Archivists* 4 (1973): 650–52.

38. *Darlington Pamphlet*, September 4, 1772; *The Original Ipswich Journal*, December 17, 1774.

39. S. Bendall, *Dictionary of Land Surveyors and Local Map-Makers of Great Britain and Ireland 1530–1850*, 2 vols., 2nd ed. (London, 1997). This contains far more information than

the first edition but remains incomplete. A useful pamphlet example is provided by B. S. Smith, "The Dougharty Family of Worcester, Estate Surveyors and Mapmakers, 1700–60," *Worcestershire Historical Society Publications*, new series, 5 (1967); A. S. Mason, *Essex on the Map, the 18th century Land Surveyors of Essex* (Chelmsford, UK, 1990); H. M. Thomas, *A Catalogue of Glamorgan Estate Maps* (Cardiff, 1992); Bendall, *Maps, Land, and Society: A History with a Carto-Bibliography of Cambridgeshire Estate Maps c. 1600–1836* (Cambridge, 1992); D. R. Hainsworth, *Stewards, Lords, and People: The Estate Steward and His World in Later Stuart England* (Cambridge, 1992); M. R. Ravenhill and M. M. Rowe, eds., *The Acland Family: Maps and Surveys 1720–1840* (Exeter, UK, 2006).

40. D. H. Fletcher, *The Emergence of Estate Maps: Christ Church Oxford, 1660 to 1840* (Oxford, 1995).

41. M. R. Ravenhill and M. M. Rowe, eds., *Devon Maps and Map-Makers: Manuscript Maps before 1840* (Exeter, UK, 2000), 43.

42. M. Reeves and J. Morrison, eds., *The Diaries of Jeffery Whitaker, Schoolmaster of Bratton, 1739–1741* (Trowbridge, UK, 1989).

43. P. Barber, "Five Unusual Maps of the Falklands," *Map Collector* 20 (September 1982): 50–51; J. Pritchard, "An Addition to Ravenhill and Rowe's *Devon Maps and Map-Makers: Manuscript Maps before 1840*," *Devon and Cornwall Notes and Queries* 40 (autumn 2009): 176–82.

44. P. D. A. Harvey and H. Thorpe, *The Printed Maps of Warwickshire 1576–1900* (Warwick, UK, 1959); P. Laxton, "The Geodetic and Topographical Evaluation of English County Maps 1740–1840," *Cartographic Journal* 13 (1976): 37–54; D. Kingsley, *Printed Maps of Sussex, 1575–1900* (Lewes, UK, 1982).

45. W. Ravenhill, ed., *A Map of the County of Devon, by Benjamin Donn, 1765* (Exeter, UK, 1965).

46. E. Pettis, *Survey of St. Ives, 1728*, edited by M. Carter (Cambridge, 2002).

47. M. Gibbs and B. Morris, *Thomas Rothwell: Views of Swansea in the 1790s* (Cardiff, 1991).

48. R. Hyde, ed., *A Prospect of Britain: The Town Panoramas of Samuel and Nathaniel Buck* (London, 1994); K. Cavers, *A Vision of Scotland. The Nation Observed by John Slezer 1671 to 1717* (Edinburgh, 1993).

49. R. Stanes, "Devon Agriculture in the Mid-Eighteenth Century: The Evidence of the Milles Enquiries," in M. A. Havinden and C. M. King, eds., *The South-West and the Land* (Exeter, UK, 1969), 43–65.

50. T. Milne, *Land Use Plan of London and Environs* (London, 1800), BL. Maps K. Top. 6.95; G. B. G. Bull, "Thomas Milne's Land Utilisation Map of the London Area in 1800," *Geographical Journal* 122 (1956): 25–30; C. Delano-Smith and R. J. Kain, *English Maps: A History* (Toronto, 1999), 127–32. See also H. C. Darby, *An Historical Geography of England before AD 1800* (Cambridge, 1936), 475.

51. W. J. Petchey, *A Prospect of Maldon 1500–1689* (Chelmsford, UK, 1991).

52. M. J. Braddick and J. Walter, eds., *Negotiating Power in Early Modern Society: Order, Hierarchy, and Subordination in Britain and Ireland* (Cambridge, 2001); J. Beattie, *Policing and Punishment in London, 1660–1750: Urban Crime and the Limits of Terror* (Oxford, 2001). For a more traditional approach to cultural appropriation and the marginalization of popular culture, M. E. Fissell, *Patients, Power, and the Poor in Eighteenth Century Bristol* (Cambridge, 1992).

53. T. Harris, ed., *The Politics of the Excluded, c. 1500–1850* (Basingstoke, UK, 2001).

4

The Public Sphere

> Here people of property march sword in hand,
> To protect their King's rights and defend their own land,
> And with rapture we view smiling commerce alive,
> While the spirit of British forefathers revive!
>
> —Verse three of James Whitley's "A Song on the Lincolnshire Militia," from *The Union Journal: or, Halifax Advertiser*, December 25, 1759

EXISTENTIAL GEOGRAPHIES OF GOOD AND EVIL

The world was very much an object of public consideration, the means and practices of which varied greatly. Traditional religious exposition remained highly significant in what was a Christian state and society. This exposition provided themes of the world as an aspect of a divine Christian plan and also of the world as a literal and metaphorical expression of the struggle between competing realms of good and evil. Although far from uniform, these themes continued to be very important. The Port Royal and London earthquakes of 1692 were both seen as a warning of God's anger with sin. This reflected the extent to which the breach in the succession in 1688-89, and the strains of war with France in 1689-97, provided occasion and cause for bitter debate about the role of Providence.[1] What could later be termed the Enlightenment, and notably the assault on fanaticism and prejudice, was often forged in the heat of zealous partisan conflict.[2]

In spatial terms, themes of good and evil were both long-standing and most clearly represented by the idea of an underworld that was literally under the ground, an idea that continued to have popular vitality even as astronomy had greatly weakened comparable beliefs in heaven. The underworld was a world that was deep in the collective psyche and the individual imagination, the two interacting to sustain each other. This was a world of decay, evil, and spirits, one to which bodies were consigned once their souls had departed. Death was not a close. Space and time were both part of the matrix of life and the afterlife, and each provided a dynamic, although the character of the afterlife varied greatly as a matter of emphasis and understanding.

Indeed, the afterlife posed particular questions for the geography of both the everyday and of human life as a whole. The imaging of other worlds and of the underworld varied by culture and place within Britain (as well as more generally) and sometimes by individual. Discussion in the world of print was usually limited or elusive, but at times, there was a full-scale and instructive discussion. Reverend Robert Kirk, Episcopalian minister in Aberfoyle, Perthshire, published in 1691 his *The Secret Commonwealth; or an Essay on the Nature and Actions of the Subterranean (and for the most part) Invisible People heretofoir going under the name of Faunes and Fairies, or the lyke, among the Low Country Scots, as they are described by those who have the second sight.* For revealing this knowledge, he was allegedly abducted by the "little people" in 1692. As an instance of the range of concerns, an Edinburgh report in the *Newcastle Courant* of February 4, 1764, noted:

> We learn that a great many people, who have little sense and a great deal of superstition, are in a prodigious panic on consulting their almanacs when they find Easter Sunday happens on Lady-day, grounding their fear on the prophecy.

"When our Lord falls in our Lady's lap,
England beware of a great mishap."

In contrast, scientific accounts of the weather became more prominent during the century.[3]

Belief in witchcraft, and discussion about it, diminished, or at least appeared to do so, although there were still instructive episodes. *Lloyd's*

Evening Post and British Chronicle, a major London newspaper, on January 2, 1761, carried a report from Wilton in Wiltshire, which was not a remote "marginal" environment: "A few days ago, one Sarah Jellicoat escaped undergoing the whole discipline usually inflicted by the unmerciful and unthinking vulgar on witches (under pretence that she had bewitched a farmer's servant maid, and a tallow-chandler's soap, which failed in the operation) only by the favourable interposition of some humane gentlemen, and the vigilance of a discreet magistrate, who stopped the proceedings before the violence thereof had gone to a great pitch, by binding over the aggressors by recognisance to appear at the next assizes, there to justify the parts they severally acted in the execution of their pretended witch law."

A stronger note of skepticism, in this case about wise men, was struck by the *Leeds Intelligencer* of March 16, 1790, which, notably, was published near the close of the century. The item, bylined Leeds, threw light on rural credulity, a frequent theme of urban commentators:

> A carrier, between Aldstone and Penrith, lately had some goods stolen out of his wagon. In order to detect the thief, he made a pilgrimage to Rumbles Moor near Skipton in Craven, to consult the Wise Man who resides there, and, who, having received the carrier's offering, dismissed him with the consolatory assurance, that if the thief did not restore the property before a certain day— "it should be worse for him!" The carrier's reports of these oracular words had a wonderful, and, as it happened, a beneficial effect on his neighbours; for, Thursday the 25th ult. being the day they having wisdom enough to know that in order to effect this the Wise Man must inevitably raise the devil,—and the devil, through vexation, would most probably raise the wind,—they loaded the thatched roofs of their houses with harrows, etc which prevented the fatal consequences of a violent hurricane that came on in the night, and was felt in the most parts of the kingdom. There can be no doubt that this circumstance will add considerably to the high opinion already entertained of The Wise Robin of Rumbles Moor. The stolen goods have *not* been refunded; but that is a trifle. Nobody will dispute the rigorous execution of the Wise Man's sentence, which extended not to the actual recovery of the property, but denounced only a conditional punishment on the offender, which may have been severely inflicted; for (in the judgement of some) the wind was strong enough to blow into—the Red Sea.

The last added a biblical reference. At the same time, the *Westminster Journal* in 1773–74 published articles on the need in light of thunder and lightning to contemplate the Day of Judgment and on the Torments of Hell.[4]

Despite varied beliefs about the afterlife, there were common spatial themes. Notable ones included the presence of means of access, especially via entrances that had no apparent end or bottom. Caves and pits provided key examples. In Viterbo in Italy, the locals discerned an entrance to the underworld accordingly. Sacred wells were a converse element in the spatiality of good and evil. Belief in these traditional sites and in the magic, good or bad, associated with them, remained strong in Britain. There was particular interest in Wales. The St. Winefride's well at Holywell in North Wales, an old saintly site, became associated with fertility after James II prayed there, helping Queen Mary to conceive "James III," the "Warming Pan Baby." The decline of pilgrimages meant that, in a process that had begun in the 1530s, one form of religious geography was largely lost. At the same time, pilgrimage continued. Lieutenant Richard Browne wrote to his father in 1765 about a visit to St. Patrick's Purgatory, an island in Lough Derg in County Donegal where each year more than ten thousand Irish Catholics made a pilgrimage, a practice expressly forbidden under the Popery Act of 1704. He found

> a multitude of both sexes mostly indeed of the poorer sort ... in one place the penitents are obliged to run so many times round barefoot on sharp pointed rocks repeating so many ave marias etc, in commemoration of the seven deadly sins ... in other parts they are obliged to wade to the middle in the water and stand there for a stated time repeating a certain number of prayers, when this is over the next penance is to retire to a vault made purposely, where they must remain 24 hours without eating, drinking, speaking or sleeping, for they are sure if they do either the Devil has a power of carrying them away, and to prevent sleeping, everyone that goes in there supply themselves with pins which they thrust into anyone found dosing ... the last ceremony is washing in the lake, when they wash away all their sins.[5]

A commitment to such traditional, and still, vital forms of knowledge as astrology was not only a matter of oral transmission but was catered for in the culture of print. Astrology offered a geography that linked the earth to astral elements and in a very direct fashion. The role of astral links was also suggested by the iconography of symbols of the zodiac, an iconography that was much reproduced. The foundation of freemasonry in London in 1717, its rapid spread thereafter in Britain and its empire, and its prominence in social and intellectual circles ensured that it was not only conservative elements and understandings that were at issue in the discussion of astrology.

FORMS OF POWER

The subject of existential geographies deserves a book in itself, but it is not the topic explored in this chapter. Instead, the approach taken is that of the world as an object of public consideration via a culture of print the content of which changed as it adapted to new topics and information. A focus will be on newspapers and on how they acted as a clearing-house to disseminate knowledge, opinion, and ideas. However, other issues must also be addressed in understanding senses of place and the structures and dynamics with which they were linked.

Despite the constitutional differences between the British Isles and most Continental states, the shared reality at the local level was self-government by the notables and their supporters and, at the national level, a political system that was largely run by the elite. The associated power was present and expressed at the local level as well as at the national. In particular, in rural society, stately homes proclaimed hierarchy, longevity, and status and, therefore, legitimacy, perhaps even providential sanction.

Nevertheless, the stately homes also reflected a concern to be up to date. This was present with the redefinition of taste and style, a long-standing theme, now strongly seen as classical designs were interpreted for, and incorporated into, British architecture and landscape design.[6] Whether new or rebuilt, the model for stately homes was of a harmonious unity. This generally required building on a large scale, and not the incoherence of a tacked-on extension, and this building proved expensive. Proportion was a key aspect of a number of styles. Such an impression captured inherent harmonies that were regarded as natural and culturally significant, with balance acting as a means, as well as symbol, for an appropriate politics. The tightly controlled symmetry of Palladianism was an architectural language that worked on a variety of building and interior scales and outer symmetry lent itself to the symmetry of interior layout. This was seen in colonial as well as "home" architecture.

At the same time as this potent display to others, there was a degree of elite withdrawal from the bulk of the population, not least by the aristocrats not living all year in cities and by their developing strategies of separation including through marriage.[7] To an extent, elite withdrawal, where it occurred, was a matter of the decline of baroque show and its replacement with more intimate sensibilities.

The segregation of the world of the landed elite was one in which the game, notably deer, rabbits, and birds, avidly hunted on private land under the Game Laws, had to be protected from poachers. The Game Act of 1671 gave the exclusive right to hunt game to freeholders worth £100 a year or to leaseholders worth £150 a year, which restricted this sport to wealthy landed gentry. There was supplementary legislation in 1707, 1771, and 1773. Much work was devoted to walls, gates, and lodges that provided bounds to the estate and, therefore, agrarian segregation, and these, both features and bounds, were clearly depicted in estate maps. From the late 1770s, game preserves were increasingly protected by spring guns and man-traps. In part, this was to protect privilege, but the demands of the market economy also played a role.[8]

There was scant sense that members of the elite had to fear personal attack and thus needed a strong "personal space" of safety. With the exception of socially licensed fighting in the shape of duels, this was indeed the case as far as death and injury were concerned. Theft, however, was a problem, notably in the form of highwaymen and pickpockets, although it was rarely violent. The presence of servants acted to protect members of elite, as, often, did that of dependents and friends.

Indeed, new houses no longer bore defensive features, while those on old houses were not preserved. This was true in Ireland, Scotland, and Wales as well as England. Fortification was reduced to fantasy, as in fortified walls—for example, at Castle Howard—to garden follies, and to mock Gothic castles. The approach from landscaped grounds to the houses, with the major obstacle being the ha-ha, a ditch to keep cattle away from the house itself, was easy for people. The new neo-Gothic style of the later eighteenth century was not designed to provide such strength and was almost a parody of it. A very different image of fortification was provided in the political contention of 1780: "Newspapers I consider as centinels, placed upon the outposts of the constitution, centinels who should never be punished but for sleeping, neglect of duty, or giving intelligence to the enemy."[9]

Landscape gardening, inescapably linked to wealthy landed patronage, and to the politics involved in such patronage,[10] flourished despite the cost and time involved in new projects. To a degree, alongside similarities, notably looking back to the classics,[11] there were distinct Tory and Whig styles of gardening and landscaping. The architect William Kent (1684–1748) developed and decorated parks (grounds of houses) in order to provide an appropriate setting for buildings. In turn, Lancelot "Capability" Brown (1716–83) took forward the rejection of the rigid formality associated with Continental models, contriving a setting that appeared natural but, nevertheless, was carefully designed for effect. His landscapes of serpentine lakes, gentle hills, and scattered groups of newly planted trees represented a less insistent conquest of nature by man. Brown swiftly established a fashion in a world where the small number of patrons, and their interest in new artistic developments, permitted new fashions to spread swiftly, while their wealth enabled them to realize and develop the new fashions.

Looked at less positively, Brown's reshaping of the landscape was an aspect of manipulation and control, one that indicated the ambiguous nature of "improvement" as both ideology and practice. Rephrased, this ambiguity was not apparent for contemporaries, or at least most contemporaries, but can be seen by modern commentators. Indeed, this reshaping has been compared to policies of imperial and domestic control, while the environmental damage that resulted has lately also attracted critical attention. This was most clearly in terms of damage to the natural habitat—for example, the drainage of boggy areas. Much of the effort involved in landscaping related to water features.

The theme of reshaping was very much one taken by contemporaries. In his *Observations on Modern Gardening* (Dublin, 1765; London, 1770), Thomas Whately, MP, a key figure in George Grenville's political group, noted that in both a park and a garden there could be

> a state of highly cultivated nature. . . . The same species of preservation, of ornament, and of scenery, may be introduced; and though a large portion of a park may be rude; and the most romantic scenes are not incompatible with its character; yet it should seem rather to be reclaimed from a forest, than a neglected corner of it; the wildness must not be universal; it is but a circumstance; and it is a happy circumstance only when it is kept within due bounds; some appearance of improvement is essential; and a high degree of polish is at times expected, and is generally agreeable.[12]

Thomas Jefferson took this book with him when he toured English gardens in 1786.

At the same time, there was damage to the human habitat, most brutally in the movement of villages, as with that of Nuneham Courtenay in Oxfordshire in 1759 away from the newly landscaped park of Earl Harcourt, and also the case of Milton Abbey in Dorset, although some deserted villages were already depopulated.[13] Less dramatically, the routes of canals and roads were altered to the benefit of the parkland of stately houses, as with the London to Portsmouth canal and the London to Holyhead road. On top of this, there has been criticism of the aesthetics of the new landscaping, and notably of straight avenues driven through woodland in order to provide vistas.[14] The extent to which this interpretation deserves positive attention, not least as a more general critical guide to elite culture in the period, is worthy of consideration as it raises significant issues about assessment. There is a parallel to this criticism in the modern academic view of maps and other works as slanted knowledge systems that inherently reflected and involved considerations of power, views advanced by J. B. Harley and others that have already been referred to. Brown certainly offered a new form of garden iconography, one that was different to that earlier in the period.[15]

Brown's ideas were developed further from the 1790s by Humphry Repton (1752–1818), in accordance with the concept of the "picturesque." This concept stressed the individual character of each landscape and the need to retain it, while making improvements to remove what were judged blemishes and obstructions, and to open up vistas.[16] Repton also produced a map in 1788 titled "A general view of the influence operating in the elections for the county of Norfolk," which included the names of those who had an annual income of more than £1,000 and who were supposed to influence more than twenty voters, along with the candidate they were likely to support.[17]

All landscaped forms were celebrated by painters,[18] who offered accordingly a visual guide to geographies of elegance. Changing tastes affected the interest in particular landscapes. Written in 1770, and first published in 1780 in the fourth volume of his *Anecdotes of Painting in England*, Horace Walpole's essay "On Modern Gardening" looked back to classical Roman origins but very much emphasized modern British achievements. He continued: "Since we have been familiarised to the study of landscape we hear less of what delighted our sportsmen-ancestors, *a fine open country*. Wiltshire, Dorsetshire and such ocean-like extents were formerly preferred to the rich blue prospects of Kent, to the Thames-watered views in Berkshire, and to the magnificent scale of nature in Yorkshire. An open country is but a canvas on which a landscape might be designed."[19]

This was a view relevant to colonialism. Stately homes dominated the countryside, visually and socially, and were designed to do so, even if the British domesticated them by not calling them palaces. These homes were a testimony to confidence and wealth, each of which was a key factor in the tone of British politics. While "establishment" politics was about far more than landed society,[20] the assumptions and practices of this society were very important to it. The stately homes were the nodes of this order and, as such, helped set its tone.[21] Their contents recorded, and disseminated, family glory, displaying the impact of longevity as well as of the present. Furniture, porcelain, cutlery, paintings, maps, and decorations frequently bore crests and other motifs that proclaimed ownership and linked the family with taste. Portraits recorded and proclaimed family status, splendor, and glory. At Knole in the Grand Hall hangs John Wootton's *The First Duke of Dorset Returning to Dover Castle after Taking the Oath as Lord Warden of the Cinque Ports*. Painted immediately after the event in 1729, the painting was sumptuously framed with the family devices of the Sackville family. That Knole now belongs to the National Trust ensures that even more people can see such family regalia.

In a complex interaction with time, these palaces represented the quest both to be ancient and to be modern. This was a transference into time of the spatial pattern of being both specific to the site and generic as a model. Neoclassicism was particularly important in this respect as it provided an architectural idiom to support the relationship between the modern elite and its supposed classical forbears. Neoclassicism was an architectural language that worked on a number of scales and in towns as well as the countryside.[22] Outer symmetry lent itself to the symmetry of interior layout. Neoclassicism should be seen not only in the formal style of that name in the late eighteenth century but also, more generally, as an approach to architecture, although there were tensions between the professionalizing power of the architect and the concerns and skills of the craftsmen.[23]

Interest in the character of stately homes and their grounds led to engravings, guides, and maps. Later famous for his survey and map of London, John Rocque, at first described himself as a *dessinateur de jardins* (garden designer) and surveyed the gardens of royalty and the aristocracy mostly near London. Smaller versions of his plans appeared in a volume of *Vitruvius Britannicus* (1739) dedicated to Frederick, Prince of Wales. These plans included Claremont and Esher, the seats of Thomas, Duke of Newcastle, and his brother Henry Pelham, key figures in the ministry.[24]

In the sixteenth canto of his ironic poetic epic *Don Juan* (1824), the Romantic poet Lord George Byron (1788–1824) stressed the dominance of electioneering by the elite, whatever their theoretical political differences: "the 'other interest' (meaning / The same self-interest, with a different leaning)." As the radical Thomas Spence claimed in 1800, "Are not our legislators all landlords?" He continued by stating, "It is childish to expect ever to see small farms again, or ever to see anything else than the utmost screwing and grinding of the poor, till you quite overturn the present system of landed property." The vitality and economic value[25] of the earlier reliance on shared land use and common field land helped explain the transforming nature of enclosure and the popular resistance to it. This resistance included hostility to the processes, such as the theft of new landmarks, surveys, and field books, and the destruction of gates, posts, and rails.[26]

So also with politics: enclosure and elite dominance of electioneering were aspects of a more general concentration of landholding in fewer hands,[27] although opposing economic priorities and social assumptions did not necessarily lead to what would later be termed class conflict. Moreover, elite dominance was qualified, as far as politics and parliamentary rule were concerned, by strong traditions of popular independence, especially in the major towns, by the activism of the propertied "middling orders,"[28] by the constant renewal of power structures,[29] and also by divisions within the elite.[30] At the same time, reciprocal assumptions of paternalism and subordination were significant.[31] Confronting the challenge of the French Revolution, John Trevor, British envoy to Savoy-Piedmont, reported from Turin in 1792: "the misfortune is that in this country the whole society is divided into two classes, the *Court and Nobility*, and *the Bourgeoisie*, and the line drawn between them is so rude and marked that the two parties have long been jealous and might too easily become hostile; there are none of those intermediate shades which blend the whole together into one harmonious mass as in our happy country."[32]

Much urban and industrial property was owned by aristocrats—for example, by the Dukes of Bedford in Tavistock. Whereas individual aristocrats were important in many small towns such as the Earls of Bristol in Bury St. Edmunds, there was a very different situation in London. The long-established pattern of a court, and therefore metropolitan, presence for the aristocracy was maintained there. The expansion into the West End seen during the reign of Queen Anne (1702–14) continued and led to the building of grand houses, as well as a larger number of homes designed for the fashionable. The construction of grand houses reaffirmed the aristocratic stamp on that part of the city. Devonshire House was built in the 1730s, Chesterfield House in 1747–52, and the new Norfolk House in 1748–56. This move of the nobility west from the Covent Garden area closer to the royal palace at St. James's was an important realignment socially and politically, as well as being a major shift in land use: the Haymarket, originally the source of feedstuff for horses, was cleared for development in the early eighteenth century. Underlining the role of the landed aristocracy and the urban oligarchs, this was the era in which London's episcopal houses were sold, including York Place, Ely House, and Winchester House.

There were, and are, different ways to conceptualize the social relations of the period. Any emphasis on sociopolitical control as a whole provided a uniform account of differentiation, with the geography of control being one of social dynamics and political means. In contrast, regional differentiation in the nature of control was underplayed. London, however, a region in itself, was an exception, as its special character received considerable attention and specific analysis. The extent to which London offered different prospects to those of landed society was captured by George Lillo in his play *The London Merchant* (1731), which deliberately focused on ordinary people. "A London apprentice ruined is our theme," declared the prologue. London was also very obviously different because of the diversity of its population. By 1690, Huguenots were about 8–10 percent of London's population, with strong concentrations in particular areas, notably Spitalfields, and by the late 1690s, there were forty-five Huguenot churches in London. New ideas came with them, as well as unfamiliar foods, including caraway seeds, garlic, oxtail soup, and pickles.[33]

At the same time, there were clashes in values within London, as in other individual localities, with cities taking on literary weight because of their use for these clashes. Social tension in London, in part, was linked to the uneasy neighborhood of the City and the West End. The interplay of the two was a long-established moral and literary theme, one with classical roots. The journalist and novelist Henry Fielding saw London in terms of a corrupt court and aristocracy at its West End, with their commerce in vice, and, in contrast, the more acceptable commercial metropolis of the City of London. In the February 14, 1747, issue of *Old England*, a leading opposition London newspaper, the writer Horace Walpole attacked Thomas, Duke of Newcastle, the leading minister, who lived at Lincoln's Inn Fields. Walpole contrasted "a frugal citizen in Cornhill [in the City], whose whole family lives on a single dish of meat, while he cheerfully pays his taxes towards pulling-down the French King," with whom Britain was then at war, with a minister of state keeping a French cook and dining every day "more sumptuously than a City livery company." Newcastle was notorious for favoring the products of his French cook and expected James, 1st Earl Waldegrave, the envoy in Paris from 1730 to 1740, to send truffles for his cook.

These themes, of court vice and city diligence, continued to be reiterated during the century, although they became less striking in the last decades. There were also contrary themes. For example, the virtues and values summarized as "sensibility" were frequently contrasted with the commercialism and crassness of new money which was very much associated with London.

TRANSFORMATIONS

"London, which place governs the value of all grain in England." This letter, published far distant from London in the *Newcastle Journal* of July 19, 1740, testified to the economic dynamics that comprised an important element of the geography of power. The dynamics very much focused on London, in part due to the unique market it offered and in part due to financial considerations, notably the possibility of charging far more for goods there.[34] Growth and specialization in the market economy were intense near large centers—for example, in Essex, Middlesex, and eastern

Berkshire near London—but also affected more distant places. Published in London, the *Public Advertiser* of January 6, 1757, reported grain prices in Salisbury, Warminster, and Devizes markets. Indeed, trade within Britain provided profit and propelled economic development. Cattle were driven south to London from Yorkshire, and Welsh cattle were driven to Kent to be fattened for the London market. Welsh drovers had "secret knowledge" of routes to London and of where the cattle and other animals could be grazed—knowledge handed down from father to son. Turkeys walked to London from Norfolk. Cheshire cheese was shipped to London.[35]

The operation of a national market economy benefited from the transmission of information—for example, of the commodity prices in London—which became a staple item in the provincial press, notably that of grain on Bear Key. In Moll's *The World Described*, a map of England and Wales, presented as the southern part of Britain, included a comprehensive gazetteer arranged in pairs of columns listing the names of each market town, their coordinates, market days, and distance from London.[36] Land use responded to distant markets, on a long-established pattern that became more intense, with the decline of household subsistence and autonomous local markets linked to change in the seasonality of marriage, a method that enables the use of marriage records in parish registers to study agricultural integration.[37] However, there are major problems with mapping agricultural data accurately even after the introduction of an annual agricultural survey in 1866.[38] In Lancashire, in North-West England, pasture was profitable because of sales thence of meat to London and to industrial towns in the North of England. Similarly, Irish dairy and livestock production developed in response to external demands, with substantial exports of beef and butter to England and of salted pork to colonies such as Newfoundland. Creating a dense network of links, these exports helped to bring considerable prosperity to sections of Irish society and were an aspect of the growing commercialization of Irish agriculture as it was drawn more fully into the market economy both within Ireland and more widely.[39]

Across Britain, landowners benefited, but so did agricultural workers. These processes, nevertheless, led to differentiation within rural society, creating new regional and local contrasts. Not all areas, localities, or farms changed or changed at the same rate.[40] Booming parishes were different to their less successful counterparts, not least in population movements and in the formation of new family units. Throughout Britain, the parishes that attracted immigration and held on to population growth tended to be those that offered opportunities for cottage industry, notably textile manufacturing. In some places, the availability of common land could be very important in providing scope for a bigger population. There were also areas where the soil was poor and population limited, such as the Breckland near Thetford: local variations that had persisted for centuries continued, as many still do.

On a long-standing pattern,[41] transformation was most notable at the regional level, whether in agriculture, industry, mining, or transport, as in East Shropshire, the North-East of England, and Strathclyde for mining and industry. Indeed, change in new crop rotations, especially the resulting enhancement of East Anglian farming,[42] and the building of canals and turnpike roads all exacerbated contrasts between and within regions,[43] as well as helping define and redefine regions. In this respect, the turnpikes prefigured the later impact of other technologies, such as the internet. As illustrated later in this chapter and discussed in chapter 9, historians need to devote more attention to the concept of the "region."[44] Economic change and the development of communications were means by which the reality of a region and its bounds were expressed, understood, and redefined.

But however different in particular localities and individual regions, the sense of transformation was national and to a greater degree than in the present day. A clear sign of integration was the rise of post office revenues: from £116,000 in 1698 to £210,000 in 1755. This rise, in a period of low inflation, reflected the foundation of new routes and an increase in the use of existing ones. The post was able to play a dramatic element in the plots of many novels—for example, those of Samuel Richardson, especially *Pamela* (1740), which helped establish a pattern for other novels. Moreover, the nature of letters changed. The length of a letter could be determined by how much time was available to the writer before the post was collected, a point to which correspondents referred. The arrival of letters became more predictable, both in timing and in reliability. Letter writers were aware that much of their correspondence took the form of a sequence and also made regular reference to letters from others.

Alongside a national urban network dominated in 1700 by the south of England, East Anglia, and the Midlands, the role of agriculture ensured a population distribution that was very different from that of Britain in 1900 when it was a great industrial power. By the standards in 1900, and still now, a relatively low percentage of the British population lived in northern England in 1700 and, even, 1750. Instead, much of the British population lived in the most fertile areas: eastern England; the fertile lowlands of South Wales, notably the Vale of Glamorgan; and the Central Lowlands of Scotland. Nevertheless, the dominant role of agriculture also ensured that a greater percentage of the population than today lived in areas that were less attractive for farming but where a living could still be earned from the soil. This was true of upland pasture areas, such as Exmoor and the Scottish Highlands, where mixed farming (arable and pastoral) was followed including the animal husbandry for which they were to be prominent later.

Enclosure represented a major change in much of the rural economy and led to much mapping. The regularization of field boundaries was an important aspect of the change. The emphasis on geometric forms was also seen in land distribution in the colonies. There was, however, nothing comparable in the political field within Britain. In particular, there was nothing similar to the ideas advanced in North America after independence as the state system was spread in a series of ordinances in the 1780s. Uniformity then was to the fore. The ordinance of 1784 for the government of the Western Territory, the product of a congressional committee chaired by Thomas Jefferson, proposed that all states have boundaries based on the precision of mathematics, rather than the variations of topography. The idea was taken further in the Land Ordinance of 1785, which proposed a grid system for the allocation of land, an allocation designed to fulfill congressional hopes that the rapid development of the frontier and the spread of commercial connections would strengthen the Union and prevent separatism.[45] Prior to independence, linear colonial boundaries had already been very important, and notably so as the colonies' westward expansion was planned—for example, between Virginia and North Carolina and between Pennsylvania and Maryland.

Social difference within the British world took many forms and most notably with slavery, which, for the British colonies, grew to an unprecedented scale with Britain also the most active slave-trading state in the world. Writings about the slave trade, including narratives of African slaves in the British world, were to prove important in stirring up abolitionist concern in the 1780s. These narratives demonstrated the cruel nature of the power that the slave trade and slavery imposed. Print therefore offered slave conditions, if not generally slaves themselves, at least an element of representation, however very restricted. Difference extended to slave narratives, which included those concerning British slaves in North Africa as well as those about the far far more numerous (and in general more harshly treated) African slaves in British America. There were significant comparisons between the two types of narrative, but they were not apparent to most contemporaries in large part because of the habit of excluding slaves from any consideration of Britishness.[46]

ELECTORAL SPACES

Within Britain, very differently, electoral politics added another dimension to the politics of place. A contrasting spatial prospectus had briefly been introduced during the Interregnum period. In 1653, a nominated "Parliament," better known as the Barebone's Parliament after a radical member, Praise-God Barebone, was appointed. In the sole systematic reform of the electoral system before the First Reform Act of 1832, "rotten boroughs" (constituencies with very few electors) were replaced by more county seats (which all had more votes) and by separate representation for expanding industrial towns, such as Bradford, Leeds, and Manchester. In addition, the franchise (right to vote) was extended. This Parliament was also the first to have representatives from Scotland and Ireland, although they were mostly Englishmen serving there. Most Members of Parliament (MPs) in this Parliament were not from the traditional ruling elite but instead were minor gentry. If anything, though, they were less representative than the usual parliamentarians, as they were not elected by any process but chosen by the council of military officers that was central to the government. However, that particular Parliament, compromised by its radicalism and divisions, was swiftly dissolved, while the very idea of refashioning the franchise and electoral system, and redrawing constituency boundaries, was discredited.

Thus, the established electoral system, both in terms of the distribution of constituencies and with reference to the electorate, remained, both with the Restoration of 1660 and also as an aspect of the Revolution Settlement that followed the Glorious Revolution in 1688–89. Nor was the new political geography enforced by Oliver Cromwell in 1655 acceptable. Himself the product and expression of military power, he had divided the country among areas under the control of individual major-generals, who were instructed to preserve security and to create a godly and efficient state. This was a very different political geography, but it was unacceptable, even when the country was threatened by Jacobite invasion from the 1690s on, and notably in 1745–46. Instead, the attempt to supplement British regular troops took the form of bringing allied troops in from the Continent, in this case from the United Provinces (Netherlands) and Hesse-Cassel; of raising the militia, which, in 1745, proved singularly unsuccessful in resisting the Jacobite invasion of Cumbria; and of turning to the aristocracy. William III had used Dutch, Danish, and Brandenburg forces to assist in his conquest of Ireland in 1690–91.

Turning to the aristocracy was a highly traditional form of raising troops and of defining and demonstrating local power and its national consequences. In the crisis of the Glorious Revolution, the lords lieutenant had played a key role in the overthrow of James II. There was some criticism in 1745–46 of the turn to the aristocracy and notably of the benefits, especially patronage, they obtained.[47] However, the new regiments both added mass and relieved more experienced troops of garrison duties, while, because the crisis did not last, this turn did not become a structural aspect of military power. Instead, the aristocracy essentially came to play a domestic military role through the militia and through the volunteer forces raised for subsequent conflicts: their command roles in both were crucial. The regional and local power, direct and indirect, bound up in such activities has not attracted scholarly attention, which is a marked contrast with the situation during the Middle Ages and as late as the Civil War. This means that the character of the political geography of the eighteenth century has not been adequately probed. More generally, the discussion of the aristocracy and of landownership does not consider the military dimension. This is a contrast with the emphasis on war as a factor in industrialization, trade, and economic cycles.

Across Britain, alongside individual financial and political failures—for example, of Henry, 2nd Duke of Chandos in the 1740s—the big landowners as a group increased their electoral power across the eighteenth century and notably from the late 1720s to the 1770s. The opinion of "the gentlemen of the greatest weight and property" was referred to positively in election literature.[48] Aristocrats such as Newcastle, who, in 1719, claimed, with much reason, to control sixteen Commons' seats, could choose or greatly influence the choice of many MPs, in his case in Sussex and Yorkshire. The Courtenays, Earls of Devon, were lords of the manor of Honiton, a Devon borough which returned two MPs, and they appointed the returning officer, as well as town officials. Members of the family sat for the borough in Parliament from 1734 until 1742 and from 1754 until 1763. The geography of electoral power very much focused on the prestigious county seats and thus had to match the traditional county divisions—for example, the two halves of Sussex, West and East. West Sussex was very much influenced by the Dukes of Richmond from their seat at Goodwood and East Sussex by Newcastle.

The situation in Yorkshire, the largest county, is instructive. The tone of electoral correspondence makes it clear that the county dimension was crucial to local political concerns and maneuvers. The dynastic rivalries of the leading families, such as the Marquesses of Rockingham, from their seat at Wentworth Wodehouse, a massive palace, and the Earls of Carlisle, from theirs at Castle Howard, a baroque masterpiece, were central to county politics and meant that they had to have interests and allies across the county.

The electoral position of the elite was significant in the more numerous borough seats, although it had "faltered" in some of the larger boroughs before 1832.[49] Certain "pocket boroughs," such as Amersham, Marlborough, and Newton, were controlled by Tory families, but most of these seats were at the disposal of the ministerial Whigs or were heavily influenced by the government. Yet, influence was not always predictable. Alongside regions, counties, and localities where the aristocracy was dominant, such as Northamptonshire, there were others that were largely under the control of the gentry—for example, Dorset. The relationship between aristocracy and gentry could involve tension as in the notorious Oxfordshire election in 1754 in which Whig peers, notably the Duke of Marlborough and the Earl of Macclesfield, challenged the habitual dominance of the Tory gentry, leading to great controversy and subsequently to a sharing out of the county representation, albeit one resented by many of the gentry.[50] In Wales, the Anglican gentry were dominant, whereas the peerage was sparse and relatively unimportant, although the Tory Dukes of Beaufort controlled Monmouthshire. Gentry families, such as the Wynns of Wynnstay, who dominated Denbighshire; the Morgans of Tredegar, who had estates in Monmouthshire and Breconshire; and the Pryses of Gogerddan, Lloyds of Peterwell, and Powells of Nanteos in Cardiganshire were central to Welsh politics, as were their bitter and lasting feuds.

Influence was a complex process. Patrons could control some borough seats, by purchase or other means, but management was generally required. This included treating the voters at election time but also managing constituency interests in the meantime. In Bedford, John, 4th Duke of Bedford, established an electoral interest by granting favors to freemen, as did William Nicholson, bishop of Carlisle in Carlisle in 1701. Thanks to such influence, many elections were uncontested. As a result, the absence of readily apparent activity was a key aspect and means of the geography of power.[51] At the same time, it is possible to map contested elections and to analyze the data accordingly. This, in turn, can still be misleading, as a lengthy preelection canvas and debate might not lead to an election day poll, but the results can still be instructive.[52]

Aside from the question of how far spatial awareness, let alone a politics of place, had a class dimension, there is that of a gender one. There has been discussion of this point,[53] but it is made difficult by the disproportionate nature of the surviving sources, which are very heavily biased—for example, in press authorship—toward men. In addition, all parliamentarians and diplomats were male. Moreover, for women, as for nonelite men and for non-Westerners, there was a common facet—namely, the tendency to underplay or ignore their contribution to the accumulation, understanding, and dissemination of knowledge, including geographic knowledge.

THE PRESS

There is a pronounced tendency to treat the press and, indeed, the world of print, in a Whiggish fashion—in other words, to adopt a progressivist and teleological approach, with the press as a political space separate to that of established authorities.[54] Such an approach is in line with the use of the term, the print, or printing, *revolution*. Like most usage of the language of revolution to describe a long-term process, there is much that is problematic about the concept. In practice, the context for the press was set by limited wealth and restricted literacy, such that only a minority of the population could, or did, read newspapers, even though they could be borrowed or read aloud, and thus read or listened to by many. Taxation accentuated the cost element, while the technological limits on mass production and distribution were not overcome until the nineteenth century. Furthermore, in the eighteenth century, oral culture remained to the fore for the bulk of the population in determining how information was communicated and ideas formed and debated. What the outside world meant in oral culture is far harder to disentangle than for written culture and not least because the sources for oral culture were, and are, largely mediated through the latter.

To read newspapers from this period is to be taken into the news, the hopes, the fears, and the culture of these years. There are of course many limits to the coverage by newspapers and to the value of newspapers, and it is a responsibility of the scholar to draw attention to them. At the same time, to do so can entail a failure to understand, or at least a tendency to underplay, the major impact of the press of the period. In opposition to the earlier theme of an early-modern printing revolution has come that of a slower and more qualified process.[55] There is considerable basis for this revision but also a danger, if adopting it, of underplaying both the significance of change in an age before mass literacy and, in particular, the importance of change as an incremental process rather than a revolutionary one.

Surviving newspapers reflect the enormous differences brought by the combination of a new regulatory regime after the Glorious Revolution of 1688–89 with the entrepreneurial drive of newspaper producers in the decades from the 1690s. The lapsing of the Licensing Act in 1695 led to a situation in which anybody could start a newspaper. It was relatively simple for printers to test a market by setting up a newspaper and, if it failed, concentrating on other activities. This lack of specialization reflected the absence of any need for specific equipment or trained staff for newspaper production (although authorization in the form of stamped paper was required) and, therefore, the relatively limited investment required when founding a paper. The absence of a system of privilege, akin to that on the Continent, permitted a growth in the number of titles. A saturated market ensured a competitive atmosphere and a large number of newspaper failures.

These differences are more impressive because much of the context was largely fixed. Despite the efforts of John Walter of the *Times* in the 1780s,[56] this was especially the case with the technologies at stake. A wide range were involved, not only the printing that conventionally engages attention but also other production technologies, such as papermaking and energy provision, as well as distribution technologies, both those of vehicles and those of routes. Low sales and limited profitability for individual titles reduced the capital resources available for investment in new work processes and technology and also the need for such investments. Thus, even when steam technology became available, there was no hurry to apply it. The first newspaper that embraced the new technology, in the shape of steam presses, was the *Times*, in 1814, because, in having the largest sales, it had both the need and the capital for technological change, as well as wishing to differentiate itself from other newspapers.

The fundamental market constraints did not alter. There was no significant growth in population until the mid-eighteenth century and none in per capita literacy until the nineteenth. In addition, taxation remained a key constraint on newspaper operations until the start of 1861 when the last of the "taxes on knowledge," duties on newspaper sales and advertising revenues, was finally lifted. In the meanwhile, the real costs posed by this taxation had risen greatly during the eighteenth century.

Change within a context of fundamental continuity is particularly interesting and so also in the case of the press. Rather than being able to respond to greatly increasing demand and only needing to hold on to the share of the market in order to make a profit, as is sometimes the case across history, entrepreneurs had to shape a largely fixed, as well as competitive, environment. Economic problems, notably, but not only, in the 1690s, contributed to the problem. At the same time, the opportunities were great. These took a number of forms. The provision of, and demand for, news and advertising are the focus of attention. The two can be readily put side by side, and readers clearly read both, but they were different as were their economic contexts. What was the largest press in the world, in terms of number of titles and circulation, provided particular opportunities for the spread of new ideas, including of products. In doing so, the press also offered opportunities for a national representation, and would-be standardization, of material. This was true not only of opinions but also of information. Advertisements contributed greatly to this. Thus, on May 26, 1744, *Old England*, a London newspaper, advertised *A Complete Tything Table* that would also be available from named agents in Reading, Gloucester, Northampton, Salisbury, and Birmingham, each of which was a city prominent in the provincial press.

There was a democratic, or at least representative, character to the press in that it was dependent on readers for sales and for advertising revenue and advertised its popularity. This popularity entailed a receptiveness to the public mood and to defining a particular tone of writing accordingly. In providing readers with a considerable range of information and opinion about politics, newspapers offered the continual refrain that the views of the readers counted, which also directed attention to the significance of the press.

There were also important organizational changes alongside essential technological continuity. In particular, prior to the age of rail, the national distribution of London newspapers became more rapid and reliable as a consequence of improvements in the road system and in the provision of post office services. This improved availability of London newspapers helped the provincial newspapers provide news more speedily in a process that underlined the cooperation between these types of newspapers.[57]

Britain was involved in war for most of the period 1689–1720 and, subsequently, in frequent war panics, notably in 1723, 1725–27, 1729–31, and 1733, until full-scale hostilities revived in 1739, lasting until 1748. This situation pressed on the anxieties and interests of the public, and the press responded. Moreover, this response was intertwined with political partisanship. As a consequence, the newspapers of the period were not only full of foreign news but also reported and commented on it in a fashion that would have meant much to a politically informed reading public.

The press was the prime means to report, and comment on, foreign news. Parliament only sat for a small portion of the year, while there were major limits on the reporting of its debates. Political parties did not have national organizations or memberships of the modern type. Thus, far from being tangential, the press served to provide a key means to create a sense of party identity and of an identity that was able to respond to changing circumstances. This helped explain the degree to which politicians believed it important to support, influence, or control the press. These processes were readily apparent during the reign of Queen Anne (1702–14) and contributed greatly to the press wars of these years, if that is not too grand a term for the serious rivalries between newspapers. These wars focused on party differences and foreign, military, and ecclesiastical policies, all of which were discussed in the press in a far more continual fashion than was possible for Parliament which sat for less than half the year. In the press, moreover, all sides, interests, and literate individuals could initiate discussion and seek to control the agenda in a fashion that was not possible in Parliament.

On August 7, 1733, in the aftermath of the Excise Crisis of that spring, a major episode in domestic politics, the *Hyp-Doctor*, a London newspaper, reported, "The article of public papers is now swelled to a considerable size, and, among them, the political is not the least considerable. They have multiplied in proportion to the contests of parties, bred from the warmth of opposition."

The press's role in electioneering helped to ensure the dissemination of reports and opinions about politics. In 1733, in light of the campaigning for the 1734 general election, a Kent vicar wrote, "The enclosed Canterbury newspaper (which is dispersed over the county) will do us a great deal of mischief unless the edge of it be taken off by something handsomely written on the other side." That he wrote this to Lionel, 1st Duke of Dorset, at once the local Whig political grandee and a figure in national politics whose house at Knole has already been mentioned in the chapter,[58] indicated the overlap of different types of politics. The inclusion of items from newspapers in commonplace books was another indication of their influence.

Electoral politics was more than a question of Tories and Whigs, for each was divided, and notably the Whigs when they were in government. Moreover, politics was a broader process than simply electioneering. Whereas only a very small portion of goods and services were advertised, most political groups and single-interest lobbies sought to use the culture of print in order to transmit their messages and to organize, encourage, and recruit supporters. Linked to these and other divisions, there were quarrels between particular newspapers—for example, those supporting

Hanoverian or Jacobite Tories—or government and opposition Whigs. Reading newspapers in bulk provides the best means to chart and understand these alignments and tensions, not least because this approach helps explain the adversarial source, as well as character, of much reporting. The particular value of an approach to newspapers by period, rather than the more usual focus on individual titles, is that it becomes possible to see newspapers in terms of the contention of the time. This is of great value as it offers a means to assess the significance of responsiveness to content and context and the success with which this responsiveness was pursued.

For example, the battles between the papers of Nathanael Mist and what he called the "Lying Post"—in other words, the Whig *Flying Post*—emerge more clearly in this context. There was little consistency between newspapers adopting the same political view, for individual titles were very dependent on the energy of particular writers and on the interplay of circumstances. Thus, *Mist's Weekly Journal*, a Tory, pro-Jacobite, London newspaper produced by Mist, was written in an accessible, often jocular, form. It was not a paper that adopted, as for example the other leading opposition newspaper, the *Craftsman* did, the straightjacket of long front-page editorial articles to the diminution of other means of conveying opinion. In the late 1730s, the opposition press was regrounded around effective new newspapers, mainly the *Champion* and *Common Sense*, after its key newspapers of the late 1720s, the *Craftsman* and *Fog's Weekly Journal*, had lost direction and vigor.

The newspapers of the period offer comments on the specific factors guiding individual newspapers and therefore the press as a whole, as the latter was a contradictory aggregate of the former.[59] Although in a nonsystematic fashion, there are many remarks of relevance. These include comments located within the text, as well as more coherent accounts when newspapers were launched or, far less consistently, ceased production.

The press was located in commercial society. Its news, of sailings and battles, adverse winds and privateers, was of immediate relevance to merchants and others involved in commerce. Indeed, given the significance of exports and imports for the economy as a whole, for much industry, and also for agricultural sectors, news of trade, and thus of the wider world, was of far wider importance. These relevances linked directly to politics, as the risk of disruption to trade owed much to Britain's international position. This linkage was debated extensively in the press as part of its political coverage.

The broader significance of newspapers helps explain the limits of Whig oligarchy, which throws light on the geography of power suggested by the stately homes of the landed elite. Both J. H. Plumb and J. P. Kenyon[60] discussed the 1710s in terms of the formation of such an oligarchy, it thereby constituting a background to the strength of the Whig establishment during the Walpole ministry (1720–42) and the Pelhamite ascendancy which ran from 1743 and, more clearly, 1744 to 1754 with an important after-echo to 1762. This account, however, emerges from a consideration of the press as far too limited. It underplays the dynamism of public politics as well as its contents. An understanding of both is best offered by the press, and this provides a useful way to approach the supposed novelty of midcentury politics, especially that of the 1760s. This latter standard approach, as developed in particular by John Brewer,[61] asserts a novelty that cannot be justified if the nature of politics earlier in the century is appreciated. Indeed, the 1690s, 1700s, 1710s, and 1720s included both episodes of public agitation, such as the Sacheverell disturbances, but also, more profoundly, a growing habit of very regular reception and discussion of the news by means of more frequent newspapers. This was especially true at the London level but was also the case across provincial England, as well as elsewhere in the British Isles.

This discussion was central to a transformation of political culture, one that was important to the development of British society, to the grounding, through debate and usage, of the Revolution Settlement, and to the growing gaps between political culture in the Anglosphere and that in the remainder of the world. To contrast the English newspapers of the period with their French counterparts is to be struck by the extent to which the latter were more rigid and uniform in content, coverage, and tone. The last may seem an intangible factor, but it was of great significance. An appreciation of the tone of discussion rests on reading newspapers in bulk.

So also with a guide to content. For example, an understanding of the role of history in the thought of the period is best served by looking at the repeated reference to historical examples. Journalists indeed frequently traded arguments in terms of historical analogies. Thus, allegedly bad ministers were discussed in terms of Sejanus, or Wolsey, or Buckingham. This was not because it was impossible to address the supposed ills of Walpole, but rather because historical analogies were regarded as relevant. They were more potent than their spatial equivalents. Contemporary first ministers abroad were less well known to British readers, while there was also the danger of provoking a hostile diplomatic response, as with the discussion of some foreign rulers, such as Charles III of Spain.[62]

The weight of historical reference reflected the extent to which the present and the future were very much seen in terms of a continuity in which the past played a key role. In particular, there was an assumption that historical processes occurred across time and could recur. Critics of the government, such as Mist or, later, in the 1760s, John Wilkes, argued not only that the Glorious Revolution was imperfect but also that a return to whatever was held reprehensible was more than probable. In short, history was a lesson about the inherent possibilities of the future, in a way that geographical works could not be. Newspapers did not simply record; they also warned about danger.

The extent to which the press contained and represented the hopes, fears, and experience of the age richly repays attention to it. Accepting all the caveats, print culture was of great importance. Moreover, there was a fundamental shift in accessibility and scale during the century, in part due to the lapsing of the Licensing Act in 1695. This lapsing brought prepublication censorship to a close. The total annual sale of stamped papers in England, in million copies, rose from 2.5 in 1713 to 14.0 in 1780, and there were also increases in Ireland, Scotland, and Wales. As a result, there was a larger number of people that could be reached through the press, for this rise greatly exceeded that in population. The press provided an increasingly national forum for the expression of political views and for much else, including financial news. A major aspect of the growing national focus of political culture was provided by the reporting of aspects of the integration of Britain. The press helped to stretch the social and geographical boundaries of the political nation as well as to change its nature, but this did not necessarily or directly threaten traditional forms of politics because the latter were changing at the same time as the political system developed.[63] Newspapers familiarized the public with the idea that print was both attractive and authoritative, and this process encouraged the development of the press.

In addition, the press could interact with other means of conveying information. For example, the *Birmingham Commercial Herald* of January

4, 1813, noted, "Whoever will take a map of the Russian Empire and examine the space contained between Vilna, Riga, and the lately existing Moscow, will see how considerable a tract of country has within the last six months been subjected to all the horrors of war," as a result of the French invasion: Moscow had been burned down. Furthermore, whereas French newspapers had few advertisements, those in British newspapers, and, notably, successful ones, were numerous and important to their profitability. Advertisements also helped ensure the multiple sales of both books and the tickets for lectures upon which knowledge relied as an alternative to that of individual patrons. Advertisements therefore provided part of the infrastructure for geographical information and activity and notably so in the provinces. This infrastructure was inherently dynamic as individual newspaper proprietors probed new opportunities.

The interest in foreign news in the press was strong and not only when Britain was at war. It is significant that cheap papers carried nearly as much foreign news as their more expensive counterparts, although far fewer of these cheap papers survive, so that analysis of change in their contents is not easy. The headpiece of the *London Farthing Post*, a newspaper of the late 1730s, depicted four hawkers shouting "Great News," the second "From Spain," the third "From France," and the fourth "From Holland," There are numerous suggestions in the established, more expensive London press of foreign news being read by men of unexalted social status. For example, the *English and French Journal* of September 12, 1723, referred to a tobacconist reading press reports about Russo-Swedish relations in a coffeehouse: the two powers were then close to war. Similarly, the *St. James's Evening Post* of September 1, 1726, reported that "on Monday night a barber and a porter being discoursing of the present posture of affairs in Europe, at an alehouse in Chancery Lane, they quarrelled . . . the porter stabbed his antagonist . . . so dangerously that his life is despaired of." Europe was then close to war.

The idea of coffeehouses and alehouses as sites for the discussion of foreign news, and thus for an understanding of political geography and for a presentation of geography as political, is instructive. Like barbershops, they were also places where newspapers could be read (or listened to being read aloud) as part of the facilities, thus extending press readership to those who could, or would, not buy papers. Thus, the diary of Dudley Ryder in

1715–16 was full of his coffeehouse conversations on news and religion. In the *Darlington Pamphlet* of June 19, 1772, there was a notice of a new Hartlepool coffeehouse "regularly supplied with all the newspapers." Coffeehouses could also have books available for customers to read or borrow.[64]

References to ordinary or plebeian readers were designed to drive home the idea that there had been a democratization of the following of the news,[65] even if some of the reports were critical of the process, and notably so on a social basis. Interest in foreign news was indeed mocked by some writers. The *Plain Dealer* of July 13, 1724, printed a letter from Thomas Tiresom, the name at once instructive. He had gained money by "selling out my India stock[66] very seasonably upon this melancholy story is whispered about, so cautiously, concerning the Great Mogull's entering into an alliance against Prince Tockmas and the Czar of Muscovy [Peter the Great]." Other news made him fearful for South Sea stocks: shares in the South Sea Company. Such items reflected the role of commercial matters in interest in the wider world, but this interest also drew on wider currents of concern and fascination. What was instructive in this item was the range of interest and report. So also with the satirical discussion of London tradesmen in Henry Fielding's play *The Coffee-House Politician* (1730) (see chapter 1).

When newspapers sought to advertise their value and to obtain more readers, they often stressed the quality of their foreign news, as in 1728 when the *Post Boy* (a leading London newspaper) became a daily. Under the heading "Foreign Affairs," the *Weekly Medley*, on June 21, 1729, commented, "The favourable reception our lucubrations meet with from our readers (which we sensibly find by the increase of the sale of the *Medley*) has encouraged the Society to procure the best intelligence possible, as well with respect to our literary as to our foreign news." In contrast, the limited amount of domestic news in many papers was notable. Reader demand and political opportunity both played a role in such choices. Thus, the pro-government *London Journal*, a major newspaper, in its issue of November 6, 1731, referred to "the close alliance with France, which the writers against the [royal] Court own to be the chief cause of their papers, and that which gave rise to their numerous productions." This alliance had ended, and thus the question was whether opposition attacks would cease or were simply opportunistic. What claimed to be a reader's letter published in the *Newcastle Courant* of March 3, 1733, at a time of rising international tension, urged the paper to "by no means let a rhapsody upon the Test Act jostle the Emperor [Charles VI, ruler of Austria] and his dominions out of your comment." The nature of the sources means that it is unclear how far such items were indeed sent in by contributors, who were anonymous or pseudonymous in the fashion of the period, rather than being inserted by the editor.

The press developed and sustained public interest in international affairs and foreign policy, giving an added depth to political debates in London and elsewhere. Such interest was long-standing. However, the tempo increased with the growth of the press. So also did the interest displayed in peacetime as well as wartime.

Thanks to the press, the correspondence and diaries of individuals living in the provinces could include references to foreign affairs. More generally, the political nation, those interested in politics, a tranche of society that owed much to the press, became fairly well informed about the wider world, including its basic political geography, and concerning the issues in British foreign policy.

In a pamphlet of 1717, Robert, Viscount Molesworth, a prominent Whig, attacked Charles XII of Sweden as a supporter of the Jacobites, adding, in a reference to public opinion and its response to the Great Northern War: There is scarce a Jacobite schoolboy, or poor tradesman's wife about our streets, who has not been instructed how conveniently Norway lies to Scotland, and how much it was for their masters' interest, that the brave King of Sweden should succeed in his undertakings. . . . They were as sorry for his loss of Rugen and Stralsund (places which they never before had heard of, but which they then were made to understand, and know how to distinguish from the map) as they were for King George's accession to the Crown."[67]

Such developments were greatly eased by the press, as it provided far more coverage than that offered by manuscript newsletters. Background information was included. The *Worcester Journal* of June 29, 1749, began an item about Kazan in Russia: "The dreadful conflagration by which the great city of Casan has lately been reduced entirely to ashes (as mentioned in our last journal), may render a short description of it, extracted from the most modern writers, not unacceptable to the public." On August 31, 1749, an item of news from Malta was followed by a note giving a brief account of the island, its history, and the Knights of St. John. The news could also be nonpolitical, as in the account of ginseng in the *Flying Post* of September 20, 1722:

> The Root Jing-Seng or Gem-Sem ie Man-Plant, which is thought a worthy present for the Greatest Princes in Europe, is by the learned Chinese esteem'd the most incomparable cordial in the world, and called the *Spiritous simple*, the *pure spirit of the Earth*, the *Fat of the Sea*, the *Panacea*, the *Remedy that dispenses Immortality*, and the like. Their Physicians, who have whole Witness of its different virtues, use it particularly in Fainting or Swooning, and make it into Broths, Electuaries, Lozenges and Syrups. They infuse small bits of about the weight of a shilling in boil'd water, cover it up till 'tis luke-warm, and Drink it in a Morning Fasting. They say it is a Bitter-Sweet, purges the Blood, fortifies the Stomach, quickens the Pulse, excites Natural Heat, and augments radical moistures.

Newspapers spread news and opinion round the country, including about foreign policy. The *Worcester Journal* accordingly reprinted items from the *London Evening Post*.[68] Many newspapers sought to include background information in order to aid readers to understand the news and no doubt also to fill space. Thus, the *Weekly Journal or British Gazetteer* of March 16, 1717, printed an account of Sweden as events there had become a topic of interest, while the *St. James's Post* of the previous day carried an account of the Electorate of Hanover. The successful Spanish invasion of Sardinia in 1717 led to accounts of the island appearing in the *St. James's Post* of September 11, the *Flying Post* of September 12, the *St. James's Weekly Journal* of September 14, and the *Weekly Journal or British Gazetteer* of September 14. The account in the *Flying-Post* provides a useful instance of the general approach:

> Since the island of Sardinia is not only like to become a subject of war betwixt the Emperor and the King of Spain, but may probably rekindle a general war in Europe... it is thought proper to give the following account of that island.
>
> It lies in the Mediterranean, betwixt the 27th and 29th degrees of longitude, and Lat. 34 and 41.15. Geographers differ about the length and breadth. Some make it 170 miles from south to north, and 92, where broadest, from east to west. Others make the greatest length 135 miles, and the greatest breadth about 52. It is separated from the Isle of Corsica, which belongs to the Genoese, by a narrow straight of about six miles. So that 'tis not the interest of the Genoese to have it possessed by any maritime potentate. It lies also conveniently for invading Naples by a fleet, and in like manner either to invade or support Sicily. This is enough to show the importance of the place by its situation, and that the Emperor [Charles VI of Austria, then ruler of Naples and Sicily], and

the Maritime Powers [Britain and the Dutch], have very good reason to oppose its being possessed by the Spaniards....

As to the history and geography of it, the best ancient and modern authors give the following account. It was anciently subject to the Carthaginians, from whom it was taken by the Romans [in the First Punic War], who used to banish such persons thither as they had a mind to be rid of, because its air was reckoned pestilential. It was taken from the Romans by the Greeks [Byzantium], and from the latter by the Saracens, from whom Pisa and Genoa took it; and falling into a dispute which of them should possess it, Pope Boniface VIII allowed James II of Aragon to make a conquest of it, which he accomplished, after a stout resistance made by four petty Princes of the country, assisted by the Genoese and Pisans, so that the best title the Spaniards had to it, was from this Pope's Bull. The Emperor Frederick II made it a Kingdom in the thirteenth century for his son Elzo, who never enjoyed it, nor have any of its particular Kings ever since resided in it. It continued afterwards under the Crown of Spain, who governed it by a viceroy, but it was treacherously given away [by the Peace of Utrecht of 1713] by our last Tory ministry, from the House of Austria [which had a claim on the Spanish Succession], to the Elector of Bavaria, whom they designed to make King of it, as they did the Duke of Savoy, King of Sicily; though the Tories always said, that none could make Kings, but God.

The soil is in many parts fruitful, and produces corn in such abundance, that in some years they are reckoned to have transported a million of bushels to Spain and Italy. It abounds also with wine and [olive] oil, black cattle and horses less than those of Italy, but more nimble; and they have plenty of wild beasts for game, but no lions, wolves, or other beasts of prey, except little foxes; nor are they infested with any venomous creature. The air is reckoned unhealthy, especially in the summer, because of the high mountains on the north-side, which hinder its being purified by the northern winds. It had once mines of silver, and coral is still found on its coasts, where there were formerly eleven sea-ports, and 94 watch-towers.

The ancient inhabitants were accounted very mercenary, which occasioned the Latin proverb, *Sardi Venales*. The present inhabitants are of the Church of Rome, and both clergy and laity so ignorant and prophane, that they have a Book of Sports for Sundays, according to which they dance, and sing bawdy songs in their churches, after worship. This does not proceed however from their want of a hierarchy, for they had formerly 18 bishops, and have still no less than seven, three of whom are Arch.

The capital city is Cagliari, on the side of a hill, at the bottom of a bay, near the south-east corner of the island. This town which was founded by the Carthagenians, is large, handsome, populous, divided into three boroughs, has a pretty good trade and harbour, defended by a citadel, is the seat of an university, and the see of their metropolitan, reckoned one of the oldest in Christendom, since their famous Bishop Lucifer assisted at the Council of Milan in 355. He was a great defender of the Athanasian Creed, and as stout an opposer of Passive Obedience, and apostate and persecuting emperors, whose authority he would not own, so that though our High-Churchmen do more agree with him in the damning clauses, than in the Orthodox Articles of his creed, it is certain he damned their politics.

The cathedral is beautiful, exempted from the jurisdiction of the Viceroy, though he resides there, and governed by its own Common-Council, alias Coxcombs, who plead an independency on the state, though fed and supported by it.

Information was also offered on the other towns. The references to the church used Sardinia to attack Tory High Church ideas, while those to the Peace of Utrecht were also anti-Tory. Thus, geography served for present-day polemics.

The Spanish invasion of Sicily in 1718 had the same effect in leading to the publication of news items. Moreover, as examples of this general process, the *Flying Post* supported its news of hostile Turco-Persian relations on December 10, 1724, with a description of the town of Erivan, which was in the area of strife, while the *Northampton Mercury* of March 18, 1723, likewise produced a description of Saint Lucia when it became a contentious issue in Anglo-French relations. The outbreak of plague in the Ionian Islands led to their description in the *Flying-Post* of May 9, 1728.

Domestic political divisions played a role in press descriptions, as in the account of Florida in the *Monitor* of January 8, 1763. By article 19 of the Peace of Paris of February 1763, Britain restored to Spain the island of Cuba, which it had conquered the previous year in the closing stages of the Seven Years' War. Article 20 gave it the Spanish colony of Florida in compensation. The terms of the treaty were generally criticized by the British opposition, but very little was said about Florida. The *Monitor* condemned the exchange when the terms of the treaty were already known:

> For what equivalent? the fagg end of North America; for a promontory, which enjoys not one internal or external advantage; dangerous for shipping to approach its shore; without trade; without revenue; without power; not capable of being rendered useful to our merchandize and manufactures; possessed but of the untenable fortress of St Augustine, in which the Spaniards are cooped up continually by the native Indians, who never submitted to the Spanish government . . . the poor, starving, weak, defenceless, unsafe, depopulated town of St Augustine, and an uncultivated savage land as far as the Mississippi, to which the Spaniards could never make out any right, further than they could command within the length of their great guns.

The process of being informed was especially significant in wartime. Edward Owen, printer of the *Gazette*, looked back to the experience of conflict, with, first, Spain and, then, also France in 1739–48, when, in 1757, he commented on the new Stamp Act, which led him to put up the price of his paper: "which high price will doubtless diminish the sale, and greatly reduce it, I am certain, in time of peace; for in wartime we always keep up a little; for though there is scarce ever anything in it, yet the continual lies that are thrown out by the other papers, keep up the expectations of the people, who are eternally damning the printer for not giving them more news."[69]

Two years later, at the height of the war, *The News-Reader's Pocket-Book, or Military Dictionary* was published. The same year, *The Union Journal: or, Halifax Advertiser* was launched. Puffing his paper, John Watson wrote in the first issue, that of February 6, "Another singular advantage to the encouragers of this paper will be, that they may there see, the lives of the brave King of PRUSSIA [Frederick II], and other great men, who are now treading the stage of action, in various countries; As also, the substance of many valuable writers, who have best described the different nations of the world." That issue included a description of Gorée, the West African slaving base captured from France. The issue of February 13, 1759, similarly carried an account of Guadeloupe. Thus, the political nation was relatively well informed, although on points of details regarding negotiations and operational matters, the information was less reliable.

The Seven Years' War encouraged the engagement with the outer world. A sardonic 1765 postwar pamphlet, *Remarks on the Importance of the Study of Political Pamphlets, Weekly Papers, Periodical Papers, Daily Papers, Political Music, etc* (1765) claimed, "in this land of liberty, of general wealth, curiosity, and idleness, where there is scarce a human creature so poor that it cannot afford to buy or hire a paper or a pamphlet, or so busy that it cannot find leisure to read it; where every man, woman, and child, is, by instinct, birth, and inheritance, a politician."[70]

Although sometimes easy to satirize, the evaluation of foreign news for economic information appears to have been common among readers. The importance of foreign trade to the economy, and the dependence of this trade on war and on events, such as the early onset of Baltic ice or the loss of galleons in Caribbean hurricanes, led to a greater interest among the mercantile community in news from abroad. The press was well placed to serve this as a result of its drawing on foreign newspapers and also of the access of London papers to information from the private correspondence of leading merchants. Newspapers stressed their economic information, including the advertisements,[71] and the relative importance of such information increased during the century, in part as a consequence of the greater provision of literary, humorous, and social items by the magazines, which were mostly monthlies. Thus, the geography of attention by title, as measured by the attention devoted in print, owed much to the time scale involved in presenting information in the shape of the frequency of appearance. As another instance of economic news, there was also discussion of agricultural improvement.[72]

Devoting much of its attempt to publicize itself to its economic news, the *London Evening Post*, a triweekly (appearing three times a week) commented, on March 30, 1762, on "an account of the arrival of British ships at, and their departure from, the several ports of the habitable world." In Fanny Burney's novel *Cecilia* (1782), Mr. Hobson, the opinionated, practical man of business, declares: "as to not letting a lady speak, one might as well tell a man in business not to look at the *Daily Advertiser*; why, it is morally impossible."[73]

News was not simply political and economic. There was also a mass of material on other subjects, some of it highly eclectic. This could lead to issues of accuracy and authentication, as in 1765 with accounts of a wild beast in France, which led the *St. James's Chronicle* to receive complaints from its readers. On June 13, it responded:

> we never imposed anything of our own. . . . Whatever has been said by us at any time concerning it, is literally translated from one or other of the foreign gazettes, in which practice we have been upheld by every one of our brother newswriters. If our correspondents, therefore, should think proper to change, we know not where they will not find cause for the same objection; but in justice to ourselves, we can arrogate further merit, vis. that of having endeavoured, on every occasion, to ridicule it. When the news of the beast first came over, we took particular pains to acquaint our readers, that all the accounts of it, were generally taken from the Brussels Gazette, of very dubious authority; and, to point out the absurdities of them still more strongly, never failed to print the most incredible parts in italic. After all, we are well assured, that the French Ambassador has accounts daily brought to him of a beast, or beasts,

which commit great ravages in France. How far his relations agree with those given in the foreign gazettes, we do not pretend to determine. Probably the latter are at least very much exaggerated, or, for anything we know, there may not be one syllable of truth in the whole. We only thought it our duty to lay the accounts before our readers, as they came to our hands; and, with respect to the print [illustration] in question [issue of June 8], it was copied from one in a magazine for last month, sent over from France.[74]

Abroad was a regular source of horror items, as with the story, carried in *Berrow's Worcester Journal* of April 10, 1766, of Frenchmen eating a baby.

The quantity of information provided in the world of print was not restricted to newspapers. For example, readers interested in Dutch politics were given much material in Onslow Burrish's well-informed book *Batavia Illustrata: or, A View of the Power and Commerce of the United Provinces* (1728). Other books also provided a mass of information. However, costs could be considerable. When Charles Brockwell's *The Natural and Political History of Portugal* was offered for subscription in 1724, five shillings was requested from subscribers. The sum was far too large for ordinary readers, and the subscription basis for Brockwell's book, or that by John Morgan on the history and much else of Algiers (1728), illustrated the limited nature of their sales. When Guthrie's *New Geographical, Historical and Commercial Grammar* was published in 1770 as one large octavo volume, the price was six shillings bound or 5s 3d (5.25 shilling) in boards. The eleventh edition of Salmon's *New Geographical and Historical Grammar* appeared the same year, also in one large volume, and at a price of six shillings bound.

Aside from purchasers, the significance of books was increased by the rise of libraries as a means of information and a forum of sociability. Libraries tended to contain a certain number of books that can be classified as geographies, whether as descriptive books or as travelogues. Knowledge was also to be communicated. The growing emphasis on the transoceanic world helped encourage the increased publication of geographical works, which indeed rose from midcentury,[75] although this in part reflected a more general increase in reading, book purchase, and libraries. The growth of circulation, proprietary, and subscription libraries (which were preceded by parish libraries), as well as the serial publication of books permitted those who could not afford, or did not choose, to purchase them to read them. The first English circulating library opened in 1757, and there were about one thousand such libraries by the end of the century. The first of the many proprietary libraries, whose members owned shares, was the Liverpool Library, formed in 1758: membership was more than four hundred by 1799, and between 1758 and 1800 the library acquired an average of almost two hundred books annually. Proprietary libraries followed in other towns, including Warrington (1760), Manchester (1765), Leeds (1768), Sheffield (1771), Hull (1775), and Birmingham (1779). Towns, moreover, offered their potential readers institutional choices. In Kendal, where a book club was formed in 1761, a newsroom followed in 1779, a subscription library in 1794, and an "Economical Library" for the less affluent in 1797.[76] Libraries were also founded in the British colonies.[77]

Libraries were regarded as especially important for female readers. The standard criticism (by men) was that women's reading was subversive of good behavior and far too much devoted to imaginative literature.[78] These views were referred to in *The Young Lady's Geography* (1765), which was dedicated to the young Queen Charlotte, wife of George III, with the confidence that she would support "every endeavour to entice from the hands of the Fair, obscene and ridiculous novels, (which serve only to vitiate their morals, inflame their passions, and eradicate the very seeds of virtue) by persuading them to the study of a science both useful and amusing, and without some knowledge of which they cannot read even a public paper or intelligence with pleasure or advantage." The preface promised to provide the means "of speedily acquiring a thorough knowledge of maps, as well as of the natural and political state of the world."

Magazines could provide not only comments on books, but also excerpts. Thus, the *Gentleman's Magazine* of September 1770 noted Guthrie's *New Geographical, Historical, and Commercial Grammar*: "The author's principal view ... has been to bring a general and comprehensive knowledge of geography, history, and commerce within the reach of those who have neither much leisure nor much money ... as the Turks are now become objects of public attention in consequence of the war carried on against them by Russia, and as it is not very improbable at present, that the war will terminate in the total subversion of their empire, we have abridged this author's account of its origin."[79]

In fact, the Russo-Turkish War of 1768–74 saw major defeats and important losses for Turkey but not the destruction of its empire.

Pamphlets could also be significant, not as geographies but in the discussion of foreign policy and, therefore, of international relations. Geographical information could be deployed in order to support assertions. In 1718, the engraver and impressive mathematician Reeve Williams wrote a pamphlet in defense of British intervention in Mediterranean power politics. The inclusion of a map added to the interest of his *Letter from a Merchant to a Member of Parliament, Relating to the Danger Great Britain is in of Losing her Trade, by the Great Increase of the Naval Power of Spain with a Chart of the Mediterranean Sea Annexed*. The lord chancellor, Thomas, 1st Earl of Macclesfield, who had a strong personal interest in mathematics, allegedly ordered the printing of seven thousand copies and Williams a further two thousand.[80] This pamphlet was designed to explain the commercial rationale for British geopolitics, and particularly a defense of a major act of power projection. The impact of the pamphlet was increased by press coverage, the *Worcester Post-Man* of November 21, 1718, reporting:

> Last Saturday a notable book was delivered to the Members of Parliament, with a chart annexed of the Mediterranean Sea, whereby it demonstrately appears of what importance it is to the trade of Great Britain, that Sicily and Sardinia should be in the hands of a faithful ally, and if possible not one formidable by sea. That these two islands lie like two nets spread to intercept not only the Italian but Turkey and Levant trade. . . . That should the naval power of Spain increase in the manner it has lately done, that kingdom may assume to herself that trade of the Mediterranean Sea, and impose what she pleases as the King of Denmark does at Elsinore [at the entrance to the Baltic].

Reporting in other newspapers, such as *Whitehall Evening Post* of December 2, 1718, reflected the arguments of the pamphlet. As another form of news, political ballads could also be significant.[81]

DEPICTIONS

The world of print was far from alone in the public sphere. There were many other ways to depict and arrange reality. For example, museums acted as display guides to what was judged significant. This process was enhanced by their layout and the juxtaposition of objects.[82] The British Museum was a notable instance, but so were other museums.

There were other respects in which the depiction of the world was more dynamic, reflecting new technologies and entrepreneurial activity. Thus, astronomy was illustrated by orreries. The panorama was a 360-degree visual medium patented (under a different name) by the artist Robert Barker in 1787. His ambition was to create, from a given spot, a picture of every object visible within the entire circle of the horizon with such fidelity that it could scarcely be distinguished from what it represented. The inaugural exhibition, *View of Edinburgh*, was first shown in that city in 1788, then transported to London in 1789. By 1793, Barker had built the Panorama rotunda at the center of London's entertainment district in Leicester Square, where it remained until closed in 1863, providing, while open, collective experiences. Mostly, these experiences centered on war. Battle panoramas taught collective audiences that courage in battle was glorious and dying for one's country the ultimate glory, which was a potent form of nation-building.[83]

Much of this entrepreneurial world did not address the world abroad, but it rested on the sense that knowledge brought wisdom and profit and that this knowledge needed to be validated by the accuracy of new material. Moreover, the backdrop to items was frequently that of placing them in space and time.

RETHINKING BRITAIN

The pursuit of information was very much defended in utilitarian terms. For both men and women, knowledge could be impressionistic, but measurement also played a role. Looking back to the ideas associated with Francis Bacon in the early seventeenth century, "political arithmetic" gained authority as a form of discourse about statecraft, with rationality understood as grounded in mathematics.[84] Geographical knowledge played a role in these processes, both in the formulation of government policy and in the argumentation required in the lobbying that followed the more frequent meeting of Parliament after the Glorious Revolution of 1688–69, and, notably, the passage of the Triennial Act in 1694. This was especially so as Parliament came to play a key part in the politics and processes of foreign policy and of commercial regulation. The latter helped ensure another aspect of the local reach for Parliament, while representation offered the reverse process.[85]

There was tension between (and within) rural and urban presentations of interests and values, but, comprehending the two, came a sense of utilitarianism, of an improving usage that could also be depicted in the broader spread of British power. Linked to this came a hostile view toward ignorance and waste and a willingness to see both in all areas that were not improved or being improved. This approach presented human society as in a constant tension with an uncivilized other that threatened to drag all down. This was a different form of existential challenge to that proposed in religious terms and discussed at the outset of this chapter. Heaven and hell were not present, but there was a clear moral stance, a struggle between clashing values and practices and an ability to integrate different items into the general schema.

These views could be mocked, at least in the case of out-of-touch metropolitan types, but, nevertheless, were insistent. In 1755, the fictional Dolly Dimple complained, "Rocks, deserts, wastes, savages, and barbarians, make up the sum total of the odious country."[86] Although this outsider's view might capture the experience of some travelers, it did not, however, present the extent of regionalism within Britain or the linked extent to which Britain offered different environments.[87] Some of them were far from the duality and conventions of "politeness" and savagery, about place and values, suggested by Dolly and others, both fictional and real.

Regionalism could be a key element of contemporary presentations of geography. For example, geography as advertisement, booster, and boast was very much seen with newspapers as they sought to establish that their circulation areas were extensive and growing. Thus, the Hereford-based *British Chronicle* of January 28, 1779, named agents, by whom advertisements were taken in and the newspaper distributed, in thirty-one places. Their extent, across Wales and the Welsh Marches, demonstrated the degree to which some provincial newspapers had a regional span. So also with the circulation of newspapers such as the *Sherborne Mercury* and the *Cumberland Pacquet*. The former circulated across the South West[88] and in a fashion greater than the Exeter papers, which focused more on their urban market.

The lists of places with agents offer a basis for a presentation of local and regional geography in terms of economic opportunity, at least in terms of advertising and the spread of news. They also provide a way for modern commentators to delimit areas of influence. While a topic that awaits comprehensive coverage across the century, and notably for the period 1760–1800, considerable information is available. For example, the *Bristol*

Chronicle, Or, Universal Mercantile Register, a Bristol weekly launched on January 5, 1760, added a list of named agents at Bridgewater, Taunton, and Wells, all in the county of Somerset, in the issue of May 3, 1760. On May 23, 1761, the list was expanded to include Haverfordwest and Pembroke, both in Pembrokeshire in South-West Wales, and, on June 20, 1761, agents were added in Abergavenny, Caerleon, Chepstow, Exeter, Newport, Pontypool, and Raglan. Distribution to Pembrokeshire was presumably by sea, the Bristol Channel serving as an economic unit, but the expansion into South-East Wales was due to the journeys of a man on horseback, the paper explaining in June: "this paper will, for the future, be constantly vended through . . . Chepstow, Newport, Ragland, Abergavenny, Pontypool and Caerleon, by John Powell . . . will deliver any message or small parcel if properly directed and left at the Printing-Office." Other newspapers also provided information. The *Gloucester Journal* of April 13, 1756, named agents in Brecon, Bristol, Carmarthen, Hereford, London, and Salisbury. The issue of June 16, 1766, announced, "Advertisements for this paper are taken in by Mr Morgan Bevan in Swansea, by whom all persons in the counties of Carmarthen, Brecon and Glamorgan, may be supplied with grocery goods." At the beginning of 1773, *Drewry's Derby Mercury* named agents in Ashbourne, Ashby-de-la-Zouch, Bakewell, Burton-upon-Trent, Chesterfield, London, Loughborough, Rotherham, Utoxeter, Winster, and Wirksworth and announced that it was "dispersed by Joseph Housely, through the towns of Alfreton, Higham, Chesterfield, Dronfield, Sheffield and numerous intermediate villages." This was a more constricted circulation zone than those of the Hereford, Bristol, Gloucester, and Sherborne newspapers. In contrast, on January 16, 1773, the *Newcastle Journal* claimed, "The circle of this Journal's distribution is near 600 miles, within which circumference are upwards of 250 towns." There were no effective and lasting rivals to the Newcastle press closer than newspapers published in Edinburgh, Glasgow, York, Leeds, and Manchester.

That summer, the *Cambridge Chronicle and Journal* named agents in Bedford, Boston, Bungay, Bury St. Edmunds, Caistor, Downham, Ely, Gainsborough, Grantham, Huntingdon, King's Lynn, Leicester, Lincoln, London, Louth, Newark, Newmarket, Norwich, Peterborough, Retford, St. Ives, St. Neot's, Spalding, Stamford, and Wisbech—a very extensive area and, in effect, a greater East Anglia. The newspaper also offered an account of its distribution network, an account that threw light on the variety of means involved: "This paper is distributed northwards every Friday night, by the Caxton post, as far as York, Newcastle, and Carlisle; through the counties of Cambridge, Huntingdon, Bedford, Buckingham, Rutland, Leicester, Nottingham, Lincoln, Northampton, Norfolk, Hertford, Essex, and the Isle of Ely, by the newsmen; to London the next morning, by the coach and fly; and to several parts of Suffolk etc by other conveyances—persons living at a distance from such places as the newsmen go through, may have the paper left where they shall choose to appoint."[89]

By January 1777, the *Bristol Journal* was listing named agents in Abergavenny, Bath, Brecon, Bridgwater, Carmarthen, Chippenham, Exeter, Gloucester, Haverfordwest, Liverpool, London, Marlborough, Sherborne, Taunton, and Wells[90]—again, a very extensive area. Like other newspapers, the *Salisbury Journal* had a complex administrative network that radiated from the hub of the newspaper printing office. Underlying this was an associated system of smaller news agency centers.[91] Diaries and accounts shed further light. In 1791, Thomas Fenwick of Burrow Hall, Lancashire, was reading the Leeds newspaper.[92]

Such papers can be termed provincial if that is taken to mean the regional rather than local.[93] The provincial, rather than local, nature of newspapers is in part explained by the extent to which the news published was national or international, rather than local however defined. Newspapers were read in order to discover news of the outside world, and this world was one that was essentially defined by the metropolis and foreign countries, rather than one by other parts of provincial England, near or far. Nevertheless, alongside the underreporting of parts of the country,[94] it was certainly the case that the space devoted, both to local news and to news from other provincial parts of England increased greatly toward the close of the century, with the news from other parts derived in part from other provincial papers. Between May 4 and September 14, 1749, the *Worcester Journal* carried news about Shrewsbury, Birmingham, Stratford-upon-Avon, Cheltenham, Benson, Breedon, Stow on the Wold, Droitwich, Cardiganshire, Gloucester, Hereford, Warwick, Pershore, Lichfield, Horton, and Marlborough. Booksellers at a number of towns, including Bridgenorth, Shrewsbury, Warwick, Stourbridge, Stafford, and Evesham, took in advertisements or sold this newspaper. Much local news was of economic value. The *Portsmouth and*

Gosport Gazette and Salisbury Journal reported the price of corn at Devizes (February 24, 1752) and ship news at Poole (May 25, 1752) and also pressed policies—for example, the enforcement of the law against the buyers and hawkers of smuggled goods, a practice that hit fair traders (September 18, 1752). The *Leeds Mercury* of August 18, 1775, included, in its local news, items from Newcastle, Selby, Thirsk, and Wooler, which provided considerable coverage.

Higher levels of information availability and flow became more common. For example, the *Dorchester and Sherborne Journal* of November 27, 1801, noted, "In compliance with the request of many of our readers, and it being our wish to render our journal as extensively useful as possible, we have inserted the current prices of all the leading articles of merchandise, which we mean to continue weekly; and as the greatest care will be taken as to accuracy, we have no doubt it will prove highly interesting to merchants and traders to every description." As an example of the resulting regional net, *Drewry's Derby Mercury* of October 8, 1773, carried details of the price of cheese at nearby Nottingham fair and of the willingness of the principal inhabitants of the nearby industrial town of Wolverhampton to take Portuguese coins, while *Woolmer's Exeter and Plymouth Gazette* of November 30, 1809, provided not only London grain, meat, and butter prices but also Salisbury, Basingstoke, Devizes, Newbury, Andover, and Warminster grain prices. Both economy and society benefited from newspaper advertisements about crime—for example, horse stealing.[95]

Although reaching across a considerable rural hinterland, newspapers were more available in towns, which was where they were published. Literacy rates were higher there, while newspapers were less expensive as it was not necessary to pay for delivery by newsmen. Regional and local reporting focused on the towns. This emphasis was taken further in newspaper titles, as with the *Kentish Post* which was subtitled the *Canterbury Newsletter*. Moreover, the towns were the source of news. Thus, in 1791, responding clearly to interest after the Priestley riots, the *London Chronicle* of July 23 printed an account of Birmingham:

> Birmingham being unhappily at present a general topic of conversation, we are favoured with the following short account of it from a correspondent who has long resided there.

> Birmingham is a large town in Warwickshire, and the most flourishing of any in England for all sorts of iron-work and curious manufactures. It has no corporation, being only governed by two constables and two bailiffs, and therefore free for any person to settle there, which has contributed greatly to the increase of its trade and inhabitants.
>
> The town stands on the side of a hill forming nearly a half-moon. The lower part is filled with the workshops and warehouses of the manufacturers, and consists chiefly of old buildings. The upper part of the town contains a number of new and regular streets, with a handsome square, elegantly built.
>
> It has two churches, one in the lower part of the town, which is an ancient building with a very tall spire; the other is a very grand modern structure, with a stone tower, cupola, a set of bells and musical chimes, which play seven different tunes, being one for each day in the week. It has many meeting-houses for every denomination of dissenters, who are very numerous there.
>
> The houses in this town are supposed to have increased within these 20 years above 10,000; so that admitting the inhabitants then were 80,000, at the rate of five to a house, they must now be increased to 130,000. It is 109 miles north-west from London.

Despite expanding local and regional coverage, the press at the end of the eighteenth century was still dominated in its reporting by national and international news. At the same time, as a reminder of the overlapping character of spheres of influence due to the simultaneity of different factors, a strongly local character was provided by the advertisements: both notices and details of items or services for sale. This material overlapped with the single-sheet ephemera and more lasting printed forms produced by local printers, ephemera that was of growing importance in government and business and thus, in turn, helping deepen the authority of print.[96] The relative absence of companies providing services on a national scale helped to ensure that individual advertisements (except those for medicines and books) were generally specific to particular newspapers or to papers published in a single town.

The press also represents a way to come at the issue of national culture. Taste and emulation certainly focused on London. This focus was linked by commentators to improvements in transport. For example, George Colman wrote in the *St. James's Chronicle* of August 6, 1761:

> Stage-coaches, machines, flys, and post-chaises are ready to transport passengers to and fro between the metropolis and the most distant parts of the kingdom . . . the manners, fashions, amusements, vices, and follies of the

metropolis, now make their way to the remotest corners of the land. . . . The effects of this easy communication have almost daily grown more and more visible. The several great cities, and we might add many poor country towns, seem to be universally inspired with an ambition of becoming the little Londons of the part of the kingdom wherein they are situated: the notions of splendour, luxury, and amusement that prevail in town are eagerly adopted; the various changes of fashion exactly copied; and the whole manner of life studiously imitated . . . every male and female wishes to think and speak, to eat and drink, and dress and live, after the manner of people of quality in London.

More mundanely, the *Worcester Journal* of April 20, 1749, advertised the start of a twice-weekly, each way, two-day stagecoach service with London.

London's publications spread designs, while London craftsmen were in demand across the country. Facilities for, and patterns of, social activity responded to the example of London, which was presented as the benchmark for conditions elsewhere. Thus, the Royal Academy of Arts helped to develop a national style that the provinces and colonies sought to emulate. This was very much a geography of soft power. It was one in which bright provincials went to London and had their ideas and talents validated there. For example, in about 1790, Thomas Sheraton (1751–1806), from Stockton in County Durham, established himself in distant London and began publication of a series of manuals of furniture design. Thanks to such books of designs, fixtures, fittings, and furniture became more standardized, and London fashions had a national scope.

The literary equivalent included works such as Charles Vyse's *New London Spelling Book* (1776). The norms of the language were set in London by these and other methods and books, which, in turn, were advertised in provincial newspapers and sometimes sold by them. Thus, the *Worcester Journal* of March 23, 1749, announced that its printer sold *The Royal Primer: Or, Easy Guide to the Art of Reading*. The dictionaries and encyclopedias published during the century were very much London activities: it was the site of a busy publishing industry.[97] This process was not restricted to England. Thus, it was in London in 1780 that William Shaw published his *A Gaelic and English Dictionary. Containing all the words in the Scotch and Irish dialects of the Celtic, that could be collected from the voice, and old books and manuscripts*. More generally, London helped promote the interaction of bourgeois/middle-class and aristocratic thinking and values. It did so more successfully than in the seventeenth century, in part because religious and political tensions were less prominent than they had been then.

The press, and other sources of news, also took valuable information to London. John Black, a cleric hunting preferment, was able to write from Chiswick just outside London in 1751: "You will see by the papers that a prebend of Worcester is vacant by the death of Dr Smaldrige."[98] Such reports, which reduced a dependence on private information, were a major source of clerical speculation.[99] Sometimes the reports were corrected—for example, those that Lancelot Blackburne, Archbishop of York, had died.

The issue of influence has to be handled with care. Metropolitan influence did not prevent autonomous developments elsewhere in Britain. Thus, provincial silversmiths, such as those in Exeter, were influenced by London designs but also produced works with unique features. It would be mistaken to ignore the capacity in the provinces both to preserve local practices and to take initiatives. Most notably, the Newcastle press created a distinctive regional platform for the exchange of ideas about cultural value, an exchange that was not simply about emulating metropolitan developments. So also with domestic culture in Scotland and more generally with provincial culture.[100]

In part, moreover, London's impact was itself a product of its openness to influences from outside, both within Britain and from further afield. London's influence anyway owed much to the extent that the social basis of London's development, a major expansion in the middling orders, and a growing practice by the rural elite of spending part of the year there, was matched in regional capitals, such as Norwich and Nottingham; in county centers, such as Warwick; and in developing entertainment towns, such as Bath and Buxton.[101] London's role and image was made more prominent by the greater importance of provincial towns within their particular regions, as the city was thus seen to exemplify a national trend. National and regional interdependence could both develop at the same time,[102] while the reconciliation of polite and civic culture could take different forms.[103]

Cities were a major topic for cartography, and notably the most prominent, London. It was particularly well served by John Rocque's new survey in the 1740s, which was designed to replace the most recent large-scale map on the market, that published in 1682 by William Morgan, which was the product of an original survey. Financed by subscription, the subscription list including twenty-nine dukes and ninety-six lords, the Swiss-born Rocque began his surveying in 1738, the methodology of which included trigonometrical surveying to build up a lattice measured between church steeples, which provided the prominent points. Differences between those measurements and his detailed ground survey slowed down the project, which was not available until 1747. The resulting *Survey of London, Westminster, and Southwark*, engraved by Rocque's partner, John Pine, is the most accurate and detailed representation of the eighteenth-century metropolis that exists, with some fifty-five hundred street and place names. Churches were scrupulously recorded, but industrial buildings were not. The map had a scale of twenty-six inches to the mile and was largely accurate for the most densely developed parts of the city, such as the West End, although many smaller streets and courts were omitted. This contrast underlines the difficulty today of mapping historical data precisely. Rocque's work was replaced in turn by Richard Horwood's thirty-two sheet map which appeared between 1792 and 1799. This map, which included street numbers, extended farther east than that of Rocque.[104]

It was not only London that was mapped. James Corbridge's map of Newcastle (1723) offered both precision and an attractive image, illustrating the map with pictograms of the major buildings—for example, the leading churches. Isaac Taylor followed the same policy in his map of Wolverhampton (1750). Chadwick's map of Liverpool was, in 1725, the first detailed one of the city produced by survey. In the case of John Eyes's map of Liverpool (1765), the pictograms were of ships in the docks. The inset showed the south elevation of the city's new Exchange (1749–54), which confirmed the port's devotion to commerce.[105] Rocque published a new map of Bristol in 1742, followed by Benjamin Donn in 1773. Urban improvement commissions, which became common in the second half of the century, such as the Wide Streets Commission established for Dublin in 1757, produced maps as well as architectural drawings.[106] Rocque also produced surveys on which maps of Bath, Bury St. Edmunds, Chester, Chichester, Exeter, Lewes, Shrewsbury, and York were based. Other cities were also covered. *A Plan of the City of Coventry* was based on a survey by Samuel Bradford in 1748–49, before being engraved for publication by Thomas Jefferys in 1750.

The depiction of New World cities varied greatly. Peter Gordon's picture plan of Savannah in 1734 captured a city, or rather a settlement, en route from conception to construction. The depiction also showed the nature of spatial organization where prior ownership rights did not have to be considered. Founded in 1733 by James Oglethorpe as the capital of the new colony of Georgia, the settlement was laid out on a bluff overlooking the Savannah River. The layout used a basic urban neighborhood unit of square-based blocks, known as wards. Each ward was bounded by streets. The plan allowed for the logical expansion of the settlement over time and endowed the city with a great deal of open space. Central Savannah still reflects the original plan and is very attractive as a result.

In contrast, the maps of Boston—for example, by John Bonner (1722) and William Price (1743)—depicted a larger and older city that did not correspond to such geometric regularity. In the Price map, the detailed index of major buildings was an important supplement. The mixture of forms was seen in *A Description of the Situation, Harbor etc of the City and Port of Philadelphia*, a work, produced in London by Thomas Jefferys at the close of the colonial period. This included an east prospect of Philadelphia recorded by Nicholas Skull, surveyor-general of Pennsylvania, accompanied by a plan of the city, as well as vignettes of the battery and the statehouse. The accompanying key identified fourteen places of interest.

Moving from cities to the scale of individual buildings, the functions of the latter reflected new emphases. New stone and brick buildings offered definitions with an emphasis on leisure and retail and, more generally, on private space open to those who could pay—such as shops, subscription libraries, and assembly rooms—rather than spaces and places open to all, such as market places and churches. At the same time, this contrast should be employed with care. There was a degree of social segregation in each of these cases, not least with Church of England churches as their pews were allocated on the basis of ownership and payment. There was also social segregation in burial rights. Moreover, churches were for members of particular religious groups. Conversely, spaces open to those who could pay were more open than those closed other than to those invited to be present. Thus, there was a degree of inclusiveness, at least based on payment, comparable to that advocated by writers on "politeness." With both public and private spaces, there was the question of how they were used. Promenades were developed but, although generally public spaces, were used to affirm status and strengthen elite cohesion.[107]

As very different forms of location and access, there were the questions of prominence and visibility. Increasingly, buildings in town centers could be seen and admired into the evening, as the night was thoroughly lit after the introduction of street lighting. Some buildings and functions, however, sought a degree of privacy, if not secrecy. This was especially so of masonic lodges.

In a world of "things," where increasing numbers could afford to purchase objects and services of utility and pleasure, towns played a central function as providers of services, as much as of commercial and industrial facilities. It was scarcely surprising that towns dominated the geography that was presented of the British Isles. This was notably so before the Romantic era lent new and exciting interest to the "wilder" parts of the country and to related emotions and experiences.

Notes

1. C. Rose, *England in the 1690s: Revolution, Religion, and War* (Oxford, 1999).
2. M. Knights, *The Devil in Disguise. Deception, Delusion, and Fanaticism in the Early Enlightenment* (Oxford, 2011).
3. J. Golinski, *British Weather and the Climate of Enlightenment* (Chicago, 2007).
4. *Westminster Journal*, June 19, 1773, April 9, 16, 1774.
5. Browne to his father, August 24, 1765, BL. RP. 3284. For a different account including a hollow Earth, plant-men and much later found in science fiction, see *A Journey to the World Underground* (London, 1742), the first English edition of Ludvig Holberg's book. Book originally published in Latin in 1741.
6. P. Willis, *Charles Bridgeman and the English Landscape Garden* (Newcastle, UK, 2002).
7. J. Rosenheim, *The Emergence of a Ruling Order: English Landed Society, 1650–1750* (Oxford, 1998).
8. R. Williams, "Some Aspects of Summary Justice in Eighteenth-Century Rural Berkshire," *Archives* 26 (2001): 52; P. B. Munsche, *Gentlemen and Poachers: The English Game Laws 1671–1831* (Cambridge, 1981).
9. Anon., dedication to Charles, 3rd Duke of Richmond, in Anon., *A Letter to John Dunning* (London, 1780), 12.
10. B. Wragg, *The Life and Works of John Carr of York* (York, UK, 2000).
11. D. C. Chambers, *The Planters of the English Landscape Garden: Botany, Trees, and the Georgics* (New Haven, CT, 1993).
12. T. Whately, *Observations on Modern Gardening* (London, 1770), 183–84.
13. T. Williamson and L. Bellamy, *Property and Landscape* (London, 1987).
14. R. Mabey, "The Great Earth-Mover: Just How Capable Was Capability Brown?," *New Statesman*, July 29–August 11, 2016: 84–86. See also N. Everett, *The Tory View of Landscape* (New Haven, CT, 1994).

15. A thematic issue titled "Georgian Landscapes of Treason and Virtue: Dynastic and Party Political Rivalry between the Jacobite Wentworth Castle and Whig Wentworth Woodhouse," *New Arcadian Journal* (1991): 31–32.

16. S. Copley and P. Garside, eds., *The Politics of the Picturesque: Literature, Landscape, and Aesthetics since 1770* (Cambridge, 1994).

17. This is used in the spread on voting in the late eighteenth century in P. Wade-Martins, ed., *The Historical Atlas of Norfolk* (Norwich, UK, 1993).

18. T. Gray, *The Art of the Devon Garden: The Depiction of Plants and Ornamental Landscapes* (Exeter, UK, 2013).

19. H. Walpole, *On Modern Gardening* (London, 1975), 30.

20. I. R. Christie, *British Non-Elite MPs, 1715–1820* (Oxford, 1995).

21. C. Christie, *The British Country House in the Eighteenth Century* (Manchester, 2000); R. Wilson and A. Mackley, *Creating Paradise: The Building of the English Country House 1660–1800* (London, 2000).

22. K. Grady, *The Georgian Public Buildings of Leeds and the West Riding* (Leeds, 1989); A. White, *The Buildings of Georgian Lancaster* (Lancaster, UK, 1992).

23. J. Ayres, *Building the Georgian City* (New Haven, CT, 1998).

24. R. Hyde, ed., *The A to Z of Georgian London* (London, 1982), v.

25. R. C. Allen, *Enclosure and the Yeoman: The Agricultural Development of the South Midlands 1450–1850* (Oxford, 1992).

26. M. Chase, *The People's Farm: English Radical Agrarianism 1775–1840* (Oxford, 1988); J. M. Neeson, *Commoners: Common Rights, Enclosure and Social Change in England, 1700–1820* (Cambridge, 1993). For an approach employing the techniques of historical geography, D. Grigg, *The Agricultural Revolution in South Lincolnshire* (Cambridge, 1966).

27. C. F. Foster, *Four Cheshire Townships in the Eighteenth Century: Arley, Appleton, Stockton Heath, and Great Budworth* (Northwich, UK, 1992).

28. P. Langford, *Public Life and the Propertied Englishman 1689–1798* (Oxford, 1991).

29. H. R. French, "The Creation of a Pocket Borough in Clitheroe, Lancashire, 1693–1780: 'Honour and Odd Tricks,'" *Northern History* 41 (2004): 301–26, esp. 326.

30. B. Coward, "The Social and Political Position of the Earls of Derby in Later Seventeenth-Century Lancashire," *Transactions of the Historic Society of Lancashire and Cheshire* 132 (1983): 150.

31. S. W. Baskerville, P. Adman, and K. F. Beedham, "The Dynamics of Landlord Influence in English County Elections, 1701–1734: The Evidence from Cheshire," *Parliamentary History* 12 (1993): 142.

32. Trevor to William, Lord Grenville, Foreign Secretary, October 8, 1792, NA. FO. 67/10.

33. D. Kelly and M. Cornick, eds., *A History of the French in London: Liberty, Equality, Opportunity* (London, 2013).

34. *St. James's Chronicle*, May 26, 1764, re: price of butter.

35. T. Pennant, *A Tour in Scotland*, 4th ed. (London, 1776), 11.

36. J. E. Crowley, "Herman Moll's *The World Described* 1720: Mapping Britain's Global and Imperial Interests," *Imago Mundi* 68 (2001): 18.

37. A. Kussmaul, *A General View of the Rural Economy of England, 1538–1840* (Cambridge, 1993).

38. J. T. Coppock, *An Agricultural Atlas of England and Wales*, 2nd ed. (London, 1976), 18, 24–31.

39. T. P. Power, *Land, Politics, and Society in Eighteenth-Century Tipperary* (Oxford, 1993).

40. For a slower pace, D. E. Jordan, *Land and Popular Politics in Ireland: County Mayo from the Plantation to the Land War* (Cambridge, 1994). For a variety, R. J. Brien, *The Shaping of Scotland: Eighteenth-Century Patterns of Land Use and Settlement* (Aberdeen, 1989).

41. C. Husbands, "Regional Change in a Pre-Industrial Economy: Wealth and Population in England in the Sixteenth and Seventeenth Centuries," *Journal of Historical Geography* 13 (1987): 345–59.

42. S. W. Martins and T. Williamson, *Roots of Change: Farming and the Landscape in East Anglia, c. 1700–1870* (Exeter, UK, 1999).

43. R. Dean, *Inland Navigation: An Historical Waterways Map of England and Wales* (London, 1993).

44. M. Huggins, "Popular Culture and Sporting Life in the Rural Margins of Late Eighteenth-Century England: The World of Robert Anderson, 'The Cumberland Bard,'" *Eighteenth-Century Studies* 45 (2012): 203.

45. P. S. Onuf, "Liberty, Development, and Union: Visions of the West in the 1780s," *William and Mary Quarterly*, 3rd ser., 43 (1986): 712.

46. A. Beach, "African Slaves, English Slave Narratives, and Early Modern Morocco," *Eighteenth-Century Studies* 46 (2013): 333–48.

47. John Tucker, MP, to Richard Tucker, November 2, 1745, Bod. Ms. Don. c.7 fol. 157.

48. Flysheet of meeting at Crown Tavern, June 18, 1747, Middlesex election printed papers, Warwick, Warwickshire CRO. CR136 B25/7.

49. J. V. Beckett, "Aristocrats and Electoral Control in the East Midlands, 1660–1914," *Midland History* 18 (1993): 84.

50. D. Eastwood, "The Triumph of Toryism in Oxfordshire Politics, 1754–1815," *Oxoniensia*, 54 (1989): 355–62.

51. F. O'Gorman, *Voters, Patrons, and Parties: The Unreformed Electorate of Hanoverian England, 1734–1832* (Oxford, 1989); A. Phillips, *Electoral Behavior in Unreformed England* (Princeton, NJ, 1982).

52. J. Barry, "Towns and Processes of Urbanisation in the Early Modern Period," in R. Kain and W. Ravenhill, eds., *Historical Atlas of South-West England* (Exeter, UK, 1999), 424.

53. I. Baudino, ed., *Les Voyageuses britanniques au XVIIIe siècle: L'Étape Lyonnaise dans l'itinéraire du Grand Tour* (Paris, 2015).

54. Christopher Wyvill to Charles, 2nd Marquess of Rockingham, November 26, 1779, Sheffield, Public Library, Wentworth Woodhouse papers, R140-27-1; *York Chronicle*, December 17, 1779.

55. A. Pettegree, *The Invention of News: How the World Came to Know about Itself* (New Haven, CT, 2014).

56. J. Walter, *An Address to the Public, Shewing the Great Improvement He Has Made in the Art of Printing, by Logographic Arrangements* (London, 1789).

57. *Sheffield Advertiser*, September 7, 1787.

58. Dr. Thomas Curteis to Dorset, August 29, 1733, Maidstone, Kent Archive Office U269 C148/2.

59. Will Slauter, "A Satirical News Aggregator in Eighteenth-Century London," *Media History* 22 (2016): 371–85.

60. J. H. Plumb, *Political Stability in England 1675–1725* (London, 1967).

61. J. Brewer, *Party Ideology and Popular Politics at the Accession of George III* (Cambridge, 1976).

62. J. Black, "'A Contemptible Piece of Ribaldry':*The Gazetteer and New Daily Advertiser* Offends the Bourbons," *Publishing History* 12 (1982):77–86.

63. B. Harris, *Politics and the Rise of the Press: Britain and France, 1620–1800* (London, 1996); L. Neal, "The Rise of a Financial Press: London and Amsterdam, 1681–1810," *Business History* 30 (1988): 163–78.

64. M. Ellis, "Coffee-House Libraries in Mid-Eighteenth-Century London," *The Library* 10 (2009): 3–40.

65. H. Barker, *Newspapers, Politics, and Public Opinion in Late Eighteenth Century England* (Oxford, 1998).

66. Shares in the British East India Company.

67. [Molesworth], *Observations upon a Pamphlet Called an English Merchant's Remarks upon a Scandalous Jacobite Paper* (London, 1717), 37.

68. For example, *Worcester Journal*, September 14, 1749. See also July 20 issue of *Westminster Journal*.

69. Owen to Edward Weston, "Writer" of the *Gazette*, March 26, 1757, Weston Underwood papers.

70. Anon., *Remarks* (London, 1765), 3.

71. *Owen's Weekly Chronicle*, July 22, 1758.

72. *Sheffield Advertiser*, June 4, 1790.

73. F. Burney, *Cecilia* (London, 1782, 1904 ed.): 857.

74. J. M. Smith, *Monsters of the Gévaudan: The Making of a Beast* (Cambridge, MA, 2011). See also http://betedugevaudan.perso.sfr.fr/histoire.htm, accessed August 21, 2016.

75. P. Stock, "America and the American Revolution in British Geographical Thought, c. 1760–1830," *English Historical Review* 131 (2016): 67.

76. P. Kaufman, *Libraries and Their Users* (London, 1969); M. K. Flavell, "The Enlightened Reader and the New Industrial Towns: A Study of the Liverpool Library, 1758–1790," *British Journal of Eighteenth-Century Studies* 8 (1985): 17–35; P. Sturges, "The Place of Libraries in the English Urban Renaissance of the Eighteenth Century," *Library and Culture* 24 (1989): 57–68.

77. R. Cave, "Early Circulating Libraries in Jamaica," *Libri* 30 (1980): 53–65.

78. J. Pearson, *Women's Reading in Britain, 1750–1835: A Dangerous Recreation* (Cambridge, 1999); J. Martin, *Wives and Daughters: Women and Children in the Georgian Country House* (New Haven, CT, 2004), 238.

79. *Gentleman's Magazine* 40 (1770): 428–29.

80. Cambridge, University Library, Cholmondeley Houghton papers, Mss 73/4/1.

81. *St. James's Chronicle*, January 4, 1766.

82. R. G. W. Anderson, M. L. Caygill, A. G. MacGregory, and L. Syson, eds., *Enlightening the British: Knowledge, Discovery and the Museum in the Eighteenth Century* (London, 2004).

83. D. B. Oleksijczuk, *The First Panoramas: Visions of British Imperialism* (Minneapolis, MN, 2011).

84. T. McCormick, *William Petty and the Ambitions of Political Arithmetic* (Oxford, 2009); G. Maifreda, *From Oikonomia to Political Economy: Constructing Economic Knowledge from the Renaissance to the Scientific Revolution* (Farnham, UK, 2012); P. Slack, *The Invention of Improvement: Information and Material Progress in Seventeenth-Century England* (Oxford, 2015).

85. P. Gauci, ed., *Regulating the British Economy, 1660–1850* (Farnham, UK, 2011).

86. *The Connoisseur* 52 (1755), quoted in P. J. Corfield, "Small Towns, Large Implications: Social and Cultural Roles of Small Towns in Eighteenth-Century England and Wales," *British Journal of Eighteenth-Century Studies* 10 (1987): 125.

87. J. Money, *Experience and Identity: Birmingham and the West Midlands 1760–1800* (Manchester, 1977); D. Hey, *The Fiery Blades of Hallamshire: Sheffield and Its Neighbourhood, 1660–1740* (Leicester, UK, 1992).

88. I would like to thank Robert Goadby for lending me a copy of his unpublished paper "The *Sherborne Mercury* and the Urban Renaissance in South-West England."

89. For example, see also *Newark Journal*, October 5, 1791.

90. For example, see also *Salisbury and Winchester Journal*, February 23, 1789.

91. C. Y. Ferdinand, *Benjamin Collins and the Provincial Newspaper Trade in the Eighteenth Century* (Oxford, 1997).

92. J. S. Holt, ed., *The Diary of Thomas Fenwick*, 4 vols. (London, 2011–12).

93. R. M. Wiles, *Freshest Advices: Early Provincial Newspapers in England* (Columbus, OH, 1969): 29–30; G. A. Cranfield, *The Development of the Provincial Newspaper, 1700–1760* (Oxford, 1960); I. Maxted, "Printing, the Book Trade and Newspapers c. 1500–1860," in R. Kain and W. Ravenhill, eds., *Historical Atlas of South-West England* (Exeter, UK, 1999): 242–45; M. E. Knapp, "Reading the *Salisbury Journal*, 1736–99," *Yale University Journal* 56, 3–4 (April 1982): 13. For the situation in France, J. Sgard, ed., *La Presse provinciale au xviiie siècle* (Grenoble, 1983); G. Feyel, "La Presse provincial au XVIIIe siècle: Géographie d'un réseau," *Revue Historique* 272 (1984): 353–74.

94. C. J. Griffin, "Knowable Geographies? The Reporting of Incendiarism in the Eighteenth- and Early Nineteenth-Century English Provincial Press," *Journal of Historical Geography* 32 (2006): 38–56 and "'Cut Down by Some Cowardly Miscreants': Plant Maiming, or the Malicious Cutting of Flora, as an Act of Protest in Eighteenth- and Nineteenth-Century Rural England," *Rural History* 19 (2008): 47.

95. J. Styles, "Print and Policing: Crime Advertising in Eighteenth-Century Provincial England," in D. Hay and F. Snyder, eds., *Policing and Prosecution in Britain 1750–1850* (Oxford, 1989), 55–111.

96. I. Maxted, "Single Sheets from a Country Town: The Example of Exeter," in *Spreading the Word: The Distribution Networks of Print, 1550–1850* (Exeter, UK, 1990), 109–29; J. Raven, *Publishing Business in Eighteenth-Century England* (Woodbridge, UK, 2014).

97. J. Raven, *Bookscape: Geographies of Printing and Publishing in London before 1800* (London, 2014).

98. Black to Edward Weston, October 31, 1751, Weston-Underwood papers.

99. Reverend Samuel Jackson to Reverend William Wickham, May 2, 1763, G. Eland, ed., *Shardeloes Papers of the Seventeenth and Eighteenth Centuries* (London, 1947), 42; see also Currey to Wickham, July 8, 1769, 47. I would like to thank Daniel Reed for sending me a copy of a forthcoming piece, "Spread the News within the Clerical Profession—Newspapers and the Church in the North of England, 1660–1760," in S. G. Brandtzaeg, P. Goring, and C. Watson, eds., *News in an Expanding World, The Transformation of News from the Renaissance to the Age of Enlightenment* (Leiden, 2017).

100. D. Wahrman, "National Society, Communal Culture: An Argument about the Recent Historiography of Eighteenth-Century Britain," *Social History* 17 (1992): 43–72; H. Berry, "Promoting Taste in the Provincial Press: National and Local Culture in Eighteenth-Century Newcastle upon Tyne," *British Journal of Eighteenth-Century Studies* 25 (2002): 14; P. Borsay, "The London Connection: Cultural Diffusion and the Eighteenth-Century Provincial

Town," *London Journal* 19 (1994): 21–35; S. Nenadic, "Middle-Rank Consumers and Domestic Culture in Edinburgh and Glasgow 1720–1840," *Past and Present* 145 (November 1994): 122–56.

101. P. Borsay, *The English Urban Renaissance: Culture and Society in the Provincial Town, 1660–1770* (Oxford, 1989).

102. J. Langton, "The Industrial Revolution and the Regional Geography of England," *Transactions of the Institute of British Geographers* 9 (1984): 145–67.

103. P. Borsay, "The English Urban Renaissance: The Development of Provincial Urban Culture c. 1680–1760," *Social History* 5 (1977): 581–603.

104. R. Hyde, "Portraying London Mid-Century—John Rocque and the Brothers Buck," in S. O'Connell, ed., *London 1753* (London, 2003), 28–38; H. Carter, "The Map in Urban History," *Urban History Yearbook* (1979): 19.

105. See also E. Stuart, *Lost Landscapes of Plymouth: Maps, Charts, and Plans to 1800* (Stroud, UK, 1991); E. Baigent, "Fact or Fiction? Town Maps as Aids and Snares to the Historian," *Archives* 29 (2004): 24–37 and "Revealing the City in Maps: Bath Seen, Built, and Imagined," *Journal of Historical Geography* 37 (2011): 385–89.

106. N. McCullough, ed., *A Vision of the City: Dublin and the Wide Streets Commissioners* (Dublin, 1991); Edel Sheridan, "Designing the Capital: Approaching the Morphology of Eighteenth-Century European Capitals," paper given at Institute of British Geographers Annual Conference, 1995.

107. P. Borsay, "The Rise of the Promenade: The Social and Cultural Use of Space in the English Provincial Town c. 1660–1800," *British Journal for Eighteenth-Century Studies* 9 (1986): 125–40, esp. 131–32.

5

The Debate on Tourism, Religion, and Culture

"SHALL WE BE driving post from place to place, living in noisy dirty inns, grumbling (perchance swearing) at postboys and visiting vast snowy mountains.... And all this to acquire what? At best a little knowledge of Geography—Alas Alas! How strange a system of Education have I engaged in." A much traveled, and therefore somewhat jaundiced, "bearleader" or traveling tutor, Thomas Brand was inclined, in 1790, to put geographical knowledge as costly:[1] swearing was unacceptable to Brand as a clergyman.

In practice, foreign travel offered an experience of abroad, indeed the major such experience, not only for those who traveled themselves, but also for those who heard or read about these travels, or saw the artefacts brought back, or, more broadly, who considered the national impact of the experience of travel. As such, the debate over the merits of tourism was an aspect of the discussion of the value and values of cosmopolitanism. This was a discussion in which xenophobia, and the range of responses that can be comprehended in that term, could have full rein. However, direct experience of abroad was particularly significant because there was no equivalent in the eighteenth century to the incessant visual stimulus now offered by cinema, television, social media, and photography. This extended to the objects brought back. Classical statuary and vases proved especially important.[2] They influenced writers, such as John Keats and Percy Shelley, and also those, such as Josiah Wedgwood, designing furniture, pottery, clothes, and other products. This indirect impact thus greatly extended the sway of the Grand Tour in Britain, chronologically, socially, and geographically.

As with much else discussed in this book, this topic and the varied responses to it were not new, but they became more pronounced in the early eighteenth century. Separate to the growth in foreign tourism in the seventeenth century, a tourism focused on France, Italy, and the Low Countries (Belgium and the Netherlands), although extending more widely, contrasts between Britain and France were an established theme in political geography, with institutions, culture, history, and events all conflated in discussing the contrasts. These contrasts were a major theme in British public discussion, with France the principal "other" against which Britain was defined and happily so by most British commentators. This contrast was also central to the comments by British tourists and about them.

The contrasts between Britain and France were complicated by the theme of betrayal from within. In France, there was concern about the Huguenots as a "fifth column," although this concern did not extend to foreign tourism or to British tourists in France. In Britain, the theme of betrayal was important to the debate about tourism. Traditionally, this anxiety focused on Catholicism, which continued to be a major issue. However, in the early eighteenth century, elite francophilia, already an important theme from the reign of Charles II (1660–85), and a major contrast to popular francophobia, became a more prominent issue in Britain. In part, the social dimension was that of gentry attacks on the aristocracy and, in part, what can be seen as an actual or incipient critique by the middling orders or a proto-middle class. There was also the theme of a development of Puritanism in a new guise.

Anxieties about elite betrayal were not eased until the conspicuous display of aristocratic gallantry in winning national success in the Seven Years' War (1756–63). Even then, doubts were to remain, but concerns about betrayal from within had been lessened greatly by the dramatic series of victories in 1759–62, as well as by the total defeat of Jacobitism with the defeat of the French invasion scheme in 1759. As a result, the geography of paranoia altered greatly from the early 1760s. In place of an earlier theme of betrayal from within, linked to an ideological threat to Britain and its future from autocratic and Catholic France, succeeded that of a geopolitical challenge from France. In the early 1760s, the ideological threat came to be associated not so much with France as with the alleged challenge from autocratic forces close to George III, a challenge also perceived in the American colonies.

The debate on tourism related essentially to the earlier situation when Britain was more vulnerable and poorer, although elements of it continued throughout the century. The debate was an aspect of the idea of abroad as existing at home, as well as on the European Continent, not least with dangerous assumptions allegedly picked up abroad being also at play at home. Thus, the Frenchified returned tourist, as satirically depicted on the stage in the person of Jack Broughton by Arthur Murphy in 1756 in *An Englishman from Paris*, was matched by criticism of foreign servants, music teachers, craftsmen, prostitutes, and so on. The fashion for Italian opera was attacked. Toward the close of Murphy's play, Broughton is urged to "take honest Nature for your guide."[3]

Moreover, this challenge, one that could be readily extended, was presented as a particular aspect of the allegedly pernicious consequences of metropolitan and/or court tendencies and circles. Although with earlier British sources, and, indeed, with echoes back to antiquity, this critique had been developed against the Stuart court in the seventeenth century and more particularly against court life under Charles II (r. 1660–85). It was ironic, therefore, that this criticism was to be employed against the Whigs when they were in government in 1714–60, for the Whigs had developed their identity in opposition to Charles during the Exclusion Crisis (1678–81) and, subsequently, had reached their self-styled apogee in playing a key role in displacing James II in 1688 and in securing the new settlement in 1689. However, the willingness of the Whigs to ally with France in 1716–31 and the refusal, thereafter in the decade, of the Walpole government to act against France, especially in the War of the Polish Succession (1733–35), helped ensure that it appeared possible to suggest that the alleged governmental and elite betrayal of national interests was linked to cultural treason.

These themes were frequently reiterated: in newspapers and caricatures, in Parliament, and on the stage. Demonstrations against foreign actors, notably, in the presence of a secretary of state, James, Earl Harrington, and the French ambassador, at the Haymarket Theatre in London in 1738 against French actors, exemplified this approach. Indeed, cosmopolitanism was defined as a threat and was frequently presented as such. It therefore, and thereby, provided both theme and language for what can be termed *political geography*.

This situation, however, posed a series of issues, as there were cosmopolitanisms and xenophobias. Most clearly, the xenophobia directed against Catholicism did not share the same identity as the criticism of alignment with foreign Protestants. This criticism was generally far less acute than that directed against Catholics, although it could be very strong as in the Tory opposition to Palatine refugees in 1709, an issue employed by the Tories in the election of 1710.[4] Moreover, as a linked point, hostility to Jacobitism was very different in character and in political context to that to the House of Hanover. Religion, in particular, was a key theme, one especially significant for hostility to Jacobitism. Religion, in the shape of Protestantism, offered an identity for what Daniel Defoe, writing in 1701 in defense of William III, referred to as a "mongrel half-bred nation," a presentation of England as ethnically composite but one that continues to be cited as a key instance of the essential character of English nationalism. There is a need to remember often serious rivalry among Protestants, especially between the Church of England and Dissenters, and between the Church of Scotland and Episcopalians, as well as friendship with individual Catholics. Nevertheless, anti-Catholicism was a central language and practice in public culture and, therefore, in the spatial placing, understanding, and expression of concern, anxiety, and danger.[5] Anti-Catholicism was also dynamic, a flexible ideology influenced by local circumstances.

This placing was particularly pronounced in the early decades of the century, as the theme of a "Protestant Interest," an interest allegedly under serious threat from an assertive Catholicism, enjoyed considerable traction then. The domestic and international placing of this threat, however, varied. In the 1700s, it focused in Britain, as in the Netherlands, on France which was very much the supporter of the Jacobite cause. Moreover, France under Louis XIV (r. 1643–1715), represented a continuity across the century divide and was important to the placing of danger and to the related understanding of strategic risk. The apparent challenge from France was no longer gauged largely in terms of a military threat to the Low Countries (modern Belgium and the Netherlands), as had been repeatedly the case from the thirteenth century. Instead, this challenge was discussed with reference to the stability of the British Isles, especially, from 1688, as Louis XIV supported James II when he resisted William III in Ireland, and to the wider European and global ambitions posed by Louis's attempt to put a grandson, Philip, Duke of Anjou, on the Spanish throne as Philip V (r. 1700–46). Closely contemporaneous to his backing for Philip, Louis recognized "James III" when his father James II died in 1701. The British government gained control of Ireland in 1690–91, but the dispatch of forces to Spain in the 1700s failed to lead to Philip's defeat. Instead, French forces defeated their opponents and established Philip, a result that has tended to be written out of British military history. Ideologically, French support for Jacobitism could be readily related to moves against Protestantism within France, especially the Revocation of the Edict of Nantes in 1598 by means of the Edict of Fontainebleau of 1685. This revocation spawned a series of horror tales, often accurate, about cruelty to Protestants as well as a large number of refugees, many of whom settled in Britain.

The placing of France was complicated when Britain and France allied from 1716 to 1731, but instead of that leading to a willingness to accept Catholicism as part of a stable European power system, there was then a continued concern about Catholic power politics. This concern focused on Austria, which appeared motivated by an anti-Protestant drive, as well as Spain. Alongside France, Britain fought Spain in 1719–20 while being the target of a Spanish invasion attempt on behalf of the Jacobites in 1719. Britain allied against Austria and Spain from 1725 to 1729 and against Austria from 1725 to 1731. At the same time, concern about international Catholicism was encouraged by the actions of a number of other Catholic states, notably Poland, the Palatinate, the Prince-Bishopric of Salzburg, and Savoy-Piedmont (the Kingdom of Sardinia).

This sense of danger led to a double spatial perception. The simple one was of Catholic versus Protestant Europe, but the more complex one highlighted areas of and in danger from Catholics. In response, there were calls for Protestant awareness and activity. This pressure and activity ranged considerably in character, including diplomatic support for oppressed co-religionists—for example, the Waldensians of Savoy-Piedmont—and, as mentioned in chapter 1, frequent public demands for a Protestant alliance, notably with the United Provinces (Dutch Republic) and with Prussia. This pressure led to a diplomatic focus on northern Europe. Russia could be treated as an add-on to any Protestant league as it was not a Catholic power.

There was also a determination to protect, police, and use the Protestant home space, although, for some commentators, this was a matter of England or the British Isles, and not of the Protestant world. Nevertheless, the latter could be significant. Thus, calling for a robust approach, the *Protestant Intelligence*, in its issue of January 9, 1725, argued that the best way to protect Protestants was to take reprisals against Catholic prelates in Protestant countries. Effectiveness was a key theme. It was argued that this method would be more successful "than the most pathetical and cogent memorials delivered at any Diet, or Congress, by Protestant Ministers [envoys]." The calls for such an approach became more prominent in the late 1730s, as the War of the Polish Succession ended in 1735 with a Franco-Austrian agreement, and there was then much talk in Britain of the dangers of a Catholic league, talk that lasted until France attacked Austria in 1741. Contrary interest in a Protestant one looked toward support in Britain among the public for Frederick II of Prussia when he attacked Austria in 1740.

This anti-Catholic approach made, and makes, it necessary to confront the question of the cultural and other relations between Britain and the Continent. This is a topic that is vexed at the present moment due to controversy over British membership in the European Union and related attempts to create or contest a backstory of close British links.[6] There may well, indeed, be issues of relevance from the eighteenth century for the present, or, indeed, from the present for our understanding of the eighteenth century. However, while being aware of these dimensions, it is more useful to consider the period without being bound up in the controversies of the present. This is particularly so as an emphasis on the latter can become all absorbing and can lead to a failure to come to any valid conclusion.

The eighteenth-century debate about foreign influences was multifaceted, but tourism was particularly significant as it led to British people going abroad and being exposed, it was claimed, when most vulnerable, to those influences. Most of these themes could be found across the century. This was the case for structural aspects, both of tourism and of the debate about it, notably the cost and loss of wealth to the country in the first place and the character of xenophobia in the second. Criticism of foreign tourism was strongest in the 1720s and 1730s, and, as already indicated, that was a lessening of ideological prejudices from the 1760s[7] and a reconceptualization of fears; however, criticism can be found throughout the century. Indeed, foreign tourism was frequently treated as but one example of an allegedly generalized and dangerous failure to defend the integrity of British life and society in the face of all things foreign.

In practice, in so far as British tourists made ideological remarks, they tended to concentrate on religious factors, which were more overt and more obviously different from the situation in Britain than their political counterparts. It was easiest to note and comment on the respect for implausible relics;[8] the plentiful presence of crucifixes and wayside shrines; the pomp, magnificence, and alien quality of Catholic ceremonies; the large number of clerics; the inappropriate nature of withdrawal from the world in monasteries;[9] the presence of nunneries; and the extent of popular devotion, notably at wayside shrines, than it was to perceive the role of the French *parlements*, the nature of political power in German principalities, or the fiscal system in their Italian counterparts. Changes in British religious culture were also significant, notably the rise of Evangelicalism toward the end of the century. This led to a changing emphasis, as in tourism to Rome, where piety placed greater stress on accounts of the testimony offered by early Christians.[10]

Politics, like religion, entailed a specific geography. In the former case, much tourist comment centered on states that were republics: the United Provinces (Dutch Republic),[11] the Swiss Confederation, Geneva (then separate), Genoa, Venice, Lucca, and San Marino. Venice in particular offering a different account to the general response to Italy.[12] Very few tourists traveled to the new American republic established on the other side of the Atlantic. Comments on republics, as on monarchies, reflected the usual issues involved in expanding geographical information. There were the problems of assessing foreign political systems (and other aspects) when most of the attempt to do so had to be conducted in a foreign language. British knowledge of foreign languages was limited, a process encouraged by the role of Latin in education. The ability to speak foreign languages was particularly limited. Some tourists spent time being educated abroad, with this including the acquisition of language skills, notably for French in the Loire Valley, but most did not.

Another problem was that, as also with Britain, visitors tended to visit only the major cities of states and so could often only grasp a metropolitan perspective on political and other developments.[13] This was a process encouraged by the extent to which royal courts were a tourist destination and experience, while British envoys could introduce tourists there, as well as providing hospitality, but not so readily elsewhere. More generally, comfortable facilities for travelers, all travelers, as well as interest for tourists, focused on major cities. This led tourists to rush from city to city, frequently treating what lay in between as difficult and wasteland, a theme also seen with travel within Britain. The theme that Paris was not France was repeated by several writers because they feared that the attractions, or apparent attractions, of life in Paris would blind susceptible tourists to the realities of life elsewhere in the country. Tourists who visited Berlin and Vienna and stopped elsewhere in the Prussian and Austrian dominions merely to sleep (apart usually from a day in Prague)[14] would only have a limited understanding of the political systems of these countries. The same was even truer for the very small number of tourists who visited Denmark, Portugal, Russia, and Sweden.

Capitals displayed the power and prestige of monarchy and gave the impression of autocratic, often efficient, states. Capitals, however, were a poor guide to the compromises between monarchical centralization and aristocratic particularism that underlay so much of the so-called absolutisms or absolute monarchies of the period. This was true, for example, of France, where the authority and, still more, the power of the monarch were limited (although less so than for British monarchs) but also of other states. If they realized this contrast, let alone understood it, few tourists recorded the fact, and this was an aspect of a more general misperception. This misperception was important to the ideological understanding of abroad and thus to the sense of the spatial patterning of politics.

Tourists, and other commentators, did, however, capture the ideological, as opposed to functional, dimension of power. They stressed the manner in which Catholicism aided state authority, a view that prepared them for a similar approach toward religion in non-Western societies. States such as France, Austria, and Spain owed much of their political stability not so much to coercion, as to the ideological consensus of obedience and community that stemmed largely from Catholicism. In France, this consensus was compromised by the Gallican and Jansenist controversies, but these were not really understood by British tourists, although aspects of them were covered in the press. By drawing attention to the interrelationships of

Catholicism and political power, tourists both perceived the strength and stability of many states and clarified the established spatial perception of Britain as separated from the Continent. However, their conclusions about the consequences of this interrelationship with Catholicism, especially its supposed deleterious effect on the economy, society, and morality, were often shallow and inaccurate, which reflected the extent to which perception was guided by established prejudice.

Foreign visitors in Britain noted major differences. A midcentury French visitor wrote: "Arrival in England seems to announce liberty. The towns are not shut, nothing constricts trade, travelers are not asked where they go or whence they came and there are no internal customs."[15] Indeed, there were not the internal tariff systems seen in France or the locked gates of towns where travelers were confronted by questioning guards. French visitors also commented on the relative freedom of women in social gatherings. Moreover, Baron Pöllnitz was impressed by the social mixing possible as a result of the convention that at grand coffeehouses, such as the Chocolate House in St. James's Street, London, admission required nothing more than to be dressed like a gentleman.[16] The same was true of being received at court by the monarch.

British travel writing, in contrast, often emphasized the inhumanity of the French social system.[17] This travel writing could expand the information publicly available on foreign countries, as in David Macnab's *An Exact Description of the Island and Kingdom of Sicily* (Falkirk, 1784; London, 1786).

The dynamic nature of cultural geography was very much captured by the successful Anglicization seen in Britain in the second half of the century and notably after victory in the Seven Years' War (1756–63), especially the successes of 1759. That sentence possibly confuses issues of cause and effect. The theme of Anglicization was already strong in the first half of the century, as with the controversy surrounding Italian opera and was also very present in the early 1750s.

At the same time, Anglicization had a recognizably partisan character, and this proved both invigorating and limiting. The cult of the national past, and, therefore, of a distinctive present, was seen in the masque *Alfred* which appeared in 1740, at a time of marked contention about the direction of British policy and notably as to whether Sir Robert Walpole had been sufficiently robust against Spain, both in peace and in war. *Alfred* was most famous for the song "Rule Britannia." In the 1730s and 1740s, simply to mention King Alfred, the ruler of Wessex in the late ninth century, who had victoriously resisted Danish invaders after the other English monarchies had been overrun, was to deploy "deep history" in order to redefine the present. It was to make a political point about the need for national integrity and the defense of national honor in the face of foreign influences and attacks. The very imprecision of the imaging increased the value of Alfred, as his Danish opponents could serve to contemporaries as a prefigurement of Hanoverian influence but also could be deployed with reference to the Jacobite challenge. In the 1730s, Aaron Hill pressed for the revitalization of English culture, a theme linked to Frederick, Prince of Wales, and the idea of the patriot king. A "Patriot Gothic" rejection of Walpolian corruption reflected the idea of culture as a means for, and product of, renewal.[18]

The rise of an English nationalism and exceptionalism is an established feature of the scholarly literature, with an elite cosmopolitanism challenged by a national consciousness whose bourgeois champions sought to proclaim and define an English culture that would be recognizably superior to any other.[19] While well founded, this approach risks underplaying a much longer-term tension between cosmopolitanism and nationalism. Moreover, at many levels, the relationship between English nationalism and a British one is complex, and notably so as the use of England was treated in England as interchangeable with Britain. This was an approach that was not due to migration within the British Isles, migration that in practice was disproportionately to England and consistently so. A resilient English nationalism was, if not an obstacle to a truly popular sense of Britishness taking root in England, at least probably a complication. The extent to which this approach comprehended the other parts of Britain in terms of their views is more problematic. Examples can be found both ways.[20]

The Seven Years' War led to changes in attitude in both France and Britain. In France, the war resulted in a rethinking of Britain as both a rival and an example, with a newly energetic patriotism focused on opposition to Britain and increasingly looking to the idea of a French nation.[21] In Britain, after the decisive victories over France and Spain in the Seven Years' War, there was a self-confident vigor that greatly affected cultural life. In specific artistic terms, rococo influences, which very much bound Britain to France, and which had been strong in London in the 1720s–1750s, were displaced in favor of a less obviously derivative art and dependent culture, one that was national and national whether presented in terms of Britishness or of an Englishness designed to serve as Britishness. In 1772, Joshua Reynolds depicted England as more dynamic than France, presenting this as the key relationship of respective influence but also one that counterpointed contrasting values: "There is at least a dozen of their most able academicians come over to try their fortune among us and we hear of more coming. There is no employment for them in France, either from the poverty of the nation or from the declining of all arts amongst them except that of furnishing Europe with bauble."[22]

The domestic English cultural tradition became stronger in the second half of the century, in part thanks to the institutionalization of art. Established in 1768, and typically in London, the Royal Academy was the realization of long-held ideas for an institution that would combine artistic education with national glory. Already, in 1749, John Gwyn had published a proposal for founding a "Public Academy" to provide education in the arts. That would lessen the need to travel for artistic education and awareness and thus permit an Anglicization of painting.

Founding president of the Royal Academy, Reynolds, popularized a modernized classical style that was taught at the academy. He was particularly impressed by Raphael and by what he saw as a grand style that could be introduced into English painting. This was a historic Italian style in comparison with which the art of France could be made to appear weak. In contrast to his focus on past Italian painters, Reynolds displayed little interest in contemporary Italian artists, a preference that was more generally shared. This was a key aspect of a process that was geographical and chronological: modern Britain was depicted as the heir to classical Rome,[23] although there were tensions between different models of Rome.[24] Furthermore, there were comments in 1787 on the speed with which "an aversion" to Greek had spread.[25] The Roman inheritance reflected the glories of modern Britain and, in particular, its imperial destiny but also the extent to which modern Italians were held to be debased and notably so in comparison with classical Romans. Moreover, it was the British who had the ability to discern the value and values of past Italian culture. If the Renaissance offered an Italian revival of classical values and qualities, that revival was repeated but also exceeded in the case of modern Britain.

Edward Gibbon commented, "The footsteps of heroes, the relics, not of superstition, but of empire, are devoutly visited by a new race of pilgrims from the remote, and once savage, countries of the North."[26] Thus, a notion of descent was offered, one in which civilizational succession provided all sorts of subliminal messages about the placing of Britain in time and space. This was different to the stadial ideas of sociological development offered by Enlightenment thinkers, notably Adam Smith. In the idea of civilizational succession between Rome and Britain, a succession in which Britain was superior as Christian and as global, time and space were both parts of the same continuum. Architecture and landscape gardening captured these elements. At Painshill, near London, where the Honorable Charles Hamilton (1704–86) developed a much-applauded landscape garden, which was visited, in 1786, by Thomas Jefferson among many others, before falling into a decay from which it has recently been rescued, the grounds included not only North American plant species but also a Roman mausoleum, a temple of Bacchus, and a set of busts of the Roman emperors, as well as a Gothic tower, a Gothic temple, a Gothic folly in the shape of a ruined abbey, and a Chinese-style bridge.

At the same time, as a reminder of cultural complexity, Anglicization could also encompass resistance to classical Rome, as with William Mason's play *Caractacus* (1776). Johann Christian Bach, the "English Bach," also paid tribute to this first-century CE/AD hero resisting the then-pagan Romans, writing the opera *Carattaco* (1767) for the King's Theatre in London. This was an instance of the placing of history with cultural relationships that were located in space. Gibbon's use of the book *Agricola* by the Roman historian Tacitus in praising the vigor of the Caledonians/Picts who successfully resisted Roman conquest was an aspect of the same process. An interest in Caractacus can be set alongside that in the (fictional) Celtic hero of the 1760s Ossian, both sharing in a non-Roman and non-Christian national history. Although Alfred was a Christian, he was also part of this national pantheon, as, in a more shadowy fashion, was Arthur.

The Shakespeare cult, a cult that included adaptation to match the moods of the moment, was an important instance of the process by which cultural identity and nationalism were redefined and expressed across time. Shakespeare could be made to work for a range of political movements, including, in the 1790s, both radicals and their opponents. This expression was very much in a spirit of national rivalry focused on France, as with the letter from "An old-fashioned Englishman" printed in the *St. James's Chronicle* of May 13, 1769.[27] Although English, and therefore problematic as a British exemplar,[28] Shakespeare had a British reception.[29] The year 1769 also saw the publication of Elizabeth Montagu's *An Essay on the Writings and Genius of Shakespeare*, as well as the staging at Stratford-on-Avon by David Garrick of a Shakespeare Jubilee. Garrick had developed a naturalistic school of acting that was presented as superior to Continental acting methods—in other words, those of France. This was a counterpart of the earlier critique of Italian opera in the shape of vernacular British opera and Handel's oratorios. Handel's works were strongly revived in the 1780s and 1790s, with George III offering conspicuous personal support for the revival.

Shakespeare, meanwhile, provided the narrative source for many painters, and thus for an Anglicized classicism, one, moreover, set in British backgrounds rather than in the Mediterranean. These paintings depicted scenes from the plays, as well as famous actors playing particular roles. Macbeth proved especially popular, both because of its drama and due to its wildness, notably the strengthening in interest toward the close of the century in the wilds of Britain.

Alongside the varied politics of space came its literary and individual perception. In Britain, the second half of the century saw the literary trope of the rambler. Thus, geography as inspiration was the key theme, rather than geography as a clearly objective account of circumstances and/or as the means of transport. The rambler's return to familiar places was presented as simultaneously focusing his own sense of time passing and of the gains and losses of intervening months or years. In turn, the Romantic era saw a heightening of the drama as the wanderer had a more adventurous frame of mind than the rambler. The fictional capture of place and space was important to the understanding of them.[30]

Tourism, which had a long background,[31] was increasingly common in Britain in the latter decades of the century and notably with the rise of interest in what was seen as the picturesque and with the rise of sea bathing, as in Devon.[32] The Lake District, the Peak District, Snowdonia, the Wye Valley, and Teesdale were key mountainous areas of interest to tourists. They were presented as akin to Switzerland. William Coxe described Monmouthshire in terms of "luxuriant vallies and romantic hills." The

Scottish Highlands were part of the process, not least with related interest in the cult of Ossian.[33] The focus on these areas led to a new geography of attention, with publications accordingly, such as Thomas Pennant's *Tour of Scotland* (1771) and *Tour in Wales* (1778–81).

Alongside attention to these areas in particular, there was also the question of the routes to them. In part, these routes reflected changes in the possibility of travel within Britain created by new turnpike roads and related bridges. There had been travelers for pleasure around Britain earlier in the century—for example, Celia Fiennes. They tended in their writings to focus on the difficulties of travel. That focus was less apparent by the close of the century, in part because of the improvements to communications and what was seen as a process of continuing improvement.

At the same time, to read from materialist, functional criteria, notably better communications, to clear cultural consequences is problematic. The cultural dynamics were in part a matter of the relationships between the Continent on the one hand and Britain on the other, with greater interest in Britain an aspect of a rejection of sections of modern Continental culture and that prior to the major disruption to travel caused by the French Revolution. Yet, there were parallels between the concerns of British tourists abroad and at home—for example, with rising interest by tourists in the Alps and, indeed, Iceland[34] and in mountainous or hilly regions of Britain. This interest can be described in terms of proto-Romanticism or Romanticism.

More broadly, both of these terms can indeed be applied to the reconceptualization of areas of Britain from semi-barbarian to, instead, an important expression of national values, not least as a critique of London's dominance. Dr. Johnson's response to the Scottish Highlands was an aspect of this newfound appreciation of earlier and different social mores. He understood the attempt to hold on to Gaelic. These were "noble savages" close to home and, in his eyes, a fit complement to the rugged landscape. Conversely, traveling through Cumbria in 1773 as part of a tour that also included Scotland and Ireland, John Drake was not particularly attracted to the Lake District. He wrote from Carlisle:

> From Manchester we travelled through Westmoreland, for about 15 or 20 miles over a country beyond conception mountainous and barren, and lay at a village called Shap consisting only of three or four houses nigh to Sir James Lowthers, by whose park we travelled, but not within sight of the mansion,

which we were informed was not at all worth seeing, the old habitation being formerly burnt down and the present made out of the offices, and reached this place by dinnertime yesterday, the situation of which is very pleasing, being situated upon a hill with the river Eden running at the bottom; there is nothing at all worthy of notice here except the castle (which was taken and retaken by the rebels three or four times,) from the walls of which you have a very fine view to the Northumberland hills and the country round about; the Cathedral is very small but neat.[35]

Somewhat differently, as an engagement with another part of Britain, William Bingley, a Cambridge undergraduate, traveled in the vacation of 1798, then publishing Welsh songs that had been arranged for the piano, before writing extensively on natural history and travel. Ireland was not treated so favorably,[36] while in the Isle of Man, there was a campaign against Manx Gaelic.[37]

Cultural and intellectual history is not easy to map with precision, as if one is dealing with communications, but such history could be understood by contemporaries in spatial terms. Cultural nationalism and its relationship with place offered a way to shape, confront, and define differences between Britain and the Continent, and thus to establish a geography that was at once positive and negative, with each, in part, a definition of the other. This process was not new but became more pronounced from the 1760s. At the same time, this shift was not simply a matter of Britain but also related to the British Empire as a whole. In particular, the idea of transoceanic destiny and, specifically, the possession of North American colonies, were a more prominent part in the shaping of Britain after midcentury, only for the latter relationship to collapse totally from 1775.

Notes

1. Brand to Robert Wharton, April 9, 1790, Durham, University Library, Wharton papers.

2. M. D. Sánchez-Jáuregui Alpañés and S. Wilcox, eds., *The English Prize: The Capture of the Westmorland, an Episode of the Grand Tour* (New Haven, CT, 2012).

3. T. McGeary, "Farinelli in Madrid: Opera, Politics, and the War of Jenkins' Ear," *The Musical Quarterly* 88 (1998): 384–85.

4. H. T. Dickinson, "The Poor Palatines and the Parties," *English Historical Review* 82 (1967): 464–85.

5. L. Colley, *Britons: Forging the Nation, 1707–1837*, 2nd ed. (New Haven, CT, 2009).

6. B. Simms, *Three Victories and a Defeat: The Rise and Fall of the First British Empire, 1714–1783* (London, 2007).

7. H. J. Müllenbrock, "The Political Implications of the *Grand Tour*: Aspects of a Specifically English Contribution to the European Travel Literature of the Age of Enlightenment," *Trema* 9 (1984): 7–21. The German version is in *Arcadia* 17 (1982): 113–25.

8. J. Lough, "Regency France seen by British travellers," in *Enlightenment essays in memory of Robert Shackleton* (Oxford, 1988): 152.

9. J. Lough, "France in the 1780s seen by Joseph and Anna Francesca Cradock," *Studies on Voltaire and the Eighteenth Century*, 267 (1989): 436.

10. R. Sweet, *Cities and the Grand Tour: The British in Italy, c. 1690–1820* (Cambridge, 2012).

11. H. Dunthorne, "British Travellers in Eighteenth-Century Holland: Tourism and the Appreciation of Dutch Culture," *BJECS* 5 (1980): 77–84.

12. B. Redford, *Venice and the Grand Tour* (New Haven, CT, 1996); J. Eglin, *Venice Transfigured: The Myth of Venice in British Culture, 1660–1797* (Basingstoke, UK, 2001).

13. C. Chard and H. Langdon, eds., *Transports: Travel, Pleasure, and Imaginative Geography, 1600–1830* (New Haven, CT, 1996).

14. This excludes those who visited Austrian-ruled Lombardy.

15. Undated, anonymous, "Mémoire sur l'Angleterre," AN. AM. B^{7}455.

16. Pöllnitz, *Lettres et memoires* (5th ed., Frankfurt, 1738): III, 309; E. Dziembowski, "L'Angleterre inexportable. Le comte de Gisors face à la vie politique britannique du milieu du XVIIIe siècle," in J.-P. Genet and F.-J. Ruggiu, eds., *Les idées passent-elles la Manche?* (Paris, 2007), 129–42; D. A. Ross, "The Early Career of Etienne de Silhouette" (Ph.D. diss., University of California, Los Angeles, 1973).

17. T. Smollett, *The Adventures of Peregrine Pickle* (London, 1751; Oxford, 1969), 210–12.

18. C. Gerrard, *The Patriot Opposition to Walpole: Politics, Poetry, and National Myth, 1725–1742* (Oxford, 1994).

19. G. Newman, *The Rise of English Nationalism: A Cultural History 1740–1830*, 2nd ed. (Basingstoke, UK, 1998).

20. A. Murdoch, *British History 1660–1832: National Identity and Local Culture* (Basingstoke, UK, 1998); J. Smyth, *The Making of the United Kingdom 1660–1800* (Harlow, UK, 2001).

21. E. Dziembowski, *Un nouveau patriotism français, 1750–1770. La France face à la puissance anglaise à l'époque de la guerre de Sept Ans* (Oxford, 1998).

22. Reynolds to Lord Grantham, April 3, 1772, Bedford, Bedfordshire Record Office, Lucas papers, 30/14/326/1.

23. P. Ayres, *Classical Culture and the Idea of Rome in Eighteenth-Century England* (Cambridge, 1997).

24. R. Browning, *Political and Constitutional Ideas of the Court Whigs* (Baton Rouge, LA, 1982).

25. *English Chronicle; Or, Universal Evening-Post*, April 5, 1787.

26. E. Gibbon, *The History of the Decline and Fall of the Roman Empire*, edited by J. B. Bury (London, 1900), VII, 324–25; J. Black, *Italy and the Grand Tour* (New Haven, CT, 2003).

27. See also F. De Bruyn, "Shakespeare, Voltaire, and the Seven Years' War: Literary Criticism as Cultural Battlefield," in De Bruyn and S. Regan, eds., *The Culture of the Seven Years' War: Empire, Identity, and the Arts in the Eighteenth Century Atlantic World* (Toronto, 2014).

28. L. Colley, *Shakespeare and the Limits of National Culture* (London, 1999), 10–12.

29. J. Bate, *Shakespearean Constitutions: Politics, Theatre, Criticism, 1730–1830* (Oxford, 1989); M. Dobson, *The Making of the National Poet: Shakespeare, Adaptation and Authorship,*

1660-1769 (Oxford, 1992); J. Brewer, *The Pleasures of the Imagination: English Culture in the Eighteenth Century* (London, 1997), 406-23.

30. J.-P. Forster, *Eighteenth-Century Geography and Representations of Space in English Fiction and Poetry* (Oxford, 2013).

31. Nicholas Orme, "Place and Past in Medieval England," *History Today* 58, no. 7 (2008): 24-30.

32. J. F. Travis, *The Rise of the Devon Seaside Resorts, 1750-1900* (Exeter, UK, 1993).

33. M. Andrews, *The Search for the Picturesque: Landscape, Aesthetics, and Tourism in Britain, 1760-1800* (Aldershot, UK, 1989); W. Coxe, *An Historical Tour of Monmouthshire* (London, 1801), 402.

34. G. Mackenzie, *Travels in the Island of Iceland during the Summer of the Year 1810* (London, 1811); A. Wawn, ed., *The Iceland Journal of Henry Holland 1810* (London, 1987).

35. John Drake to his father, William Drake, August 3, 1773, Aylesbury, Buckinghamshire Record Office, D/DR/8/5/2.

36. D. Hayton, "From Barbarian to Burlesque: English Images of the Irish c. 1660-1750," *Irish Economic and Social History* 15 (1988): 5-31.

37. P. Clamp, "Bishop Wilson's Discipline: Language, Schooling and Confrontation in the Isle of Man, 1698-1755," *Journal of Religious History* 15 (1988): 188-98.

6

Responding to Novelty

RUSSIA'S RISE

General trends can, and should, be anchored with more specific examples, not least because these trends were in part an accumulation of such instances and the related efforts and experiences. A classic case of the engagement of geography with power was provided by the public, and notably press, response to Russia's rise. This was very much an aspect of a new geography of awareness and concern. Russia itself was scarcely an unknown country for the English and, indeed, was better known than the Balkans. Elizabeth I of England had pursued links with Ivan the Terrible (Ivan IV) in the late sixteenth century. Moreover, Russian expansionism had already been an issue for the European powers in the late sixteenth and late seventeenth centuries, both under Ivan and under Alexi. Nevertheless, the situation was transformed under Peter the Great (r. 1689–1725) and, more particularly, as a consequence of extensive Russian gains after the crushing victory over Charles XII of Sweden at Poltava in Ukraine in 1709. When Peter visited England in 1698, he was a curiosity. By the 1710s, he was a dramatic conqueror.

In the mid-1710s, Russian forces moved into northern Germany (to use the modern term) and Denmark with Peter, spending several months in Copenhagen in late 1716. He planned a joint Danish-Russian conquest of southern Sweden that was not brought to fruition, but then overwintered his army in Mecklenburg. The British government, under the influence of

George I (r. 1714–27) and his Hanoverian concerns, became conspicuously hostile to the possibility of a new-modeling of the international system by Peter, and notably so after George and these Hanoverian concerns were crucial to ministerial changes in 1717 and to the linked Whig split. Mecklenburg bordered Hanover.

Indeed, there was no suggestion that there was any natural boundary that could, or would, block Russia's advance. In that respect, international/political and physical geography appeared as one. A political barrier to Russian expansionism had to be established. More particularly, in order to ensure that such a geographical boundary to Russian expansion did in fact pertain, it was clearly necessary, to those who supported this stance, for Britain to act: by diplomatic or military means, or by both. *The Political State of Great Britain* for September 1719 argued that "the interest of our British trade does demand the Czar's being again shut out of the Baltic."

However, the British attempt to organize a coalition to restrict Russian gains failed totally, in part due to its contradictions and in part to the impact of fiscal crisis in Britain in the shape of the South Sea Bubble. In 1721, by the Treaty of Nystad, Russia's acquisition of Ingria, Estonia, and Livonia (eastern Latvia including Riga) were confirmed. Finland was returned to Sweden.

Thereafter, Russian expansion continued to be regarded as a threat until Russia more commonly became an ally of Britain, its power thereby employed against other threats. International relations, indeed, proved the key focus for British attention to Russia, and that focus was very much reflected in the press. Governmental changes, religious disputes, and metallurgical discoveries in Russia all received coverage. Nevertheless, it was foreign policy and related military steps that attracted most attention.

In part, this attention was a reflection of anxiety about the emergence of an apparently new power, at least to the extent of the unprecedented success it enjoyed. There was no awareness of any comparison in terms of the Russian advance across the Urals and Siberia and to the Pacific from the 1580s to the 1630s or of the Russian advance southward in the late seventeenth century toward the Black Sea.

The capacity of political geography to deal with disconcerting novelty was the issue. In part, the discussion was, more specifically, in terms of the divisions of British politics and, more especially, the argument that whatever George I and his ministerial supporters might suggest, British interests from 1714 were being sacrificed for the sake of Hanover. This argument was not without foundation. The handling of political geography, its content, context, language, and tone, by contemporary commentators had to address the specific politics as well as the more general, and that need greatly complicated the discussion of causation and consequences.

As an instance of the range of media in which the wider world and, more particularly, foreign policy were discussed, ballads offered a media that was not dependent for its appreciation on literacy. The sources for ballads are somewhat limited because not all were written down, but those that were suggest that a good range of subjects were tackled. The survival of ballads in manuscript and/or printed versions highlights the range of the form and the issues of survival. "Safety and Tranquillity—An Excellent New Ballad" of 1722 ably expressed the agitation of the period and the sense of unprecedented Russian power:

> Well, well, sail off, Replied the Czar
> Tho digne de Chatiment;
> But when you want your naval stores
> You'll not ride top Gallant.
> Full of it the Russian monarch wish'd
> To have him in his Paw;
> And swore he instantly would Roast,
> A Minister so Raw.[1]

Tensions in Anglo-Russian relations continued in Peter's last years, with particular fear of a Russian attack on Sweden in 1723, as well as under his successors: his widow, Catherine I (r. 1725–27); his grandson, Peter II (r. 1727–30); and, initially, under his niece Anna (r. 1730–40). These tensions interacted with political differences within the London press, helping ensure that the accuracy of news from Russia became an issue. For example, the *Weekly Journal, or British Gazetteer* of January 25, 1718, attacked Mist for his paper of a week earlier: "See how his scribbling blockheads are stumbling in profound ignorance, saying the Czar is going to Muscovy with 50,000 men, when he is at home already; but they meant Moscow, the chief city of his country."

The British newspaper-reading public was kept informed of developments. For example, the *Flying Post* of September 1, 1726, a pro-government

London newspaper, printed the memorial presented by the Danish envoy in St. Petersburg complaining of Russian naval preparations and of the threat to peace they represented. Such a war would probably have involved Anglo-Russian hostilities as Britain was then committed to the support of Denmark and Sweden. Furthermore, from 1726, Russia was allied to Austria and aligned with Prussia, both of which were then opposed to Britain and Hanover. Indeed, there was a war panic in the case of Prussia in 1729. Relations with Russia remained poor until the negotiation of a commercial treaty in 1734, and this opening had been made possible by Britain's alliance with Russia's ally Austria in 1731 and by the easing of Hanoverian disputes with Russia in 1731–32.

Despite the atmosphere of diplomatic tension, reports in the British press were, by the mid-1720s, reasonably free of prejudice, in part, possibly, because by then, Russia was seen as already an established part of the European system and certainly a well-known news story. Moreover, there was not the ideological threat to Britain posed by France, Spain, and the papacy. Russian expansion per se did not appear to challenge the nature of British society and culture, in large part because Russia was not Catholic. Moreover, Russia was distant. There were reports about Russian support for Jacobitism, but nothing to compare with anxieties about such backing from France, Spain, Austria, and Sweden, each of which provided assistance, or the prospect of assistance, between 1700 and 1730. Indeed, the willingness of the Protestant Charles XII of Sweden to discuss such help in 1717 helped make his opponent Peter appear less menacing.

Rather than hostility toward Russia, although that was expressed, there was, increasingly, as immediate political crises ebbed, and notably from 1727, the uncertainty and rumor that characterized territories on the margins of established political geography. For example, the *Flying-Post*, in its issue of July 4, 1727, printed a report from The Hague, the leading center of European news: "The accounts that have been published as from Petersburg of the indisposition of the young Emperor [Peter II],[2] of the assassination of the Duke of Holstein,[3] and of the mobbing and insurrections there, prove all of a piece, and to have been without foundation; all things have been very quiet, his Imperial Majesty has been, and is, very well; they are quiet and easy at home."[4]

These rumors of instability, and other reports of hostile Russian intentions, owed more to confusion as to Russian developments than to any campaign of defamation directed against Russia. Thus, the *St. James's Evening Post* of July 13, 1727, reported Russian intentions of supporting Austria, then adopting a hostile stance toward Britain, while other papers flatly contradicted these reports, which, indeed, captured the confusion of international relations on this juncture. Reports as to Peter II's intentions toward Britain were confused.

More helpfully, Russian policy was not presented as a single entity but as a product of complex factional feuds. In the discussion of the latter, the interests of major aristocratic families and the rifts between the old "Russ" nobility and the westernizing foreign advisers were all described, which was a reasonable approach. So also were the probable consequences in terms of foreign policy.

There was also an attempt, as for other powers, to assimilate Russian developments to British patterns and examples, an instance of a frequent approach to deny or overcome the conceptual distance involved in geography. For example, the accessions of Peter II in 1727 and of Anna in 1730 led to reports of intended constitutional changes in Russia and to the possibilities of an Anglo-Russian rapprochement. At times, though very briefly in each case, these two monarchs appeared as model, even Whiggish, sovereigns, rather than as some cross with an Oriental despot as Russian rulers had invariably earlier appeared. *Applebee's Original Weekly Journal*, a Whig London newspaper, reported on August 5, 1727, that Peter II "hath openly declared in Council, that the end of government is chiefly designed to redress grievances, and to contribute as much happiness as possible to the people, because in their prosperity consists that of his own." This represented a parallel to the recent accession of George II.

In 1730, much attention was paid to the attempt by the aristocratic Great Council to limit Anna's powers as part of the conditions for her accession to the throne. The *Daily Post Boy* of March 28 devoted two and a half columns to these changes. Anna's apparent support for constitutional reform and the fall of Prince Menzikof, who was presented as an autocratic minister, were cited as examples of the "moral" qualities of foreign news in the *British Journal* of May 30.

In general, however, such Whiggish episodes appeared as brief moments, and Russia, instead, was seen as a despotic autocracy. This situation was not usually criticized on the grounds of difference to British circumstances. Instead, on a pattern adopted throughout the earlier "early-modern" period, this situation was regarded as pertaining naturally to the country and to its inhabitants: "the savage Muscovites," as the *Flying Post* described them in its issue of September 5, 1727.

This approach contrasted with the attitude to Western European states that were regarded as ruled autocratically. The view that autocracy was a natural response to the supposed innate national characters of the French, Spaniards, and Italians did exist, but it was contradicted by a strong "historical" approach to the problem. In the latter case, autocracy was presented as the result of evil misgovernment at a certain period—for example, of France by Cardinal Richelieu. In British accounts, the destruction of representative institutions commonly provided a key historical cause and occasion.

This was a warning about what could happen in Britain and also a marked reminder of the time-space nature of the understanding of political geography: in this way, where peoples and states appeared was not structurally determined by their physical geography but was an aspect of their historical trajectory, a trajectory that was highly contingent. The latter approach was to recede in the nineteenth century, in part due to Social Darwinism, in part to an increased focus on the non-Western world, and in part to a greater understanding and usage of physical geography and the employment of it to classify and explain circumstances and developments, sometimes misleadingly so.[5]

In the eighteenth century, Russia could be readily presented as a different state to the rest of Europe, having elements, instead, in common with the Turkish and Persian Empires, both of which were reported in the British press, although with only limited analysis. In the case of all three, the relative ignorance of their histories by Western Europeans permitted, and made necessary, a treatment that was different to that of other Western European states. For example, the accounts, sometimes apparently dispassionate discussion, sometimes conspiracy theories, used in Britain to blame French autocracy on Richelieu, or Mazarin, or on Louis XIV's passion for warfare, could not be so readily applied in Russia.

A certain amount of confusion was the result, as Russian news tended to be presented without as much explanation or background information as was put forward in the case of Western European news. Coupled with the natural tendency of Russian news to be confined to events in St. Petersburg and Moscow, this situation helped to ensure coverage that was not terribly sensitive to the degree to which Russian developments were affected by factors other than territorial expansion or factional strife. This was a failing, but it was a failing shared by the dispatches of foreign diplomats, and it was partly a consequence of the size of the country, the largest with which Western commentators came into regular contact, and also of the parlous nature of Russia's internal communications. Furthermore, the policies of the Russian government with which Britain had diplomatic relations did not appear to be dependent on the wishes of any section of the people. Thus, the political factions could be seen as ones that only needed to be understood in terms of the Russian court.

Opinions of the stability and effectiveness of the Russian government were of importance because of their relationship to the issue, and sometimes problem, of Russian military power—problem as seen by other powers. The information available as to the scale of this power made it clear that Russia could readily confront and defeat its various bordering countries, and that, indeed, repeatedly proved the case.[6] Moreover, it was apparent that Russia could project its power even further.

After the Great Northern War (1700–21), Russia fought Persia in 1722–23 but next engaged in a major war in 1733–35, the War of the Polish Succession, followed in 1736–39 by war with the Turks. Both received extensive coverage in the British press, whereas Peter the Great's campaign against Persia in 1722–23 did not attract comparable attention, although it was discussed. The coverage reflected the shaping, and continual reshaping, of a geography of interest and concern in light of British interests and priorities. These interests became more pressing because of greater concern about France from 1731 and, even more, 1733, concern that included invasion fears in both years. Better relations between Britain and Russia's ally Austria from 1731 were a major factor, as was the Anglo-Russian trade treaty of 1734, a treaty that was much welcomed in Britain. Trade permitted a reshaping of mental geographies (and also its strengthening): it was a key element in British public discussion.

The fate at the hands of Russia of the Poles, a nation notorious in Britain for the persecution of Protestants, with the Thorn massacre of 1724 receiving particular attention, aroused very little sympathy in Britain. Comment on the fall of Danzig (Gdansk) to a Russian siege army in 1734 was not marked by any extravagant trumpeting of a danger to European civilization. The *Daily Post Boy* of July 8, 1734, was particularly phlegmatic: "The Dantzickers, like other people, must suit their spirits to their circumstances, must cut their coat according to their cloth."

In contrast, the French consistently regarded the Russian successes as an appalling triumph of barbarism. There was much support in Paris for the Polish cause, whereas Britain was delighted by the humiliation of France's Baltic policy. This contrast looked to Catholic internationalism as well as to the long-standing French idea of Poland as an ally against hostile powers, variously Austria, Prussia, Russia, and Sweden. Differences over Poland between Britain and France remained the case later in the century and notably at the time of the First Partition of Poland at the hands of Austria, Prussia, and Russia in 1772: Britain proved less critical of the partition than France. The geopolitics of nearby antagonism in part dictated the response to more distant geopolitics. This factor helped explain why, in 1791, there was only limited support in Britain, in the Ochakov crisis, for war with Russia. The French notion of a *barrière de l'est* lacked traction.

Nevertheless, the crisis led the British government to gather information on the Black Sea region, acquiring reports from George Frederick Koehler, a German in the British artillery; Sir William Sidney Smith, a naval officer; William Lindsay, resident at Venice; and George Monro, in particular.[7] Smith's report on the defenses of Wallachia and the Danube was especially important. He had been sent on the secret mission by William, Lord Grenville, the foreign secretary.[8] Monro sent plans of the Dardanelles he had made and a chart of the Sea of Marmora.[9] Smith produced a sketch and soundings of the Danube delta.[10] The effort involved reflected a determined engagement with the need to gather geographical information.

Broader geopolitical considerations also encouraged an inclusion of Russia in Europe by British commentators. This proved a key instance of the extent to which the balance of power, the measure by which international relations were best explained, could, as already discussed, be variously defined and, in particular, had a dynamic quality in response to new threats and possibilities.[11] Russia was variously both as far as British commentators were concerned. More generally, the significance of the balance of power for political geography was strong. This was not only because it influenced British policy, but also as it conveyed apparent meaning to states and provided both a structural and a dynamic quality to the assessment of them.

Russian success in Poland in 1733–34 led to the possibility that, unlike in 1716–17, Russian forces would be employed further west against the French army and thus prevent the French exploiting successes in campaigning in Germany. This was a policy repeatedly pursued, as in 1748, 1799, and 1805, one that culminated in 1815 when the westward move of a large Russian army was the ultimate guarantor of Napoleon's failure whatever happened at Waterloo. That autumn, 150,000 Russian troops were reviewed at Châlons-sur-Marne, near the modern Euro Disney. Moreover, this westward power projection was very much one sought by Britain between 1734 and 1755 and from the 1793 to 1815 and, therefore, served as a way to present a strong positive account of Russia.

The immediacy of this need took precedence over questions about the nature of Russia as a political system. On October 28, 1734, the *Daily Post Boy* asked, "Must Christendom always owes its safety to the North? And must Russia come now, and save it from slavery, as the Polanders once did under the brave Sobieski?" This was a politically charged comparison with the relief of Vienna from Turkish siege in 1683, one that readers were expected to understand.

In threatening a potentially benign (and, earlier, apparently hostile) outcome, anti-Russian international policies were given a comparison with the attempts by the "Old Russ" to turn Russia away from Europe and to reverse the policies of Peter the Great. Both for the press and for Western diplomats, this drive was encapsulated by the attempt to return the capital to Moscow, which was very much seen as a linked set in political geography. The *British Journal* of March 21, 1730, claimed that the state of Anglo-Russian commerce depended on the policy of the new czarina (Anna) and on whether the capital was moved to Moscow. The writer argued that if so, Russia would lose control of its Baltic provinces, which, indeed, had only been recently conquered from Sweden, and continued:

> was the city of Petersburg swallowed up in the sea, as is not unlikely to be its fate in a few years; and were the ports of Riga, Narva, Tallinn and Viborg lost to the Russians and become Swedish again, as they were before, yet we should

never want for hemp, potash, Russian leather, and other valuable imports from thence, as we had them before, when those towns were in the hands of the Swedes.

But the inland trade of Russia for the consumption of British manufactures, that will never be restored, unless the Empire of Russia rouses itself from under the lethargic slumber, which is now fallen into; their furred gowns and long petticoats will return upon them, and all the sordid affectation of a singularity from all the world, which made them so truly contemptible before, will do the like again, and where shall our trade be carried on?

The theme of a possible Russian return to barbarism was a common one. Each change of monarch led to such comments, they reflected a genuine belief in the mutability of Russian power and of the achievements of Peter the Great, and the more general conviction that power was not fixed and that empires in particular rose and fell. This attitude toward Russia was particularly pronounced up to, and including, the early 1740s, but less pronounced after Czarina Elizabeth gained power in 1741. She provided a welcome note of political continuity until her death in 1762. In practice, the capital remained in St. Petersburg and this helped guarantee the Western focus of Russian politics and elite culture. The relationship between the location of the capital and general Russian westernization was a given as far as Western commentators were concerned. In this, there was nothing distinctive to British views.

Earlier in the century, the rise of Russia, and the consequent reshaping of Europe, had not been accepted as permanent. Russia, indeed, tended to be viewed as an especially unstable part of a dangerously unstable system. The latter was such that the *Hyp Doctor*, a London newspaper, with a comparison resonant for the period, argued, on October 8, 1734, "states and kingdoms have their periods of duration, their bounds of existence; they are infants, young, in manhood, grow old, decay and die, like the mortals that compose those fleeting societies." The sense of stability was one that was essentially addressed in the early 1740s, when Russia faced and overcame a serious crisis compounded of domestic problems and foreign attack, the latter by Sweden. There was also a greater awareness and recognition of Russian attainments and importance,[12] as well as the publication of travel accounts by merchants and a diplomat: James Spilman's *Journey through Russia into Persia* (1742), Jonas Hanway's *Historical Account of the British Trade over the Caspian Sea* (1753), and Charles Whitworth's *Account of Russia, as It Was in the Year 1710* (1758).

Russia proved a key item when Edward Gibbon, in his *The History of the Decline and Fall of the Roman Empire* (1776-88), addressed the question of whether Europe could fall anew to the attacks of "barbarians" from Central Asia, as classical Rome had done. This was but one instance of Gibbon's play with counterfactuals (what ifs?), as in his famous passage about Islam advancing northward in Western Europe but for Charles Martel's victory over the Moors at Tours in 732, although Gibbon was willing to be sympathetic about Islam.[13]

Counterfactualism offered not only a way to rethink history but also to reshape the relationship between history and geography, as well as indicating the contingent character of history (and thus political geography) in the present and future or the limits to that character. The "barbarian" assault question was fundamental for the *Decline and Fall* as it related centrally to the issue of development in world history and, in particular, whether cyclical patterns of growth and decline, or rise and fall, had been overcome, and if so, how and why. This issue was a potential major qualification to Enlightenment optimism and to the project of finding purpose in history. The latter did not necessarily preclude the idea of that purpose being an aspect of a divine plan, but that interpretation was not to the fore in terms of most specific developments.

Gibbon answered his question of whether Europe could fall again in the affirmative. In part, he did so by arguing that Russian westernization under Peter the Great ensured that there was a new barrier to "barbarian" advance into Europe. In Gibbon's view, civilization had led to science and a process of invention, application, and diffusion, such that "cannon and fortification now form an impregnable barrier against the Tartar horse."[14] In short, the political geography of Eurasia had fundamentally changed and very much for the better. There was a linkage with progress in his account but also with British views on the need to redress the risks of a French-dominated Europe, views that repeatedly left much space for cooperation with Russia. As a result, despite some ministerial interest, the British government did not respond positively to French approaches in 1772-23 to cooperate in opposing the First Partition of Poland and/or Russian pressure on Sweden.[15]

Gibbon offered another consolation, one in which geography and history were combined: the Europeans' "easy victories over the savages of the new world" ensured that in the unlikely event of civilization collapsing in Europe before new barbarian inroads, it would be sustained "in the American world."[16] This very much took the theme of civilizational progress forward on the global scale and provided a way to bring the future into the pattern. Incorporating North America offered another way to establish the prominence of British political culture, on the global scale, or, more basically, its ability to survive decline. This was a very different welcoming of North America to that offered by British sympathizers with the cause of American independence. What, however, both had in common was a willingness to adapt the conventional space of geographical attention to the possibilities offered by North America. This reflected a strong sense that the European world did not stop at the Atlantic. This sense was very different to the acceptance of Russia as part of that world because there was a more positive view of North America. The latter was a consequence of its Britishness, and notably the political culture there. Thus, as Gibbon suggested, and in his mention both of Russia and of America, Europe was a matter of values, and not a set geographical space. This approach also reflected the open frontiers and expanding territory of both, a situation that contrasted with that in Western Europe.

FRENCH REVOLUTION

Another, and far-more-unexpected novelty, ironically, for Gibbon's readers, was the "barbarism" in Western Europe seen with the aftermath of the outbreak of the French Revolution as it became increasingly radical and notably from 1791. The varied response to the revolution offered new geographies of concern, commitment, and action, as well as the revival of the "Western question," the issue of dominance in Western Europe which had been in abeyance since the Peace of Aix-la-Chapelle of 1748 and the subsequent diplomatic reconfigurations of the 1750s. Agreements between Austria and France, and Austria and Spain had frozen political space, leaving issues in Italy or the Rhineland to be settled peacefully or placed in abeyance. When conflict did break out involving Austria, notably the War of the Bavarian Succession with Prussia in 1778–79 and rebellion in the Austrian Netherlands in 1787, France did not intervene. As a result, the extent to which French expansion triggered British concerns about European political geography had ceased to be a factor.

The situation changed with the French Revolution. To radicals, French, British, and others, a new international order appeared a prospect, indeed an imminent one. To conservatives, most prominently Edmund Burke, there was a need to intervene in France in order to destroy a threatening canker in the European world. This was a political geography outlined in his *Reflections on the Revolution* (1790). In contrast, the government of William Pitt the Younger sought to define a more cautious response. This was essentially one of nonintervention, but that was tested as France advanced new principles about international relations and then, in 1792, appeared willing to put them into effect. By that time, the governmental policy was one of a measured, peaceful opposition to French policy, one that aimed to limit French expansionism without being committed to the overthrow of the new republic—in short, containment, not political reaction.

Claims over the role of ideology in international relations directly related to the possibility of transforming previous geopolitical realities. Thus, in the House of Commons on April 15, 1791, at a time of contention over a deteriorating situation with Russia and the apparent imminence of war with Britain, Charles James Fox, the leader of the opposition Whigs in the House of Commons, told the House that the French Revolution had totally changed Britain's international situation but in a benign fashion: "He had been a strenuous advocate for the balance of power, while France was that intriguing, restless nation which she had formerly proved. Now, that the situation of France was altered, that she had erected a government, from which neither insult nor injustice was to be dreaded by her neighbours, he was extremely indifferent concerning the balance. . . . No man could say that Russia was the successor of France in this respect."[17]

To Burke, on the other hand, space was, as it were, collapsed because the ideological toxin of revolutionary France was revolution, not France. Thus, according to Burke, Britain was at risk irrespective of the precise territorial advance of revolutionary France, and revolution in France was very different to that earlier in the United States or, indeed, in Britain in 1688. The key element to Burke was neither geography nor history but ideology. In September 1792, Burke wrote to James, 1st Earl of Malmesbury, a senior former diplomat, indeed the James Harris who had briefed the Cabinet with a map in 1787 (see chapter 1): "The English assassins of the Jacobin faction are working hard to corrupt the public mind in favour of their brother murderers in France—and not *one* person, either on the part of government, or opposition, makes the slightest effort, of any kinds, to prevent the ill effects of these poisons. I am, I confess, sick at heart from all horrors and perfectly disgusted with the conduct or rather no conduct of both parties, at a time when neutrality does not nor cannot produce neutral effects."[18]

At one level, geopolitics had been transformed as a result of France pushing the nation to the fore in identity and decision making, becoming a republic in 1792 and consciously ending dynastic considerations. The habitual bases of legitimate rule in territory, whether inherited or conquered, were to be renounced by revolutionary France in favor, instead, of popular will and the ideology of "liberation," which provided potent rationales for control and transformation.[19] In practice, specific geographical-legal factors were also to play a key role. In particular, the French reopening of the navigation of the River Scheldt in defiance of international agreements and the French threat to the neutrality of the Netherlands became crucial issues for Britain in the winter of 1792–93: the closure of the Scheldt, which the French saw as unnatural, was designed to benefit Amsterdam at the expense of Antwerp (which sits on the Scheldt) and was therefore crucial to Dutch interests. The Dutch, moreover, were allies of Britain. These issues helped lead to the final breakdown in relations.

The resulting outbreak of war with France in early 1793 both greatly affected the tourism already disrupted by the revolution[20] and encouraged a stronger interest in Continental news. Indeed, faced with a wealth of material, newspapers frequently referred to having to choose what material to insert. The *Courier*, a leading London paper, in its issue of January 6, 1795, noted, "We have received a great number of letters, and of Dutch, German, and French papers, of which the extreme length of the debate in the House of Commons prevents us at present from entering into detail." In addition, the Terror created lasting images of horror for the benefit of British caricaturists.[21]

Reporting the war created problems for the press similar to those in earlier conflicts with France but with the additional problem that the conflict rapidly became wide ranging. In contrast to the War of American Independence, when, in Europe, fighting was restricted to Gibraltar and at sea, there was now widespread fighting on the Continent. In contrast to the Seven Years' War, there was conflict in Italy and the Low Countries.

Furthermore, the French Revolutionary War was particularly intense, lengthy, and wide ranging and also more unsuccessful for Britain on the Continent than any since the last stages of the Hundred Years' War in the mid-fifteenth century.

The use of foreign correspondents, mostly British correspondents abroad, was very rare. Most foreign news came from traditional sources: the foreign press and the British government, the latter being particularly important for transoceanic campaigning. Rather than seeking the news themselves, newspapers continued to be derivative, competing for primacy in government information, or struggling to obtain copies of the French papers as speedily as possible. Newspapers remained totally dependent on the Continental mails, with concomitant problems of delayed information and uncertain news. Yet, there was less disagreement about what had happened than in the case of more distant America during the War of Independence.

Moreover, the central geopolitical concern remained. Should Britain pursue regime change, as Burke wanted, or simply firm containment, as Pitt sought, or cooperation with France of some type, as the radicals wished? This was a debate fully reflected in the press and one that linked domestic and foreign news and that encouraged knowledge of political geography. As the government remained in power and set the agenda, the outcome, containment, was scarcely surprising.

The major development occurred, instead, due to the threatening expansion of French military power. Whereas, in 1792–93, British concern had focused on the Low Countries and France's eastern border, by 1796–97 attention had switched to Italy, where Napoleon was dramatically successful at the expense of Austria, then, in 1798–99, to Egypt and the Middle East, where he was campaigning, and, in 1800, back to Italy, where Napoleon again defeated the Austrians. Each sphere and stage of the war had to be covered by the press and thus understood by its readers. There were problems with obtaining and verifying news. Wellington won a great victory at Salamanca in Spain on July 22, 1812. On August 3, the *Times* reported that dispatches bringing the news of a victory had reached Falmouth, the major port in Cornwall and the closest to Spain and Portugal, but that no confirmation or details were available. Two days later, the paper could offer a fuller report, but the official dispatches did not arrive until the morning of August 16.

Britain was left isolated in 1801 when Austria was forced to peace, a situation that led to the unsatisfactory Anglo-French Peace of Amiens of 1802. This situation was best understood in light of a knowledge of political geography. In 1800, George Canning wrote to his successor as Undersecretary in the Foreign Office, about French campaigning in Italy: "What do you think of the Italian news? And what consolation does Pitt point out after looking over the map in the corner of his room by the door?"[22] The reference to the map is instructive.

As war news came to the fore from 1793, the French Revolution, while still an ideological issue, was increasingly subsumed, for many British commentators, within the established pattern of conflict with France or, at least, interpreted in these terms. This pattern had been somewhat in abeyance as the war of 1778–83 had not been waged on the Continent, while, in 1756–63, French forces had not operated in Italy or the Low Countries but, instead, in Germany. As a result, there was, in the 1790s, a recurrence in political geography, one reminiscent of rivalry with Louis XIV. This came alongside an ideological novelty in the face of the French Revolution, albeit an ideological rift that was to be lessened under Napoleon. With his armies in Vienna in 1805, Berlin in 1806, Madrid in 1808, and Moscow in 1812, he posed an even greater geopolitical threat but did not match the ideological challenge of the revolutionaries he overthrew in 1799. Nevertheless, the intractability of the war and the extent to which the French system encompassed most of Europe helped encourage "an extraordinary chauvinism in the British."[23] At the same time, there were distinct processes of modernization, industrialization, and politicization in Britain.[24] They were linked to the war but also separate.

MAPPING AND WAR

There were intimations of new moves in warfare, moves that might have entailed novel needs of, and means for, mapping. In particular, manned balloon flight began in 1783, in France, with Britain following rapidly; and, in the 1790s, the French used reconnaissance balloons, notably at the Battle of Fleurus south of Brussels (1794). However, this innovation was not responsible for French success and was abandoned after Napoleon seized power in 1799. In large part, this was due to the time it took to inflate the balloons and the impossibility of controlling them. As with submarines and semaphores, it was the potential for the future that was notable, and not the situation in the 1790s.

One of the most lasting legacies of the war was the Ordnance Survey in Britain. The Board of Ordnance, the government department responsible for the artillery, was given responsibility for mapping in order to help cope with a possible French invasion, which, indeed, was planned. This process predated the French Revolutionary and Napoleonic Wars, although it was greatly encouraged by them. The Trigonometrical, later called Ordnance, Survey—the basis of the detailed maps of Britain to this day—began in 1791, although it continued triangulation work first begun in 1784 for peaceful purposes in order to link the observatories of London and Paris. The Corps of Royal Military Surveyors and Draughtsmen was founded in 1791, and by 1795, they had completed a double chain of triangles from London to Land's End in Cornwall. A one-inch-to-the-mile map of Kent, a key invasion area on the south coast, was published in 1801. Indeed, in 1804–5, French troops were deployed by Napoleon in northern France, ready to invade southern England as soon as naval superiority in the Channel could be obtained. In the event, the French were thwarted by the British navy.

After 1801, the surveyors moved to the southwest of England, another potential invasion area, which was covered by about 1810. Mapmaking was significant as part of the infrastructure of defense, and this offered a major impetus to the remapping of provincial England,[25] as had not been the case to the same degree in the sixteenth century. The French Revolutionary and Napoleonic Wars also encouraged the acquisition and use of other aspects of spatial information, as in the detailed feasibility study carried out for the East India Company in 1796 concerning the best location for a military depot in southern England.[26]

There was a considerable emphasis in the mapping of the period on depicting "strong ground": terrain that could play a role in operations. This emphasis reflected the importance of relief and slopes, not only to help or impede advances, by infantry and cavalry, but also for determining the sightlines of cannon and at a time when they had to focus on direct, not indirect, fire: only howitzers and mortars employed the latter and their range was less. Artillery became more important in field operations from the 1790s as the major improvements made in the French artillery from the 1760s, notably in response to failure in the Seven Years' War (1756–63), affected campaigning in Europe. Napoleon in particular made adroit use of artillery, which he massed to that end. Direct fire remained the key element for cannon, ensuring that it was necessary to understand terrain, a point exemplified by the Duke of Wellington's repeated success in deploying on reverse slopes where his infantry was protected from such fire, notably at Waterloo.

The mapping of topography was to be more common and more precise by the late nineteenth century, by when the surveying and mapping of height had improved, not least with the use of contours. Nevertheless, there were useful devices prior to that. One such was the example of the use of numbers to indicate the relative height of the ground. Important to locating artillery, and to sheltering infantry and cavalry, this technique, known as "relative command," was taught by François Jarry, a French émigré (refugee) who became topographical instructor at the newly established British Royal Military College in 1799. Jarry influenced the teaching of reconnaissance to the Royal Engineers, and this helped Wellington as he planned in 1815 how best to respond to a French invasion of Belgium. Earlier, Wellington had used a mobile lithographic printing press in the Peninsular War (in Portugal and Spain) in 1808–13 in order to produce maps.

British officers found it helpful to have maps and referred to them in their correspondence. They also assumed that the public was using maps to follow the campaigning. Captain John Hill, an infantry officer, serving in the expedition to Holland in 1799, wrote to his father, "I am sorry you should have lost your maps of Holland as they were on a larger scale than any I have seen, though old, would have shown you every inch of the country." In 1813, he wrote to his mother from the Peninsula: "There is a new and very highly finished map of Portugal published that will show you the bearings of the sierras which are various."[27] This map clarified the options available if invading Portugal from Spain and vice versa.

CONCLUSIONS

The French Revolution had therefore led to particular military demands and responses focused on mapping. These were essentially operational and tactical in character, rather like those stemming from the War of American

Independence. However, in each case, there were strategic considerations that were closely linked to geopolitics, with the latter understood both as geographic and as political. The latter was the key element as it was the new political challenges that forced a greater degree and range of engagement, whether the dispatch of a large British army to New York in 1776 or of another to Egypt in 1801. Each entailed particular and unprecedented needs for geographic information. Thus, the narrative for the search for, and use of, geographic information that is adopted here is different to that offered in chapter 1. The emphasis here is on urgent problems, rather than on a quest for information almost for its own sake, although that element should not be exaggerated when considering exploration.

The topic, moreover, can be reconceptualized in order to lessen this apparent contrast. The key similarity is that of responding to circumstances, with the latter providing very different contexts for the use of, and need for, power. In the 1760s and early 1770s, there was no challenge for Britain comparable to what was to follow, and Britain was not at war with other European powers between 1763 and 1778. As a result, there was no immediate need for geographical data for military purposes, although there was a more general concern for the preparedness that might be possible and permitted in the fiscal aftermath of the Seven Years' War. This concern helped lead to a determination to improve this aftermath, a determination that led to the Stamp Act crisis of 1765. That was an aspect of preparedness that was very different in character to the naval voyages to the Pacific, but the context was similar. Against a background of sustained fears about France and Spain, fears that drew on their naval preparations and on a series of crises, there was a strong commitment to a form of geopolitical "improvement," one that was governmental, political, and military.

This was different to the "improvements" pursued by landowners or turnpikers, but there was a similar sense that the protection of position required action and a related reluctance to accept an unchanging situation. This attitude became more marked in Britain from midcentury, although it did not begin them, and there had been important reform impulses after the "Glorious Revolution." The possibilities and problems of the transoceanic world were particularly to the fore from the 1760s, but as this chapter has indicated, this world was in part to be understood as an aspect of the dynamic power politics of the competitive European state system.

Notes

1. Verses 15 and 16, Hertford, Hertford Record Office, Panshanger Manuscripts, papers of First Earl Cowper, Miscellaneous Items, D/EPF 240.
2. See, for example, *Post Man*, June 24, 1727.
3. See, for example, *Post Man*, June 22, 1727.
4. For inaccurate newspaper reports from St. Petersburg, BL. Add. 33540 fol. 240.
5. R. Drayton, "Science and the European Empires," *Journal of Imperial and Commonwealth History* 23 (1995): 503–11.
6. J. Black, "Anglo-Russian Relations 1714-1750: A Note on Sources," in J. M. Hartley, ed., *The Study of Russian History from British Archival Sources* (London, 1986), 67–87.
7. Koehler to James Bland Burges, Under Secretary in Foreign Office, September 22, October 5, 1791, March 23, April 21, 1792, Koehler memorandum, Lindsay report, 1791, Monro memorandum, Bod. BB. 36 fols 94–160, 41 fols 38–83, 58, pp. 1–43, 67, pp. 1–41; Koehler to Burges, January 10, 1793, Smith to Burges, February 22, 1793, NA. FO. 78, 14 fols 7, 14. On Koehler's appointment, Charles, 3rd Duke of Richmond, Master-General of the Ordnance, to William, Lord Grenville, Foreign Secretary, January 25, 1791, BL. Add. 58937 fol. 130.
8. Grenville to Smith, June 19, 1792, Bod. BB. 41 fols 6–8.
9. Bod. BB. 52 fols 104–6.
10. Bod. BB. 41 fol. 73.
11. J. Black, "The Theory of the Balance of Power in the First Half of the Eighteenth Century: A Note on Sources," *Review of International Studies* 9 (1983): 55–61.
12. A. G. Cross, "British Knowledge of Russian Culture (1698–1801)," *Canadian-American Slavic Studies* 13 (1979): 412.
13. G. Fowden, "Gibbon on Islam," *English Historical Review* 131 (2010): 261–92, esp. 291–92.
14. Gibbon, *Decline and Fall*, edited by J. B. Bury: IV, 167.
15. C. Brooks, "British Political Culture and the Dismemberment of States: Britain and the First Partition of Poland 1762–1772," *Parliaments, Estates, and Representation* 13 (1993): 51–64.
16. Gibbon, *Decline and Fall*, IV, 166.
17. *Cobbett*, 29: 247–48.
18. Burke to Malmesbury, September 10, [1792], Winchester, Hampshire County Record Office, Malmesbury papers, vol. 145.
19. D. A. Bell, *The Cult of the Nation in France: Inventing Nationalism, 1680–1800* (Cambridge, MA, 2001).
20. S. Bending and S. Byrave, eds., *Women's Travel Writings in Revolutionary France* (London, 2007). J. Black, *The British Abroad: The Grand Tour in the Eighteenth Century* (Stroud, 1992), 306–25.
21. D. Bindman, "The War of Images: British Caricatures of the French Revolution," *Franco-British Studies* 6 (1988): 58.
22. Canning to John Hookham Frere, June 20, 1800, BL. Add. 38833.
23. A. D. Harvey, "European Attitudes to Britain during the French Revolutionary and Napoleonic Era," *History* 63 (1978): 361.
24. H. Barker and D. Vincent, *Language, Print and Electoral Politics, 1790–1832: Newcastle-under-Lyme Broadsides* (Woodbridge, UK, 2001).

25. K. Barker and R. Kain, eds., *Maps and History in South-West England* (Exeter, UK, 1991).

26. J. H. Thomas, "Housing East India Company Troops in the 1790s: A Forgotten Survey," *Archives* 26 (2001): 123–33.

27. Hill to father, September 23, 1799, Hill to mother, March 24, 1813, Hill papers, private hands.

7

Responding to the Transoceanic World

MUCH OF THE maritime globe, more recently termed the "water planet,"[1] and certainly the configuration of the Atlantic world and much of the Indian Ocean, and an understanding of parts of the Pacific, was largely known to Europeans by 1700. However, in the eighteenth century, there was not only more knowledge about the distant world, a topic discussed in chapter 1, but also a stronger interest in, and understanding of, its significance for Europe, a significance linked to the role of this distant world in both geopolitics and in long-range trading networks.[2] This appreciation led to greater interest in the transoceanic world but also underlined the relevance of the problems involved in trying to understand this world and in assessing the importance of developments there. Indeed, the frame of reference for political discussion was not restricted to places in the Western world. George, Lord Lyttelton's *Letters from a Persian in England, to His Friend at Ispahan* (1735), which included a bitter attack on Sir Robert Walpole, one by an opposition Whig on a government one, closed with a suggestion that the threats to freedom were global in their span: "if slavery is to be endured, where is the man that would not rather choose it, under the warm sun of Agra [in India] or Ispahan [the capital of Persia], than in the northern climate and barren soil of England?" The journalist and man of letters Oliver Goldsmith used a fictional wise Chinaman, Lien Chi Altangi, in his periodical *The Citizen of the World* (1762).

GEOGRAPHY AND DEEP HISTORY

As an aspect of the time-space continuum that was so important to the significance of geography, there was also a "deep history" of places in international relations as well, one very much linked to political controversy and to the course of events. Classic instances of such places included Dunkirk, Minorca, Ostend, and Louisbourg. The significance of places in this "deep history" shifted for Britain toward the transoceanic world. For example, captured from France in 1745, Louisbourg, on Cape Breton Island, France's major base on the Atlantic coast of Canada, was returned to France under the subsequent peace treaty of Aix-la-Chapelle of 1748. This return caused outrage in New England, whose militia had played a key role in its capture, and also among opposition political circles in Britain, both genuinely angry and looking for an issue. Porto Bello and Cartagena, Caribbean fortresses of the Spanish empire, also became part of this "deep history," as a consequence of the role they played in campaigning against Spain in 1739 and 1741, respectively: British forces had succeeded in the first case, ensuring the war with Spain began on a triumphalist note, and failed abysmally in the second helping to focus criticism of the Walpole ministry.

Claims of betrayal about Louisbourg contributed to the paranoia in New England about the British government. These claims were seen more clearly from 1763, albeit in a very different context linked to tax policy. This unjustified paranoia in 1748 reflected the geography of political concern because in New England there was a lack of engagement with the wider course of the war and the linked geopolitics of the British government, one similar to that of Australia in World War II. The return of Louisbourg was as part of a peace treaty largely focused on the status quo ante bellum, or return to the prewar situation. However disadvantageous for New England, this basis involved France returning its wartime gains: Madras (Chennai) in India, as well as much of modern Belgium and two major fortresses in the modern Netherlands: Bergen-op-Zoom and Maastricht. These latter French gains of 1745–48 represented a threat to the British alliance system and to British security. Discussion of the trade-off, and by the public as well as ministers, involved the need to understand political geography but also underlined the problems of establishing value and discussing policy in such cases. These issues were to recur with the trade-offs in subsequent peace treaties, notably in 1763 and 1802: the Peace of Paris and the Peace of Amiens.

THE BRITISH PRESS AND EMPIRE

The British reading of transoceanic lands was an aspect of a wider process of discussion of information and opinion within the British world as a whole. This was the case with correspondence, the culture of print, and, indeed, the information systems and communication routes that were crucial to imperial government.[3] Moreover, the development of English-language newspapers in the British Empire indicated the extent to which an active press was an aspect of British civilization. This press very much helped to create links and to define the identity of a British world. The identity both sought to convey a sense of solidity and stability and yet also proved fluid in terms of the people included (and on what terms), and with reference to the relationships between the constituent parts. These points were also pertinent for the French, Spanish, and Dutch Atlantics. However, compared with the French and Spaniards, the British proved exceptionally open to those of different peoples and regions. The identity of a British world was one of the most significant geographical elements of the period, that, in particular, of the British Atlantic, for, although they existed, newspaper links were weaker in the world of the East India Company and, indeed, remained so.

English news serials were shipped across the Atlantic in the seventeenth century, while sermons were reprinted in America. As in the British Isles, the situation changed radically after the Glorious Revolution of 1688–89. In 1690, an unlicensed, and swiftly suppressed, newspaper, *Publick Occurrences Foreign and Domestic*, had been published in Boston, a city whose population had a high rate of literacy and who were highly politicized. As in Britain, the situation changed when prepublication censorship was abandoned with the lapsing of the Licensing Act in 1695. In 1704, appeared the *Boston News-Letter*, the first regular newspaper in the Thirteen Colonies published by authority. It was followed in 1719 by the *Boston Gazette* and by Philadelphia's *Weekly Mercury*.[4] Separation, between Britain and its colonies, was not the major theme. Instead, the colonial press was to be a buoyant aspect of the eighteenth-century British press, dependent on it for staff and equipment and, increasingly, on the pattern of news between England, Scotland, and Ireland,[5] exchanged information with it, although news flows within the colonial world were also highly significant. War with France and Spain increased identity with Britain.[6]

So also with other forms of literature. After the Glorious Revolution, sermons were much more widely published in the colonies. These included sermons of major figures in Britain, such as Tillotson and Hoadly. Published in London, their sermons were reprinted soon after in Boston and Philadelphia.

With their large population of white settlers, their wealth, and their "empowerment,"[7] the North American colonies provided both readers and also copy for British newspapers. In 1735, the *London Journal*, one of the leading London newspapers, carried colonial items under a heading "News from the Plantations," announcing, on August 23, that "the British Colonies are of so much importance to the trade and commerce of Great Britain that we shall continue . . . to make a separate article." Moreover, "Plantation News" was a heading employed in a number of British newspapers and of a variety of types, including the *Newcastle Courant* and the *Penny London Morning Advertiser* in the 1740s. On February 26, 1732, the *Weekly Register* carried a "Letter from a merchant in Jamaica to his friend at London" about competition from the French colony of Saint-Domingue.

The development of a colonial press greatly affected the geography of British news space, although it did not transform the newspapers in Britain. The colonial press provided a source for items of news that was as regular and predictable as the increasingly regular and predictable transoceanic sailings that carried the news. The colonial press reduced the significance of information provided by personal letters, information that, while valuable, had a different authority and was less regular and predictable. As an alternative, however, *Felix Farley's Bristol Journal* announced in 1747 that it had engaged Boston and Philadelphia correspondents, which was a means and announcement of trying to claim particular authority to itself. The developing transoceanic pattern corresponded to the news geography of the British Isles and, notably, the improvement in the network of provincial newspapers and their value for the London press. By the 1780s, the frequency of items in the British press with acknowledgment to transoceanic newspapers, including the distant *Calcutta Gazette*, had markedly increased. This was a process encouraged by the range of British activity.

The intensification of news sources can be readily seen in the case of the West Indies, a key area of the empire and one with many British settlers, although with far more slaves than elsewhere, slaves who had very little access to formal education and only rarely access to newspapers. Newspapers began on Jamaica, Britain's largest colony in the West Indies, with the *Weekly Jamaica Courant* (1718).[8] The number of towns on the island supporting a newspaper increased with the *St. Jago Intelligencer* (1756) and the *Cornwall Chronicle* from Montego Bay (1773), and with the foundation of newspapers at Savanna-la-Mer (1788) and Falmouth (1791). Other British Caribbean colonies acquired their first newspapers later in the century than Jamaica. The *Barbados Gazette* (1738) was followed by the *St. Christopher Gazette* (1765), the *Bermuda Gazette* (1784), and the *Bahama Gazette* (1784). Moreover, as in Britain, competing titles developed in existing centers, as with the *Barbados Mercury* (1762) and the *St. George's Chronicle and New Grenada Gazette* (1789).

The need for newspapers, and the extent to which they were an expression of the British world, were shown by the launching of newspapers in newly conquered colonies, as with the *St. Lucia Gazette* (1780), the *Royal Essequebo and Demerary Gazette* (1796) in the Guianas in South America, the *Trinidad Weekly Courant* (1800), and the *Cape Town Gazette, and African Advertiser* (1800) after they had been seized from France, the Dutch, Spain, and the Dutch, respectively. These and other newspapers provided war news for British papers, the *St. Lucia Gazette* doing so for the *Leeds Intelligencer* of July 24, 1781.

The empire was a term that was capable, both to contemporaries and subsequently,[9] of a range of meanings and resonances and with variations according to place and social rank.[10] The empire was a matter not only of curiosity but also a framework for intellectual speculation and power politics, as well as for cultural engagement which included competing historical references.[11] Indeed, the empire was both the means of such cultural interaction and its subject. The empire was only under state control to a point, and then largely in particular places. With regard to the latter, there were crucial sites and conjunctures in imperial power politics, notably the North American colonies, and, more particularly their ports, in 1763–75 as the Stamp Act led to a series of crises. As an important aspect of these sites and means, the circulation of information was a facet of the political contention. On the side of radicals, printers and their "Patriot" allies criticized the post office as an oppressive imperial abuse limiting the free circulation of news and correspondence. American newspapers increasingly moved from offering an imperial vision to one that had a more clearly American concern.[12]

THE WAR OF AMERICAN INDEPENDENCE

The American Revolution or War of Independence (1775–83) created both stronger demand for news and comment and more problems for those providing information. The British world and its potent sense of community was split in a civil war in which competing sympathies did not lead to clear geographical blocs, despite the partisan attempts to suggest that they did, although the ability to express beliefs and sympathies was limited by political pressures.[13]

Within Britain, there was much coverage of differences there over how to respond to the American crisis. This interest encouraged reporting of the configuration of domestic criticism of the ministry, as with the *Leeds Mercury* of October 31, 1775, which carried, under a Leeds byline, an account of a general meeting in Newcastle, a major provincial center, over the American crisis. In other words, this was not an item of news that came via the London press. Instead, the ascendancy of the latter over the national geographies of news, one already affected by the growing sophistication of the provincial press, was challenged with the War of Independence, both in the Atlantic world and within Britain. The imperial geography of news was transformed.

The most clear-cut challenge took the form of the foundation of "Patriot" newspapers in the American colonies, the dissemination of their news, and moves in the colonies against the circulation of British newspapers. These changes defied, circumvented, and overcame the authority of British-based and -oriented institutions and opinions.

However, the situation was more complex, at least in so far as the circulation of news was concerned, not least because, certainly initially, the

"Patriot" press drew on criticism of the ministry from within Britain, including in the British press. Indeed, General Thomas Gage, the commander in chief in North America, complained to Viscount Barrington, the secretary at war, in 1772: "Your papers are stuffed with infamous paragraphs which the American printers, especially those of Boston, seldom fail to copy with American additions." Two years later, Gage added from Boston, where he was based, "The seditious here have raised a flame in every colony which your speeches, writings, and protests in England have greatly encouraged."[14] In this, Gage captured the degree to which the American crisis was an aspect of civil struggle within the empire and that information was regarded as part of the process. He also reflected a military viewpoint that does not generally receive much attention.

This civil struggle can be differently "mapped" or located, for the American Revolution (or War of Independence) involved tensions between different "kinds of spaces," or geographical imaginations. In a fascinating version of the later Turner thesis on the American frontier, these spaces and tensions have been presented as the oceanically oriented British Atlantic and, in contrast, the settler empire of the "American Frontier." The intermediate eastern seaboard is presented as providing a crucial sphere of tension and therefore is brought to the fore. It has been suggested that, although in the seventeenth century, English merchants and proprietors had begun the colonization of New England, the Chesapeake, and the Carolina low country, they had subsequently lost control over the process of settlement to the colonists. This loss has been attributed to structural geographical factors, rather than to political ones. In particular, it has been claimed that the English merchants and proprietors were defeated by the enormous availability of agricultural land and the related difficulty of commanding immigrant labor, notably indentured workers from England. As a result, more autonomous economies had developed in North America. Moreover, the spaces of the American interior provided colonial elites with a "much greater geographic context in which to maneuver than existed on the islands of the British Atlantic"—for example, Jamaica—with such maneuver seen as a way to limit the power of the British state.[15]

There are problems with such a reading, notably that it is too easy to read from geography to an outcome in a somewhat deterministic fashion. It is necessary, in particular, to remember that the frontier had a variety of meanings and locations.[16] Moreover, the economies of the interior were heavily dependent on transoceanic politics and economics in the shape of fighting for, and securing, trade routes and, therefore, seeking supplies. Both in colonial times and subsequently, trans-Appalachia was linked to the Atlantic world by, and through, America.[17] Separately, if there is to be a focus on geography and causation, then the latter can be traced to more than one process and outcome. For example, rather than a colonial economy, there were colonial economies linked more closely with London than with one another. South Carolina and Massachusetts, for example, had relatively little trade with each other.[18]

Yet, it is also necessary to understand the major role of political geography and its particular significance for imagining and defining new political entities, both as states and as communities. It may be going too far to claim that "the fracturing of empire was along structural faults embedded in the continent's evolving human geography,"[19] but nevertheless, these faults were significant, and it is pertinent to assess what meaning they had to contemporaries. Although there were also tensions in the West Indies over government policy, notably, as in North America, strong opposition to the Stamp Act of 1763, there was no rebellion in these colonies. In part, this was due to a dependence by the colonies on the British state arising both from the presence of large numbers of slaves and from the threat from nearby French and Spanish colonies. These elements introduce significant aspects of geopolitics and "space," especially the extent to which the latter was demographically constructed and also the role of strategic competition.

The American crisis led to a marked increase in news about America, and this increase can be seen in Britain, Continental Europe, and the American colonies themselves. Due to the importance of the crisis and the character of the British news world, which was independent, entrepreneurial, competitive, and extensive, this crisis meant that there was considerable demand, both for news as a whole and for distinctive news items. In its issue of November 24, 1774, the *Cumberland Pacquet* stressed the particular quality of its American reporting, while focusing this reporting on access to American newspapers: "A respectable merchant in this town has favoured us with several American newspapers, and particularly the *Boston Gazette, Pennsylvania Journal, Massachusetts Gazette*, and the *Virginia Gazette*." In short, a new Anglo-American news world was developing or being strengthened, even as the political link was broken, with the two processes being closely linked.[20]

War itself increased the channels of information. Thus, the *Leeds Mercury*, a major provincial newspaper, produced in an English manufacturing center that was not on the coast, in late 1775 printed items derived from a letter received by a gentleman at Berwick-on-Tweed from his friend at Boston (July 18); a letter from Boston to someone at Halifax, Yorkshire, another nearby manufacturing center (August 1); a ship from Boston arriving at Liverpool (September 19); a letter from a soldier at Boston to his father in Chester (October 10); and a letter from Virginia to a correspondent at Whitehaven (October 24). The significance of West of England ports as intermediaries for news was clear with the role of Chester, Liverpool, and Whitehaven. So also was the number of channels of communication.

Similarly, the *British Chronicle or Pugh's Hereford Journal* (the title sinking in significance as it proceeded), published, under its Hereford byline, items that were not received from the London press, which again emphasized the multilateral character of the British newspaper world. On May 20, 1779, news about the French Brest fleet (the major French naval force) was published from a Bristol correspondent, while, on July 8, further maritime news appeared, under a Bristol byline, as an "extract of a letter from a gentleman of Plymouth to his friend in this city," and, that September, news of American privateers appeared from Cardigan, Haverfordwest, and Swansea. Each was also in the newspaper's circulation network.

The *Gloucester Journal* of August 28, 1780, printed news of the unsuccessful British attempt to advance across Central America via Lake Nicaragua: "By the *Grantham* packet which is arrived at Falmouth, we have the following accounts: From the *Jamaica Gazette*. Extract of a letter from Fort St Juan, to a gentleman at Jamaica, May 18." This item captured the chain of links that could lay behind a news item. Such a chain also offered possibilities for the movement of news in opposite and other directions. It also captured the density and multifaceted character of the British Atlantic. That was also seen in news that did not relate to the war. For example, the *Leeds Intelligencer* of January 16, 1781, carried a piece from the *Liverpool Advertiser* about the extent of damage done by a hurricane in the Caribbean. The eagerness of provincial newspapers to print distinctive items from abroad, and thus emphasize their particular value, continued, as with the Dutch Crisis of 1787.[21]

The divisive character of the War of American Independence took its conduct further into British domestic politics than that of earlier wars, however divisive they had been. As with previous wars, this divisive character was encouraged by commercial, personal, and political rivalries between newspapers, both metropolitan and provincial. For example, some newspapers, such as the *Cambridge Chronicle*, *Leeds Mercury*, and *Newcastle Courant*, supported the American Patriots, while others were loyalist and very self-consciously so, for example the *Newark and Nottingham Journal* and the *Newcastle Courant*. Newspapers founded during the war tended to take sides. Thus, the *Nottingham Gazette*, launched in 1780, supported the Patriots.[22] Competition encouraged the mustering of evidence, which therefore spread information about Britain and the world. For example, a Leeds item in the *Leeds Intelligencer* of May 8, 1781, provided details of West Riding cloth production in order to refute opposition claims of economic crisis in the region.[23] News of the progress of the war was also contested, as in the issue of May 29, 1781, which, inaccurately as it turned out, refuted opposition claims that Pensacola, the major center in West Florida, had fallen to Spain. The British press expanded in titles and total circulation during the war, from 12,680,000 copies published in 1775 to 15,272,519 in 1782.[24]

British popular interest in North America after the Seven Years' War (1756–63) had continued to encourage the publication of maps. Thomas Jefferys published a number of atlases, including *A General Topography of North America and the West Indies* (1768), and, using his maps, Robert Sayers and John Bennett published *The American Atlas, or a Geographical Description of the Whole Continent of America* (1775), with subsequent editions dated 1776 and 1778.

The first major battle of the American Revolution, Bunker Hill in 1775, was rapidly followed in London by the publication of maps of the battle, the earliest appearing four days after the report of the engagement reached London. This was eased by Bunker Hill being just outside Boston and thus readily reported. The struggle for Boston was also followed on the Continent, with Samuel Holland and George Callender's *Chart of the Harbour of Boston*, published by J. F. W. Des Barres, being used by Jean, Chevalier de Beaurain, to produce a map. The latter map was soon re-engraved and printed in Leipzig. More generally, the French relied in part on the availability of British printed maps sold through the map trade.[25]

In 1776, detailed maps of New England enabled British readers, anxious about the civil war in the empire, to follow the course of the conflict in its initial theater, while the British naval victory on Lake Champlain led to the publication of a map and supporting description. In 1777, William Faden published a large-scale map of New Jersey and, in the following year, a plan displaying the recent campaign on the Delaware River, which had been waged by the British in order to ensure Philadelphia's access to the sea. Faden did the same for other campaigns and engagements, such as the unsuccessful British attack on Fort Sullivan, South Carolina, in 1776 and George Washington's operations at Trenton and Princeton in New Jersey in the winter of 1776–77. These operations delivered a crucial check to the British forces after their earlier success in exploiting success at New York in order to overrun New Jersey.[26] Maps, however, did not capture the key element of the political affiliations of the American public or the major difficulties facing the two sides: the British failure to create an effective pacification policy and the deficiencies of the American war machine.

Public attention to the war took other forms as well—for example, caricatures.[27] The pantomime of "Harlequin Junior, or the Magic Cestus," seen in Leeds and York in 1784, showed the repulse of the Spanish attack on Gibraltar in September 1782.[28] This victory was also celebrated in other forms. *A Plan of the Town and Fortifications of Gibraltar with the Spanish Lines and Attacks*, published in London in 1782, included, as scene setters, maps of the Straits of Gibraltar and the Bay of Gibraltar. The large attacking force was supported by warships and by floating batteries. The main map illustrated the design of these batteries, including with a cut-away view, showed their position, and added the text "Anchored on the 13 of September at half past nine in the morning, and were all blown up or sunk on the 14th at noon." The British used heated shot against them. A large and dramatic painting, John Singleton Copley's *The Defeat of the Floating Batteries at Gibraltar* (1791), commissioned by the City of London in 1783 and originally hung in the Common Council Chamber there, was also reproduced in engravings. However, it is symptomatic of changing attitudes to the period that, as a result of the wartime destruction of the Guildhall Art Gallery in

London due to German air attack and the loan of the painting to the governor's residence in Gibraltar, it has only recently been restored to view in the rebuilt Guildhall Art Gallery.

There were also maps of British naval engagements during the war and notably of the victory over the French fleet at the Saints in 1782. This was a victory late in the war and one that proved crucial to British morale and to the fate of the West Indies. A map showing the location of the battle was published in the June 1782 issue of the *Political Magazine*.

There is the need today to understand maps in terms of the communications as well as the politics of the period: issues of strategy were greatly exacerbated by poor communications. Before the telegraph produced the nineteenth-century communications revolution, instructions could go no faster than the swiftest horse or the speediest boat. This was an aspect of the situation in which Britain's need to confront a number of serious challenges, both in North America and around the world, placed considerable burdens on its ability to control and allocate resources and to make accurate threat assessments. The cumulative nature of information was readily apparent.

Because of the failure of the British government, what would otherwise have been a great rebellion became a War of Independence. This failure had a larger impact in Britain because it was a civil war within the empire. Indeed, in 1782, the response to failure led to the fall of the long-standing Lord North ministry, despite its success in the 1780 general election, as, earlier, in that of 1774. This failure was strongly against the trend of recent British history. There had been no failure to overcome domestic rebellion since 1688. Moreover, in a step that, at once, reflected both discontinuity and adaptability, the overthrow of James II (and VII of Scotland) in 1688–89 had been incorporated into the constitution, political system, and national heritage as a result of the sanitizing remodeling that was described in terms of the Glorious Revolution and the Revolution Settlement. In contrast, the success of the Americans could not be incorporated in this fashion because George III, who regarded flexibility, including what might have saved the situation, as failing in his constitutional and religious obligations, felt unable to make the concessions of self-government necessary to preempt independence. Nor, for Britain, was there any experience of defeat in a war on this scale since the 1620s. From a different perspective, the Revolution Settlement had been imposed by force, and notably in Ireland and much of Scotland in 1689–91. A new verdict imposed by force on the American colonies would not have been different in character.

The establishment of a new American state, however, indicated the role of geography as well as war in asserting and defining nationhood, and specifically in fixing and conveying a sense of place and its possibilities. Prior to independence, geographic ideas served for British Americans to encompass the mass of North America and to shape it into a coherent and explicit whole. This process had to make sense in terms of difference and geopolitical ideas but also took them forward. Geographical ideas, the relevant ideas of the collective imagination, therefore, were important to an incipient American nationalism that helped justify a sense of difference. This sense made British rule of the North American colonies appear alien or could be employed to that end. Moreover, notions that geography had somehow bound the mainland colonists together had gained credence by 1774–75.[29] In contrast, North America did not have a pre-(European) contact identity as the indigenous societies had only limited knowledge of each other.[30] As a result, North America, and indeed America as a whole, owed much to the conceptual process by which Westerners arranged the world, and notably as the New World.

Nevertheless, it is important not to explain independence in light of the outcome, or to be instrumentalist in explanation. There were competing geographies, particularly those of continued and strong trans-Atlantic links, and of potent and violent tension between (and within) the colonies. These might have become more prominent had the war had a different outcome. Moreover, in effect, they very much did so in the case of Canada. The colonies that became Canada took a very different course to the thirteen that became the United States, while East and West Florida were returned by Britain to Spain in 1783. This difference was further entrenched when American expansionism at the expense of Canada failed in the War of 1812. The protean, unfixed nature of North American geopolitics was repeatedly to be apparent until the settlement of Anglo-American differences in 1871.

There is considerable evidence of the role of geographic awareness in helping influence identity formulation in the new American state, but also of a major contrast between the world of print and rhetoric in which this idea was advanced,[31] and a reality in which there was not a consolidated national sphere or a unified economy but, rather, a set of localities that was best represented by the federalism of the political system.[32] These localities, moreover, contributed to sectional, more than national, views, and both political movements, such as Federalism, and regional presentations of the country reflected this sectionalism, as did the response to the War of 1812 in which much of New England was not really or readily engaged.[33] Sectionalism was to play a major role in divisions over the incorporation of new territory. Moreover, there was a tension between an advancing frontier creating new territory to incorporate, politically, economically, and psychologically, and existing views of country and people, state and nation.

NEW ATLANTICS

In one sense, two new British geographical worlds came from the American Revolution. One was that of the new American state. This new state, to some the outcome of an immutable historical process, was celebrated in *A New and Correct Map of the United States of North America*, "agreeable to the Peace of 1783," that was published in New Haven, Connecticut, in 1784. Produced by Abel Buell, a silversmith there, it was advertised by him as "The first ever published, engraved and finished by one man, and an American," and as designed for the "patriotic gentleman." The map presented a new land reaching to the Mississippi and offered a potent prospectus of American independence followed by national expansion. This prospectus reflected the dynamic presentation of the country.[34]

This state owed much to its colonial origins as part of the empire but had violently rejected that empire[35] and, as a result, was sundered from the British colonies that became Canada. The second new British geographical world was that of a Britain, and its remaining empire, notably the Loyalist diaspora, that had to adjust to the Revolution, if only in the depiction of America.[36] Contrasts emerged rapidly[37] but should not be made too stark.[38] For example, as the Anglosphere was reimagined, British newspapers continued to take items from American counterparts.[39] Interest in Canada grew and was presented to the public, as in *An Account of the Present State of Nova Scotia* (1786), which discussed the possibilities of the production of naval stores due to the abundant forests.[40] The Loyalists helped to take the empire in a more conservative direction, but because Loyalism as an identity was greatly transformed by the challenging conditions of migration and exile, no single, monolithic Loyalist tradition could be passed on to subsequent generations, even in Canada.[41]

The focus on North America suggests a view of British Atlantic and, indeed, transoceanic history that centers on North America. That, indeed, is a common approach.[42] At the same time, there is a tendency in Britain and the United States to overlook the South Atlantic. It looked toward India, via the British-ruled island of St. Helena, and toward the Pacific, via the Falklands, and is an important correction to the geography commonly meant by the British Atlantic. There were also other South Atlantics, as with the Portuguese one of Brazil and Angola, which looked both to the Portuguese Indian Ocean, of Mozambique and Goa, and to a mid-Atlantic of Portuguese Guinea and Madeira. The Spanish Atlantic was the subject of Robertson's *History of America* (1777), for which he sent out questionnaires to colonial informants, both British and Spanish.[43] Moreover, even the standard British coverage of the North Atlantic has gaps, with Newfoundland, the Maritimes (Nova Scotia, Prince Edward Island, New Brunswick), and fishing repeatedly underplayed, and particularly recently. That they no longer appear of great consequence to British commentators and the British public is a testimony to changing perceptions of economic activity and imperial links.

Scale is also a factor in some cases of attention and its lack, although not in the neglect of fishing. The Atlantic and Indian Oceans can be linked, notably in the 1690s in the case of Atlantic pirates who had moved to Madagascar, operating there, and who traded with New York merchants, creating an "Indo-Atlantic World." However, there were only two voyages most years in this particular nexus, and, thereafter, it declined.[44] More generally, this factor of scale is worth considering when assessing the bold claims often made on behalf of transnational and transoceanic links.

The disruption caused to British political geographies (and much else) by the loss of part of the empire was to be taken further in political terms within a decade by the challenge of the French Revolution, and, even more, the French Revolutionary Wars to which it led and in which Britain engaged from 1793. These forced Britain to confront not only developments on the Continent, but also a wide-ranging challenge in which the fates of British, French, and other European colonies were, or appeared, intertwined. This was especially so with the case of whether the fate of Saint-Domingue (now

Haiti), the leading French West Indian colony, where the slaves rebelled and successfully resisted reconquest, would become a prospectus for British colonies, as was much feared.

The uncertainty about Saint-Domingue interacted with a more general sense of change that arose in the 1780s and 1790s from rapidly mounting criticism of the slave trade and, indeed, of slavery itself. That was not an issue that necessarily depended on information about the situation outside Europe. In particular, religious views, including Protestant providentialism, contributed to abolitionism. Nevertheless, much information was offered and both for Africa and for the slave colonies and thus for the slave trade and slavery. The imaginative extent, geography, and character of the British world altered as a result. Slaves had been part of the British world but, essentially, despite significant missionary activity, as objects. This approach was transformed as abolitionist sympathies spread. Abolitionists focused on a concrete activity, the slave trade, applied it to particular moments and places in Britain,[45] and sometimes related this discussion to the broader, less defined questions of who the imperial peoples were, on what terms, and with what futures.

These were not new questions, but they became more acute in the crisis linked to the French Revolution. This crisis encouraged existential questions about the intentions of Providence, not least as Britain suffered repeated defeats from 1794, questions that focused on sin, which was found in a range of practices, including the slave trade. Sin, indeed, was an aspect of the existential geography of the slave trade, a geography that reflected the significance of religion. This existential geography was linked to an existential history in the shape of the workings of Providence. These themes were defined, asserted, negotiated, and democratized in a range of media including books, pamphlets, newspapers, prints, caricatures, sermons, theatrical acts, and pottery.[46]

DEVELOPMENTAL STAGES

Although a concern with the workings of Providence was scarcely new, the ability to inscribe it on the slave trade was. Indeed, geographical perceptions and the geographical imagination were constantly dynamic. Alongside changes within the Western system, there was the need to assess the non-Western world, which was not seen as constant. Indeed, the Western stadial thought of the period assumed that there were very distinct and clearly progressive stages in development, stages that set the background for Western consideration. "Barbarians" were presented as lacking the more formal state structures and settled economies of those regarded as more opulent and more civilized.

These views, for example, were expressed by Edward Gibbon, William Robertson, and Adam Smith as they sought to provide an account of human history, and thus development and purpose, that was not dependent on a Christian approach and that therefore extended to non-Christian societies in a fashion that paid attention to their strengths and agency.[47] In his *The Wealth of Nations* (1776), Smith began book five, "On the Revenue of the Sovereign or Commonwealth," by arguing that

> the first duty of the sovereign, that of protecting the society from the violence and invasion of other independent societies, can be performed only by means of a military force. But the expense both of preparing this military force in time of peace, and of employing it in time of war, is very different in the different states of society, in the different periods of improvement.
>
> Among nations of hunters, the lowest and rudest state of society, such as we find it among the native tribes of North America . . . an army of hunters can seldom exceed two or three hundred men. . . . An army of shepherds on the contrary, may sometimes amount to two or three hundred thousand.[48]

Smith linked complexity to the socioeconomic developments that permitted the establishment of professionalized regular armies able to sustain themselves and presented this establishment as an inevitable consequence of these developments. He referred to the "opulent and civilized" in contrast to the "poor and barbarous."[49] Smith's developmental model was not one with a clear close. Indeed, in some respects, Smith articulated a new imperial formation: an imperial network integrated through exchange. This was an aspect of the relationships among imagination, expression, and activity in the creation of imperial images and realities.[50]

Far from simply being abstract considerations, there was also an often violent cutting edge to "development." An account from this cutting edge was offered by Dean Mahomet, a quartermaster with the powerful Bengal army of the British East India Company. He recorded the advance of a brigade of this army from Bihar to the British base of Calcutta in 1772–73 and the response to resistance by the hill people of the passes through which Bengal was entered. Mahomet clearly thought weaponry and discipline were important and also commented on the savagery of the conflict. After the "licentious savages" had attacked those cutting grass and gathering fuel for the camp, two companies of sepoys (Indian infantry paid by the East India Company and trained to fight like their Western counterparts) advanced: "Our men, arranged in military order, fired . . . the greater part of them [savages], after a feeble resistance with their bows, arrows, and swords, giving way to our superior courage and discipline, fled . . . two hundred . . . prisoners . . . severely punished for their crimes; some having their ears and noses cut off, and others hung in gibbets."[51]

Less violently, a stadial approach (in stages) to history offered the opportunity of travel to see the past of one's own civilization, as Samuel (Dr.) Johnson did, at least in his own eyes, when he visited the Scottish Highlands in 1773.[52] To Johnson and others, such regions offered a vista of the "primitive" origins of modern Britain. This vista apparently conformed to the "noble savages" depicted by Gibbon when he wrote about the Picts valiantly resisting the Romans in the first century CE (AD) and also to those found in the Pacific by the European explorers of the present day. A comparable view was not provided for Ireland.

Smith's approach offered a way to discuss "barbarians," a way that remains influential today. This method was (and is) one that, alongside frequently discussing them as virtuous, primitivized them and treated them as objects and thus made them apparently easy to dissect and explain. This approach was misleading in a number of respects, and notably because the strategies of these peoples were well developed and fit for purpose, although lacking the form of public political discussion seen in the West.

There is a related tendency that minimizes the "barbarians," one in which they are seen as unsuccessful because anachronistic (whether virtuous or not) and as largely irrelevant as a consequence. In short, they were allegedly motivated by primitive drives, and strategy was "done" to them. This tendency is linked to, and, to a degree, stems from, the argument that the power of major states increased in the eighteenth century, in part as a consequence of growing population and improving climate. It is argued that this increase ensured that the "barbarian" peoples or nomads or semi-nomads or pastoralists were driven back by the expanding territorial sway of the major settled peoples and their states. This process was linked to a general territorial consolidation of these states that was seen in the spread of agriculture, settlement, and military service.[53]

There is a parallel in the contemporary and later treatment of "pirates," as with the British response to the predatory coastal powers on the west coast of India.[54] Contemporary accounts of these and other powers and peoples brought out potent ethnographical assumptions on the part of the British, and the same was true for others. In turn, these assumptions and categories were applied to new groups that were encountered, as when the British extended their scope northward along that coast, an extension that required more effective naval power. At the same time, there was also an ability to respond to local circumstances and to alter treatment and response accordingly.[55]

Public attitudes, however, did not always adapt so readily. For example, there was a widespread reluctance to accept the extent or consequence of high European death rates in the Tropics, notably the West Indies. Indeed, there was an almost willful ignorance.[56] This was linked to a failure of adequately considering disease as a major element both in social development and, even more, in environmental adaptation.

RELIGION

Religion was a key element in the perception of the non-Western world and, as such, an aspect of the continuity with the perception of the Western world. The British Empire itself was spanned by the same movements—for example, the Protestant and evangelical proselytizing of the 1720s and 1730s, which led George Whitefield and the Wesleys (John and Charles) to North America. At the same time, this proselytizing was not restricted to the empire or to British-born people, as the "Great Awakening" was also found in parts of the German lands. The extensive missionary effort, both within and outside areas of colonial control, attracted support from both clergy and laity and was an important link between Britain and the transoceanic world and one, furthermore, that conveyed providential meaning. This link encompassed Continental Europeans.[57]

There was an institutional trajectory. The Society for the Promotion of Christian Knowledge, founded in 1698, was followed by the Society for the Propagation of the Gospel in Foreign Parts, established in 1701, which was particularly active in the colonies. Other societies included the Baptist Missionary Society founded in 1792, the London Missionary Society (1795), the Scottish Missionary Society (1799), and the Church Missionary Society (1799).

Spreading the faith was presented as a providential purpose[58] that earned rewards such as trade and land and that also held Catholicism at bay. The vitality of religious explanations for overseas expansion looked toward the role of missionaries and religious conceptions of a civilizing colonial role. Arthur Dobbs, the highly active governor of North Carolina, was, like Joseph Banks, a commentator more than happy to speculate across geographical space and to seek to define and, thus, use it. In 1762, he sent the government a memorandum in which he called for liberating and improving the New World by free trade and Christianization, including "to send missionaries to civilise and Christianise the natives where the Spaniards have no settlements and to form them into regular polities under the direction of governors truly Christian and educated for that purpose in Britain at the expense of the public."[59]

On a long-standing pattern, religion offered one way to structure the outside world and Christianity the way to understand other religions. For example, George Sale published an English translation of the Koran in 1734, arguing that "to be acquainted with the various laws and constitutions of civilised nations, especially of those who flourish in our own time, is perhaps the most useful part of knowledge."[60] This approach was not, however, intended by Sale to suggest any equivalence, for he was certain that Providence had reserved the glory of the overthrow of Islam to the Protestants, a view that was a significant strand in providential thought. Interest in Islam was suggested by Joseph Pitts in the preface to the third edition of his *A Faithful Account of the Religion and Manners of the Mahometans* (1731): "I have been informed that there hath been a great demand for it (especially in London)."[61] At the same time, it was common to puff books.

PACIFIC ISLANDERS

Very differently but also overlapping with Christian views and with stadial thought, the Pacific and its islands posed a challenge to established views, not least Tahiti and the idea of islanders as noble primitives. The seductive European, notably French and British, portrayal of innocent children of nature was true only in part, but it served to help question conventional views and particularly about sexuality. This positive portrayal was supported by the powerful visual images provided by painters who accompanied explorers, notably William Hodges and John Webber who traveled with Cook. The Pacific, as in Hodges's *A View taken in the bay of Oaite Peha, Otaheite [Tahiti]* or *Tahiti Revisited* (1775) and *The War Boats of the Island of Otaheite* (1777), offered a vista of paradise, one full of drama, and of truly noble figures—for example, in Joshua Reynolds's portrait of Omai, a Pacific Islander brought back from Cook's second expedition. The talented Hodges also painted in India between 1778 and 1784. His Indian paintings were engraved for a British market fascinated by distant lands, a market whose interest in India was also met by other painters such as Johann Zoffany. In 1793, Hodges published an account of his *Travels in India*.

Alternative readings of the Pacific Islanders were downplayed. Wallis's expedition had in fact discovered not a primitive utopia, but, indeed, a complex society with rulers, aristocracy, private property, priestcraft, and feuding. Cook also stressed the presence of private property, law, and social ranks in the Pacific. Thus, the South Seas had a civilization with many, although not all, fundamentals similar to those of Europe. However, the ability of Hawaiians to connect human life with divinity seemed disturbing. More dramatically, the discovery of human sacrifice put the stress on a savagery without appeal, and the killing of Cook in 1779 contributed to a sense of brutishness. Modern visitors continue to be troubled by the sites and descriptions of such sacrifices.

Yet, favorable accounts still appeared in print. George Keate's *Account of the Pelew Islands, from the Journals of Captain Henry Wilson and some of his officers, shipwrecked there in the Antelope in August 1783*, published in 1788, had five editions by 1803. Wilson and his crew found a friendly reception and brought back to Britain the "Prince," Lee Boo, who became a celebrity before dying of smallpox in 1784. Favorable accounts were matched by the depiction of Britain and its relationship to the Pacific. In his *History of the Decline and Fall of the Roman Empire* (1776–88), Edward Gibbon sought to place British voyages of exploration in a historical context that reflected particular credit on the Britain of the present day: "The merit of discovery has too often been stained with avarice, cruelty and fanaticism; and the intercourse of nations has produced the communication of disease and prejudice. A singular exception is due to the virtue of our own times and country. The five great voyages, successively undertaken by the command of his present Majesty [George III], were inspired by the pure and generous love of science and mankind... introduced into the islands of the South Sea the vegetables and animals most useful to human life." To modern commentators, however, this account ignores the ecological imperialism presented by such an introduction. For example, the rats introduced by British ships did much damage to islands where they had no predators.

INDIA

The British response to India was very different to that to the far-less-familiar South Seas. The obvious weakness of the Mughal Empire, after the death in 1707 of Aurangzeb, the emperor, made India seem weak and in disorder. Modern scholarship has greatly questioned the degree to which the crisis of Mughal power or, more generally, the problems of eighteenth-century India, were signs of failure, let alone degeneracy.[62] However, many British commentators were apt to suggest that India was in marked decline. This appeared to make way for a British role there, as, earlier, with that of the Romans in the Hellenistic world as the empires there, notably the Ptolemaic and Seleucid ones, allegedly declined into self-indulgence. This was a Roman view that the British readily repeated and applied.

India became more important to the practice and imagination of the British world both as Britain became an imperial power there, greatly changing former patterns of Anglo-Indian hybridization,[63] and because, with some exceptions, the positive account of China was replaced by one of China as inferior.[64] A sense of a new triumphant destiny for India was offered by the cartouche to a map of India published in 1782 by James Rennell, former surveyor-general of the Bengal Presidency, after his return to England. It showed Britannia receiving the sacred scriptures of India from a Brahman. Four years earlier, Spiridion Roma had been commissioned by the directors of the East India Company to paint the ceiling of their Leadenhall Street headquarters. His *The East Offering its Riches to Britannia* depicted India and China, both as women, presenting their riches to a more dynamic present. At the same time, there was considerable uneasiness about the political corruption and social dissolution that wealth gained in India offered, uneasiness most clearly presented in Samuel Foote's play *The Nabobs* (1772), in other plays, and in caricatures.[65]

A sense of Indian political weakness was compatible with growing British cultural interest in India, a pattern also seen with the British response to Italy. The Scottish deist Alexander Dow, author of the *History of Hindustan* (1766–72), was anxious to demonstrate the moral superiority of Hinduism to Christianity. Most commentators who were willing to adopt a favorable view saw India in terms of a glorious past, akin to classical Greece or Rome, rather than as an advancing modern society. That view did not necessarily encourage a determination to change Indian society. Warren Hastings, the able governor of Bengal from 1772 to 1774 and, from then to 1784, the first governor-general, believed that each society had its own politico-cultural genius, and that it should be adhered to, and not violated. This conservative notion of institutional authority did not encourage any attempt to impose British laws and institutions.

The notion was qualified under Charles, Marquis Cornwallis, governor-general from 1786 to 1793, especially in his creation of the Permanent Settlement in Bengal in 1793. Cornwallis had been defeated by the Americans and French at Yorktown in 1781. He was to go on to defeat the Irish rebels in 1798. His career, which included representing George III at the Prussian military maneuvers in 1785, reflected the extent to which very different places or spaces of empire could be linked by the careers of specific individuals. This process occurred at all social levels and in the navy as well as the army.

From the mid-eighteenth century, more was published on India, while information became more rapidly and regularly available. Books were most significant, although there was also newspaper and magazine material. Thus, Henry Vansittart's *Narrative of Transactions in Bengal, 1760–1764* was published in 1766. Sir William Jones, who made his reputation translating Persian works in the 1770s, producing a *Grammar of the Persian Language* in 1771, mastered Sanskrit the following decade and translated several Hindu classics. Founding the Bengal Asiatic Society in 1784, Jones studied Indian languages, literature, and philosophy. His retrieval of Sanskrit texts and reconstruction of India's past helped introduce a significant

Oriental strand to the development of Romanticism. Jones also developed knowledge of the connection between Sanskrit and Western languages.[66] His fame reflected an understanding of the impressive quality of his work.

Hastings and members of his circle were willing to engage with Hindu and Persian literature, thought, and mysticism.[67] Such an approach potentially challenged the ideas and practice of Christian superiority and more so than the long-standing example set by a Jewish presence in Britain, a presence that was enhanced by recent immigration.[68] However, Hinduism, like Judaism, could be viewed through a "successionist" lens: as valid but as replaced by Christianity. Closer involvement in India brought firsthand acquaintance with contemporary Hindus and Zoroastrians, whose faiths were found to have some of the same components in their stories as Judeo-Christianity—for example, the story of a great flood, which for Jews and Christians was that of Noah. In this approach, Christianity became merely one among a number of religions that took their place in a comparative universal history in which the biblical account was no longer central.[69] This approach represented a significant rewriting of religious geography. That rewriting was one of the most important aspects of the changing geographical assessment during the period, although this change is underplayed due to a tendency to underrate the significance of religious perceptions.

This rewriting took a number of forms, some of them silent. For example, the origin account of Christianity, as well as the classical typologies, appeared less plausible as exploration led to the "discovery" of more animals and plants. The idea that they had all come from Noah's Ark, or been described by classical writers, appeared increasingly incredible, and, to many commentators, faith, or faith alone, did not seem a reasonable basis for incredible truths. This perception, and the related excitement and concern, led to a search for a new history and geography to describe and explain the distribution of animals and plants.[70] Moreover, such a search encouraged interest in the stages by which the present-day distribution had been reached. Geology was to be part of the same process.

The "discovery" of difference encouraged the idea of the exotic as a way to understand and classify the outside world. Geography played a role in this ordering, with two linked visions of the world. One conception of the non-Western world—of a disorderly space filled with exotic contents—invited the response of a more clearly demarcated world, a world that could be readily described in terms of geography and, in a less clear-cut fashion, the response of related explanatory notions.[71] Religious concerns helped to reset the world. For example, a focus on religious issues in India offers a very different feel to the geography of British interest and concern in the early years of the century when the overwhelming attention had been on a challenge from Catholicism.

CHANGING POLITICAL GEOGRAPHIES

In part, this sense of change is misleading because concern about the British Isles and "near Europe" was to revive greatly in the 1790s with the spread of French Revolutionary forces. Indeed, this situation helped create a bifurcated British view about the outside world. This was one in which a strong concern about Europe was counterpointed with a similar concern about the transoceanic world and sufficiently so to create serious issues about the prioritization of competing national issues when attempting to plan strategy. Nevertheless, the two elements could be linked, as with the Dutch Crisis of 1787, for this was also seen as significant for the situation in the Indian Ocean where the Dutch were important in Sri Lanka, Malaya, and Sumatra. The crisis led to much press discussion of the details of Dutch politics, including descriptions of particular places.[72] The *London Chronicle* of August 23, 1787, reported, "As many people in this country remain in perfect ignorance, with regard to the principle and nature of the melancholy disturbance in Holland, and confound the States of Holland with that of the States General,[73] it will be of infinite service to many people to be set right on this point, to prevent their being the dupes of Exchange-Alley etc. The fact is this, their Noble Puissances the States of Holland are composed of a number of rich merchants . . . without an iota of nobility amongst them."

Despite the revival of interest in Europe, the drift in attention, the geography of concern, across the century as a whole, had been one in which more than hitherto was devoted to the transoceanic world. In part, this was a product of the failure of Jacobitism. Moreover, when a major challenge within the empire recurred in the second half of the century, it initially did so in North America, and not in the British Isles. The Irish Rising of 1798 partly countered this, but it was a short-term crisis and not as serious as the Fifteen or the Forty-Five. The geography of British concern and attention had changed toward the transoceanic world, although this was not as much as was to be the case after 1815. Nevertheless, to make the latter point should not lead to a downplaying of the earlier change. The gain and profits of empire, including recruiting for and supplying both army and navy,[74] helped to win support for Britishness, both in Scotland and Ireland.

THE NAVAL WORLD POWER

The range of British warfare led to a greater interest in countries that were not well covered and that were newly interesting. This can be seen with Egypt, which Napoleon invaded in 1798 and where Britain sent an expeditionary force in 1801. The former consul-general in Egypt, George Baldwin, published in 1802 *Political Recollections relative to Egypt, containing Observations on its Government under the Mameluks; its Geographical Position; its intrinsic and extrinsic Resources; its relative Importance to England and France; and its Dangers to England in the Possession of France; with a narrative of the campaign in 1801.*

This was very much a political geography by an individual who had long sought to develop Egypt as a means for Britain to trade to India via the Red Sea. This scheme had led Baldwin to publish *The Communication with India by the Isthmus of Suez, vindicated from the Prejudices that have prevailed against it* (1784). The same year, Colonel James Capper of the East India Company army published his *Observations on the Passage to India through Egypt; also to Vienna through Constantinople and Aleppo, and from thence to Bagdad, and across the Great Desert to Bassora* [Basra], *with occasional Remarkes on the adjacent countries, and also sketches of the different Routes*, a work reprinted in 1785. This included an argument in favor of the importance of the Egyptian route, which competed with the overland route via the Persian Gulf. There was also growing French interest in the strategic importance of Egypt.[75]

As a reminder of the multiple links of the period, links that included frequent overlaps in interests, Capper (1743–1825) was to take much interest in meteorology and (separately), agricultural improvement, publishing *Observations on the Winds and Monsoons, illustrated with a chart, and accompanied with Notes, Geographical and Meterological* (1801), *Observations on the Cultivation of Waste Lands, addressed to the gentlemen and farmers of Glamorganshire* (1805), and *Meterological and Miscellaneous Tracts applicable to Navigation, Gardening, and Farming, with Calendars of Flora, for Greece, France, England, and Sweden* (1809).

The nineteenth century saw Britain become increasingly dominant on the world stage, with particular impact in Asia, Africa, and Australasia. This process was related to Britain's use of the information it could gather, deploy, and apply, while, in turn, this usage reflected the potential offered by British power and notably maritime strength. This relationship was seen not only in political effectiveness but also in other aspects, including economic activity. There were also attempts to advance a cultural dominance over non-Western peoples and to frame, discuss, and use information accordingly.

The charting of the oceans was a key instance of this process and theme of the nineteenth century, one that brought together the search for information, its accumulation, depiction, and use. This charting was linked to power, as Britain's global commitments and opportunities, naval and commercial, made it both easiest and most necessary for Britain to acquire and use the information. Indeed, throughout the century, Britain played the major role in charting the oceans. In 1808, while Britain was at war with Napoleonic France, and very much dependent on its navy, the Charting Committee of naval officers was appointed by the Admiralty to advise on how best to improve the situation. This provided an instructive instance of the manner in which state agencies took on new functions and, in doing so, transformed the amount and reliability of available information. The committee recommended the provision of a set of charts for each British naval station as rapidly as possible but also the superseding of reliance on the private sector.

This superseding entailed the purchase of charts from commercial map publishers and the buying back of the copyright of charts made by naval officers and produced by entrepreneurs. The latter practice, which had been very important in the eighteenth century, was symptomatic of the close relationship between the state and commerce in British map publishing. Underlining the complementarity sought between institutions acquiring information, there was also an effort to obtain information on the British coastline from the Ordnance Survey, which was the branch of the British military responsible for the mapping of the land. The coastline was a key zone as it was there that an invasion would land and where it would be resisted if earlier opposition had been unsuccessful at sea. An atlas of *Charts of the English Channel*, containing thirty-one charts for naval use, appeared in 1811.

There was also the checking of earlier charts, as the British did with the Dutch charts of the Molucca Islands in the East Indies in 1797. This proved necessary as the British conquered them in 1812–13 during the Napoleonic Wars. Around the world, running aground was a major problem for warships mounting inshore operations, notably supporting amphibious attacks, enforcing blockades, and chasing shallower-draft vessels. The Royal Navy was particularly prone to losing ships this way as it very much mounted such operations and was also the largest navy in the world. During the French Revolutionary and Napoleonic Wars, the British lost more ships running aground than from enemy action. European waters were important sources of such loss, in large part because of the importance of the British blockade of France and its allies there, but other waters also saw significant losses, including the Indian Ocean.

After the Napoleonic Wars finally ended in 1815, the British pressed on to chart coastal waters across the world. This was part of the process in the West by which formal, state-directed, information-gathering replaced earlier, ad hoc, means of assembling information that had been gathered in a nonsystematic fashion. Much of the existing situation was in practice unsatisfactory. Robert Sawyer reported of the Straits of Sunda, a major route through the East Indies: "until the extent of the dangers off the south end of Banca are better known, the approach of it must be dangerous and we seem to be equally ignorant of what dangers may lie off the numerous islands to the south east." In 1817, en route to Guangzhou (Canton), HMS *Alceste* hit a coral reef just north of Sunda.

Alongside key surveys, such as that of the Thames estuary, much of the charting was far flung. Moreover, much of it was not a question of charting coasts controlled by Britain. For example, a British coastal survey of 1822–24 brought back much information about East Africa. There was also a continuing relationship with the private sector in Britain, although the terms of exchange were now different to those of the eighteenth century. From 1821, the extensive range of charts produced by the Admiralty was offered publicly for sale, a policy designed to produce funds for more surveying. Indeed, catalogs of material for sale were published from 1825.

The careers of the individual naval officers and ships responsible for such surveys reflected the range of British activity but also the extent to which surveying was linked to British power. This situation looked toward the later dominance of Britain in submarine telegraphy, a dominance that was a matter not only of charting the oceans, of the ownership of telegraph lines, and of the related production and laying of cables but also of the key role of Britain in establishing practices and setting standards.

Sir Francis Beaufort (1774–1857), whose father, Reverend Daniel Beaufort (1739–1821), had published a map of Ireland in 1792, a map that was useful at the time of the suppression of the 1798 nationalist rising, entered the Royal Navy in 1787, receiving nineteen wounds in 1800 when he cut out a Spanish warship. In 1807, on the pattern of James Cook's surveying of the St. Lawrence prior to the British attack on Québec in 1759, Beaufort surveyed the entrance to the Plate estuary. This was a valuable aid to the warships in preparing for what was to be a large-scale, but ultimately unsuccessful, British attack on Buenos Aires, one that was successful in the naval stage but not on land, with an attempt to storm the city leading to the surrender of the attacking force. More lastingly, knowledge of these waters was also important for what was to be a major destination for British trade.

As a frigate captain, Beaufort was active in 1810–12 in Turkish waters, seeking to suppress pirates and to survey the coast, only to be badly wounded in a clash. He subsequently produced charts based on his survey and, alongside William Smyth's hydrographic surveys, his *Karamania* (1817) was an aspect of the process by which the British controlled the Mediterranean through naming it. Smyth published the *Hydrography of Sicily, Malta, and the Adjacent Islands* (1823) and also surveyed the Adriatic and the North African coast. He rose to be a rear-Admiral and to be president of the Royal Geographical Society and the Royal Astronomical Society.

In 1829, Beaufort became hydrographer to the navy, a post he held until 1855. Soon after his appointment, Beaufort plotted on a map of the world the coasts already covered by surveys. This was an aspect of the systematic approach to information gathering that became more important in the nineteenth century. Concerned by the length of the coastline not yet tackled, a length clarified by the map, Beaufort pressed on to fill the gaps.

The results were shown in the flow of information received. For example, Edward Belcher surveyed the coast of West Africa in the early 1830s, an area of major concern as Britain sought to suppress the slave trade. This was to be a naval commitment during much of the century. William Fitzwilliam Owen and Alexander Vidal surveyed the coastline of Africa from 1821 to 1845. Later in the 1830s, Belcher surveyed the west coast of South America, his surveying an aspect of Britain's important informal empire in Latin America. Trade was helped, and British naval power acquired not only practical knowledge but also considerable prestige.

Robert Moresby surveyed the Red Sea in 1829–33. Seeking to support military action from India, British warships operating there in 1799 against the French in Egypt had run aground. This was a classic instance of charts playing a role in the negotiation of treacherous waters for trade and power projection. As an instance of the cumulative nature of change, the impact of the new charts of the Red Sea, published in 1834, was enhanced by the development of steam navigation, which enabled ships to overcome both northerly winds in the Red Sea and calms in the Mediterranean. This capability demonstrated the flexibility of steam and its multipurpose value.

In turn, power considerations came into play, with Britain determined to control the shortest route to India. This represented a new strategic responsibility and new operational tasks. The army was ultimately dependent on the navy's ability to support a greater range of commitments and a large number of positions. Mauritius was conquered from the French in 1810, Aden was annexed in 1839, and control was taken over the Suez Canal soon after it was opened in 1869. Cyprus followed in 1878 and Egypt, with its major naval base at Alexandria, in 1881.

The quest for accuracy was also seen in the Royal Navy's patronage of the work of Charles Babbage, a key figure in the development of computing. The navy wanted astronomical tables that did not have printing errors, which would allow it to plot positions with certainty. Originally, Babbage's difference engine was to have a tool for molding papier-mâché type that could be used for printing, so cutting out human error in typesetting.

Charts were extensively used in war. The British capture of Mauritius was preceded by the careful charting of the waters round the island. Earlier in 1810, in a major blow that reflected a lack of information, two frigates from the British blockading squadron had run aground and been destroyed. Similarly, the collection of the influential Royal United Services Institute (of London) includes a *Chart of the island of Chusan enlarged from a chart by*

Alexander Dalrymple [Hydrographer to the Navy, 1795–1808], *and corrected in many places by observations made during an expedition under Captain Sir H Le Fleming Senhouse on HMS* Blenheim *between 30th August and 4th September 1840.* This information was both used and improved in Britain's First Opium War with China, a conflict that also led to the charting of the seas round Hong Kong in 1841 by HMS *Sulphur*, under the command of Edward Belcher. Moreover, Britain's new presence in China led to an extension of information on the region. As commander of the *Samarang* in 1842–47, Belcher surveyed the coasts of Borneo, the Philippines, and Taiwan, the last then a part of China. This surveying reflected the newfound projection of British power notably into northern Borneo.

Charts were not only used in war. They also helped in understanding the opportunities offered by the oceans. Information about the availability and distribution of whales, seals, and fish led to an expansion of maritime activity. In time, however, this expansion hit the sustenance of local people—for example, the Yaghan of Tierra del Fuego. More famously, British charting voyages contributed to the development of the theory of evolution. Charles Darwin found his voyage of 1831–36, as naturalist on HMS *Beagle*, a formative experience, notably the journey to the Galapagos archipelago. This was a formative period akin to that for Joseph Banks on James Cook's *Endeavour*, also in the Pacific.

The captain of the *Beagle*, Robert FitzRoy, was a prominent figure in the development of meteorological services, becoming, in 1854, chief of the meteorological department of the Board of Trade, a post he held until 1865. FitzRoy, who placed a great reliance on barometers, helped design an inexpensive one. Writing on how best to use barometers, he founded, in 1861, a system of storm warnings, which became the basis of what he called the "weather forecast." The first telegraphic weather reporting was carried out in 1865. As an instance of the continuing process of nomenclature, the sea area Finisterre was renamed FitzRoy in 2002.

CONCLUSION

The world was increasingly understood by Europeans and with only limited advance or advantage by non-Europeans. The understanding of the world was expressed in a matrix of power in which the categorization was in

Western terms, as in lands as wet or dry, too hot or too cold, as understood in the West. The information was spatially encoded accordingly, and mapping of environmental characteristics began. Moreover, on a long-standing pattern, anthropological ideas developed as an expression of a spatially related idea of ethnic vitality and quality. These ideas were linked to racist perceptions of slaves, South Sea islanders, Native Americans, and others.[76] British power played a major role in making such a context and practice appear obvious.

Notes

1. A. Spilhaus, "Maps of the Whole World Ocean," *Geographical Review* 32 (1942): 431–35; A. Spilhaus and J. P. Snyder, "World Maps with Natural Boundaries," *Cartography and Geographic Information Systems* 18 (1991): 246–54.

2. J. Brotton, *Trading Territories: Mapping the Early Modern World* (London, 1997); M. Ogborn, "Historical Geographies of Globalisation, c. 1500–1800," in B. Graham and C. Nash, eds., *Modern Historical Geographies* (London, 2000), 52–59.

3. I. K. Steele, "Moat Theories and the English Atlantic, 1675 to 1740," *Historical Papers* (1978): 18–33; K. J. Banks, *Chasing Empire across the Sea: Communications and the State in the French Atlantic, 1713–1763* (Montreal, 2002).

4. C. E. Clark, "Boston and the Nurturing of Newspapers: Dimensions of the Cradle, 1690–1741," *New England Quarterly* 64 (1991): 243–71.

5. Samuel, Bishop of Killala, to Sir Robert Wilmot, Secretary to the Lord Lieutenant of Ireland, January 28, 1762, Matlock, Derbyshire CRO. D 3155 WH3461.

6. C. E. Clark, "The Newspapers of Provincial America," *Proceedings of the American Antiquarian Society* 100 (1991): 367–89, and *The Public Prints: The Newspaper in Anglo-American Culture, 1665–1740* (New York, 1994); M. Eamon, *Imprinting Britain: Newspapers, Sociability, and the Shaping of British North America* (Montreal, 2015).

7. J. P. Greene, *The Intellectual Construction of America: Exceptionalism and Identity from 1492 to 1800* (Chapel Hill, NC, 1993).

8. The extensive printing stock of the printer Robert Baldwin can be seen in R. Cave, "An Inventory of the First Jamaican Printing House," *Papers of the Bibliographical Society of America* 69 (1975): 562–64.

9. I. Hampsher-Monk, "Edmund Burke and Empire," *Proceedings of the British Academy* 155 (2009): 117–25.

10. P. Woodfine, "'Suspicious Latitudes': Commerce, Colonies, and Patriotism in the 1730s," *Studies in Eighteenth-Century Culture* 27 (1998): 45–46.

11. D. Armitage, "The Cromwellian Protectorate and the Languages of Empire," *Historical Journal* 35 (1992): 553–55.

12. J. M. Adelman, "'A Constitutional Conveyance of Intelligence, Public and Private': The Post Office, the Business of Printing, and the American Revolution," *Enterprise and Society* 11 (2010): 709–52; J. A. Smith, *Printers and Press Freedom: The Ideology of Early American Journalism* (Oxford, 1988); C. E. Clark and C. Wetherell, "The Measure of

Maturity: The *Pennsylvania Gazette*, 1728–1765," *William and Mary Quarterly*, 3rd ser., 46 (1989): 301–3.

13. P. N. Miller, *Defining the Common Good: Empire, Religion, and Philosophy in Eighteenth-Century Britain* (Cambridge, 1994).

14. Gage to Barrington, September 2, 1772, July 18, 1774, BL. Add. 73550.

15. S. J. Hornsby, *British Atlantic, Atlantic Frontier. Spaces of Power in Early Modern British America* (Lebanon, NH, 2005), 226.

16. C. Cangany, *Frontier Seaport: Detroit's Transformation into an Atlantic Entrepôt* (Chicago, 2014).

17. F. Furstenberg, "The Significance of the Trans-Appalachian Frontier in Atlantic History," *American Historical Review* 113 (2008): 647–77.

18. J. J. McCusker and R. R. Menard, *The Economy of British America 1607–1789* (Williamsburg, VA, 1985); R. C. Nash, "South Carolina and the Atlantic Economy in the Late Seventeenth and Eighteenth Centuries," *Economic History Review* 45 (1992): 677–702.

19. Hornsby, *British Atlantic*, 7.

20. W. Slauter, "Forward-Looking Statements: News and Speculation in the Age of the American Revolution," *Journal of Modern History* 81 (2009): 759–92.

21. *Leeds Mercury*, July 10, 1787.

22. T. Bickham, *Making Headlines: The American Revolution as Seen through the British Press* (DeKalb, IL, 2009).

23. See also issue of July 17, 1781.

24. *Gazetteer*, August 11, 1783, cited in A. Grant, "The Middling Men, the British Press, and America, November 1781–August 1783. An Association of Reader and Newspaper" (MLitt diss., Edinburgh, 1989), 16–17.

25. M. Pedley, ed., *The Map Trade in the Late Eighteenth Century: Letters to the London Map Sellers Jefferys and Faden* (Oxford, 2000).

26. K. Nebenzahl, *A Bibliography of Printed Battle Plans of the American Revolution, 1775–1795* (Chicago, 1975); M. T. Capps and T. G. Stroup, *United States Military Academy, West Point: The Library Map Collection: Period of the American Revolution 1753–1800* (West Point, NY, 1971).

27. R. T. Haines Halsey, "'Impolitical Prints': The American Revolution as Pictured by Contemporary English Caricaturists," *Bulletin of the New York Public Library* 43 (1939): 797–821.

28. *York Courant*, April 27, May 4, 11, 1784; *Leeds Intelligencer*, May 25, June1, 1784.

29. J. D. Drake, *The Nation's Nature: How Continental Presumptions Gave Rise to the United States of America* (Charlottesville, VA, 2011).

30. F. Fernàndez-Armesto, *Continuity and Discontinuity in the Sixteenth-Century New World* (Minneapolis, MN, 2001), 19.

31. C. Eastman, *A Nation of Speechifiers: Making an American Public after the Revolution* (Chicago, 2010).

32. T. Loughran, *The Republic in Print: Print Culture in the Age of United States Nation Building, 1770–1870* (New York, 2007).

33. S. Kermes, *Creating an American Identity: New England, 1789–1825* (New York, 2008).

34. J. R. Short, *Representing the Republic: Mapping the United States, 1600–1900* (London, 2001).

35. M. Brückner, *The Geographic Revolution in Early America: Maps, Literacy, and National Identity* (Chapel Hill, NC, 2006).

36. P. Stock, "America and the American Revolution in British Geographical Thought, c. 1760–1830," *English Historical Review* 131 (2016): 64–91.

37. R. A. Burchell, *The End of Anglo-America: Historical Essays in the Study of Cultural Divergence* (Manchester, 1991).

38. N. L. York, *The American Revolution, 1760–1790: New Nation as New Empire* (New York, 2016), 129.

39. M. Meranze and S. Makdisi, eds., *Imagining the British Atlantic after the American Revolution* (Toronto, 2015); *Newcastle Chronicle*, February 24, 1787, from *Norfolk Journal* in Virginia.

40. S. Hollingsworth, *An Account of the Present State of Nova Scotia* (Edinburgh, 1786), 139–42, 148–50.

41. J. Bannister and L. Riordan, eds., *The Loyal Atlantic in the Revolutionary Era* (Toronto, 2012).

42. D. Armitage and M. J. Braddick, eds., *The British Atlantic World, 1500–1800* (Basingstoke, UK, 2002).

43. M. Duckworth, "An Eighteenth-Century Questionnaire: William Robertson on the Indians," *Eighteenth-Century Life* 11 (1987): 37–49; I. F. Pugliese, "From Antagonism to a Common Fate: Guillaume-Thomas Raynal and William Robertson," in C. Courtney and J. Mander, eds., *Raynal's 'Histoire des deux Indes': Colonialism, Networks, and Global Exchange* (Oxford, 2015), 165–66.

44. K. McDonald, *Pirates, Merchants, Settlers, and Slaves: Colonial America and the Indo-Atlantic World* (Oakland, CA, 2015). For parallels and contrasts, see H. V. Bowen, E. Mancke, and J. G. Reid, eds., *Britain's Oceanic Empire: Atlantic and Indian Ocean Worlds, c. 1550–1850* (Cambridge, 2012).

45. J. R. Oldfield, *Popular Politics and British Anti-Slavery: The Mobilisation of Public Opinion against the Slave Trade, 1787–1807* (Manchester, 1995). For Bristol, M. Dresser, *Slavery Obscured: The Social History of the Slave Trade in an English Provincial Port* (London, 2001).

46. J. M. Gibbs, *Performing the Temple of Liberty: Slavery, Theater, and Popular Culture in London and Philadelphia, 1760–1850* (Baltimore, 2014); G. Quilley, "Art History and Double Consciousness: Visual Culture and Eighteenth-Century Maritime Britain," *Eighteenth-Century Studies* 48 (2014): 21–23.

47. J. G. A. Pocock, "Gibbon's *Decline and Fall* and the World View of the Late Enlightenment," *Eighteenth-Century Studies* 10 (1977): 287–303 and *Barbarism: Triumph in the West*, volume six of *Barbarism and Religion* (Cambridge, 2015); K. O'Brien, "Between Enlightenment and Stadial History: William Robertson on the History of Europe," *British Journal of Eighteenth-Century Studies* 16 (1993): 53–63.

48. A. Smith, *An Inquiry into the Nature and Causes of the Wealth of Nations* (Oxford, 1976 ed.): 689–91. See also W. Robertson, *The History of the Reign of the Emperor Charles V: With a View of the Progress of Society in Europe* (London, 1769; 3 vols., 1782 ed.), I, 5–6; E. Gibbon, *The History of the Decline and Fall of the Roman Empire* (1776–88), edited by J. B. Bury (7 vols., 1897–1901 ed.), I, 93, V, 358–59, VII, 2.

49. Smith, *An Inquiry into the Nature and Causes*, 708.

50. D. Ryan, *Technologies of Empire: Writing, Imagination, and the Making of Imperial Networks, 1750–1820* (Newark, DE, 2013), 34.

51. M. H. Fisher, ed., *The Travels of Dean Mahomet: An Eighteenth-Century Journey through India* (Berkeley, CA, 1997), 55.

52. T. M. Curley, "Johnson's Tour of Scotland and the Idea of Great Britain," *British Journal of Eighteenth-Century Studies* 12 (1989): 137.

53. T. Barrett, *At the Edge of Empire: The Terek Cossacks and the North Caucasus Frontier, 1700-1860* (Boulder, CO, 1999); W. Sunderland, *Taming the Wild Frontier: Colonization and Empire on the Russian Steppe* (Ithaca, NY, 2004); B. J. Boeck, *Imperial Boundaries: Cossack Communities and Empire-Building in the Age of Peter the Great* (Cambridge, 2009).

54. P. Risso, "Cultural Perceptions of Piracy: Maritime Violence in the Western Indian Ocean and Persian Gulf Region during the Long Eighteenth Century," *Journal of World History* 12 (2001): 293-319; D. Elliott, "Pirates, Polities, and Companies: Global Politics on the Konkan Littoral c. 1690-1756," Economic History Working Papers, London School of Economics, 136 (2010).

55. L. Subramanian, "Whose Pirate? Reflections on State Power and Predation on India's Western Littoral," in S. Davies, D. S. Roberts, and G. S. Espinosa, eds., *India and Europe in the Global Eighteenth Century* (Oxford, 2014), 241-65.

56. T. Burnard, "'The Countrie Continues Sicklie': White Mortality in Jamaica, 1655-1780," *Social History of Medicine* 12 (1999): 67.

57. A. S. Fogleman, *Two Troubled Souls: An Eighteenth-Century Couple's Spiritual Journey in the Atlantic World* (Chapel Hill, NC, 2013).

58. For the complexities of this, A. Crome, "The 1753 'Jew Bill' Controversy: Jewish Restoration to Palestine, Biblical Prophecy, and English National Identity," *English Historical Review* 130 (2015): 1449-78.

59. Dobbs to John, 3rd Earl of Bute, June 2, 1762, Mount Stuart, [Bute papers] papers of the 3rd Earl, 2/74.

60. G. Sale, ed., *The Koran* (London, 1734), iv.

61. Pitts, *A Faithful Account of the Religion and Manners of the Mahometans* (1731), xv; P. Auchterlonie, *Encountering Islam: Joseph Pitts: An English Slave in 17th-Century Algiers and Mecca* (London, 2012).

62. H. V. Bowen, M. Lincoln, and N. Rigby, eds., *The Worlds of the East India Company* (Woodbridge, UK, 2002).

63. S. Davies, D. S. Roberts, and G. S. Espirosa, eds., *India and Europe in the Global Eighteenth Century* (Oxford, 2014).

64. U. Hillemann, *Asian Empire and British Knowledge: China and the Networks of British Imperial Expansion* (Cambridge, 2009); C.-M. Yang, *Performing China: Virtue, Commerce, and Orientalism in Eighteenth-Century England, 1660-1785* (Baltimore, 2011); J. L. Hargrave, "'To the Glory of the Chinese': Sinocentric Political Reform in Eliza Haywood's *The Adventures of Eovaai*," *Eighteenth-Century Studies* 49 (2015): 31-52.

65. T. W. Nechtman, *Nabobs: Empire and Identity in Eighteenth-Century Britain* (Cambridge, 2010).

66. M. J. Franklin, *Orientalist Jones: Sir William Jones, Poet, Lawyer, and Linguist, 1746-1794* (Oxford, 2011); A. Murray, ed., *Sir William Jones, 1746-94: A Commemoration* (Oxford, 1998).

67. R. Rocher, *Orientalism, Poetry and the Millennium: The Checkered Life of Nathaniel Brassey Halhed, 1751-1830* (Delhi, 1983).

68. R. D. Barnett, "Diplomatic Aspects of the Sephardic Influx from Portugal in the Early Eighteenth Century," *Transactions of the Jewish Historical Society of England* 25 (1973-75): 210-21.

69. U. App, *The Birth of Orientalism* (Philadelphia, 2010).

70. J. Browne, *The Secular Ark* (New Haven, CT, 1983).

71. B. Schmidt, *Inventing Exoticism: Geography, Globalism, and Europe's Early Modern World* (Philadelphia, 2015).

72. *Times*, July 3, *London Chronicle*, August 2, 1787.

73. The distinction is between the provincial government of Holland and that of the United Provinces as a whole.

74. C. Buchet, *Marine, économie, et société: Un exemple d'interaction: l'Avitaillement de la Royal Navy durant la guerre de sept ans* (Paris, 1999).

75. H. Furber, "The Overland Route to India in the Seventeenth and Eighteenth Centuries," *Journal of Indian History* 29 (1951): 105–33, esp. 123–33; F. Charles-Roux, *L'Angleterre, L'Isthme de Suez et l'Egypte au XVIIIe siècle* (Paris, 1922).

76. N. Hudson, "From 'Nation' to 'Race': The Origin of Racial Classification in Eighteenth-Century Thought," *Eighteenth-Century Studies* 29 (1996): 247–64; J. Chaplin, "Natural Philosophy and an Early Racial Idiom in North America: Comparing English and Indian Bodies," *William and Mary Quarterly*, 3rd ser., 44 (1997): 229–52; T. Bickham, "'I Shall Tear Off Their Scalps, and Make Cups of Their Skulls': American Indians in the Eighteenth-Century British Press," in T. Fulford and K. Hutchings, eds., *Native Americans and Anglo-American Culture, 1750–1850: The Indian Atlantic* (Cambridge, 2009), 56–73; M. Hunt, "Racism, Imperialism, and the Traveler's Gaze in Eighteenth-Century England," *Journal of British Studies* 32 (1993): 333–57

8

Responding to Coal and Commerce

> Your Patriots I will straight inspire,
> And touch them with commercial fire.
>
> —John Watson, *Union Journal: or, Halifax Advertiser*

JOHN WATSON, A Yorkshire curate, in his 1759 verses on the navigation of the River Calder, had Neptune, the god of the sea, address a Britain, then in the throes of war with France, in terms that clearly linked commercial activity to patriotism.[1] Inland Halifax was a major cloth-manufacturing center, not a port like Bristol or Liverpool, but the improvement of rivers, the prelude to canal building, would allow it to play its role. Halifax was also an instance of the local forcing houses of a variegated middle-class culture.[2]

Despite such awareness, the maps and gazetteers of the period, however, generally paid insufficient attention to the transformation in British power and geography that was occurring. This transformation owed much to the major development of coal production and the economic and geographical changes, notably in the second half of the century, that arose as a direct result. This was a long-term trend and, possibly as a consequence, one that did not force a new geography of attention onto eighteenth-century commentators. Looked at differently, there was a conventional character to the depiction of the country, and notably to the emphasis on county units and landed seats, a depiction that did not respond to coal, even though individual landowners frequently did. This point relates to how a changing, particularly industrializing, urbanizing, and imperial society learned, or did not learn, about its own changing nature, and, especially, how far the traditional frameworks of knowledge, such as the parish, borough, and county, still adequately represented that new society. Geography thus emerges both as an aspect of a changing society and as an aspect of the developing generation of information.

Coal production rose in the sixteenth and, even more, the seventeenth century. The major production area was the North-East of England. The amount of coal shipped from the River Tyne rose to 400,000 tons by 1625 and to over 600,000 in 1730–31. Seventy percent of this coal went to London in 1682, and King's Lynn and Great Yarmouth, the ports for East Anglia, took half of the rest. When the Scots invaded England in 1644, one of their objectives was to capture the North-East and thereby secure coal supplies for their parliamentary allies in London. Domestic heating was a key use for coal and notably in London, but there was also increasing use for manufacturing. Coal, for example, was the main fuel in sugar refining, brewing, salt boiling,[3] and brick making by 1700. As a result in part of local coal, Newcastle produced about 40 percent of all the glass made in England in the seventeenth century.

Coal production also rose in Lancashire, Wales, and Central Scotland. Landlords sought to profit. Searching for coal, William, 6th Earl of Derby, ordered surveys on his Lancastrian property at Knowsley Park in 1602, and Sir Richard Molyneux followed suit nearby in 1610. Much Lancastrian coal was exported through Liverpool and Wigan to Ireland, especially to Dublin, an export that was to be joined by coal from Cumberland and Ayrshire.[4] This was an important aspect of the extent to which, despite serious problems facing ships,[5] the Irish Sea operated as an economic zone. Sea routes, like inland waterways, were important, for the overland transport of bulky goods remained expensive.

Sales to national markets brought money and workers into areas that produced coal and increased local demand, especially for food. For example, the development of coal and lead mining in County Durham in the North-East of England in the sixteenth and seventeenth centuries led to a rise in population, from about 35,000 in 1550 to about 70,000 in 1700, and to the enclosure of land, so that it could be more easily farmed and adapted to new agricultural methods in order to feed this rising population. By the end of the century, most of the lowland east of the county was enclosed.

In 1700, British coal production, of about three million tons, was largely for domestic heating. The North-East of England accounted for nearly half the national output. East Shropshire, South Yorkshire, and South Staffordshire, in that order, all in England, were the next three leading production areas.[6] Output rose by just over 1 percent a year to 5.2 million tons by 1750, and then by more than 2 percent a year for the rest of the century.[7]

This growth was far greater, in absolute and relative terms, than that in any other country, and coal production helped to make the British economy distinctive, providing a cheap energy economy. This opened up a powerful comparative advantage over Continental economies where energy remained largely dependent on wood supplies, although, as in Britain, water and wind power were also valuable. By 1750, it has been calculated, coal provided 61 percent of all the energy used in England, was six times more significant than wood, and produced energy equivalent to that from 4.3 million acres of woodland.[8] Even if the figures can be queried, the trend is clear. The availability of investment capital,[9] as well as mercantile organization and state activity, facilitated this trend, whereas the Chinese state did little to promote the use of coal, and in India, there was an emphasis on wood, not coal.[10]

Coal offered many advantages. It was readily transportable, and certainly more easily so than wood, and notably in energy equivalence, and thus coal altered the pressures of distance. Coal was also a controllable fuel, especially in comparison with wood, and therefore more useful for manufacturing that required a controllable heat. Coal could be mined throughout the year, whereas water mills were affected by ice, flooding, and summertime falls in water flow. Without transport, coal was of limited value, but coal with transport could serve as the basis for the creation of buoyant mixed-industrial regions with large pools of labor and demand and special services. Separately, by raising labor productivity, cheap energy made it easier to pay high wages and thus to sustain demand.[11]

The need to move coal acted as a spur for innovation, especially for the construction of canals and of railways with horse-drawn wagons. Coal was also crucial for the powering of steam engines, which were potent symbols of a new age and a means of, and for, power. The steam pump demonstrated by Thomas Savery in 1698 was of little importance, but, in 1712, Thomas Newcomen, a Dartmouth ironmonger, produced his Atmospheric Engine.

In essence, this steam engine consisted of a beam with a cylinder. The injection of water condensed the steam, causing the piston to descend under the weight of the atmosphere, and thus lift the pump rods at the other end of the beam. The piston was returned to the top of the stroke by the weight of the pump rods. Simple compared to what was to come but also a major change. Successive developments in technology, including in related engineering, were highly significant but so also was the availability of investment.

The regional consequences of coal power were to be manifold, but it is important not to read back from later developments with coal, on the national, regional, and local scales. For example, South Wales was responsible for 19 percent of British coal production in 1900–13 but only 2.7 percent in 1750. Communications were crucial in this transformation: successively, a road from Cardiff along the Taff Valley, the Glamorgan Canal (1793–94), and the Taff Valley railway (1841). Coal was important to the development of the South Wales iron industry. There were 25 furnaces by 1796 and 148 by 1811. Merthyr Tydfil, a hamlet in 1750, was, by 1801, the leading center of iron production in the world. The demand for iron encouraged the mining of coal. Scotland also saw significant industrial growth linked to coal.[12]

Whereas foreign visitors in the early decades of the eighteenth century very much focused on London and South-East England, a greater number came to take an interest in industrial sites and new technology. This was true, for example, of Thomas Jefferson's visit in 1786, a visit in which he toured industrial sites in the West Midlands and London. Also, after the War of American Independence, the brothers François and Alexandre de La Rochefoucauld went as far north as Sheffield, Manchester, and Liverpool and, in addition, also visited such centers as Northampton, Leicester, Derby, Shrewsbury, Birmingham, Coventry, Bristol, Bath, Exeter, Plymouth, and Dorchester. Their travels were not as far flung as those of Count Karl von Zinzendorf, who provided a lengthy account of British industry, but in 1784–85, they saw much of England. The La Rochefoucaulds saw John Wilkinson's mill at Birmingham, describing it in detail, and discussing it with his agent. He also reported on the progress of nail manufacture in the city noting that the majority of workers were women and that they generally turned out two thousand a day, earning a shilling. Similarly, ribbon manufacture at Coventry was described by the brothers, as were Liverpool slavers, the Bridgewater Canal, coal mining, and the Sheffield metal industry.

This demonstrated the degree to which travelers in Britain were particularly interested in technological progress and signs of modernity,[13] a process that had reached its royal apogee at the close of the seventeenth century with the visit of Peter the Great who saw a ship being constructed at Deptford in 1698. A Newtonian world of applied science and the dramatic new utilitarian buildings of, for example, Greenwich and the Bank of England were of interest, or at least note, to many travelers, British and foreign.

Although there was much that was not dependent on steam-powered factories—for example, in Birmingham[14]—industry was increasingly attracted to the coalfields, as with South Wales and South Staffordshire. Coal-based industry helped produce a new regional economic geography of Britain, one of expansion and decline, winners and losers.[15] By the 1790s, industrial change had a clear regional pattern that was reflected in indicators such as expenditure on poor relief by head of population. Seasonally unemployed laborers, many of whom worked in farming, were a major call on poor relief, although the poor elderly also required relief. In 1801, the average expenditure on poor relief per head[16] for England and Wales was 9s 1d (45p in modern money), but in the industrial counties, it was far lower: 4s 4d in Lancashire and 6s 7d in the West Riding of Yorkshire. In contrast, counties with hardly any industry, such as Sussex, or with declining industries, such as Essex, Norfolk, and Suffolk, had to pay far more than the average. The Suffolk yarn industry had collapsed by 1800, unable to compete with the uniform quality and lower prices of machine-spun yarns from the West Riding of Yorkshire.

In addition to these divisions, there was also the long-standing opposition between cloth manufacturers and wool producers. Thus, supporting the former, the *Leeds Intelligencer* in the winter of 1781–82 produced a number of items critical of the wish of Lincolnshire farmers to export wool.[17] The paper looked at the reporting on the items by other newspapers—for example, the *Cambridge Chronicle*.

Population numbers rose rapidly in the areas of industrialization. In contrast to an annual average increase in population in England and Wales in 1750–70 of 0.75 percent, the percentage for the West Riding of Yorkshire was 1.7 percent. In addition, urban manufacturing was very important, with towns such as Derby, Newcastle, Nottingham, and Stockport becoming major centers of activity: in Stockport, the population rose from 3,144 in 1754 to 14,830 in 1801. In Liverpool, the trading center for the British Atlantic, it rose to 83,250 in 1801. Ten years earlier, William, Marquess of Lansdowne, formerly, 2nd Earl of Shelburne, Prime Minister in 1782–83, wrote from his splendid country seat at Bowood, "If you think of Wales, you should see Liverpool. It is an amazing phenomenon."[18]

In place of the earlier emphasis on rural manufacturing districts,[19] districts that lessened the urban-rural divide,[20] the relationship between urbanization and industrialization became closer, with the growing cities closely associated with manufacturing or with related commerce and services. Industrialization involved much disruption and hardship, often with scant improvement in real wages or labor security.[21] Although small towns remained important, not least in the goods and services they could provide,[22] industrialization involved developments to which the conventional presentation of the country's geography did not really rise, and that situation encourages modern treatments that are not county based.[23]

ROADS AND CANALS

So also with other aspects of economic transformation. Roads could be presented in traditional terms, being long marked on maps. However, the idea of a rapidly dynamic road system, carrying more traffic and more speedily,[24] was different. In the latter case, most of the links took on their logic, and finance, at the regional or national level. So also even more with canals. These links are not adequately covered if the level of analysis is that of the county. For example, the comparatively slow growth of many Cheshire towns in part was due to their relatively poor links with the more dynamic centers in Lancashire. This reflected not only the significance of regional dynamics but also the extent to which what stimulated growth was not necessarily intrinsic to particular towns but to do with external relationships in the shape of their linkages with town and country across at least a regional range.[25]

In the eighteenth century, steam was not applied to provide locomotive power as was to be the case on land and at sea in the nineteenth century. Nevertheless, despite qualifications about revolutions, there were major changes in transportation in a number of respects. These were very important because it was partly through transport that the geography of Britain was experienced, while, in turn, efforts were made to shape it. One of the most significant was the improvement in communications and, in particular, in roads and in coach services. Better communications within Britain ensured that demand could be met and for both people and freight.

The inherited situation had frequently been dire, although there could be a complex road network, as in pre-turnpike Wiltshire, and, as long as there had not been heavy rainfall, most English roads were passable, even in winter.[26] Nevertheless, the complex physical geography of the country posed crucial geographical limits in the shape of terrain and drainage. Steep climbs were difficult for packhorses and wagons. Many roads were narrow paths on which packhorses often could not pass each other. The quality of the roads reflected local circumstances. Road construction and maintenance were of limited effectiveness in marshy regions, such as the Fens or the Somerset Levels, each extensive regions, where there were no real roads. In the Somerset Levels, trampsmen and -women carried packs of goods to villages that were inaccessible to wagons or even packhorses. Roads were also an issue in areas with a high water table, such as the heavy clays of the Midlands, South Essex, and the Vale of Berkeley in Gloucestershire, where wheels churned up the mud into impassable quagmires. The need to avoid damp river valleys, such as the Severn, ensured that roads tended to stick to high ground in a pattern that went back many centuries, indeed to pre-Roman days.[27]

Poor roads tied up scarce capital in goods in transit and led to a reliance on carts or packhorses, rather than wagons that could carry more but that required a better road surface. Despite their legal obligations, parishes generally failed to maintain their roads to the standards required by heavy through traffic. The resulting situation required local knowledge and could not be mapped. Indeed, the mapping of the quality of transport routes has always been poor.

The limitations of road transport, notably for bulk goods, encouraged coastal and river traffic, but they also owed much to the possibilities provided for routes across bays, estuaries, and rivers that were otherwise water obstacles. Both coastal and river traffic make a contribution to an appreciation of the strength of regionalism in the period. Thus, Bristol's port books show that the city acted as the focal point of an extensive coastal and river network, notably in the Bristol Channel and the valley of the Severn, that linked the economies of the city's far-flung hinterland, both with Bristol and with each other. Bristol's twice-yearly fairs provided important commercial "spaces," helping create and sustain a hinterland serving the market offered by the city and its links.[28]

Improvements to the roads, which had been neglected during the Civil War, began in the late seventeenth century but became much more pronounced in the eighteenth. The improvement of the road system assisted postal services which, in turn, enabled newspapers, both London and provincial, to meet provincial demand and thereby helped London newspapers to establish their claim to be a national voice. Postal services, notably the cross-country system, also permitted learned and literary societies, such as the Spaulding Gentlemen's Society founded in 1712 and its Peterborough counterpart founded in 1730, to develop a network of correspondents.[29]

In 1663, the first turnpike trust was created on part of the Great North Road, and if a national turnpike network was not a reality until the mid-eighteenth century, communication links had already been improved. For example, the first Cheshire turnpike act of Parliament had been in 1705, and the next one was not till 1724, but, from the 1750s, the situation in the county improved: cross routes were turnpiked, including Macclesfield to Buxton in 1758 and Chester to Northwich in 1769. Such an account may appear seamless, but there were controversies over routes, both in Cheshire and elsewhere. These extended to bridges, including, in Yorkshire, whether there should be one at Selby, as the city of Ripon wanted, or not, as the city of York recommended.[30] Moreover, once turnpikes were established, there was still the need to improve them, notably against flooding.[31]

By the end of the eighteenth century, much of lowland England was within ten miles of a turnpike.[32] This process helped collapse space and lessen difference, as well as distance and a sense of distance. For example, in 1702, visiting the distant town of Helston in Cornwall, John Evelyn noted: "where we dined was the Royal Oak Lottery which one could hardly have expected to have found in a country town so remote from London."[33] Maps depicted the new and improved roads, as in Daniel Paterson's *A New and Accurate Description of All the Direct and Principal Cross Roads in England and Wales* (1771). At the same time, narrow wheels damaged the road surfaces, so that projectors such as James Sharp pressed the case for broader wheels claiming they would consolidate the road surface. Sharp argued that his rollers approached the efficiency of "railed roads" as the road and the vehicle were in effect part of the same "mechanism."[34]

Improved roads and coach services were also important to travelers in the colonies, although far less so than more frequent transoceanic voyages, while coastal voyages were also highly significant. This was especially so for islands, notably in the Caribbean but was also seen in North America—for example, between New England and the southern colonies. This situation matched that of maritime links between individual colonies and Britain and contributed to a situation in which these links were as, or often more, important than those between the colonies. Bodies of water that were especially significant were Chesapeake and Delaware Bays and Long Island Sound. In addition, major rivers, such as the Hudson, were not bridged.

Better roads and coach services, in terms of more extensive, regular, and reliable services, as well as regular and more reliable maritime links encouraged a sense of improved communications as normative. Moreover, space was reshaped. For example, faster and higher capacity road transport in Britain aided national integration or, at least, the sense that it was occurring. The development of post roads can be linked to a differing understanding of travel and space on the part of writers. As a result of travel, an appreciation of topography on the local, regional, and national levels improved.[35]

At the same time, there was significant regional variation. For example, the road links were particularly apparent in South-East England, the wealthy area closest to the capital. New and improved roads made it easier for Londoners to travel into the surrounding countryside. This led, in 1790, to the publication of John Cary's *Survey of the High Roads from London to Hampton Court* and twenty-five other places around the metropolis, a volume, on the pattern of the 1675 Ogilby road atlas *Britannia*, divided into forty strips covering, for example, London to St. Albans in three maps. This work was reissued in 1799, 1801, and 1810. There was also road building in London in order to improve circulation and maintain access. The versatile Cary was a map seller who also produced terrestrial and celestial globes, astronomical books, road books and maps, and canal plans. In 1798, he printed a new edition of Ogilby's *Britannia* and, in 1815, William Smith's *Delineation of the Strata of England and Wales with Part of Scotland*.

As a separate improvement for communications, one of consequence primarily for freight, there was a major expansion in the use of internal waterways. Canals played a major role in improving the transport of bulky goods, notably coal and, therefore, in satisfying and, in turn, creating demand, and literally being an aspect of the geography of power. The Bridgewater Canal, begun in 1761 to bring coal from Francis, 3rd Duke of Bridgewater's mines at Worsley to the major market of Manchester, was particularly influential. Having viewed it in 1767, Joseph Banks reflected, "The benefits accruing to the country are almost invaluable. Trade is opened between two very large towns [Manchester and Liverpool] before labouring under great inconveniences . . . and a plan is struck out before deemed impracticable which has already been followed in several parts of the kingdom."

In contrast to the earlier emphasis on improving rivers, there was a rapid expansion in canal provision, and, unlike with river improvement, this led to the creation of a system that spanned much of the country. In 1790, indeed, the Oxford Canal linked Oxford and the Midlands, creating the final link in a network joining the rivers Trent, Mersey, and Thames. The network enhanced the significance of relevant ports that acted as tranship-ment points, notably Liverpool and Hull: nodes were as important as routes. In turn, the requirement for more capacity and the availability of investment led to the decision to improve the London–Birmingham route by digging a new canal, the Grand Junction Canal, from the Thames near London, to join the Oxford Canal. The legislation passed in 1793, the same year in which the opening of the Monkland Canal stimulated the development of the Lanarkshire coalfield to serve the rapidly growing Glasgow market. More generally, canals permitted the movement of larger amounts of coal.

Whereas the possibilities for improving rivers were very much determined by the course of the latter, although still involving rival economic and political interests, as with the River Dee in Cheshire in 1732–34,[36] canals provided a "new-build" capability that offered the possibility of reconceptualizing spatial links and therefore creating a new geography. This creation involved national, regional, and local understanding of space. These were very different to road travel. In addition to the new links, there was much speculation about others. Some were attempted and unfinished— for example, the canal between Exeter and Taunton—while others only remained ideas. However, the net effect was to create the possibility of new geographies of power.

Surveying was a key skill for canal construction, and issues of terrain, slope profile, drainage, and soil type proved highly significant at the local level and therefore could affect more general issues of the viability of particular routes. Aside from making particular places of significance as nodes, prefiguring the later impact of railways, canals also altered the economic consequences of being landlocked. Thus, the area around Stoke-on-Trent, an area hitherto noted for poor roads, could become a major production center for pottery because pots could be transported out by canal, an opportunity that was profitability grasped by Josiah Wedgwood.

Canal construction involved the press, which built up public interest, and also the landed elite. Thus, in the March 16 and April 6, 1789 issues, the *Salisbury and Winchester Journal* praised the plans for a Bristol-London canal via Salisbury, before adding on April 13: "We are happy to hear that most of the gentlemen of rank and fortune in the neighbourhood of the proposed Great Western Canal intend to support the undertaking with all their weight and influence, not only as an object of private emolument, but on the noble and patriotic principle of public good."[37]

Like most newspapers, the *Union Journal: or, Halifax Advertiser* supported better transport links—for example, a post road from Halifax via Sheffield to Mansfield in order to improve communications with London and thus focus the Kendal to London transport route on Halifax. A sense of excitement was readily conveyed with items about new transportation links and technology. The publication of one in the *Newcastle Chronicle* of January 6, 1787, probably owes something to the comment concerning the impact on the price of coals:

> A letter from Cirencester, Gloucestershire, says, "A navigable work of a most arduous and extensive nature is now carrying on in this neighbourhood, which is nothing less than a junction between the Thames and the Severn. In this undertaking a prodigious mountain, of more than two miles and a half in length will be cut through, so that barges of 60 or 70 tons burthen may pass. Near two miles of this subterraneous work are nearly finished, and the whole navigation, which is near thirty miles long, is expected to be finished in a year and a half. When completed, London will have a grand inland navigation with almost all parts of England and Wales, so that the trade thereupon must be immense. The people near the part of it that is already finished feel its good effects, by a considerable reduction in the price of coals."

The following year, George III was to see the Sapperton Tunnel through which the Thames-Severn canal runs.[38] Less dramatically, turnpikes transformed the availability of fish, as was noted in the *St. James's Chronicle* of March 16, 1765:

Extract of a letter from York, March 11

Some time ago I read a letter in your paper from this place, complaining of the dearness of provisions in this city, and particularly of the fish market, I can now tell you with truth, that the inhabitants having exerted themselves on that occasion, we now enjoy fish in greater plenty, and is mostly brought here on proper carriages, like those of Captain Blakes. The present price of fish with us is from two pence to two pence half-penny, and three pence; and other sea fish in proportion; a great relief to the housekeepers, when fresh meat bears an high price, though nothing is extravagant for this time of the year. Good wheat is retailing out at five shillings a bushel, Winchester, by a society of gentlemen, which has reduced the market a shilling a bushel. We think ourselves happy, and wait with pleasure for the next year's crop of corn, which promises well, as there has not been any extraordinary quantity of rain fallen this winter, and which most certainly was the occasion of thin crops the last year. Add to the plenty of fish at this place, that we see three or four times a week, fish machines passing through this city to Leeds, Sheffield, Doncaster, nay, as far Derby and Worcester, of so great utility to the public are turnpike roads, to which places it was impossible before they were made to carry sea-fish either with proper expedition or security.

CONSUMERISM

A key element in economic transformation, consumerism[39] occurred at a range of scales, from the international to the intimate, and was important to the more sophisticated advertising that facilitated the intensification of the whole economic effort, not least more specialization.[40] For example, advertisements helped shape the normative idea about objects and practices, thus fixing the identification of goods. Advertisements thereby affected everyday social spaces.[41] Auctions developed and were regulated by law. They allowed and facilitated a range of activities including the purchase of used items from wealthier homes by the middling and lower classes.

The expansion of cities and towns was an important instance of consumerism given the effort involved. This expansion was also an evolutionary process, with developments out of existing housing types and traditional layouts. The ability to change and upgrade the structure of houses, plus the high level of maintenance that new houses required, especially in the painting of woodwork, made them well suited to a consumer society geared toward the continued renewal and replacement of products.[42]

The supply networks of consumerism were crucial. These included traditional forms, notably fairs, which continued to be both significant and adaptive. There was also the development of newer and different forms, ranging from shops to the supply and distribution networks of transoceanic trade, such as the agents and suppliers of the East India Company.[43] Directories provided much information for contemporaries and offer much today. Significant ones included Bailey's *Western and Midland Directory* (1783) and Barfoot and Wilkes's *Universal British Directory* (1793–98).

Consumerism fed by transoceanic links reached into every parish, with shifts in taste focused on the products of empire and trade, notably tobacco, sugar, coffee, tea, chocolate, and cod. So also with mahogany and exotic woods for furniture, indigo for cloth dyeing, and other products. In turn, the development of these tastes sustained the profits of this commercial imperialism.[44]

These profits required information. Indeed, the aspects of that quest considered in this book—for example, mapping and the expansion of the press—were in part driven by the quest for profit, a quest that was inherently one of comparative advantage. This advantage was both on the international scale and also within Britain. For example, specialization, concentration, and specific lines of trade were keys to the contrasting performance of British outports. Thus, Bristol concentrated on sugar because of difficulties with other products, an outcome reinforced by time and communication lags, seasonal variations in imperfect markets, wartime disruptions, and the need to consolidate connections with specific agents in particular places to maintain secure business relations. Such issues encouraged specialization.[45]

The nature of the hinterland was also significant. Whereas a rapidly developing industrial hinterland helped Liverpool in its development as what became the leading British port on the Atlantic, Bristol's trade was not sufficiently linked to export industries that would have helped both the hinterland and the trade. The need to keep foreign and domestic demand and opportunities aligned was important. Liverpool's hinterland was such that the first number of *The Union Journal: or, Halifax Advertiser*, that of February 6, 1759, announced: "as the printer is a great well-wisher to trade, and would do everything to promote that most valuable blessing to the nation, he will oblige his subscribers with the exports, etc. at Liverpool." On April 24, the paper added: "Numbers of our worthy readers being desirous of having the Hull exports, etc. inserted, as we think it our duty to do everything in our power to please them, care will be taken, in a week or two, to comply with their request." On May 5, however, "We are obliged to leave out the Hull imports and exports for want of room." Other papers did the same. Thus, the *Sheffield Advertiser* in 1761 reported trade and shipping at the nearby port of Hull, while the *Darlington Pamphlet*, a weekly newspaper, in 1772 carried shipping news from the nearby North Sea ports of Hull, Newcastle, and Stockton.

Another form of hinterland was created by advertisements, with the printer proprietor of the *Chelmsford Chronicle*, significantly subtitled, *or, Essex Weekly Advertiser*, claiming on September 14, 1764, that "the sale is now become so very considerable that all advertisements therein inserted will be universally read all over the county of Essex, and its environs," the latter indicated by naming agents in Harwich and London. Networks became denser with time.[46] Thus, *The Bury and Norwich Post: or, Suffolk, Norfolk, and Essex Advertiser* of February 21, 1787, named agents in fifty East Anglian towns. Titles captured the significance of commerce, as in the *Hull Advertiser and Exchange Gazette* of 1795.

Similarly, financial information was very important to the networks from which the financial revolution developed. These networks were centered on the Royal Exchange in London. They provided a range of services, notably investment, mortgaging, and insurance. In turn, these networks could be disrupted by false information, notably about the imminence of war, that was planted in the press.[47] In Samuel Foote's play *The Bankrupt*, first acted in 1773, the printer, "Margin," is pleased by his gains considering the "winter has been pretty pacific."[48]

ECONOMIC DEVELOPMENT

The importance of the nature of power for all these developments emerges from comparative work, notably the question of why such change did not occur elsewhere. Whereas in France, control was more in the hands of a central bureaucracy that was not particularly responsive to local needs, the political institutions and culture of Britain were more conducive for the local initiatives and control required for the creation of new transport links. The possibility of establishing turnpike trusts by Private Acts of Parliament was significant, whereas, in France, the insistence on central government control precluded necessary private investment, led to a concentration on a small number of prestige projects and hindered regional development. The British transport system facilitated the emergence of new industries, regional development and specialization, an increase in the scale and standardization of production, and wider markets. Similarly, English law emphasized the landowner's rights to minerals and coal under their property and the right to dispose of property as thought appropriate at death.[49]

Another difference between Britain and France was provided by the free discussion of economic policy, not only in Parliament but also in print, and also the facilities offered by the latter for disseminating economic information, as in the notice by Master Hatters against embezzlement by subcontractors that was carried in the *Public Advertiser* of January 13, 1757. Six days later, the paper discussed the need to oblige distillers to use malted corn only. In addition, there were signs of increased bureaucratization in the administration of justice by justices of peace and related aspects of control. Thus, in the rural district of Lindsey in Lincolnshire, the quarter sessions were reorganized in 1749, and from the late 1760s, the documentation was fuller and much more business came before the bench.[50] Another instance of greater control and registration was offered by the Marriage Act of 1753.[51]

Legislation on economic topics formed the subject of much press attention.[52] This related both to national legislation, as with the *Edinburgh Advertiser* of June 17, 1783, and to its local counterparts. The *Shrewsbury Chronicle* of February 4, 1786, carried a letter about improvement to the navigation on the River Severn. As with other aspects of improvement, there was also a social dimension, as with the Leeds item in the *Leeds Intelligencer* of November 7, 1786, that called for vigilance on the part of the constables in order to deal with disorderly people at fairs. The press also lent itself to policing by public admonition. Thus, three weeks later, it reported, "the Court Leet belonging to his Grace the Duke of Leeds ... at Wakefield, several persons were fined for selling by false weights" before adding, in a different type, "Would it not be right to have the names of these offenders published?" Prosecution associations were part of the same drive and were praised in the press.[53] Moral strictures extended to Sabbatarianism, notably swimming on Sunday. These attitudes were linked to the moral politics of George III.

Moral strictures were significant. At the same time, consumerism was indeed, as moralists warned, a universal solvent. In particular, alongside merchantilist ideas and practices, the wish to create open and active markets was supported by legislation and notably so in the crucial field of food supply. Moreover, alongside relatively sophisticated financial institutions, the fiscal system was far more liberal than that of France, although there was also major concern about the scale of the national debt. In addition, Britain's ability, from 1762 until 1793, to avoid commitments on the European continent ensured that military expenditure could be focused on the Royal Navy, where Britain enjoyed a powerful comparative advantage, underwriting mercantilism and imperialism,[54] rather than on the army, where it did not. However constrained, the greater liberalism and flexibility of the British political and social system created opportunities for the "middling sort" which helped commercial and industrial development.[55] This situation contrasted with an agrarian paternalism in China that proved less conducive to economic transformation.[56]

Notes

1. John Watson, *Union Journal: or, Halifax Advertiser*, February 27, 1759.

2. J. Smail, *The Origins of Middle-Class Culture: Halifax, Yorkshire, 1660–1780* (Basingstoke, UK, 1994).

3. C. A. Whatley, *The Scottish Salt Industry 1570–1850: An Economic and Social History* (Aberdeen, 1987).

4. J. Langton, *Geographical Change and the Industrial Revolution. Coalmining in South-West Lancashire, 1590–1700* (Cambridge, 1979); C. A. Whatley, "The Finest Place for a Lasting Colliery: Coal Mining Enterprise in Ayrshire c.1600–1840," *Ayrshire Collections* 14, no. 2 (1983): 50–57.

5. Re: running aground and adverse winds in 1695, Journal of Edward Southwell, New Haven, Connecticut, Beinecke, Osborn Shelves f b 90; O. Wood, *West Cumberland Coal 1600–1982/3* (Kendal, UK, 1988): 53.

6. J. Hatcher, *The History of the British Coal Industry, Volume 1: Before 1700* (Oxford, 1993).

7. A. J. Rawling, *The Rise of Liverpool and Demographic Change in Part of South-West Lancashire, 1661–1760*, (PhD diss. University of Liverpool, 1986), 25–27.

8. E. A. Wrigley, *Energy and the English Industrial Revolution* (Cambridge, 2010), 94.

9. James Lister to brother Jeremy, May 19, 1772, Halifax, Calderdale Archives, SH 7/JL/25.

10. P. Parthasarathi, *Why Europe Grew Rich and Asia Did Not: Global Economic Divergence, 1600–1850* (Cambridge, 2011).

11. R. C. Allen, *The British Industrial Revolution in Global Perspective* (Cambridge, 2009); B. Trinder, *The Industrial Revolution in Shropshire*, 3rd ed. (Chichester, UK, 2000); J. Brewer and R. Porter, eds., *Consumption and the World of Goods* (London, 1993).

12. C. Whatley, *Scottish Society 1707–1830: Beyond Jacobitism, towards Industrialisation* (Manchester, 2000).

13. G. Gurtler, "Impressionen einer Reise. Das England-Itineraire des Grafen Karl von Zinzendorf 1768," *Mitteilungen des Instituts für Österreichische Geschichtsforschung* (1985), 33–69; N. Scarfe, *Innocent Espionage. The La Rochefoucauld Brothers Tour of England in 1785* (Woodbridge, UK, 1995) is more useful than J. Marchand, ed., *A Frenchman in England 1784: Being the "Mélanges sur l'Angleterre" of François de la Rochefoucauld* (London, 1995); see also, e.g., J. Gury, ed., *Marquis de Bombelles, Journal de voyage en Grande Bretagne et en Irlande 1784* (Oxford, 1989) and T. Berg and P. Berg, eds., *R. R. Angerstein's Illustrated Travel Diary 1753–1755: Industry in England and Wales from a Swedish Perspective* (London, 2001).

14. E. Hopkins, *Birmingham: The First Manufacturing Town in the World, 1760–1840* (London, 1989).

15. P. Hudson, *Regions and Industries: A Perspective on the Industrial Revolution in Britain* (Cambridge, 1989).

16. I would like to thank Henry French for drawing my attention to the drawbacks of using average expenditure.

17. *Leeds Intelligencer*, November 27, December 4, 25, 1781, January 1, 8, February 19, 1782.

18. Shelburne to John Eardley Wilmot, August 8, 1791, New Haven, Connecticut, Beinecke Library, Osborn Shelves, Eardley-Wilmot Boxes.

19. D. Rollison, *The Local Origins of Modern Society, Gloucestershire 1500–1800* (London, 1992). See also A. M. Urdank, *Religion and Society in a Cotswold Vale: Nailsworth, Gloucestershire 1780–1865* (Berkeley, CA, 1990).

20. C. Estabrook, *Urban and Rustic England: Cultural Ties and Social Spheres in the Provinces, 1660–1780* (Manchester, 1999).

21. L. D. Schwarz, *London in the Age of Industrialisation: Entrepreneurs, Labour Force, and Living Conditions, 1700–1850* (Cambridge, 1992).

22. P. Clark, ed., *The Cambridge Urban History of Britain: II: 1540–1840* (Cambridge, 2000); P. Borsay and L. Proudfoot, eds., *Provincial Towns in Early Modern England and Ireland: Change, Convergence, and Divergence* (Oxford, 2002).

23. T. Koditschek, *Class Formation and Urban Industrial Society, Bradford 1750–1850* (Cambridge, 1990); D. Hey, *The Fiery Blades of Hallamshrie: Sheffield and Its Neighbourhood, 1660–1740* (Leicester, UK, 1992).

24. D. Gerhold, *Road Transport before the Railways: Russell's London Flying Wagons* (Cambridge, 1993).

25. J. Stobart, "Regional Structure and the Urban System: North-West England, 1600–1760," *Transactions of the Historic Society of Lancashire and Cheshire* 145 (1996): 45–73.

26. D. Gerhold, *Carriers and Coachmasters, Trade and Travel before the Turnpikes* (Chichester, UK, 2005).

27. D. Hey, *Packmen, Carriers, and Packhorse Roads: Trade and Communications in North Derbyshire and South Yorkshire* (Leicester, UK, 1980).

28. D. Hussey, *Coastal and River Trade in Pre-Industrial England: Bristol and Its Region, 1680–1730* (Exeter, 2000).

29. M. Honeybourne and D. Honeybourne, *The Correspondence of the Spaulding Gentlemen's Society, 1710–1761* (Lincoln, UK, 2010).

30. *Leeds Intelligencer*, March 2, 1790.

31. J. Hartland, "The Cirencester-Lechlade Road," *Annual Report and Newsletter of the Cirencester Archaeological and Historical Society* 27 (1984–85): 7–8.

32. W. Albert, *The Turnpike Road System in England 1663–1840* (Cambridge, 1972); E. Pawson, *Transport and Economy: The Turnpike Roads of Eighteenth-Century Britain* (London, 1977).

33. BL. Evelyn papers, vol. 49 fol. 36.

34. J. Sharp, *Rolling Carts and Waggons*; descriptive advertisement, ca. 1770.

35. J.-P. Forster, *Eighteenth-Century Geography and Representations of Space in English Fiction and Poetry* (Oxford, 2013).

36. S. W. Baskerville, "The Establishment of the Grosvenor Interest in Chester 1710–48," *Journal of the Chester Archaeological Society* 63 (1980): 73.

37. *Salisbury and Winchester Journal*, April 13, 1789. See also June 22, 1789.

38. W. S. Baddeley, *History of Cirencester* (Cirencester, UK, 1924), 274. For a 1788 description, M. Barratts, "An Account of the Journeys Undertaken by the Rev. Richard and Mrs Boucher 1788–1789," *History Studies* 1 (1968): 46.

39. J. Brewer, *The Pleasures of the Imagination: English Culture in the Eighteenth Century* (London, 1997).

40. J. Smail, *Merchants, Markets, and Manufacture: The English Wool Textile Industry in the Eighteenth Century* (New York, 1999).

41. B. M. Benedict, "Encounters with the Object: Advertisements, Time, and Literary Discourse in the Early Eighteenth-Century Thing-Poem," *Eighteenth-Century Studies* 40 (2007): 193–207.

42. E. McKellar, *The Birth of Modern London: The Development and Design of the City, 1660–1720* (Manchester, 1999).

43. J. H. Thomas, *The East India Company and the Provinces in the Eighteenth Century. II. Captains, Agents, and Servants* (Lampeter, UK, 2007).

44. J. Walvin, *Fruits of Empire: Exotic Produce and British Trade, 1660–1800* (Basingstoke, UK, 1997); C. D. Edwards, *Eighteenth Century Furniture* (Manchester, 1996).

45. K. Morgan, *Bristol and the Atlantic Trade in the Eighteenth Century* (Cambridge, 1993).

46. J. J. Looney, "Advertising and Society in England, 1720–1820: A Statistical Analysis of Yorkshire Newspaper Advertisements" (PhD diss., Princeton, 1983); C. Ferdinand, *Benjamin Collins and the Provincial Newspaper Trade in the Eighteenth Century* (Oxford, 1997).

47. *Berrow's Worcester Journal*, November 30, 1769.

48. S. Foote, *The Bankrupt* (1773; published London, 1776), Act 3.

49. R. Szostak, *The Role of Transportation in the Industrial Revolution: A Comparison of England and France* (Montreal, 1991).

50. B. J. Davey, *Rural Crime in the Eighteenth Century* (Hull, UK, 1994).

51. R. B. Outhwaite, *Clandestine Marriage in England 1500–1800* (London, 1995).

52. *Newcastle Chronicle*, February 17, 1787.

53. *Leeds Intelligencer*, January 9, 1787.

54. P. K. O'Brien, "Mercantilism and Imperialism in the Rise and Decline of the Dutch and British Economies, 1585–1815," *De Economist* 148 (2000): 469–501.

55. M. Daunton, *Progress and Poverty: An Economic and Social History of Britain 1700–1850* (Oxford, 1995); J. Mokyr, *The Enlightened Economy: An Economic History of Britain, 1700–1850* (New Haven, CT, 2009).

56. P. Vries, *State, Economy, and the Great Divergence: Great Britain and China, 1680s–1850s* (New York, 2015).

9

Geographies in Retrospect

EIGHTEENTH-CENTURY BRITAIN BECAME the subject of historical geography after its passing. The period was the seedbed of British imperial greatness and industrialization, each problematic but also undoubted and, therefore, is a period of great interest. The accounts of industrialization tended to focus on the availability of resources but also on positive cultural and social factors aiding economic development. In contrast, political power relationships within Britain were not to the fore. Most of the discussion of industrialization was left to economic historians. Their approaches were ones to which commentators on sociological developments, taking forward the approach of Adam Smith, could be joined.

More generally, geography as a study of power did not engage comparable attention. Instead, physical geography as a historical enabler and explanation came to the fore in the nineteenth century, both in terms of writing and of reading. Interest in environmental influences came to play a major role in both history and geography. Greatly influenced by developments in the natural sciences, writers assumed a close relationship between humanity and the biophysical environment, and they sought to probe this relationship in terms of the environmental control that they took for granted. Environmentalism proved an attractive analytical method for the historians and geographers of successful states. Environmentalism played a crucial role in the organic theory of the state developed in the nineteenth century, and also in the treatment of culture as defined by the integration of nature and society. Aside from asserting the linkages, there was the need for geographers to demonstrate the processes. Thus, to understand the present, geographers and others looked to the past. This process was not limited to Britain, and British writers considered wider examples, a process that was to become more apparent in the twentieth century.

In his *Illuminated Atlas of Scripture Geography* (1840), William Hughes, an active mapmaker and professor of geography in the College for Civil Engineers, noted:

> the influence which physical characteristics have exercised over the formation of the national character—the modes of thought and feeling—the customary associations—the manners and institutions—of the inhabitants of a country—form elements in its condition which must be understood and appreciated before its political and religious history can be read with advantage. The different circumstances under which an island or a maritime country is placed, and the varied influences of the lofty chain of mountains or the widespread plain—the parched and arid desert or the fertile valley—the navigable river or the rapid mountain torrent—have exercised a large share in directing the progress of civilisation.[1]

In the case of English history, Charles Pearson presented geography, in his *Historical Maps of England* (1869), as playing a direct role in its history. He suggested that, although "man triumphs over the elements" (an argument that was also to be frequently employed by Mao Zedong), this triumph, which was widely applauded by Pearson, was essentially a matter only of the previous half century. He also saw geography at work in the great political divisions of the country's history and, specifically, the mountains as "the conservative element . . . in our history." Thus, for the Jacobite uprising in 1745, he wrote, "nowhere, except in the Highlands could Prince Charles Edward [Bonnie Prince Charlie] have raised an army; nowhere but in the north-western counties, still only partially civilized, did he find recruits."[2]

The theme of geography as significant, principally for environmental reasons, continued to be advanced. Thus, in his *New Student's Atlas of English History* (1903), a work published by Macmillan, a major publisher, Emil Reich argued, "the paramount importance of geography as the basis of a study of history." Two years later, in an introduction titled "Relation of Geography to History," C. Grant Robertson, an influential historian, and J. G. Bartholomew claimed that "no student of historical geography will learn what his subject can teach him unless at every stage he brings historical facts into intimate and vital connection with the condition of modern descriptive and physical geography."[3] In his *New School Atlas of Modern History* (1911), Ramsay Muir focused on his determined use of physical geography: "In the first place, great emphasis is throughout placed upon the *physical basis* of historical geography." Moreover, the notes to the atlas brought out the significance of the physical features depicted.[4] Muir's atlas, which subsequently became the *Philips' New Historical Atlas for Students*, went through further editions, for long with scant alteration. The fifth edition (1923) still used the preface to the 1911 edition.

Physical geography continued to be to the fore. In his *Man and His Past* (1921), O. G. S. Crawford stressed the geographical approach to history. He was responsible for a series of interwar historical maps produced by the Ordnance Survey that mapped locations and distributions against the background of physical geography. Similar use of geography and of distribution maps and notably the application of the concept of the distinction between lowland and highland zones was seen in Cyril Fox's *The Personality of Britain* (1932). In his *The Geography behind History* (1938), Gordon East, the Cambridge-educated lecturer in historical geography at the London School of Economics, emphasized "physical features," arguing, "It is not enough, in studying history, merely to consult the atlas." Instead of focusing on locations, the nature and impact of the environment had to be assessed.[5] The role of physical features but also of additional factors, such as the proximity to towns and the role of "improvers," continues to be stressed.[6]

East's approach is particularly significant for this book as he wrote the chapter covering the eighteenth century in the major historical geography of England. Titled *An Historical Geography of England before A.D. 1800* edited by H. C. Darby, the doyen of English historical geographers,[7] and published by Cambridge University Press in 1936, this book long remained the set text and reference work. I, for example, used it in the 1970s and still have my copy. There has been no historical geography of England that has had comparable influence, even though the Darby volume, which terminates at 1800, was therefore deliberately incomplete, and has long been dated, conceptually, methodologically, and empirically. Darby went on to produce *A New Historical Geography of England* (1973).

With the exception of a chapter specifically on London, that by East is the last in the book. The chapter "England in the Eighteenth Century" is worth consideration as an account of the geography of the period that not only needs replacing but that also set a context within which more recent work can be evaluated. First, East was concerned to note continuities rather than change. In particular, the emphasis was not on the eighteenth as the precursor to the nineteenth but rather on the eighteenth as the last in the sequence of the book's chapters before the changes brought by the Industrial Revolution. Second, this emphasis can be related to the stress within the chapter on agriculture rather than industry. Agricultural change is to the fore, notably in the form of enclosure, but that does not distinguish the period from earlier ones in which there was also significant agricultural change—for example, the sixteenth century. Third, the focus, understandable in a book with its title, was very much on England, and not on Britain or its colonies. Linked to this, the treatment of external links was less than it could, and should, have been. Fourth, in accordance with the emphasis of the period, the stress was on production as the driver of the economy and the subject for discussion, and not on consumption. Nor was there adequate attention to finance. Last, the social and political configurations and contexts of spatial activity, and of the economy as a whole, were underplayed. East discussed the role of the aristocracy but did not otherwise have enough to say about these configurations and contexts. Moreover, the aristocracy emerges in his study as agricultural innovators, and not as key players in a power system linking the center to the localities, even though the role of the aristocracy in the latter was an important background to its economic activity.[8]

It is possible to multiply criticisms of the work of East or of other historical geographers of the period. To do so is not, however, to suggest, with the condescension of posterity, that the scholarship of the past was necessarily flawed and the present inherently better. Instead, the very discussion of the past in terms of limitations necessarily both reveals the extent to which present scholarship will be judged accordingly (which undermines any claims to definitive status) and also throws light on how current concerns are different to earlier ones. Doing so directs attention to the shaping of concerns, both past and present.

In comparison with East's approach, there are a host of contrasts in modern concerns, notably the emphasis on consumption, on women, on contemporary perceptions, on international links, and, as here, on aspects of power. That these emphases may, in turn, appear of their time, indeed transient or faddish, is worthy of consideration. So, more helpfully, is the question of what may have been lost with the current focus. The detailed understanding of localities that was so important to earlier work has very largely been lost. So also with the understanding of the place and role of regions that was again so important, and that remains so in current work for the Anglo-Saxon period. In each case, the failure to address a topic leads to a lack of evidence for its significance and thus risks becoming a self-fulfilling process. This tendency has been accentuated by the emphasis on "four nations history," that of England, Ireland, Scotland, and Wales. This tendency, which became prominent from the 1980s, leads to a marked underplaying of divisions or distinctions within those units or, indeed, to links and comparisons between them at the subunit level.

That is a problem with the unit of assessment. This can be taken further, from another direction, by considering the emphasis on counties. The value of the county as a unit can be questioned from the methodological viewpoint. In practice, patterns of publication have been significant in encouraging this focus, as local architectural, archaeological, historical, and record societies have developed at this level, but can be misleading. Similarly, historical atlases of particular areas, and in the British case that tends to mean counties, are apt to assert that the area in question was both an entity and distinctive. A county approach, either covering just one county or dividing some larger area, such as England, into counties and using these as unit areas for choropleth maps and so on, implies that a county is a self-contained unit,[9] but this approach can lead to the neglect of important regional variations within, and between, counties.[10] Indeed, the fundamental significance of soils and distinct natural regions within (and also spanning counties) emerged clearly in the *Historical Atlas of Suffolk* (2nd ed., 1989).

Alternatives have been mapped, including the forty-two "farming counties of early modern England [and Wales]" and the fourteen "cultural provinces" of England,[11] although it is most appropriate to focus on open-ended and overlapping categories.[12] Regional historical atlases have much to offer, but few have appeared for England.[13] References could be made to a regional level by contemporaries. In 1763, William, Earl of Bath, referred to public pressure against a recent law: "When the angry folks of the West have tried what they can do about cider."[14] It is less clear whether such distinctions were strongly established, at least for this period.[15] Yet, there were major regional differences in a number of respects, including in the provision of poor relief, illegitimacy rates, and the distribution of dispensaries as opposed to hospitals.[16] Study of markets and fairs can offer an indication of the extent of regional economic development.[17] Moreover, a regional dimension can be seen in politics.[18] In addition, one was readily apparent in Britain's North American colonies, most clearly in New England, not least with a tendency to see abstractions of character there as products and shapers of regional identity.[19] The relationship between colonies and regions, however, is contentious.

A focus on areas other than counties, both in Britain and its colonies, certainly has its value for modern scholarly concerns. These include the growth of urban population, especially in manufacturing towns, while perceptions—for example, those of "northerners" by "southerners"[20]—also were not fixed at the country level. E. A. Wrigley has argued that the use of hundreds (smaller than counties) as units of description permits the construction of more homogeneous regional units than those offered by larger county units, and this is an approach that certainly highlights the significance of industrialization for population growth. It was also important for social indicators such as school attendance.[21] There was development in the processes of parish governance, including more uniform and regular administration.[22] There were also detailed variations in townscapes, including quasi-formal ones such as "sanctuaries" in London where groups of debtors would resist by force attempts to arrest them.[23]

However, if the units employed, notably regions, were not the basis for the collection of information, there are obvious problems with data acquisition, and this approach is therefore best for impressionistic works. It is, for example, very difficult to plot the nature and extent of control by government. Data problems are linked to the separate difficulties of statistical analysis, as in the handling of crime data in order to establish patterns.[24] At whatever level the analysis is conducted, there are crucial issues relating to data to do with the realization of different objectives, and notably those of general pattern as opposed to the local inflections that are very important to the organization and experience of local life.[25] These issues can relate to the questions of how best to present data.[26]

The county remains the best base for analysis and presentation so long as its varied limitations are appreciated. County historical atlases indeed have much to offer. The sense of change as a result of industrialization was captured in the historical atlas of Cheshire published in 1958. It addressed the value of the county unit with the argument that "the shires were artificial, and did not correspond with the old folk divisions, but ten centuries of subsequent history has in many cases shown the cohesive influence of a regional centre to have been an effective basis of division." It also argued that physical divisions had been superseded: "The related changes of the last two hundred years . . . have so altered the geographical balance of the county, that the main contrasts are no longer between the lowland and the Pennine slopes, but between the predominantly agricultural south and centre, and the industrial and residential belt of the north."[27]

This was a period of county historical atlases, as with *Kent History Illustrated* (Maidstone, 1966), which, despite its title, was a historical atlas commissioned by the Kent Education Committee and widely used in schools. For Kent, in the subsequent historical atlas, that of 2004, a map based on the Hearth Tax returns of 1664 permitted the depiction of parishes grouped as average or below average poverty, above average poverty, and well above average poverty, as well as the location of almshouses and poor relief charity. A document from the War Office papers in the National Archives provided the basis for a map of accommodation for travelers in Kent in 1686. All places with ten or more beds and stabling for ten or more horses are mapped. These data indicate the continuing importance of Watling Street, an old Roman route, as well as the cluster of accommodation near the developing spa of Tunbridge Wells.[28]

More generally, poll book analysis of the results for county elections is also significant, not least in showing how votes were distributed among particular parishes.[29] The county was the unit for an influential minority of parliamentary seats[30] and was the major unit in which local decisions were taken. Local government areas became more important as bodies that could introduce local acts of Parliament, although, at the same time, there were private acts. This process of legislation for particular localities became more significant with the transport improvements crucial to industrialization.[31]

Particular county institutions could take valuable initiatives. For example, in 1787 the Westmorland Quarter Sessions commissioned a population survey with parish constables ordered to send in returns listing the names and occupations of the members of every household in their area. The returns only survive in part, and there is a marked variation in their quality, with no two identical in form and all reflecting the different interpretation of the instructions received by the individual constables. Nevertheless, the returns capture some 12,500 named inhabitants out of a total population of about 40,000 and, for Westmorland, provide a unique source between certain 1695 lists of inhabitants and the detailed national census of 1841. A similar order was issued in Cumberland in 1787, specifying residence and age as well as occupation, but, although the listing was carried out, none of the returns survive.[32]

Counties were the units for the militia, and the militia lists can produce crucial information for scholarly purposes. For example, out of the 13,741 men recorded on the Northamptonshire militia lists for 1777, the occupations or status of 87 percent, perhaps two-thirds of the males aged eighteen to forty-five living in the county, were recorded by the parish constables. The material is not free from difficulties, not least much variation of terminology and many erratic spellings and contractions, but this is the nearest approach to an occupational census available for the county prior to the table included in the printed abstract of the 1831 census.[33]

The county had significant symbolic value. For example, the county community had a symbolic importance to its gentry families, as it provided links with a distant historical past and an anchoring for concern with pedigree.[34] Looked at differently, the emphasis on the county captured, and still captures, the impact of continuity. This is significant because stability, in the sense of continuity and adaptation, is often more difficult to grasp and evaluate than change.[35] However, the extent to which the county is to be seen as a local source and sense of "patriotism," as opposed to identity, is unclear. The gentry often held land in more than one county, a process that was both long-standing[36] and encouraged by inheritance and marriage.[37] Moreover, county autonomy and its urban counterpart were affected by links with the agencies and purposes of central government. Indeed, there was often a desire for advice and assistance from the center.[38] Given such links and the importance of Parliament, the law and the government in affecting life in the localities in a wide range of matters, from the rate of taxation to the composition of the bench (the justices of the peace responsible for local law and order), the position of Dissenters (religious Nonconformists) to turnpike legislation, it is scarcely surprising that national politics had a local dimension and vice versa. Economic lobbying focused on national bodies.[39]

The discussion of power and, more specifically, of its spatial character needs to address these and other aspects of political behavior. George Lyttelton preferred a meteorological image: "our climate is not subject to such furious wars of the elements as that of the Continent. Its disorders are more frequent, but then they are not so violent. Britannia is like a nervous lady, seldom well long together, but not dangerously ill. This comparison I hope will hold with regard to our politics as well as our weather."[40]

In practice, government, like society as a whole, relied on cooperation,[41] and politics helped define the bounds and nature of such cooperation by encompassing contention and debate. A similar pattern can be seen in the empire, where also there are issues about the validity of regions as opposed to individual colonies.

In Britain, although the intensity of individual belief could not be readily assessed,[42] another source of information was provided by religious surveys as they were classically based on dioceses, with a grouping within under rural deaneries. In the visitation of the diocese of Llandaff in 1763, the visitation returns were by county but, within each, by deanery. Nonconformity emerged as found principally in sparsely populated upland areas and thus as not particularly significant. Although declining in several areas, the role of the Welsh language emerged from the visitation in that English incumbents of Welsh parishes needed Welsh curates.[43] Visitations and parochial queries—for example, that of Archbishop Wake of Canterbury in 1706—also provided information on Dissenters/Nonconformists.[44] The processes of diocesan visitations and of returns by clerics enabled the collection of material, which was aided by their high standards of clerical literacy and by the interest in preserving material across a wide range of subjects. It was not surprising that the church was turned to when the 1676 Compton census and the 1720s census of Catholics were undertaken.[45] Successive visitations charted change, notably in local life and demography. Thus, for his visitation in 1764, Archbishop Drummond of York studied the articles used by Archbishop Herring, for his visitation tours in 1743. Visitation tours were planned and announced, with the newspapers employed for this, and bishops changed centers as the population shifted and it made more sense for people to travel to a different center. In 1755, at the behest of the Lord President, Robert Dundas, the Reverend Alexander Webster produced a census of Scotland based on information from parish clergy, although this was often only of catechized people.[46]

At the same time, there were improvements in the provision of information by the Church of England, improvements that were recorded at the parochial scale. For example, in 1777, Archbishop Markham of York introduced a more precise system for parish registers, spreading the best practice developed by a vicar, William Dade, in 1770. A different form of improvement followed in the diocese of Durham from the late 1790s. A standard national format was not introduced until an act of Parliament in 1813.[47]

Maps, however, do not appear to have played much of a role in episcopal visitations, in part because the latter often followed customary routes between centers and therefore did not need to be mapped, and also because they were (largely) local. The same had been true of heraldic visitations, which were tours of inspection by the College of Arms to regulate and register pedigrees and use of arms by the armigerous classes. They were conducted on a county basis: the first in 1530, the last in 1688.[48]

The church was particularly significant not only for religion but also for poor relief and education.[49] The church, moreover, was also a source of local taxation and discussion in the case of tithes. Passed in 1836, the Tithe Commutation Act led to the creation of a bureaucracy in the shape of the Tithe Commission, the appointment of tithe commissioners and local agents, the establishment of tithe districts, and the progress of commutation. The resulting information for the mid-nineteenth century on parish and township boundaries, field boundaries and names, settlement patterns, rights of way, land ownership, and the rural economy provides material relevant for the late eighteenth century.[50] Earlier, there were new institutions and practices producing data. Turnpike trusts were one. So also with the inspectors who reported on rural wet nursing for the Foundling Hospital in London.[51]

In practice, alongside the sense of difference created by contrasting data sets, there were multiple spatial links at the levels of individuals and institutions, as shown by household and estate accounts, diaries, autobiographies, and correspondence. Moreover, although they were most significant at the national level for the social elite, it was not only for them that these links could be local, regional (whether or not defined as county), and national.[52] Apprenticeship records in Edinburgh show Scotland-wide migration patterns and, increasingly so, as do marriage registers. In the case of Aberdeen and Inverness, the pattern was more regional.[53] So also with the impact of London, which was, variously, national, regional, and local. For example, many of the London clergy came from the West Country, Yorkshire, and Wales.[54]

Another issue, that of the mechanics and dynamics of power, is also a problem as there is a tendency not to look at this other than in the shape of control at the isotrophic (everything equal) level of England as a whole: control in terms of social dominance over, for example, women or the poor as a whole, rather than the specifics of particular localities. The latter are usually handled with regard to discussions of individual electoral interests, but such work, once a staple of Namierite political analysis, that inspired by the work of Sir Lewis Namier, is no longer of much consequence in the literature, and it is scarcely socially comprehensive.

The value of applying conceptual approaches can be seen in the historical atlas of Oxfordshire. James Bond's spread on market towns 1700–1900 owes much to central place theory and contrasts instructively with Adrienne Rosen's spread on market towns in the 1670s. Barrie Trinder's mapping of stagecoach routes in 1830 similarly establishes primacy.[55]

Alongside conceptual issues, there are data ones, and there has been considerable progress in establishing and using data sets. For example, *London in the 1690s: A Social Atlas* (2000) shows how social geography can be re-created, not least by using the 1692 Poll Tax database. This provides an opportunity to dissect the occupational structure, showing that London had carefully defined social spheres. Although the scope of metropolitan employment was extensive, a few occupational sectors were crucial. Whereas geographical works of the period did not tend to focus on problems with the sources, the situation is very different for modern scholarship. This atlas noted the difficulty of establishing the wealth of Londoners not based on property. The 1693–94 four shilling "aid" provides a good comparative measure of individual wealth, although the assessed values are known to underestimate actual wealth. The tax levied on stocks permits study of the spatial distribution of stockholding and its relative value.[56]

There are other sources that repay examination when establishing spatial patterns. Probate records are valuable,[57] for example, to show the growth in pastoral output in Norfolk, a growth that underlines the economic significance of the county. Again, the 1723 oath of allegiance rolls after the Atterbury Conspiracy supplement better-known sources.[58] The 1801 Crop Return for England and Wales provided an arable crops census for nearly half of the total area.[59] At the same time, the data are not available to carry out projects on the range and scale of those for subsequent centuries—for example, with *An Atlas of Victorian Mortality* (1997).

The mutability of spatial patterns and the difficulties, given the institutional legacy, of understanding and analyzing them can be parallel with the comparable difficulties in understanding social structure and consciousness. As far as these were concerned, there was "diversity of debate, fluidity of language, competing interpretations," and a society "increasingly experienced as mutable and combative."[60]

A key analog in discussing sources and argumentation for the eighteenth century is provided by the nature of recent and current scholarly projects—for example, historical atlases. There is a general lack of interest in the retention of academic papers and of records of publishing projects.[61] Failure to retain and failure to collect ensure that little often is left other than the text itself. The absence of adequate background material means that those studying a subject are sometimes overly prone to extrapolate in discussing processes and links. As such, there is a contrast between the readiness to extrapolate and the important and specific role of the practical problems involved in the acquisition, analysis, and depiction of information.[62]

To turn to another approach, geopolitics, not simply at the international level but also at the subnational one, is an analytical approach that could be used, or at least considered, with greater frequency. At the international level, geopolitics is important in discussing the power political and strategic dimensions of the subject. This approach is essentially useful at the comparative level when seeking to establish the key aspects of British strategic culture. By its very nature, the latter entailed choices in, and about, space, both as far as area was concerned and with reference to distance. The importance of these on both land and sea and their role in the allocation and coordination of military units help explain the significance of their mapping, as discussed in chapter 2. This mapping represented an attempt to overcome not the conceptual problems of distance but rather the practical issues of operating across space. In this sense, geography was very much about power. It dealt with the practicalities of military power, as well as of land use, and did so in a way that brought location into a readily graspable fashion. The term *graspable* is not intended to suggest appropriation, as in seizure, in the fashion of "critical geopolitics" but, instead, the need to understand territory and thus be better able to use it.

The theme of practicality did not mean that values played no role in the geographies of the period. Far from it. Instead, whether or not conceived as an Enlightenment "project," the processes of accumulating and assessing geographical knowledge served to fulfill a series of utilitarian tasks that were designed to match, and take forward, the values of the period. These values included power, power as protection but power also as a means to implement and express the agendas of British political culture. The subnational use of geopolitics is one that has not been theoretically well developed, but it offers possibilities, as this book indicates.

In 1972, A. R. H. Baker discerned a change in historical geography from 1960, with an old, essentially classificatory, geographical tradition, focused on the reconstruction of different past geographies, and at times describable in terms of a "tree of knowledge," replaced by a model-based paradigm. He pressed the need to incorporate the decision-making process in the past and for historical geography to understand the past ideas and images of reality that underlay human actions.[63] As such, geography, it has been argued, is a special way of looking at the world.[64]

Power has very much been the theme of geography over recent decades and, indeed, the explicit theme. Maps and other geographical sources were (and are) treated as texts to be read and deconstructed in the poststructural and postmodern sense pioneered for literature, architecture, and signs by Roland Barthes and Jacques Derrida. Cartography was linked to, and to be understood with reference to, ontology, epistemology, iconography, and reception theory. As a result, cartography and geography in general were located in broader intellectual movements and, notably, in contexts other than that of the simple spread of knowledge. The influential radical French philosopher Michel Foucault proved important. His view of knowledge as struggle was to be understood in large part by reference to space: there were boundaries and spheres of contest, as ideologies colonized terrains. Foucault sought to use the notion, symbols, and language of cartography, specifically of space, boundaries, and networks, in order to understand and make dynamic his views on the politics of knowledge.[65]

These themes were taken up by those working on what was styled critical geopolitics. For them, "Geography is about power,"[66] one linked today to American imperialism, globalization, and capitalism. The value of such an approach can be variously considered,[67] but it has been brought to the fore by the revival of writing on geopolitics since 1990.[68] To give a flavor, in 1996 Gearóid Ó. Tuathail closed his critical account of geopolitics by claiming, "Critical geopolitics is one of many cultures of resistance to geography as imperial truth, state-capitalised knowledge, and military weapon. It is a small part of a much larger rainbow struggle to decolonise our inherited geopolitical imagination so that other geo-graphings and other worlds might be possible."[69]

That approach can indeed be taken to the eighteenth-century British world, but it is overly limited and slanted. Instead, a range of contexts and meanings for geography should emerge, while in terms of historical geography there is no one perspective that has been adopted through which to look at the period as a whole. At the local, as at the regional, national, and international levels, the role of physical factors, such as topography and drainage, emerge clearly. Although power considerations played a role, these factors cannot be readily explained or dismissed simply in these terms. For example, water courses and roads served to depict boundaries in part simply because they were convenient.[70] At times, indeed, the academics' emphasis on power has been somewhat crude, reductionist, mechanistic, and instrumental.[71]

The attempt here is to encourage the greater degree of subtlety that is appropriate. There are, indeed, excellent instances in the literature, and notably when an archival grounding has been provided for the discussion of power. For example, in his perceptive and wide-ranging study of Edinburgh, Rab Houston focused on the social processes that created a need, the expression of which was the building of the New Town. He argued that by the mid-eighteenth century, the formal social distinctions, based on legal status or on membership of associations, were being replaced by the less formal ones of lifestyle, wealth, status, appearance, and belief. To Houston, urban space was redefined, with the New Town setting the seal on growing economic differentiation and developing social divisions within Edinburgh and more generally.[72] Similar work on other cities is urgently called for.

So also with the need to investigate different ways to consider Britain's global position. There are many conceptual, methodological, and practical issues involved in the spatial presentation of this relationship. For example, the naval historian Nicholas Rodger once remarked to me that Atlantic history was history with the Atlantic left out. It is certainly the case that not all historians who write about globalization understand ships, winds, and currents. Separately, a focus on oceanic concerns and links, whether or not there is such an understanding, can lead to an underplaying of developments within continents, notably in Asia, Africa, and Europe. History understood from the coast into the interior, indeed, tends to come with a powerful framework of assumptions.

Nevertheless, allowing for these and other caveats and issues, the stress on the oceans, and on the worlds enacted over, across, and along them, has proved very helpful. It has brought new energy to the investigation of the European maritime empires, notably the British one, including, at times, an instructive comparative focus. The focus on transoceanic worlds has led to a greater emphasis on the interactive character of the colonial bond and on the number of human constituencies involved, including those not formally imperial subjects. As a result, the study of the British world is readily open to transoceanic stories, concerns, and methods. This is notably so with the history of migration, whether voluntary or coerced. The variety of the world being made and remade by the British (and others) emerges clearly, and this variety underlines the extent to which it is not helpful to think in terms of inevitable patterns.

Notes

1. W. Hughes, *The Illuminated Atlas of Scripture Geography* (London, 1840), 3.
2. C. Pearson, *Historical Maps of England* (London, 1869), v–vii.
3. C. G. Robertson and J. G. Bartholomew, *Historical and Modern Atlas of the British Empire* (London, 1905), v.
4. R. Muir, *A School Atlas of Modern History* (London, 1911), xix.
5. G. East, *The Geography behind History* (London,1938), 21. J. N. L. Baker, "The Development of Historical Geography in Britain during the Last Hundred Years," *Advancement of Science* 8 (1951–52): 406–12.

6. L. Leneman, "Highland and Lowland Perthshire in the Eighteenth Century—Two Different Worlds?," *Scotia* 12 (1988): 1–12.

7. H. C. Darby et al., *The Relations of History and Geography: Studies in England, France, and the United States* (Exeter, UK, 2000).

8. W. G. East, "England in the Eighteenth Century," in H. C. Darby, ed., *An Historical Geography of England before AD 1800* (Cambridge, 1936), 465–528.

9. For example, D. Dymond and E. Martin, eds., *An Historical Atlas of Suffolk* (Ipswich, UK, 1988), 7; S. Bennett and N. Bennett, eds., *An Historical Atlas of Lincolnshire* (Hull, UK, 1993; 2nd ed., Chichester, UK, 2001); D. Short, ed., *An Historical Atlas of Hertfordshire* (Hatfield, UK, 2011).

10. M. Kowaleski, *Local Markets and Regional Trade in the Medieval Exeter* (Exeter, UK, 1995), 10.

11. E. Kerridge, *The Common Fields of England* (Manchester, 1992), viii; C. Phythian-Adams, ed., *Societies, Cultures and Kinship, 1580–1850: Cultural Provinces and English Local History* (Leicester, UK, 1993), xvii–xx, 9–18; M. Overton, "Agricultural Regions in Early Modern England: An Example from East Anglia," *University of Newcastle Seminar Papers* 42 (1983).

12. N. Davie, "Chalk and Cheese? 'Fielden' and 'Forest' Communities in Early Modern England," *Journal of Historical Sociology* 4 (1991): 1–31.

13. J. A. Patmore and A. G. Hodgkiss, eds., *Merseyside in Maps* (London, 1970); R. Kain and W. Ravenhill, eds., *Historical Atlas of South-West England* (Exeter, UK, 1999).

14. Bath to Elizabeth Montagu, November 6, 1763, HL. MO. 4447.

15. H. M. Jewell, *The North-South Divide* (Manchester, 1994).

16. S. King, *Poverty and Welfare in England 1700–1850. A Regional Perspective* (Manchester, 2000); L. Leneman and R. Mitchison, "Scottish Illegitimacy Ratios in the Early Modern Period," *Economic History Review* 40 (1987): 41–63; S. J. London, "The Origins and Growth of the Dispensary Movement in England," *Bulletin of the History of Medicine* 55 (1981): 326.

17. P. O'Flanagan, "Markets and Fairs in Ireland, 1600–1800: Index of Economic Development and Regional Growth," *Journal of Historical Geography* 11 (1985): 364–78.

18. A. Goodwin, "A Comparative Study of Regionalism in Politics in Lancashire and Normandy during the French Revolution," *Annales de Normandie* 8 (1958): 235–55, esp. 235–38.

19. W. Bodle, "The 'Myth of the Middle Colonies' Reconsidered: The Process of Regionalisation in Early America," *Pennsylvania Magazine of History and Biography* 113 (1989): 527–48; W. Bodle, "Themes and Directions in Middle Colonies Historiography, 1980–1994," *William and Mary Quarterly*, 3rd ser., 51 (1994): 387; W. Bodle, "The Fabricated Region: On the Insufficiency of 'Colonies' for Understanding American Colonial History," *Early American Studies* 1 (2003): 1–27; L. Buell, *New England Literary Culture: From Revolution through Renaissance* (Cambridge, 1986).

20. R. F. Hastings, *Essays in North Riding History 1780–1850* (Northallerton, UK, 1981), 76.

21. E. A. Wrigley, "English County Populations in the Later Eighteenth Century," *Economic History Review* 60 (2007): 35–69; R. F. Hastings, *Essays in North Riding History 1780–1850* (Northallerton, UK, 1981), 182.

22. J. R. Kent, "The Centre and the Localities: State Formation and Parish Government in England, c. 1640–1740," *Historical Journal* 38 (1995): 365–404, esp. 402–3.

23. R. L. Brown, "The Minters of Wapping: The History of a Debtors' Sanctuary in Eighteenth-Century East London," *East London Papers* 14 (1972): 77–86.

24. M. D. Maltz, A. C. Gordon, and W. Friedman, *Mapping Crime in Its Community Setting: Event Geography Analysis* (New York, 1991), x, 21.

25. A. Horner, "150 Years of Mapping Ireland's Population Distribution," *Bulletin of the Society of University Cartographers* 22, pt. 1 (1988): 1.

26. H. G. Funkhouser, *Historical Development of the Graphical Representation of Statistical Data* (Bruges, 1938); A. H. Robinson, *Elements of Cartography*, 5th ed. (New York, 1984), 343, 349–50.

27. S. Sylvester and G. Nulty, eds., *The Historical Atlas of Cheshire* (Chester, UK, 1958), 2–3.

28. T. Lawson and D. Killingray, eds., *An Historical Atlas of Kent* (Chichester, UK, 2004).

29. J. Collett-White, *How Bedfordshire Voted, 1685–1735: The Evidence of Local Poll Books, I, 1685–1715* (Woodbridge, UK, 2006), *II, 1716–35* (Woodbridge, UK, 2008); P. Jupp and S. A. Royle, "The Social Geography of Cork City Elections, 1801–30," *Irish Historical Studies* 29 (1994): 13–43.

30. S. Sommers, *Parliamentary Politics of a County and Its Town: General Elections in Suffolk and Ipswich in the Eighteenth Century* (Westport, CT, 2002).

31. J. Sheail, "Local Legislation: Its Scope and Context," *Archives* 30 (2005): 36–37.

32. L. Ashcroft, *Vital Statistics. The Westmorland "Census" of 1787* (Kendal, UK, 1992).

33. V. A. Hatley, *Northamptonshire Militia Lists 1777* (Northampton, UK, 1993).

34. J. Broadway, "William Dugdale and the Significance of County History in Early Stuart England," *Dugdale Society Occasional Papers* 39 (1999).

35. B. K. Roberts, "Nucleation and Dispersion: Distribution Maps as a Research Tool," in M. Aston, D. Austin, and C. Dyer, eds., *The Rural Settlements of Medieval England* (Oxford, 1989), 61.

36. J. C. Ward, *The Essex Gentry and the County Community in the Fourteenth Century* (Chelmsford, UK, 1991).

37. A. Orde, ed., *Matthew and George Culley: Farming Letters 1798–1804* (Woodbridge, UK, 2006).

38. L. Glassey, "Local Government," in C. Jones, ed., *Britain in the First Age of Party 1680–1750* (London, 1987), 171.

39. George Chalmers to George Grenville, November 1, 1769, HL., Stowe papers, STG. Box 21 (28).

40. Lyttelton to Montagu, August 21, 1763, HL. Montagu papers, 1311.

41. D. Eastwood, *Government and Community in the English Provinces, 1700–1870* (London, 1997).

42. H. McLeod, "Class, Community, and Region: The Religious Geography of Nineteenth-Century England," in M. Hill, ed., *A Sociological Yearbook of Religion in Britain*, VI (London, 1973), 30.

43. J. R. Guy, ed., *The Diocese of Llandaff in 1763, The Primary Visitation of Bishop Ewer* (Cardiff, 1991).

44. J. Broad, ed., *Buckinghamshire Dissent and Parish Life, 1669–1712* (Aylesbury, UK, 1993).

45. W. R. Ward, ed., *Parson and Parish in Eighteenth-Century Survey. Replies to Bishops Visitations* (Guildford, UK, 1994); C. Annesley and P. Hoskin, eds., *Archbishop Drummond's Visitation Returns, 1764. I* (York, UK, 1997); J. Fendley, ed., "Notes on the Diocese of Gloucester by Chancellor Richard Parsons c. 1700," *Gloucestershire Record Series* 19 (2005).

46. R. E. Tyson, "The Population of Aberdeenshire," *Northern Scotland* 6 (1985): 113–31; I. D. Whyte, "Scottish Population and Social Structure in the Seventeenth and Eighteenth Centuries: New Sources and Perspectives," *Archives* 20 (1993): 31.

47. R. A. Bellingham, "Dade Registers," *Archives* 27 (2002): 134–47.

48. G. D. Squibb, ed., *Munimenta Heraldica* (London, 1985).

49. N. Yates, R. Hume, and P. Hastings, *Religion and Society in Kent, 1640–1914* (Woodbridge, UK, 1994).

50. R. J. Kain and H. Prince, *Tithe Surveys for Historians* (Chichester, UK, 2000).

51. G. Clark, ed., *Correspondence of the Foundling Hospital Inspectors in Berkshire 1757–68* (Reading, UK, 1994).

52. D. Fleming, *The Estate and Household Accounts of Sir Daniel Fleming of Rydal Hall, Westmorland, 1688–1701*, ed. Tyson. Cumberland and Westmorland Antiquarian and Archaeological Society Record Series, 13 (Kendal, 2001).

53. A. A. Lovett, I. D. Whyte, and K. A. Whyte, "Poisson Regression Analysis and Migration Fields: The Example of the Apprenticeship Records of Edinburgh in the Seventeenth and Eighteenth Centuries," *Transactions of the Institute of British Geographers*, new series, 10 (1985): 317–32; I. D. Whyte and K. A. Whyte, "Patterns of Apprenticeship Migration to Aberdeen and Inverness during the Seventeenth and Eighteenth Centuries," *Scottish Geographical Magazine* 102 (1986): 81–91; C. W. J. Withers, "Highland Migration to Aberdeen c. 1649–1891," *Northern Scotland* 9 (1990): 21–44.

54. V. Barrie-Curien, *Clergé et pastorale en Angleterre au XVIIIe siècle: le diocese de Londres* (Paris, 1992).

55. K. Tiller and G. Darkes, *An Historical Atlas of Oxfordshire* (Oxford, 2010).

56. C. Spence, *London in the 1690s: A Social Atlas* (London, 2000).

57. M. Overton and B. M. S. Campbell, "Norfolk Livestock Farming 1250–1740: A Comparative Study of Manorial Accounts and Probate Inventories," *Journal of Historical Geography* 18 (1992): 392–94; N. W. Alcock, *People at Home: Living in a Warwickshire Village, 1500–1800* (Chichester, UK, 1993).

58. S. Dixon, "Local History, Archives and the Public: Eighteenth-Century Devon: People and Communities Project Assessed," *Archives* 33 (2008): 101–13.

59. M. Turner, "Arable in England and Wales: Estimates from the 1801 Crop Return," *Journal of Historical Geography* 7 (1981): 291–302.

60. P. J. Corfield, "Class by Name and Number in Eighteenth-Century Britain," *History* 72 (1987): 60–61.

61. P. Wade-Martin to Black, April 1, 2003, with reference to Wade-Martin, ed., *Historical Atlas of Norfolk* (Norwich, UK, 1993).

62. J. Black, "Sources for the Mapping of History: The Case of Historical Atlases," *Archives* 29 (2004): 9–24.

63. A. R. H. Baker, "Rethinking Historical Geography," in A. R. H. Baker, ed., *Progress in Historical Geography* (Newton Abbot, UK, 1972), 11–27 and "Reflections on the Relations of Historical Geography and the Annales School of History," in A. R. H. Baker and D. Gregory, eds., *Explorations in Historical Geography* (Cambridge, 1984), 1–27. See, later, his *Geography and History. Bridging the Divide* (Cambridge, 2010). For the situation in the eighteenth century, C. W. J. Withers, "Geography in Its Time: Geography and Historical Geography in Diderot and d'Alembert's *Encyclopédie*," *Journal of Historical Geography* 19 (1993): 255–64. See also R. Butlin, *Historical Geography: Through the Gates of Space and Time* (London, 1993).

64. D. W. Meinig, *The Shaping of America. A Geographical Perspective on 500 Years of History. I Atlantic America 1492–1800* (New Haven, CT, 1986), xv.

65. F. Driver, "Power, Space, and the Body: A Critical Assessment of Foucault's *Discipline and Punishment*," *Environment and Planning D: Society and Space* 3 (1985): 425–46; D. Wood, *The Power of Maps* (New York, 1992); B. Belyea, "Images of Power: Derrida Foucault/Harley," *Cartographica* 29/2 (1992): 231–47; D. Turnbull, *Maps Are Territories: Science Is an Atlas* (Chicago, 1994); P. Laxton, ed., *The New Nature of Maps. Essays in the History of Cartography by J. B. Harley* (Baltimore, 2001); P. Kelly, "A Critique of Critical Geopolitics," *Geopolitics* 11 (2006): 28–29; J. Branch, *The Cartographic State: Maps, Territory, and the Origins of Sovereignty* (Cambridge, 2013).

66. G. Ó. Tuathail, *Critical Geopolitics: The Politics of Writing Global Space* (London, 1996), 1; D. Newman, ed., *Boundaries, Territory, and Postmodernity* (London, 1999).

67. K. Dodds, M. Kuus, and J. Sharp, eds., *The Ashgate Research Companion to Critical Geopolitics* (Farnham, UK, 2013).

68. J. Black, *Geopolitics and the Quest for Dominance* (Bloomington, IN, 2016), 211.

69. G. Ó. Tuathail, *Critical Geopolitics*, 255–56.

70. H. E. Le Patourel, M. H. Long, and M. F. Pickles, eds., *Yorkshire Boundaries* (Leeds, UK, 1993).

71. R. Braverman, *Plots and Counterplots. Sexual Politics and the Body Politic in English Literature, 1660–1730* (Cambridge, 1993).

72. R. A. Houston, *Social Change in the Age of Enlightenment, Edinburgh 1660–1750* (Oxford, 1994).

10

Conclusions

THE GEOGRAPHIES OF the past have many aspects. There is the geography of the time, the geography of the time of which people were aware, their understanding of geography, subsequent understandings of geography, subsequent understandings of their geography, and the current position for both. Inevitably, there are many overlaps, as well as ongoing permutations; and any precise typology of the geographies of the past would be misleading, not least as it could not capture the varied and shifting perceptions of realities that are so significant. The range of geographies is significant because it ensures that, at a time when Britain was changing, both internally and externally, so there were (and are) a number of ways in which this change and its impacts can be assessed. That, indeed, not only reflects, but also sustains, the range of geographies. There were educational purposes for geographical works,[1] and also the general reader, the latter appealed to in the prefaces of geographical works.

The overall reality, as far as contemporaries were concerned in eighteenth-century Britain in viewing the world, was one of dynamic concerns and no sense of stability. This process of change in part reflected the flow of new information—for example, about the South Seas. The process also created problems in acquiring sufficient information, as well as raising issues of verification, analysis, and classification.

In spatial understanding, as in other respects, new, like existing, subjects posed questions of political response. In this perspective, politics should be understood in the widest sense, including religious, social, and cultural politics. The focus is usually on partisan party politics, and that is a key element in the molding of the understanding and use of space. At the same time, a discussion of party politics has to include an appreciation that there are these other aspects of politics.

The extent to which party politics shaped responses to spatial issues, and/or gave issues a spatial dimension, invites discussion. That is very much the approach taken with the discussion of foreign policy and military strategy in the first half of the century, and, again, in response to the French Revolution. There are generally held to be Whig views and Tory views on both. In turn, these views were, and are, employed to help define, clarify and distinguish, party identities, and correctly so because foreign policy was more significant politically than is usually now the case. That approach, indeed, has much force and would have been meaningful to contemporaries. The extent of the "rage of parties," and notably in the cultural and intellectual spheres, as well as the conventional political ones, were frequently commented on.

However, there are also problems with this approach. First, there is a tendency to reify what was often a more amorphous, changeable, and fluid set (or, rather, amorphous world) of assumptions, beliefs, and arguments about foreign policy, the wider world, and everything else. If there was a big and conspicuously public riot against a company of French comedians at the Haymarket Theatre in London on October 9, 1738, the bulk of the audience who wanted to see the show were also British. So also with the tendency to politicize garden design. William and Mary certainly brought in "Dutch"-style gardening, with tulips, knot gardens, and so forth. However, the notion that "Whig landscaping" was about taming the wild and imposing the human imprint on the landscape, so that it was subject to humankind, and that "Tory landscaping" was about letting the wild aspects of the landscape remain, is problematic. More generally, this is the case with ready categorization in terms of partisanship.

Second, and as an additional qualification to any reductionist analysis, there were frequently tensions, divisions, and rivalries within party identities or would-be identities. Those between Hanoverian Tories and Jacobites and between government and opposition Whigs were the most obvious, as well as the most significant from the 1710s to 1750s, and could affect the content of geographical works,[2] but these divisions were far from the only ones. In addition, to take simply those categories, each was far from uniform in character or impact.[3] Similar points can be made about religious classifications such as Low Church or Latitudinarian.

This situation continued to pertain as new issues emerged, such as the American War of Independence (1775–83) and the French Revolution (1789). Alongside apparent clarity between radically different views, responses could be complex. Some commentators captured a regional dimension in the responses. In 1792, John Hatsell, clerk to the House of Commons, wrote about the tension between radicalism and loyalism: "I wish every county was like Devonshire—but I fear that in Ireland, Scotland, the manufacturing parts of Yorkshire, and particularly in London, there is a very different spirit rising."[4] Hatsell's mention of "manufacturing" areas reflected an awareness that industrial regions tended to have a particular politics. The government also gathered information that had a regional component. Thus, in 1784, the Irish government produced a secret "Return of the Volunteers" who had become a potentially radical force.[5]

At the same time, alongside what were partisan tensions in aggregate on the national scale, there were those tensions that arose from particular structural relationships within Britain. These relationships could be both means of success and sources of tension, as with the mutually dependent, but unsettled, relationship between the provincial book trade and its dominant London partner.[6] Repeatedly, albeit in different contexts, there are the differing perceptions of "insiders" and "outsiders," the contrast between authority figures, such as, for the nineteenth century, policemen and medical officers, and on the other hand, those under their view.[7]

Given that this degree of complexity was the case in the past, it is apparent that modern classifications of geospatial information, opinion, and usage are sometimes overly confident. This is the case both in classification and in the use, by certain geographers and historians, of material and opinion, once classified, in order to build a bigger superstructure of assessment and of the discussion of the use and "construction" of space. Such a note of caution qualifies some of the literature on historical geography. As with all branches of history and geography, however, most work is subtle on definition and causation, and this note of caution simply returns us to the complexities of the past. It is striking, for example, to see how the emphasis on transnationalism can return us to a practical and conceptual complexity. Thus, Renaud Morieux's *The Channel: England, France, and the Construction of a Maritime Border in the Eighteenth Century* (2016), an impressive recent book, presents the English Channel not as a natural frontier between Britain and France or primarily as a strategic site[8] but as a shared space that mediated Anglo-French relations in both metaphorical and material senses. The Channel thereby becomes a zone of contact and a space of exchange, with fishermen, smugglers, and merchants as transnational actors. At times, the theoretical structure is pushed too far, but, as the work of Morieux and others suggests, the reality of transnationalism, and of transnationalism as a dynamic element, needs to be added to the practice and ideology of nationalism.

So, also, for example with the argument for a clear-cut relationship between empire and geography, an argument that focuses on both ideological and instrumental arguments that can be problematic. The reality of "imperialism," instead, in practice was of a complex, varied, and divided tendency. Moreover, any relationship with geography, however described or defined, was as much bitty as coherent, let alone causative, or obviously causative. To adopt one approach and ignore the other would be mistaken, but to offer both at once does not provide the clarity that so many prefer.

An interest in geography was, at least in part, an aspect of the ideology and practice in Britain of a rational culture.[9] In this, geography was linked with both politeness and practical value and values, including the arts of measurement and an understanding of commerce. The political culture, influenced by a belief in scientific progress fed by new information, was important to a conviction of the possibility of achieving beneficial change. Information contributed greatly to the commercial strength of the British maritime system and, thus, to Britain's self-identity as a successful, free society.[10] The character of, and need for, information encouraged new means of geographical and related analysis, as did intellectual developments.

Chronological developments, and therefore contrasts, played a major role. For example, in the 1780s and 1790s, serious defeats for Britain in the War of American Independence and, later, the French Revolutionary War, and the senses of failure and crisis to which both defeats and outcomes gave rise, led to attempts not only to improve the governmental system but also to scan resources anxiously and to extend the available information. This was the case with Pitt's fiscal reforms and search for trade treaties in the mid-1780s, with the royal commission appointed to inquire into the condition of Crown woods and forests,[11] and was especially so in 1798–1801. Then the government, in the midst of a very difficult war, was concerned about domestic stability. In part, this stability was calibrated with grain prices, and the government sought details on agriculture.[12] There were fears, then, about the danger of a popular uprising, although, in practice and on a long-established pattern,[13] rioting, rather than revolution, was at issue.[14]

The search for information was an aspect of geography as utilitarianism and thus as promoting "an ideology of utility that encouraged the public use of scholarly knowledge for the good of the economic and political state."[15] This ethos and the linked situation, which existed throughout the period, were not unchanging in the resulting methods. Alongside the accumulation of information, there were new methods for its analysis and depiction. This was notably so of the comparison of British and foreign resources by William Playfair (1759–1823) by means of line, circle, and bar graphs and charts. In his *Commercial and Political Atlas: Representing by Stained Copper-Plate Charts, the Exports, Imports, and General Trade of England* (1786), Playfair included a graph showing the exports and imports to, and from, the British possessions in India.[16] This chart was an instance of what Playfair referred to as "lineal arithmetic," an important contribution to the development of "political arithmetic."[17] His *Statistical Breviary: Shewing, on a Principal Entirely New, the Resources of Every State and Kingdom in Europe. . . . To Which Is Added a Similar Exhibition of the Ruling Power of Hindoostan* (1801), which saw the first use of the pie chart and the circle graph, included the proportional representation of territory, revenues, and populations. The circle diagrams were supported by statistical tables, and the impact of British conquest in India and of French conquests in Europe was well represented.[18] This information was at once geographical, statistical, and vivid.

Playfair was not alone. In Scotland in the 1790s, taking forward considerably a 1720–21 church survey on the geography of the parish, Sir John Sinclair, a prominent political arithmetician of his day and a landlord who sought to improve his estates, used the efforts of parish ministers to produce the answers in his *Statistical Account of Scotland* (1791–99). This was an attempt to accumulate information in order to further an economic improvement that was prompted by ideological considerations, as well as by the profits offered by rising demand.[19] Enclosure maps and the information they reflected were another aspect of such depiction and statistics. Sinclair himself was scarcely separate from the world of politics. A Member of Parliament from 1780 to 1796, 1797 to 1806, and 1807 to 1811, he was a believer in the need to use systematic information for the benefit of economic development and also saw it as valuable in international relations. In 1787, at a time of deteriorating relations with Russia, Sinclair wrote to Lord Hawkesbury, the influential president of the Board of Trade, "I am peculiarly anxious that the real state of that court, and the importance of an alliance with it, should be well known in this country."[20]

More generally, the greater use of statistics encouraged more systematic investigation of social consequences and of probabilities, as well as of much else. Jeremy Bentham's *Table of Cases Calling for Relief*, which appeared in the *Annals of Agriculture* for November 1797, provided a basis for distinguishing between the inherently dependent poor and those only in poverty, a long-established distinction. The statistics also encouraged support for a fact-based approach to reforming the Poor Laws and thus looked to the more general use of the national census, which was first organized for 1801.[21] Other key works included Frederick Eden's *The State of the Poor* (1797) and Thomas Malthus's *Essay on Population* (1798).

The revival of "political arithmetic," to use a term of the late seventeenth century in a new context, might appear to have relatively little to do with geography. However, the very collection and presentation of most of the data were by means of geographical units, and statistics helped to make sense of such units and to direct attention to particular ones. New questions were suggested. Moreover, there was a more profound link between geography and statistics in that an acceptance of probability played an important role in the understanding and depiction of both. In the eighteenth century, the age of Jacob and Daniel Bernoulli, innovative Swiss mathematicians, and of Condorcet's related *General Picture of Science* (1783), probability became much more significant across a range of spheres of thought, not least as a normative value and also as a means to gauge data.[22] Geography was affected by this process, and notably as skeptical reason was applied to reports of the outside world, and to the systematization of these reports.

Geography in the eighteenth century, as in other periods, however, lacked any one meaning. The term was used, but books that included *geography* in the title, or the word *geographer*, no more exhausted the topic than was the case for history and historians. The comparison with history is instructive as the term *history*, which was longer established as a major literary theme, was frequently employed in order to describe any narrative, and thus included invented histories, as with the history of Henry Fielding's fictional Tom Jones.[23] Moreover, both geography and history were worked, and reworked, in part to respond to political developments. Changing presentations of John Stow's Elizabethan account of London provide a good example.[24]

Geography (like history) was also an element in fictional works (as is still the case), and, indeed, an important one as a sense of place had to be created for such works to succeed and in order to allow the narrative to proceed.[25] That much of the world was still being explored in the eighteenth century made this process an easier task as it was possible to locate fictional places within the areas being explored or to be explored. An overlap was also apparent between foreigners travelling to Britain or Continental Europe and fictional foreigners commenting on either. The fictional dimension is not the subject of this book, but it needs to be remembered before too coherent and clearly formed an account of geography is offered. In particular, a Whiggish perspective of steadily greater knowledge and improved perception can be questioned. Fiction was also significant in vesting topography with meaning.[26]

There is the question of the meaning of fiction and the generally overly ready separation of fiction from fact, and of the drawing of an overly simple distinction between them. For example, the belief in life elsewhere in the universe can be regarded as an early form of fiction but was also advanced by some astronomers and natural philosophers. For them, the depiction of life was not restricted to the earth, and a belief in God's purpose did not encourage the notion of useless stars and planets. These assumptions encouraged both speculation and astronomical research.[27] Geography as speculation, exploration, and analysis overlapped with astronomy and notably so in the case of mapping, beginning with discussion of the globe. The same overlap was to be true of geology.

Geographical interests were too broad ranging to be readily summarized. Fictional works and factual analyses had in common the element of spatial weight and resonances. Reading these as individual texts can be helpful, but they also have to be understood in terms of a broader engagement in spatial issues.

The relationship between history and geography was varied. For example, the changing history of the period, and the resulting impact in imperial control and geopolitical concerns, led to new geographies that had to be considered. Thus, the British gain, or, rather, conquest, of an Indian-based Oriental empire from the 1750s encouraged comparison with imperial Rome, which was one of the ways of dealing with the idea and reality of a "Greater Britain."[28] This comparison rested on a number of factors. In part, there was a reasonable perception of similarity because, unlike Britain's North American empire, but like that of imperial Rome, the new British Empire in India had no ethnic underpinning and was clearly imperial, and not consensual and representative, which was how the North American empire could be presented. As such, British perception of the empire drew not only on travelers and related sources but also on the classical Greek idea of "barbarian" inferiority and Oriental despotism.[29]

The idea of "barbarian" inferiority was particularly applied to Africa. In part, this question of geographical perception in a model of civilizational progress rested on how the British elite liked to see itself. Slavery could be subsumed into a classical model because of the major role of slavery in ancient Greece and Rome. This approach was to be taken over by independent America.

Geography amounted to more than an awareness of spatiality. It was at once heavily descriptive, yet also a form and means of analysis and of identification, both self-identification and that of others. In each form, there was considerable reliance on the culture of print. Indeed, books, notably illustrated books, provided opportunities for compendia of geographical information, and not only in Britain. Due to close intellectual and entrepreneurial links with Britain, the situation in the United Provinces was particularly important. A series of big books was published by the Dutch between 1670 and 1730. A pictorial turn in geography emerges clearly from them[30] as an aspect of geography as benign entertainment and pleasurable use, and to profitable ends. As a consequence of such publications (and also encouraged, as with science,[31] by advertising), greater consumer depth was provided to the interest in information. This synergy helped greatly to increase the attraction, and thus significance, of geography over the eighteenth century. It helped provide an important social and cultural dimension additional to that of the state and its interests. James Hamilton, archdeacon of Ross, in his *Astronomical Introduction to the Study of Geography: Principally Intended for the Use of Schools* (1800), described geography as "an elegant, and highly entertaining science, that opens the mind, and enlightens the understanding."[32] This was similar to the portrayal of history.

The provision of information has to be considered alongside its reception. For the latter, we are very much affected not only by theories that see power as inherently involving a spatial dimension[33] but also by the contentious notion of the "public sphere"[34] and, more particularly, the issues of its social and intellectual placing. In the case of eighteenth-century Britain, society and social trends, especially the role of the "middling orders,"[35] have provided a universal catch-all to describe, and apparently explain, a range of developments and characteristics, from the growth of a consumer society to the ethos of politeness, from the rise of the public political sphere to the arrival of Evangelicalism. This approach, moreover, is linked to notions of exceptionalism.

In the standard account, the culture of print is very much linked to the public sphere and to the middling orders. This approach, however, raises questions about the application of this linkage and concerning the related presentation of the "middling orders." There is also the issue of the understanding of spatiality other than by those able readily to share in the "culture of print" and notably by those of that large part of the population who were illiterate. This criterion, however, did not delimit those who did not express spatiality. Instead, at every level, it was imagination, experience, and speech that were the main forms of thought, interpretation, and discussion. Our understanding of these are limited and, necessarily, suggestive.

Part of our access to these means and forms is through the very "culture of print," although that is indirect in its account of others. Moreover, there are the very conventions of accounts in print. Any emphasis on the role of imagination, experience, and speech encourages us to consider the fictional dimension of geography not as a failed or flawed alternative to the factual one but, rather, as a key mode of developing, expressing, and probing knowledge and views. That some fictional geographies were, self-evidently, fictional to the point of satire, as with Swift's brilliant *Gulliver's Travels*, does not mean that fiction was, or should be, counterpointed with fact.

In practice, the "middling sort" was engaged in, and courted and appropriated to, all sorts of causes. These causes were, and are, best described as "improvement," while understanding that that, in practice, was an ideology and argument as much as a description. The regulation as well as enhancement of space and spaces were important to this "improvement." For example, the *London Evening Post* of February 16, 1762, published a letter accordingly by "Humphry Hint": "I understand there is now a serious intention of putting a speedy and effectual end to an old grievance: I mean the driving cattle about the streets of this metropolis, at a time when they are full of people, passing through them on their necessary and honest occasions. This is one of those reformations, which, as you have more than once observed, we owe to our newspapers." The same issue brought a call for a dog tax to stop the pest of mad dogs, an issue still today.

More particularly, the political developments of 1689–1714 proved crucial to the contentious use of the nation as a key tool in political discourse, and this usage was particularly associated with those engaged in the political system. In this context, the provision of geographical knowledge represented not a voyeuristic interest in the world that was socially inappropriate, as with the satire of Fielding's *The Coffeehouse Politician* in 1730 (see chapter 1), but rather the education of the "middling sort" to take their rightful role in the working of parliamentary monarchy.[36] This social order, and its educational and political underpinnings and consequences, provided a context within which the outer world, both in Britain and abroad, could be viewed, presented, and understood. This process was far more politicized, contentious, and politically significant than that for astronomy but was also more diffuse in its consequences. For example, alongside instability abroad, as well as changes in sensibility, the rise of travel for pleasure in Britain was encouraged by the significance of the "middling sort" and the aspirations created for them in the culture of print.

Travel in Britain became a frequent topic of publications in the late eighteenth century. The travelers included artists who, in turn, created attractive images, notably after 1800, such as those of Thomas Hewitt Williams, author of *Picturesque Excursions in Devonshire* (1801), *A Tour to the North of Devon* (1802), and *Picturesque Excursions in South Devon* (1804).

Traveling in Britain became so common that it was satirized, as in *The Tour of Doctor Syntax: In Search of the Picturesque*.[37]

In his *New Geographical, Historical, and Commercial Grammar* (1770), William Guthrie argued that a "general diffusion of knowledge" in Britain was "one effect of" the "happy constitution of government" that gave "due influence" to "the people." Accordingly, books, Guthrie argued, were adapted to a mass readership. He aimed to include "moral, or political, as well as natural geography," because he thought history and the constitution influential in "geographical performances."[38] Confidence in geography, as an expanding means of, and subject for, knowledge, increased greatly in part helped by the fame of new discoveries. In his *System of Universal Geography* (1790), Thomas Bankes emphasized the recent progress of the subject.[39]

The significance of geography was not a question of its formal or semiformal discussion by geographers but, instead, a matter of its ability to interact with wide-ranging concerns and interests. This has remained the case. It is an approach that does not deny the reality of particular geographical facts: iron was produced in Shropshire, but not in Berkshire, in the eighteenth century, and this was due to opportunity in the most basic sense that iron deposits were not present in Berkshire. However, alongside facts, the central role of perception in establishing and ordering reality, experience, *and* imagination was such that part of the emphasis in the discussion of geography should be on such perception and on its capacity and use to address these concerns and interests. In this and other respects, historical skills in analysis are important. Historical geography should be a shared task of historians and geographers and not one simply left to the latter.

Notes

1. R. Mayhew, "Geography in Eighteenth-Century British Education," *Paedogogica Historica* 34 (1998): 731–69.

2. M. Ogborn, "*Geographia*'s Pen: Writing, Geography, and the Arts of Commerce, 1660–1760," *Journal of Historical Geography* 30 (2004): 311.

3. J. Black, "Foreign Policy and the Tory World in the Eighteenth Century," in J. Black, ed. *The Tory World: Deep History and the Tory Theme in British Foreign Policy, 1679–2014* (Farnham, UK, 2015), 33–68.

4. Hatsell to John Ley, November 28, 1792, Exeter, Devon CRO, 63/2/11/1/53.

5. J. Kelly, "A Secret Return of the Volunteers of Ireland in 1784," *Irish Historical Studies* 26 (1989): 268–92.

6. J. Feather, *The Provincial Book Trade in Eighteenth-Century England* (Cambridge, 1985).

7. R. Dennis, *English Industrial Cities of the Nineteenth Century: A Social Geography* (Cambridge, 1984), 11.

8. P. Crimmin, "The Channel's Strategic Significance: Invasion Threat, Line of Defence, Prison Wall, Escape Route," *Studies on Voltaire and the Eighteenth Century* 292 (1991): 67–79. On 78–79, however, Crimmin notes the cooperation of sailors and fishermen.

9. P. Elliot, *Enlightenment, Modernity, and Science: Geographies of Scientific Culture in Georgian England* (London, 2010).

10. D. Armitage, *The Ideological Origins of the British Empire* (Cambridge, 2000).

11. R. Grant, *The Royal Forests of England* (Stroud, UK, 1991), 205–10.

12. W. Minchinton, "Agricultural Returns and the Government during the Napoleonic Wars," *Agricultural History Review* 1 (1953): 29–43.

13. A. Charlesworth and A. Randall, *Markets, Market Culture, and Popular Protest in Eighteenth-Century Britain and Ireland* (Liverpool, 1996).

14. J. Beckett, "Responses to War: Nottingham in the French Revolutionary and Napoleonic Wars, 1793–1815," *Midland History* 22 (1997): 80.

15. L. B. Cormack, "'Good Fences Make Good Neighbors': Geography as Self-Definition in Early Modern England," *ISIS* 82 (1991): 661.

16. H. Wainer and I. Spence, eds., *Playfair's Commercial and Political Atlas and Statistical Breviary* (Cambridge, 2005).

17. H. Playfair, *Lineal Arithmetic: Applied to Shew the Progress of the Commerce and Revenue of England during the Present Century* (London, 1798); J. Hoppit, "Political Arithmetic in Eighteenth-Century England," *Economic History Review* 49 (1996): 516–40.

18. I. Spence, "No Humble Pie: The Origins and Usage of a Statistical Chart," *Journal of Educational and Behavioral Statistics* 30 (2005): 354–56.

19. T. M. Devine and J. R. Young, eds., *Eighteenth Century Scotland: New Perspectives* (Edinburgh, 1999).

20. Sinclair to Hawkesbury, September 22, 1787, BL. Add. 38222 fol. 129.

21. E. Higgs, *Making Sense of the Census* (London, 1989).

22. L. Daston, *Classical Probability in the Enlightenment* (Princeton, NJ, 1988).

23. J. Black, "Ideology, History, Xenophobia, and the World of Print in Eighteenth-Century England," in J. Black and J. Gregory, eds., *Culture, Politics and Society in Britain 1660–1800* (Manchester, 1991), 184–216.

24. J. F. Merritt, ed., *Imagining Early Modern London: Perceptions and Portrayals of the City from Stow to Strype, 1598–1720* (Cambridge, 2001).

25. F. N. Smith, *The Genres of Gulliver's Travels* (Newark, DE, 1990).

26. C. Wall, *The Literary and Cultural Spaces of Restoration London* (Cambridge, 1998).

27. M. J. Crowe, *The Extraterritorial Life Debate 1750–1900: The Idea of a Plurality of Worlds from Kant to Lovell* (Cambridge, 1986).

28. D. Armitage, "Greater Britain: A Useful Category of Historical Analysis?," *American Historical Review* 104 (1999): 427–45.

29. N. B. Dirks, *The Scandal of Empire: India and the Creation of Imperial Britain* (Cambridge, MA, 2006).

30. B. Schmidt, *Inventing Exoticism: Geography, Globalism, and Europe's Early Modern World* (Philadelphia, 2015).

31. J. R. Wigglesworth, *Selling Science in the Age of Newton: Advertising and the Commoditization of Knowledge* (Farnham, UK, 2010).

32. J. Hamilton, *Astronomical Introduction* (London, 1800), iii.

33. L. Knopp, "Sexuality and Urban Space," in D. Bell and G. Valentine, eds., *Mapping Desire: Geographies of Sexualities* (London, 1995), 159; J. Duncan and D. Levy, eds., *Place/Culture/Representation* (London, 1993), 329.

34. J. A. Downie, "How Useful to Eighteenth-Century Studies Is the Paradigm of the 'Bourgeois Public Sphere'?" *Literature Compass* 1 (2003): 1–18, and "Public and Private, the Myth of the Bourgeois Public Sphere," in C. Wall, ed., *A Concise Companion to the Restoration and Eighteenth Century* (Oxford, 2005): 58–73.

35. J. Barry and C. W. Brooks, eds., *The Middling Sort of People: Culture, Society, and Politics in England, 1550–1800* (Basingstoke, UK, 1994); P. Lake and S. Pincus, eds., *The Politics of the Public Sphere in Early Modern England* (Manchester, 2007); M. Rospocher, ed., *Beyond the Public Sphere: Opinions, Publics, Spaces in Early Modern Europe* (Berlin, 2012).

36. J. Black, "The Middling Sort of People in the Eighteenth-Century English-Speaking World," *Revue d'Études Anglo-Américaines* 72 (2015): 41–56.

37. P. Howard, "Painters' Preferred Places," *Journal of Historical Geography* 11 (1985): 141–43; S. Shaw, *A Tour to the West of England in 1788* (London, 1789); T. Gray, *Travels in Georgian Devon* (Tiverton, UK, 1999).

38. W. Guthrie, *New Geographical, Historical, and Commercial Grammar* (1770), iii–v.

39. T. Bankes, *System of Universal Geography* (1790), iii.

SELECTED FURTHER READING

Earlier works can be followed up in the bibliographies of these studies. It is also valuable to consult the *Journal of Historical Geography*.

Akerman, J. R., ed. *The Imperial Map: Cartography and the Mastery of Empire*. Chicago, 2009.
Baker, A. R. H. *Geography and History: Bridging the Divide*. Cambridge, 2010.
Bayly, C. A. *Imperial Meridian: The British Empire and the World, 1780–1830*. Harlow, UK, 1989.
Borsay, P. *The English Urban Renaissance: Culture and Society in the Provincial Town, 1660–1770*. Oxford, 1989.
Bowen, M. *Empiricism and Geographical Thought: From Francis Bacon to Alexander von Humboldt*. Cambridge, 1981.
Brückner, M. *The Geographic Revolution in Early America: Maps, Literacy, and National Identity*. Chapel Hill, NC, 2006.
Claydon, T. *Europe and the Making of England, 1660–1760*. Cambridge, 2007.
Drayton, R. *Nature's Government: Science, Imperial Britain, and the "Improvement" of the World*. New Haven, CT, 2000.
Driver, F. *Geography Militant: Cultures of Exploration and Empire*. Oxford, 2001.
Elliot, P. *Enlightenment, Modernity, and Science: Geographies of Scientific Culture in Georgian England*. London, 2010.
Feather, J. *The Provincial Book Trade in Eighteenth-Century England*. Cambridge, 1985.
Fisher, R., and H. Johnston. *From Maps to Metaphors: The Pacific World of George Vancouver*. Vancouver, 1993.
Forster, J.-P. *Eighteenth-Century Geography and Representations of Space in English Fiction and Poetry*. Oxford, 2013.
French, H. *The Middle Sort of People in Provincial England, 1620–1750*. Oxford, 2007.
Gascoigne, J. *Sir Joseph Banks and the English Enlightenment*. Cambridge, 1995.
Gauci, P., ed. *Regulating the British Economy, 1660–1850*. Farnham, UK, 2011.

Gerhold, D. *Carriers and Coachmasters: Trade and Travel before the Turnpikes.* Chichester, UK, 2005.

Godlewska, A. *Geography Unbound: French Geographic Science from Cassini to Humboldt.* Chicago, 1999.

Golinski, J. *British Weather and the Climate of Enlightenment.* Chicago, 2007.

Guest, H. *Empire, Barbarism, and Civilisation: Captain Cook, William Hodges, and the Return to the Pacific.* Cambridge, 2007.

Houston, R. A. *Social Change in the Age of Enlightenment: Edinburgh 1660–1750.* Oxford, 1994.

Hussey, D. *Coastal and River Trade in Pre-Industrial England: Bristol and Its Region, 1680–1730.* Exeter, UK, 2000.

Kain, R. J., and W. Ravenhill, eds. *Historical Atlas of South-West England.* Exeter, UK, 1999.

Kain, R. J., and H. Prince. *Tithe Surveys for Historians.* Chichester, UK, 2000.

Lake, P., and S. Pincus, eds. *The Politics of the Public Sphere in Early Modern England.* Manchester, 2007.

Laxton, P., ed. *The New Nature of Maps: Essays in the History of Cartography by J. B. Harley.* Baltimore, 2001.

Livingstone, D. N., and C. W. J. Withers, eds. *Geography and Enlightenment.* Chicago, 1999.

Marshall, P. J., and G. Williams. *The Great Map of Mankind: British Perceptions of the World in the Age of Enlightenment.* London, 1982.

Mayhew, R. *Enlightenment Geography: The Political Languages of British Geography, 1650–1850.* Basingstoke, UK, 2000.

McCormick, T. *William Petty and the Ambitions of Political Arithmetic.* Oxford, 2009.

McKellar, E. *Landscapes of London: The City, the Country and the Suburbs, 1660–1840.* New Haven, 2013.

Morieux, R. *The Channel: England, France, and the Construction of a Maritime Border in the Eighteenth Century.* Cambridge, 2016.

Neeson, J. M. *Commoners: Common Rights, Enclosure, and Social Change in England, 1700–1820.* Cambridge, 1993.

Ogborn, M. *Spaces of Modernity: London's Geographies, 1680–1780.* New York, 1998.

Pedley, M. S. *The Commerce of Cartography: Making and Marketing Maps in Eighteenth-Century France and England.* Chicago, 2005.

Porter, R. *Enlightenment: Britain and the Creation of the Modern World.* London, 2000.

Quilley, G., and J. Bonehill, eds., *William Hodges, 1744–1797: The Art of Exploration.* New Haven, CT, 2004.

Reinhartz, D. *The Cartographer and the Literati: Herman Moll and His Intellectual Circle.* Lewiston, NY, 1997.

Rennie, N. *Far-Fetched Facts: The Literature of Travel and the Idea of the South Seas.* Oxford, 1995.

Schmidt, B. *Inventing Exoticism: Geography, Globalism, and Europe's Early Modern World.* Philadelphia, 2015.

Sloan, K., ed. *Enlightenment: Discovering the World in the Eighteenth Century.* London, 2003.

Spence, C. *London in the 1690s: A Social Atlas.* London, 2000.
Stock, P., ed. *The Uses of Space in Early Modern History.* New York, 2015.
Wallis, H., ed. *Historians Guide to Early British Maps.* London, 1994.
Wigglesworth, J. R. *Selling Science in the Age of Newton: Advertising and the Commoditization of Knowledge.* Farnham, UK, 2010.
Withers, C. W. J. *Geography, Science and National Identity: Scotland since 1520.* Cambridge, 2001.
Withers, C. W. J. *Placing the Enlightenment: Thinking Geographically about the Age of Reason.* Chicago, 2007.
Wolff, L. *Inventing Eastern Europe: The Map of Civilisation on the Mind of the Enlightenment.* Stanford, CA, 1994.
Wolff, L. *Venice and the Slavs: The Discovery of Dalmatia in the Age of the Enlightenment.* Stanford, CA, 2001.

INDEX

Aberdeen, 255
abolitionism, 114, 205
Account of a Portable Barometer, An (Parker), 36
Account of Russia, as It Was in the Year 1710 (Whitworth), 178
Account of the Discoveries Made in the South Pacific Ocean (Dalrymple), 14
Account of the Pelew Islands (Keate), 210
Account of the Present State of Nova Scotia, An, 203
accuracy: maps, 65–66, 70, 78, 79, 82; naval charting, 219; press, 132–133; surveys, 53, 64
Act of Union of England and Scotland, 50
Adam, Alexander, 2
Adams, John, 51, 87
Aden, 219
Admiralty Island, 87
Adventurer, 94
advertisements, 120, 125, 137–141, 237, 239
Africa, 19–21, 216, 219, 271
African Association, 20
afterlife, 100, 102
Agricola (Tacitus), 163
agriculture, 88–91, 95, 111, 113
Aitutaki, 18
Aix-la-Chapelle, 191
Alaska, 15, 19
Aleppo, 22

Alexandria, 219
Alfred, 160–161
Algiers, 133
Altamaha River, 83
Amadeus, Victor II, 29
American Atlas, The (Sayers and Bennett), 199
American colonies, 44, 82–83, 113 158, 192–193
American War of Independence, 14, 64, 72, 182, 186–187, 195–203, 266, 267
Amersham, 116
Amherst, Jeffrey, 67
amphibious operations. *See* navies/naval power
Amsterdam, 182
analogies, historical, 123–124
Analysis of a General Map of the Middle British Colonies in America (Evans), 82
Ancient/Modern debates, 1–2
André, Peter, 93–94
Anglicization, 160–164
Anglosphere, 123
Angola, 204
animals, foreign, 33
Anjou, Duke of, 156
Anna, Czarina, 173
Annapolis Royal, 87–88
Anson, George, 12, 71
anti-Catholicism, 48, 57, 61, 155–157

Antwerp, 182
Applebee's Original Weekly Journal, 173
apprenticeship records, 255
architecture: classical Roman influence, 163; on maps, 144, 145; public sphere and, 103, 107, 109; public vs. private spaces, 145–146
aristocracy: electoral politics, 114–117; elite betrayal, 153–154; national culture and, 142–143; public sphere, 103–110. See also social class; urban vs. rural
arithmetic, lineal, 268
arithmetic, political, 268, 269
Arrowsmith, Aaron, 53
art, institutionalization of, 162
artillery, 185–186
artists: expeditions, 34; travel narratives and, 273–274; landscape, 106–107; portrait, 107; topographers, 94–95
Ashe, Joseph Windham, 91
Asia, 216
Association for Promoting the Discovery of the Interior Parts of Africa (African Association), 20–21
astrology, 102
Astronomical Introduction to the Study of Geography (Hamilton), 272
astronomy, 37, 136, 270
Atlantic Neptune (Des Barres), 73
Atlantic world, post-American Revolution, 203–205
Atlas Geographus (Moll), 3
Atlas Maritimus and Commercialis (Defoe), 70
Atlas of Victorian Mortality, An, 256
atlases, 68–69, 73, 77, 217, 234, 249, 251, 255
attention, geography of, 165
Atterbury Conspiracy, 256
auctions, 237
Augmentation Returns, 54
Aurangzeb, 211
Australasia, 33, 216
Australia, 14–15, 18
Austria: Britain and, 156, 157, 159, 172, 175; France and, 176, 180, 183, 184; Jacobitism, 172; Spain and, 180
Austro-Turkish wars, 27

authority: of Bible, 37; intellectual, 16; mapping of, 77–96 (*see also* territorialization); power and, 95–96; of print, 142; state, religion and, 159–160; zones of, 55–56
autocracy, 173, 174
autonomy, 5
Ayre's Sunday London Gazette, 19
Ayrshire, 227
Azov, 64

Babbage, Charles, 38, 219
Bach, Johann Christian, 163
Bacon, Francis, 136
Baddesley Clinton, 92
Bahama Gazette, 194
Baker, A. R. H., 257
Baldwin, George, 215
balloons, reconnaissance, 184–185
Baltic, 81
Bank of England, 230
Bankes, Thomas, 274
Bankrupt, The (Foote), 239
Banks, Joseph, 18, 20, 34, 209, 220, 235
Baptist Missionary Society
Barbados Gazette, 194
Barbados Mercury, 194
barbarism/"barbarians," 178, 179–180, 206–208, 271
Barbary pirates, 27
Barebone, Praise-God, 114
Barfleur-La Hougue, 7
Barker, Robert, 136
Barking Level, 93
barometers, 35–36, 37, 220
Baroscopical Discourses (Parker), 36
Barrington, Viscount, 196
Barrow, John, 85
Barthes, Roland, 257
Bartholomew, J. G., 246–247
Bartram, John, 33
Basra, 22
Bass, George, 19
Bass Strait, 19
Batavia Illustrata (Burrish), 133
Bath, 143, 144
Bath, Earl of, 249–250

battle panoramas, 136
Bay of Bengal, 19
Bay of Gibraltar, 200
Bay of Passamaquoddy, 87
Bear Key, 111
Beaufort, Daniel, 218
Beaufort, Dukes of, 117
Beaufort, Francis, 218
Beaumont estate, 90
Beaumont maps, 23
Beck, Harry, 11–12
Bedford, 4th Duke of, 30, 117
Bedford, Dukes of, 109
Beggar's Opera, The (Gay), 10
Belcher, Edward, 218, 220
Belgium, 153, 155, 186, 191
Belgrade, 27
Belt, the, 72
Bengal, 83, 84, 206–207, 212
Bengal Asiatic Society, 212
Bengal Atlas (Rennell), 84
Bennett, John, 199
Bentham, Jeremy, 269
Bergen-op-Zoom, 191
Bering, Vitus, 9
Bering Strait, 9
Berkshire, 107, 111, 274
Berlin, 184
Bermuda Gazette, 194
Bernoulli, Daniel, 269
Bernoulli, Jacob, 269
Berrow's Worcester Journal, 133
Bhutan, 84
Bible, authority of, 37
Bihar, 84, 206
Bingley, William, 166
Birmingham, 120, 134, 140–141, 229, 230
Birmingham Commercial Herald, 124–125
Black, John, 143
Black Sea, 27, 72, 82, 176
Blenheim, Battle of, 80
Bligh, William, 18
blockades, 70
Blue Nile, 19, 20
Board of Longitude, 16
Board of Ordnance, 52, 185
Board of Trade, 86

Bogle, George, 21
Bohemia, 64
Bombay Marine, 17
Bond, James, 255
Bonner, John, 145
Boo, Lee, 210
books, 133–134, 164, 193, 212, 213, 270
Borneo, 220
Boston, 64, 68, 145, 192, 196, 199–200
Boston Gazette, 192
Boston News-Letter, 192
Botany Bay, 14, 18
bourgeois/middle-class, 142–143, 153–154
Boutflower, Thomas, 93
Bowen, Emmanuel, 82–83
Boyer, Abel, 79–80
Boyne, the, Battle of, 80
Braddock, Edward, 65
Braddock expedition, 67
Bradford, Samuel, 144
Brand, Thomas, 152
Brandywine, 68
Brasier, William, 66–67, 91
Brazil, 204
Breckland, 112
Breconshire, 117
Bremen, 48
Brest, 55
Brewer, John, 123
bridges, 51, 165, 233, 234
Bridgewater, 3rd Duke of, 235
Bridgewater Canal, 229, 235
Bristol, 58, 90, 144, 198, 232–233, 238
Bristol, Earls of, 109
Bristol Channel, 232
Bristol Chronicle, 137–138
Bristol Journal, 139
Britain: Anglicization, 160–164; Austria and, 156, 157, 159, 172, 175; Britishness, 50–58; Canada and, 67, 72–73, 86–87, 203–204; Caribbean and, 4, 58, 59, 85, 194; China and, 220; Civil Wars, 50, 52, 57, 58; Continent vs., 157, 160, 165–166; Cuba and, 130; economic development, 239–241; electoral politics, 114–117; Enlightenment, 44; expansionism, 22–23, 58–59, 83–85, 192–195, 271;

explorations by, 6–21; France and, contrast between, 153–154, 155–157, 160–164, 239–240, 241; France and, 49–50, 99, 204–205; France as threat to, 46, 50–51, 153–155, 172, 187, 191–192; French Revolution and, 180–184; historical geography, 245–259; imperialism, 44, 241; India and, 44, 83–85, 211–214, 219, 268, 271; invasion of, 52, 55, 71; Ireland and, 68, 214–215; Italy and, 212; landownership and agriculture, 88–91; London (*see* London); maps and mapping, 77–85; nationalism, 161, 163–164; North America and, 64–66, 82–83, 86, 86–87, 130, 180, 195–205, 250; in Pacific, 58, 209–211; Poland and, 176; population (*see* population); public sphere, 136–146; Russia and, 169–180; sacred sites, 102; Scotland and, 214–215; slave trade/slavery and, 20, 113–114, 194, 197, 205; Spain and, 43, 130, 156, 160–161, 187; trade within, 111; transportation routes, 231–237. *See also* transoceanic world

Britannia (Camden), 10
British Atlantic, 192, 203–205
British Chronicle or Pugh's Hereford Journal, 137, 198
British Empire, 192–195, 271. *See also* transoceanic world
British Isles, 8, 37, 38, 103, 155, 161, 192, 214–215
British Journal, 173, 177
British Museum, 21–22, 135
British Royal Military College, 186
Britishness, 50–58, 161–162, 215
Brockwell, Charles, 133
Brookes, Richard, 2
Brown, Lancelot "Capability," 105, 106
Browne, Richard, 102
Browne, William, 20
Bruce, James, 19–20, 64
Brunswick, 88
Buck's Antiquities, 94
Buell, Abel, 203
Buenos Aires, 218
Bug, the, 72
Bunker Hill, Battle of, 64, 68, 199

bureaucratization, 240
Burges, James Bland, 30
Burke, Edmund, 6, 181
Burney, Fanny, 132
Burrish, Onslow, 133
Bury and Norwich Post: or, Suffolk, Norfolk, and Essex Advertiser, The, 239
Bury St. Edmunds, 109, 144
Bute, 3rd Earl of, 34
Buxton, 143, 233
Byron Island, 87
Byron, George, 108

cadastral maps, 91
Calcutta Gazette, 194
Calcutta, 83, 84–85, 206
Calder River, 226
Callender, George, 199
Calvinism, 49
Cambridge Chronicle and Journal, 138–139, 199, 230
Cambridge University, 247
Camden, William, 10
Campbell, John, 54
Canada: Britain and, 67, 72–73, 86–87, 203–204; expansionism, 23; France and, 66, 67, 70–71, 191; post-American Revolution, 203–205; survey of, 19; War of American Independence and, 202
canals, 106, 112, 231–237
Canning, George, 184
cannon, 185–186
Canterbury, Archbishop Wake of, 253
Cape Anne, 87
Cape Breton Island, 72–73
Cape Colony, 85
Cape Horn, 19
Cape King William, 87
Cape of Good Hope, 19
Cape Orford, 87
Cape St. George, 87
Cape Town Gazette, and African Advertiser, 194
capitalism, 258
capitals, 159
Capper, James, 215–216
Caractacus, 163

Caractacus (Mason), 163
Carattaco (Bach), 163
Cardiff, 229
Cardigan, 198
Cardiganshire, 54, 117
Carew, Richard, 93
Caribbean: British expansionism, 4, 58, 59, 85, 194; expansionism, 22–23; Spanish expansionism, 81, 191; trade routes, 17; transportation links, 234
caricatures, 200, 212
Carlisle, 51, 117
Carlisle, Earls of, 116
Carolina, 72
Cartagena, 4, 191
Carteret, Philip, 14, 87
Carteret's Island, 87
cartography: city mapping, 143–145; in France, 78; geopolitics and, 46; governments and, 70; poststructuralism/postmodernism and, 257–258; wartime and, 82
Cary, John, 234
Castle Howard, 104, 116
Catesby, Mark, 32
Catholicism, 48–50, 57, 102, 153, 155–157, 159–160, 176
Cecilia (Burney), 132
censorship, 124, 192
census, 95, 252, 269
Centinel, 30
Central America, 198
Central Lowlands, 113
central place theory, 255
Chalons-sur-Marne, 177
Champion, 122
Chandos, 2nd Duke of, 115–116
Channel Islands, 50
Channel, The (Morieux), 267
Chapman, John, 93–94
Chapman, Richard, 35
Charles II, 68, 153, 154
Charles III, 124
Charles XII, 28, 127, 169, 172
Chart of the Harbour of Boston, 199
Chart of the island of Chusan, 219–220
Charting Committee, 216

charts/charting: copyright and, 216–217; language and, 70; marine currents, 9; naval power and, 215–220; navigational, 8, 9, 36–37, 73
Charts of the English Channel 217
Chatham Islands, 18
Chelmsford Chronicle, 239
Cherokees, 66
Chesapeake, 196
Chesapeake Bay, 234
Cheshire, 231, 233, 235, 251
Chester, 144, 233
Chesterfield, 4th Earl of, 50–51
Chesterfield House, 109
Chesterfield Inlet, 13
Chichester, 144
China, 34, 211, 220, 241
Chiswick, 143
Chocolate House, 160
choropleth maps, 249
Christianity, 99, 158, 208–209, 212, 213
Christmas Island 15
chronometer, 16, 19
Church Missionary Society
Church of England, 49, 145, 155, 254
Church of Scotland, 155
circulation libraries, 133–134
Citizen of the World, The (Goldsmith), 190
civilization, developmental stages/progression of, 163, 205–208, 271
Claremont, 52, 108
classical Greece, 162
classical Rome, 162–163, 179
classical style, 162
classification, 37
Clegg, John, 78
Clevland, John, 65
Clive, Robert, 83
coal industry, 226–229
Coffee-House Politician, The (Fielding), 126, 273
coffeehouses, 125–126, 160
Coke estate, 90
Coke of Holkham, 90
College for Civil Engineers, 246
College of Arms, 254
Collins, Greenville, 69–70

Colman, George, 142
colonial America. *See* American colonies
colonialism, 107
Colquhoun, Patrick, 24
commerce: consumerism, 237–239; economic development, 239–241; press and, 122–123; regulation, 136; roads and canals, 231–237. *See also* economic issues; trade
Commercial and Political Atlas (Playfair), 268
commercialism, 54, 110
Common Sense, 122
Communication with India by the Isthmus of Suez, The (Baldwin), 215
communications, transportation routes and, 231–237
Compaignes Land, 13
Compleat Geographer, The (Moll), 4
Compleat Surveyor, The (Leybourne), 92
Complete Collection of Voyages and Travels, A (Harris), 82–83
Complete System of the Commercial Geography of England, A (St. Quentin), 25
Complete Tything Table, A, 120
Comprehensive Grammar of Modern Geography and History, A (Pinnock), 2
Compton, 253
Concise System of Geography, A (Devizes), 25
confessional geopolitics, 48–50
confessionalism, 57
Connecticut, 203
Constantinople, 32
Construction of Maps and Globes, The (Green), 70
consumerism, 24, 237–239
Continuation of the History of the Late War in Germany (Lloyd), 31
continuity, 252
Convention of the Pardo, 59
Cook, James, 9, 14–16, 33–34, 87, 210, 218, 220
Cooke, Edward, 11
Copenhagen, 71, 169
Copley, John Singleton, 200
copyright, 216–217

Corbridge, James, 144
Corfu, 27
Corn-Cutter's Journal, 28
Cornwall, 91–92, 93, 183, 185, 233
Cornwall, Duchy of, 92
Cornwall Chronicle, 194
Cornwallis, Charles, 212
Corps of Royal Military Surveyors and Draughtsmen, 185
Correct Plan of the Isle of Man (Fannin), 94
correspondence, 11, 53, 112, 192, 198
cosmopolitanism, 152, 154–155, 161
Cotehele, 91–92
Council of Plantations, 69
counterfactualism, 179
county maps, 93–94
county-level analysis, 249–259
Courier, 182
Course of Lectures in Natural and Experimental Philosophy, Geography and Astronomy, A (Martin), 25
Court of Exchequer, 88
Courtenay family, 116
Covent Garden, 61, 109
Coxe, William, 164
Cozens, John Robert, 95
Craftsman, 122
Crakanthorp, John, 78–79
Crawford, O. G. S., 247
Crete, 27
crime, 104, 140–141
Crimea, 82
critical geopolitics, 258
Cromwell, Oliver, 50, 115
Crop Return for England and Wales, 256
Cruising Voyage Round the World, A (Woodes), 11
Cuba, 4, 130
Culloden, 81–82
cultural geography, 160–164
cultural nationalism, 166
culture: British, 152–166; environmentalism and, 245–246; oral vs. written, 118; political, 123–124; of print, 272; strategic, 256–257
Cumberland Pacquet, 137, 197
Cumberland, 227, 252

Cumbria, 115, 165
Cyprus, 219

Dade, William, 254
Daily Advertiser, 65
Daily Post Boy, 173, 176, 177
Daily Universal Register, 27
Dalrymple, Alexander, 14, 73
Dampier, William, 8, 33–34, 87
Danube River, 80, 176
Danzig, 176
Darby, H. C., 247
Dardanelles, 176
Darfur, 20
Darlington Pamphlet, 32, 126, 239
Darwin, Charles, 220
data sets, 255
Davidson, Robert, 25, 28
Dayes, Edward, 94–95
de Beaurain, Jean, 199
de La Rochefoucauld, Alexandre, 229
de La Rochefoucauld, François, 229
dead reckoning, 19, 36, 71
Dee, John, 43
deep history, 161, 191–192
Defeat of the Floating Batteries at Gibraltar, The (Copley), 200
Defoe, Daniel, 9, 10, 70, 155
Delaware, 200
Delaware Bay, 234
Delineation of the Strata of England and Wales with Part of Scotland (Smith), 38, 234
Denbighshire, 117
Denmark, 72, 169
depictions, 135–136
depoliticization, 12
Dépôt des Cartes, 70
Deptford, 230
Derby, 51, 230
Derby, 6th Earl of, 227
Derbyshire, 92
Derrida, Jacques, 257
Des Barres, Joseph Frederick Wallet, 72–73, 199
Description of all the Seats of the Present Wars of Europe, A (Morden), 80

Description of the Situation, Harbor etc of the City and Port of Philadelphia, A (Jeffrys), 145
Devizes, 111
Devon, 93, 95, 116, 164
Devon, Earls of, 116
Devonshire House, 109
diplomacy, 12, 30–31, 62
directories, 238
Discourse of Winds (Dampier), 8
discovery, 4, 21–22
disease, 4, 208
dissected maps, 23
dissemination: geological knowledge, 37–38; in knowledge process, 4, 6, 9; oral, 118; politics and, 121–123; public presentation, 22
Dissenters, 253
diversity, 109
Dneprovskiy Lima, 72
Dnieper River, 72
Dobbs, Arthur, 13, 209
domestic policy, 121
Dominica, 32
Don Juan (Byron), 108
Donegal County, 102
Donn, Benjamin, 93, 144
Dorchester and Sherborne Journal, 140
Dorset, 106, 116
Dorset, 1st Duke of, 121
Douglas, 94
Dow, Alexander, 212
Drake, John, 165–166
Draughts of the Most Remarkable Fortified Towns of Europe, The (Boyer), 79–80
Drewry's Derby Mercury, 138, 140
Drogheda, 80
Drummond, Archbishop, 253
Dublin, 80, 144, 227
duels, 104
Duke of Gloucester Island, 87
Duke of Portland Island, 87
Duke of York Island, 18
Dundas, Robert, 254
Dunkirk, 26, 71, 191
Durham, 94, 254
Durham County, 142

Dutch Crisis, 29, 199, 214
Dutch maps, 72, 78–79
Dutch Republic, 49
Duty of a Steward to his Land, The (Laurence), 92

Earl Harcourt, 106
earthquakes, 99
East, Gordon, 247–248
East Africa, 218
East Anglia, 89, 90, 113
East Florida, 202
East India Company, 17, 21, 56, 73, 83, 84, 185, 192, 206–207, 211, 215, 238
East Indies, 17, 217
East London, 61
East Offering its Riches to Britannia, The (Roma), 211–212
East Shropshire, 112, 228
East Sussex, 116
economic issues: commercialism, 110; consumerism, 237–239; economic development, 239–241; entrepreneurism, 78–80, 118; landownership and agriculture, 88–91; market economy, 91, 104, 110–112; press reports on, 119–120, 131–132; trade (*see* trade)
Eden, Frederick, 269
Edict of Fontainebleau, 156
Edict of Nantes, 156
Edinburgh, 51, 100, 255, 258
Edinburgh Advertiser, 240
Edward, Charles, 52
Edwards, Jacob, 14
Egypt, 17, 183, 187, 215, 219
electioneering, 108, 121–122
electoral spaces, 114–117
Elements of Geography (Clegg), 78
Elements of Geography, Expressly Designed for the Use of Schools (St. John), 25, 73
Elements of Geography, The (Davidson), 25
Elizabeth, Czarina, 178
Elizabeth I, 43, 169
Ellis, John, 32
Ely House, 109
empiricism, 6

enclosure maps, 88–89, 92, 108, 113, 269
Endeavour, 220
England: agriculture, 111; Britishness and, 50–58; coal production, 227–228; electoral politics, 114–117; Enlightenment, 44; historical geography, 246; home fortification, 104; industry, 230; invasions of, 50–51; map trade, 78–79; maps of, 94, 185; national culture, 161–162; nationalism, 155, 161; population growth, 38, 230; power dynamics, 255; Scotland and, 54, 227
English and French Journal, 125
English Channel, 267
English Pilot, The (Collins), 69–70
Englishman from Paris, An (Murphy), 154
enlightened despotism, 44
Enlightenment, 44, 99, 163, 179, 257
entrepreneurism, 78–80, 118
environmentalism, 105, 245–246
Episcopalians, 155
Erivan, 130
Esher, 108
Essay on Population (Malthus), 269
Essay on the Art of War (Orme), 84
Essay on the Writings and Genius of Shakespeare, An (Montagu), 164
Essex, 58, 93–94, 110–111, 230
estate maps, 91–93
Estonia, 170
Ethiopia, 19, 20
Europe: balance of power, 59, 156, 172, 176–177, 179–180, 180–184, 187; international relations, 44; mapping of, 64; missionaries, 208
European Union, 157
evangelicalism, 158, 208
Evans, Lewis, 65, 82
Evelyn, John, 233
evil, good vs., 99–102, 137
evolution, theory of, 220
Exact Description of the Island and Kingdom of Sicily, An (Macnab), 160
exceptionalism, 161, 272
Excise Crisis, 121
Exclusion Crisis, 154
Exeter, 90, 95, 144, 235

existential geographies, 99–102, 205
Exmoor, 113
exoticism, 213–214
expansionism: American, 202; Americas and, 22–23; British, 22–23, 58–59, 83–85, 192–195, 271; Canadian; disease and, 208; French, 181; India and, 211–214; naming and appropriation, 85–88; Pacific Islands and, 11–14, 17–19, 58, 209–211; religion and, 208–209; Russian, 169–180
exploration, 4, 6–21
Eyes, John, 144

Faden, William, 86–87, 200
fairs/markets, 238, 250
Faithful Account of the Religion and Manners of the Mahometans, A (Pitts), 209
Falkirk, Battle of, 81
Falkland Islands, 12, 93, 204
Falmouth, 194
Fannin, Peter, 94
Federalism, 203
Felix Farley's Bristol Journal, 193
Fens, 232
Fenwick, Thomas, 139
feuds, 117
fiction works, 270–271
fictional geographies, 272–273
Fielding, Henry, 26, 110, 126, 270, 273
Fiennes, Celia, 165
Fiji, 18
financial industry, 239
Finisterre, 220
Finland, 170
First Duke of Dorset Returning to Dover Castle, The (Wootton), 107
First Opium War, 220
First Partition of Poland, 176
First Reform Act of 1832, 114
Firth of Forth, 71
FitzRoy, Robert, 220
Fleurus, Battle of, 184
Flinders, Mathew, 19
floods/flooding, 35–36, 233
Florida, 16–17, 81, 82–83, 86, 130
Flying Post, 122, 128–130, 171–172, 173, 174

Fog's Weekly Journal, 122
foods, 109, 110
Foote, Samuel, 212, 239
foreign correspondents, 193
foreign news reporting, 124–127
foreign policy, 58–59, 127–128, 135, 136, 265
Formosa, 35
Forster, Georg, 16
Fort Duquesne, 65
Fort George, 52
Fort Niagara, 66
Fort Sullivan, 200
Fort William, 67, 85
fortifications, 51, 52, 81, 104
Forty-Five, the, 50, 53, 81
fossils, 37, 38
Foucault, Michel, 257–258
Foundling Hospital in London, 254
"four nations history," 249
Fox, Charles James, 181
Fox, Cyril, 247
France: American Revolution and, 14; as threat to Britain, 46, 50–51, 153–155, 172, 187, 191–192; Austria and, 176, 180, 183, 184; autocracy, 174; Britain and, 49–50, 99, 204–205; Canada and, 66, 67, 70–71, 191; cartography, 70, 78; contrast with Britain, 153–154, 160–164, 239–240, 241; Egypt and, 219; Enlightenment, 44; expansionism, 181; explorations of, 14, 18; French Revolution, 71, 108, 180–184, 204, 205, 217, 265, 266, 267; Germany and, 184; invasions of Britain, 52; Ireland and, 80; map costs, 79; navy/naval power, 7–8, 13, 27, 46, 70, 71, 198, 201, 217; North America and, 64–66, 72–73; Poland and, 176; political geography, 155–157; political stability, 159; press in, 123, 125; Prussia and, 30, 176; Revolutionary Wars, 204; Russia and, 176, 177; Scotland and, 80; Seven Years' War, 161–162; slave trade and, 20, 66, 131, 205; Spain and, 180, 183; Sweden and, 176; tourism, 153; transportation infrastructure, 239–240
francophilia, 153
francophobia, 153

Franklin, Benjamin, 9
fraud, 35
Frederick II, 157
Frederick, Prince of Wales, 108, 161
freemasonry, 102
French Revolution, 71, 108, 180–184, 204, 205, 217, 265, 266, 267
fruits, 32–33
Full and Particular Description of the Highlands of Scotland (Campbell), 54
Funnell, William, 11
furniture, geography as, 37

Gaelic language, 57, 165, 166
Gage, Thomas, 64, 196
Galapagos archipelago, 220
Gallican controversy, 159
Gambia River, 20, 21
Game Act of 1671, 104
Game Laws, 104
gardening, 32–34, 60, 61, 104–105, 106, 109, 163, 265
Garrick, David, 164
Gascoyne, Joel, 92, 93
Gauld, George, 16
Gay, John, 10
Gazette, 131
gazetteers, 2, 95, 111, 117
General and Rare Memorials Pertaining to the Perfect Act of Navigation (Dee), 43
"General Chart" (Halley), 8
General Gazetteer or Compendious Geographical Dictionary, The (Brookes), 2
General Picture of Science, 269
General Survey of British North America, 86–87
General Topography of North America and the West Indies, A (Jefferys), 199
Geneva, 158
Genoa, 158
Gentleman's Magazine, 22, 23, 66, 81, 134
gentrification, 61
Geographical, Historical, Political, Philosophical, and Mechanical Essays (Evans), 65
geographical knowledge: advertising and, 125; education and, 78; exploration and, 6–21; fraudulent, 35; gender bias, 117; geology and, 37–38; governmental stability and, 267–268; hoarding of, 68–69; imperialism and, 43–45; information society, 24–35; misinformation and, 34–35, 174; national power and, 43–45; overview, 1–6; pamphlets and, 135; paradigm of, 4–6; pedagogy, 25; population and information, 38; poststructuralism/postmodernism and, 257–258; reporting discovery, 21–22; social status and, 31, 37; statecraft, 6; subnational geopolitics and, 257; travel experiences, 23–24; types of geographical writing, 23–24; utilitarian role, 25, 38, 69, 85 136–137, 257, 268; wartime need for, 186–187; weather, 35–37
geographical satire, 26–28
Geography behind History, The (East), 247
Geography epitomized (Davidson), 28
geography(ies): agricultural, 88–91; as advertisement, 137; of attention, 165; aspects of, 264–274; as consumerism, 24; cultural, 160–164; deep history and, 191–192; as entertainment, 271–272; existential, 99–102, 205; fictional, 272–273; as furniture, 37; geology and, 270; historical, 245–259; history and, 2, 4–5, 245–259, 270, 271; imperialism and, 267; mental, 175; by omissions, 58; of paranoia, 153–154; physical, 35–37, 47, 174, 231–237, 245–248; political, 114–117, 155–157, 169–180, 214–215; power dynamics and, 235, 257–258; regionalism, 137–141; religious, 102, 213–214; retrospective view of, 245–259; science and, 5; of soft power, 142; statistics and, 269; terminology, 269–270; as utilitarianism, 268
geology, 37–38, 270
geopolitics: cartography and, 46; confessional, 48–50; critical, 258; French revolution, 180–184; geography and, 258; improvement ideology, 187; military and political power, 45–50; North American, 202–203; pamphlets and, 135; post-American Revolution, 203–205; retrospective view of, 245–259;

subnational level, 256–257; terminology, 44–45
George I, 3, 48, 53, 59, 170, 171
George II, 3, 53, 173
George III, 14, 15, 32, 33, 34, 70, 134, 154, 164, 201, 212, 237, 241
Georgia, 82–83, 144–145
Georgics (Virgil), 14
Germany, 29–30, 47–48, 184
Gheriah, 83
Gibbon, Edward, 15–16, 84, 163, 179–180, 206, 207, 210
Gibraltar, 27, 67, 81, 200
Gibson, Edmund, 10
ginseng, 128
Glamorgan, 113
Glamorgan Canal, 229
Glasgow, 235
globalization, 258, 259
globes, 15, 78
Glorious Revolution, 7, 8, 49, 115, 118, 124, 136, 187, 192, 193, 201
Gloucester, 90, 120
Gloucester Journal, 90, 138, 198
Gloucestershire, 232
Goa, 204
Gogerddan, 117
Goldsmith, Oliver, 23, 190
good, evil vs., 99–102, 137
Goodwood, 116
Gordon, Peter, 144–145
Gordon Riots, 61
Gorée, 66, 131
Gothic style, 104, 163
Gower's Island, 87
Grafton, Duke of, 89
Grammar of the Persian Language (Jones), 212
Grand Junction Canal, 235
Grand Magazine of Magazines, 66
Grand Tour, 24, 48, 152–166
Great Awakening, 208
Great Britain's Coasting Pilot (Collins), 69
Great Dismal Swamp, 82
Great Fire of 1666, 60
Great North Road, 233

Great Northern War, 127, 175
Great Yarmouth, 227
Greece, classical, 162, 271
Green, John, 5–6, 70
Greenwich Meridian, 16
Grenville estate, 92
Grinton Moor, 88
Groyne, 55
Grub Street, 23
Guadeloupe, 131
Guangzhou, 217
Guantánamo Bay, 4
Guelph, 88
Guianas, 194
Guildhall Art Gallery, 200–201
Guinea, 204
Gulf Stream, 9
Gulliver's Travels (Swift), 11, 273
Guthrie, William, 23, 133, 134, 274
Gwyn, John, 162

Habitable World Described, The (Trusler), 34–35
Hague, The, 29, 172
Hakluyt, Richard, 43
Halifax, 226, 236
Halley, Edmund, 8–9
Hamilton, Alexander, 21, 22
Hamilton, Charles, 163
Hamilton, James, 272
Handel, 164
Hanover Square, 61
Hanover, 47–48, 53, 70, 88, 122, 128, 161, 170, 171, 172, 265
Hanway, Jonas, 178
Hardy's Island, 87
Harley, J. B., 106
Harrington, Earl of, 154
Harris, James, 29–30, 181–182
Harris, John, 80, 82–83
Harrison, John, 16
Hasselquist, Frederick, 35
Hastings, Warren, 212
Hatsell, John, 266
Havana, 66
Haverfordwest, 198
Hawai'i, 15

Hawkesbury, Lord, 269
Hawley, General, 52
Hay, Michael, 85
Haymarket, 109
Haymarket Theatre, 154, 265
Hearth Tax, 251
Helston, 233
Herring, Archbishop, 253
Herschel, William, 14
Hervey, James, 28
Hesse-Cassel, 115
Hill, Aaron, 161
Hill, John, 186
Hinduism, 212, 213
Historical Account of the British Trade over the Caspian Sea (Hanway), 178
historical analogies, 123–124
Historical and Geographical Description of Formosa, An (Psalmanazar), 35
Historical Atlas of Suffolk, 249
historical atlases, 251, 255, 256
Historical Collection of the Several Voyages in the South Pacific Ocean (Dalrymple), 14
historical geographies, 2, 245–249
history: counterfactualism, 179; deep, 161, 191–192; developmental stages, 205–208; geography and, 2, 4–5, 245–259, 270, 271; terminology, 270
Historical Geography of England before A.D. 1800, An (East), 247–248
Historical Geography of the New Testament (Wells), 3
Historical Maps of England (Pearson), 246
History of America (Robertson), 6, 204
History of Hindustan (Dow), 212
History of the Decline and Fall of the Roman Empire, The (Gibbon), 179, 210
Hitchin, 92
HMS *Alceste* 217
HMS *Beagle*, 220
HMS *Sulphur*, 220
HMS *Victory*, 72
Hodges, William, 210
Holdernesse, 4th Earl of, 64
Holland, 186, 214

Holland, Samuel, 86–87, 199
Holywell, 102
homes, 104, 237–238
Hong Kong, 220
Honiton, 116
Horwood, Richard, 144
Houghton, Daniel, 20–21
House of Hanover, 155
Houston, Rab, 258–259
Howard, Luke, 37
Howe, William, 68
Hudson Bay, 12–13
Hudson River, 234
Hudson's Bay Company, 13
Hughes, William, 246
Huguenots, 109, 153
Hull Advertiser and Exchange Gazette, 239
Hull, 134, 235, 239
human sacrifice, 210
Humphry Clinker (Smollett), 28–29
Hundred Years' War, 183
Hungary, 27, 64
hunting rights, 104
Huntingdonshire, 94
Huske, Ellis, 65
Hutton, James, 37
Hydrography of Sicily, Malta, and the Adjacent Islands (Smyth), 218
Hyp Doctor, 121, 178

Iceland, 34
iconography, 102, 106
Île Saint-Jean, 86–87
Illuminated Atlas of Scripture Geography (Hughes), 246
Illustrations of the Huttonian Theory of the Earth (Hutton), 37
imperialism: American, 258; aspects of, 267; British, 44, 241; commercial, 238; Enlightenment era, 44; environmental changes and, 34; geographical knowledge and, 43–45; geography and; geography and, 5, 267
improvement ideology, 7, 34, 105, 240, 273
India: Britain and, 44, 83–85, 204, 211–214, 219, 268, 271; expansionism, 22–23;

France and, 191; maps of, 83–85, 211; tea cultivation, 34; trade and, 215
Indian Ocean, 27, 204, 214, 217
Indo-Atlantic World, 204
industrialization: consumerism, 237–239; economic development, 239–241; French Revolution and, 184; historical geographies, 245, 250, 251, 252; ideology and, 241; overview, 226–231; population growth and, 38; roads and canals, 231–237
information society, 24–35
Ingham, George, 92
Ingria, 170
Institute of Chartered Surveyors, 92
instrumentalism, 47, 202, 258, 267
international relations: geopolitics, 45–50; ideology and, 181–182; pamphlets and, 135; press reporting, 124–127; statistical information and, 269
interventionism, 48
Inverness, 255
Ionian Islands, 130
Ireland: Britain and, 68, 166, 214–215; Britishness and, 50, 54–58; coal imports, 227; electoral politics, 114–117; France and, 80; French intervention in, 7, 8; home fortification, 104; maps of, 80, 218; nationalism, 218; press in, 124; religious geopolitics, 48; Revolution Settlement, 201–202; Spain and, 156; trade, 111; War of Independence, 50; William III conquest of, 115
Irish Rising, 214
Irish Sea, 227
Irish War of Independence, 50
iron industry, 229
Irwin, Eyles, 22
Islam, 179, 209
Isle of Man, 50, 94, 166
Isles of Scilly, 50
Isthmus of Darien, 68
Italy: artists of, 162
Italy: Britain and, 212
Italy: French Revolution and, 182, 183; maps of, 81; national culture, 162; operas, 10, 154, 160, 164; Peace of Aix-la-Chapelle, 180; scared places, 102; tourism, 153, 158
itineraries, 9–12
Ivan the Terrible, 169

Jacobitism, 50–51, 52, 55, 57, 67, 71, 115, 122, 127, 153, 155, 156, 161, 172, 214, 246, 265
Jamaica, 85, 194
James II, 7, 54, 80, 102, 115, 154, 156, 201
James III, 71, 156
James VIII, 71
Jansenist controversy, 159
Jarry, François, 186
Jefferson, Thomas, 105, 113, 163, 229
Jefferys, Thomas, 144, 145, 199
Johnson, Samuel, 82, 207
Jones, William, 212–213
Joseph II, 16
Joseph Yorke, 30
Journey through Russia into Persia (Spillman), 178
Judaism, 213

Karamania (Smyth), 218
Katmandu, 21
Kazan, 127
Keate, George, 210
Keats, John, 152
Kedleston, 92
Kendal, 134, 236
Kent Education Committee, 251
Kent History Illustrated (Maidstone), 251
Kent, 107, 185, 251
Kent, William, 105
Kentish Post, 140
Kenyon, J. P., 123
Kermadecs, 18
Kett's Rising, 89
Kildare, Earl of, 92
King George the Third's Island, 14
King's Lynn, 227
Kinnoull, 7th Earl of, 32
Kinsale, 80
Kirk, Robert, 100
Kirkpatrick, William, 21
Kjellan, Rudolph, 45

INDEX

Knights of St. John, 127
Knole, 107, 121
knowledge: hoarding of, 68–69, 111; maps as image of, 6; process of, 5–6; social status and, 24–25; superstitious, 100–101. *See also* geographical knowledge
Knowsley Park, 227
Koehler, George Frederick, 176
Koran, 209

Lagos, 13
Lake Champlain, 67, 200
Lake District, 164, 165–166
Lake Nicaragua, 198
Lanarkshire, 235
Lancashire, 58, 111, 227, 231
Land Atlas (Gascoyne), 92
Land Ordinance of 1785, 113
land ownership: electoral politics and, 115–117
Land Surveyor's Club, 92
Land Tax, 91
Land Use Plan of London and Environs (Milne), 95
Land's End, 185
landownership, 88–91, 103–110
landscape gardening, 104–105, 106, 163
language: British Empire and, 192; foreign, knowledge of, 158; Gaelic, 57, 165, 166; national culture and, 165, 166; Welsh, 253
Lanhydrock, 92
Lansdowne, William, 231
Latin America, 219
latitude, 16
Latitudinarian, 266
Laurence, Edward, 92
Lea, Philip, 78
Leeds, 134
Leeds Intelligencer, 101, 194, 198, 199, 230, 240
Leeds Mercury, 140, 195, 198, 199
Leicester Square, 136
Leigh's Island, 87
Letter from a Merchant to a Member of Parliament (Williams), 135
Letters from a Persian in England (Lyttelton), 190

letters. *See* correspondence
Lever, Ashton, 21–22
Leveson-Gower estate, 90
Lewes, 144
Leybourne, William, 92
libraries, 133–134
Licensing Act, 118, 124, 192
Lillo, George, 109
Lincolnshire, 230, 240
Lindley, John, 94
Lindsay, William, 176
Lindsey, 240
lineal arithmetic, 268
Lisbon, 32
literacy, 118, 119
Literary Magazine, 82
literature, 164, 193, 212, 213, 270
Little Wallachia, 27
Liverpool Advertiser, 198
Liverpool Library, 134
Liverpool, 10, 144, 227, 231, 238–239
Livonia, 170
Llandaff, 253
Lloyd, Henry, 31
Lloyd family, 117
Lloyd's Evening Post and British Chronicle, 100–101
logbooks, 36–37
Lombardy, 64
London: earthquakes, 99; as information and publishing hub, 3; maps of, 94–95, 143–144; national culture and, 141–143; provincial press and, 120; regional dynamics, 109–110; spatial matrix of power, 59–61; surveys of, 107–108; transportation routes, 236
London Chronicle, 33, 140, 214
London Evening Post, 128, 132, 273
London Farthing Post, 125
London in the 1690s: A Social Atlas, 255
London Journal, 126, 193
London Magazine, 66
London Merchant, The (Lillo), 109
London Missionary Society, 209
London School of Economics, 247
London Underground map, 11–12
Long Island Sound, 234

INDEX

longitude, 16, 64
Lord Howe Island, 18
Lough Derg, 102
Louis XIV, 80, 155–156, 184
Louis XV, 49
Louisbourg, 191
Low Church, 266
Low Countries, 153, 155, 182, 183
Loyalism, 203–204
Lucca, 158
Lyttelton, George, 190, 253

Maastricht, 191
Macartney, Lord, 85
Macclesfield, 233
Macclesfield, 1st Earl of, 135
Macclesfield, 2nd Earl of, 116–117
Mackenzie, Alexander, 19
Macmillan, 246
Macnab, David, 160
Madagascar, 204
Madden, Samuel, 55
Madeira, 204
Madras, 13, 83, 191
Madrid, 184
magazines, 134
Mahomet, Dean, 206–207
Maidan, 85
Malaya, 214
Malmesbury, 1st Earl of, 181–182
Malta, 127
Malthus, Thomas, 269
Man and His Past (Crawford), 247
Manchester, 51, 134, 235
Manila, 13
manufacturing, 230–231
Map of the British and French Dominions in North America (Mitchell), 65
maps/mapping: agricultural maps, 88–91, 95, 111; Beaumont maps, 23; cadastral maps, 91; choropleth maps, 249; of cities, 143–145; commercial production, 64; copyright and, 216–217; dissected maps, 23; of enclosures, 92, 113, 269; entrepreneurism and, 53, 78–80; estate maps, 91–93; government involvement, 70, 78; itineraries vs., 9–12; mental maps, 62; military and political power and, 52, 61–68; misinformation, 87; naming and appropriation, 85–88; naval engagements and, 201; poststructuralism/postmodernism and, 257–258; production aspects, 79; reconnaissance maps, 64; of roads, 52, 233; route maps, 64; standardization, 70; strategic culture, 29, 256–257; territorialization, 77–85 (*see also* territorialization); tithe maps, 92; travel publications, 23–24; wartime and, 79–82, 184–186, 199–201
Marathas, 83
maritime charting, 53, 68–73
Maritimes, 204
market economy, 91, 104, 110–112
Markham, Archbishop, 254
Marlborough, 116
Marlborough, 1st Duke of, 80
Marlborough, 3rd Duke of, 116–117
Marriage Act, 240
marriage registers, 255
marriage, petty, 56–57
Marriott, Reginald, 88
Martel, Charles, 179
Martin, Benjamin, 25
Maryland, 113
Mason, William, 163
Massachusetts, 87
Mauritius, 219
Mecklenburg, 169–170
Mediterranean Sea, 27, 72, 135, 218
Memoir of a Map of the County of Surrey (Lindley), 94
mental geographies, 175
Menzikof, Prince, 173
mercantilism, 241
Mersey River, 235
Merthyr Tydfil, 229
Messina, 28
Meterological and Miscellaneous Tracts (Capper), 216
Middle East, 183
Middlesex, 110–111
Middleton, Christopher, 13
middling orders, 272–273
Midlands, 113, 232, 235

military operations/power: Britain, 50–58; electoral politics and, 115; failures, 27; French, 177, 183, 184–186; geography and, 265; geopolitics and, 45–50; innovations, 184–186; maps/mapping and, 29–30, 52, 61–68; maritime mapping and, 68–73; role of aristocracy, 115, 153; Russian, 175, 176, 177
militias, 115, 252
Miller, Thomas, 32
Milles, Jeremiah, 95
Milne, Thomas, 95
Milton Abbey, 106
minerology, 38
mining, 112
Minorca, 27, 67, 81, 191
missionaries, 9, 208–209
Mississippi River, 83, 203
Mist, Nathanael, 122
Mist's Weekly Journal, 122
Mitchell, John, 65
modernity, 230
modernization, 184
Molesworth, Viscount of, 127
Moll, Herman, 3–4, 55, 81
Molucca Islands, 217
Molyneux, Richard, 227
monarchies, 159
Monck, George, 51
Monitor, 130
Monkland Canal, 235
Monmouthshire, 164
Monro, George, 176
Montagu, Elizabeth, 164
Montagu Harbor, 87
Montego Bay, 194
Montresor, James, 67
Montresor, John, 67–68
Moor, William, 13
Moore, John 15
morality: abolitionism and, 205; economic development and, 240–241; themes of, 99–102, 137
Morden, Robert, 80
Morea, 27
Moresby, Robert, 219
Morgan, John, 133

Morgan, William, 143
Morgan family, 117
Morieux, Renaud, 267
Morris, Lewis, 54
Moscow, 175, 177, 184
Moseley, Edward, 72
Mozambique, 204
Mughal Empire, 211
Muir, Ramsay, 247
Murphy, Arthur, 154
museums, 21–22, 135
Myanmar, 21

Nabobs, The (Foote), 212
Namier, Lewis, 255
naming and appropriation, 18, 85–88, 218
Nanteos, 117
Napoleon, 177, 183, 184–185, 186, 215
Napoleonic Wars, 71, 185, 217
Narrative of Transactions in Bengal (Vansittart), 212
National Archives, 251
national culture: Britain, 152–166; England, 161–162; geography and, 5, 6, 202; press and, 141–143; social class and, 142–143
National Trust, 107
nationalism: American, 202; British, 161, 163–164; cosmopolitanism vs., 161; cultural, 166; English, 155, 161; Irish, 218; religion and, 49; transnationalism, 266–267
Native Americans, 44, 66, 226
Natural and Political History of Portugal, The (Brockwell), 133
Natural History of Carolina, Florida, and the Bahama Islands, The (Catesby), 32
navies/naval power: blockades, 70, 217; British (*see* navy, British); charting and, 215–220; French, 7–8, 13, 27, 46, 70, 71, 198, 201, 217; maritime mapping, 68–73, 201; mutinies, 61; peacetime and, 12, 17; preparedness of, 46; Russian, 27, 172; Spanish, 46, 71; Turkish, 27; world power, 215–220
navigational charts, 8, 9, 36–37, 73
navy, British: blockades, 70; Caribbean operations, 34; deficiencies, 71–72;

expenditures on, 241; French navy and, 7–8, 13, 185; logbooks, 36–37; loss of ships, 71, 217, 219; maps of engagements, 201; maritime mapping, 68–73; in Mediterranean, 27; pirates and, 208; preparedness, 46; regional role, 17; wartime exploration, 8–9; world power role and, 13–14, 215–220

Necessity of Repentance Asserted, The (Chapman), 35

Nelson, Horatio, 15

Neoclassicism, 107

Netherlands, 30, 47, 64, 153, 155, 180, 182, 191

New Account of the Alterations of the Wind and Weather, A (Parker), 36

New Account of the East Indies, A (Hamilton), 22

New and Accurate Description of all the Direct and Principal Cross Roads in England and Wales (Paterson), 233

New and Correct Map of the United States of North America, A, 203

New and Exact Plan of Gibraltar, A (Moll), 81

New Britain, 18, 87

New College, 91

New England, 191, 196, 200, 203, 250

New France, 67, 72

New General Atlas: Geographical and Historical, A (Senex), 3

New Geographical, Historical and Commercial Grammar (Guthrie), 23, 133, 134, 274

New Geographical and Historical Grammar (Salmon), 2, 133

New Hanover, 87

New Historical Geography of England, A (Darby), 247

New Ireland, 18, 87

New Jersey, 200

New London Spelling Book (Vyse), 142

New Map of Europe, A (Harris), 80

New Map of Georgia (Bowen), 82

New Map of Hindoostan, A (Orme), 84

New Map of South America, 31

New Map of the Cherokee Nation, A, 66

New Moral System of Geography, An, 5

New School Atlas of Modern History (Muir), 247

New Set of Maps Both of Ancient and Present Geography (Wells), 1

New Student's Atlas of English History (Reich), 246

New Town, 258–259

New Voyage and Description of the Isthmus of Panama, A (Wafer), 11

New Voyage Round the World (Dampier), 8

New World, 144–145, 202

New York, 68, 187, 200

New Zealand, 14, 18

Newark and Nottingham Journal, 199

Newcastle Chronicle, 236

Newcastle Courant, 100, 126–127, 193, 199

Newcastle Journal, 110, 138

Newcastle, 51, 143, 144, 195, 227, 230, 239

Newcastle, Duke of, 28–29, 32, 53, 89, 108, 110, 116

Newcomen, Thomas, 228

Newfoundland, 34, 87, 111, 204

newspapers: agents and circulation, 137–141; during wartime, 182–183; English-language, British Empire, 192; French Revolution and, 182–183; geographical writing, 23–24; loyalist, 199; misinformation and criticism, 27–28; Patriot, 195–196, 199; press and, 117–135; provincial, 120, 137–141, 193, 195, 198–199, 233; regionalism and, 137–141; Russian expansionism, 169–180; transportation and, 233

News-Reader's Pocket-Book, or Military Dictionary, The, 131

Newton, 116

Newtonian physics, 46, 47

Nicholson, John, 80

Nicholson, William, 117

Niebuhr, Carsten, 22

Niger River, 19, 21

Nile River, 20

Nine Years' War, 8

Nonconformist tradition, 49, 57, 58, 253

Nootka Sound, 18

Nore, 61

Norfolk, 89, 230, 256

Norfolk House, 109
North, Lord, 201
North Africa, 27, 114
North America: Britain and, 64–66, 82–83, 86, 86–87, 130, 180, 195–205, 250; European power dynamics and, 180; expansionism, 22–23; France and, 64–66, 72–73; maps of, 13, 64–68, 72–73, 82–83, 86–87, 199–201, 203; overland crossing, 19; post-American Revolution, 203–205; slave trade, 114; state boundaries, 113; surveying, 82–83; tourism, 158; transportation links, 234; War of American Independence, 195–203; westward expansion, 113
North Carolina, 82, 113, 209
North-East England, 227–228
North Pacific, 12–13
North Pole, 17
North Sea, 71, 239
North Wales, 54, 102
Northampton Mercury, 130
Northampton, 120
Northamptonshire, 116, 252
Northumberland, 89
Northwest Committee, 13
Northwest Passage, 12–13, 15
Northwich, 233
Norway, 28
Norwich, 58, 143
Nottingham, 143, 230
Nottingham Gazette, 199
Nottinghamshire, 94
Nova Scotia, 72–73, 81
Novaya Zemlya, 69
novelty: French Revolution, 180–184; mapping and war, 184–186; overview, 186–187; press and, 123; Russia's rise, 169–180
Nuneham Courtenay, 106

Observations on Modern Gardening (Whately), 105
Observations on the Cultivation of Waste Lands (Capper), 215–216
Observations on the Passage to India through Egypt (Capper), 215

Observations on the Winds and Monsoons (Capper), 215–216
Observer, 22
Ochakov crisis, 72, 176
Oglethorpe, James, 145
Old England, 65, 110, 120
Old Fort, 85
oligarchy, 123
omission, geography by, 58
On the Modifications of Clouds (Howard), 37
operas, 10, 154, 160, 164
opposition press, 122
Orangists, 30
Ordnance Survey, 29, 78, 93, 185, 216
Orme, Robert, 84
orreries, 136
Osnaburg Island, 87
Ossian, 163, 165
Ostend, 47, 191
Ottery St. Mary in Devon, 93
overland expeditions, 19, 21, 80
Owen, Edward, 131
Owen, William Fitzwilliam, 219
Oxford, 235
Oxford Canal, 235
Oxfordshire, 106, 116–117, 255
Ozanam, Jacques, 81

Pacific: British expansionism, 58, 209–211; explorations of, 11–14, 17–19; Spanish expansionism, 68–69
Pacific Islanders, 209–211
Páez, Jesuit Pedro, 20
Painshill, 163
painters/paintings: Anglicization of, 162; Pacific Islanders and, 210; Shakespeare cult, 164
Palatinate, 156
Palatine refugees, 155
Palermo, 28
Palk Strait, 83
Pallas, P. S., 35
Pamban Channel, 83
Pamela (Richardson), 112
pamphlets, 135
Panama, 68

Panorama rotunda, 136
panoramas, 136
paranoia, 153–154
Paris, 159
Park, Mungo, 19, 21
Parker, Gustavus, 36
Parker, John, 36
parks, 105
Parliamentarianism, 57
Parma, 81
patriotism, 161
patronage, 117
Peace of Aix-la-Chapelle, 180
Peace of Amiens, 85, 184, 192
Peace of Paris, 73, 130, 192
Peace of Utrecht, 58, 81, 130
Peak District, 164
Pearson, Charles, 246
Pelham, Henry, 108
Pelhamite ascendancy, 123
Peninsular War, 186
Pennant, Thomas, 165
Pennsylvania, 113
Penny London Morning Advertiser, 193
Penrhyn Island, 18
Pensacola, 199
Permanent Settlement, 212
Persia, 26, 174, 175
Persian Gulf, 215
Personality of Britain, The (Fox), 247
Peter II, 173
Peter the Great, 27, 64, 169–170, 175, 177, 179, 230
Peterborough, 233
Peterwell, 117
petite guerre, 64
Pettis, Edward, 94
petty marriage, 56
Philadelphia, 68, 192, 200
Philip V, 156
Philippines, 58, 220
Philips' New Historical Atlas for Students, 247
Phillip, Arthur, 18
philosophes, 44
Phipps, Constantine, 17

physical geography, 35–37, 47, 174, 231–237, 245–248
Picturesque Excursions in Devonshire (Williams), 273
picturesque, 106, 164–165
pilgrimages, 102
Pine, John, 144
Pinnock, William, 2
pirates, 27, 204, 208
Pitcairn, 14
Pitt, William the Younger, 29–30, 181
Pitt Island, 18
Pitts, Joseph, 209
place, politics of, 58–59
plague, 130
Plain Dealer, 126
Plan of the City of Coventry, A, 144
Plan of the Town and Fortifications of Gibraltar with the Spanish Lines and Attacks, A, 200
plants, 32–34, 60
Plassey, 83
Plate River, 58
Playfair, John, 37
Playfair, William, 268
Plumb, J. H., 123
pocket globes 15
Poland, 49, 156, 175–176; domestic, 121; economic, 240; foreign 58–59, 127–128, 135, 136, 265; improvement ideology, 105; maps and, 78; peace treaties, 191–192
political arithmetic, 136, 268, 269
political ballads, 135; changing, 214–215; Egypt, 215; France and, 155–157; French Revolution, 180–184; retrospective view of, 245–259; Russian expansionism, 169–180; War of American Independence, 195–203
Political Magazine, 201
Political Recollections relative to Egypt (Baldwin), 215
Political State of Great Britain, The, 170
politics: aspects of, 264–266; Britishness and, 50–58; descriptive vs. prescriptive, 46–47; electoral, 114–117; elite power in, 91; European focus, 22–23; land use, 95–96; landownership and agriculture,

89–90; landscape gardening, 104–105, 106; local dimensions, 252–253; London, 59–61; map depictions and, 65–66, 81; in "new geography," 12; of place, 58–59; political culture, 123–124; politicization, 184; press and, 120–122; publishing and, 266; regional dimension, 250; religion and, 155–157, 159–160, 169–180, 214–215; social elite and, 91, 103–110. *See also* geopolitics
poll data, 251, 255
Pöllnitz, Baron, 160
Poltava, 169
Poor Laws, 269
Pope, Alexander, 60
Pope Benedict XIV, 48
Popery Act, 102
population: distribution, agriculture and, 113; diversity, 109; industrialization and, 230; geographical knowledge and, 38; movements, 111–112
Port Hunter, 18
Port Royal, 99
Porter, Roy, 44
Porto Bello, 191
portraits, 107
Portsmouth and Gosport Gazette and Salisbury Journal, 140
Portugal, 20, 183, 186, 204
positioning, 70–71
Post Boy, 126
Post Man and the Historical Account, 27
post offices, 112
postal services, 233
postmodernism and, 257–258
poststructuralism, 257–258
Powell family, 117
power: authority and, 95–96; balance of, 46–47; forms of, 103–110; geography and, 235, 245, 257–258; ideological dimensions of, 159–160; knowledge as, 5–6; national, 43–45, 85–88; soft, 142
power, spatial matrix: Britishness, 50–58; geopolitics, 45–50; London, 59–61; maps and, 61–68; maritime mapping, 68–73; overview, 43–45; politics of place, 58–59

Pratt, Henry, 80
Present State of North America (Huske), 65
press: American colonies, 192–193; British, empire and, 192–195; colonial, 192–195; commerce and, 122–123; commodity prices, 111; correspondents, foreign, 183; economic development and, 240–241; economic news: 131–132; entrepreneurialism, 118; explorer reporting, 15–16; French Revolution and, 182–183; in wartime, 120, 125–126, 131, 182–183, 198; misinformation and, 239; politics and, 65–66, 121–123; press wars, 121; printing revolution, 118–119; provincial, 120, 137–141, 193, 195, 198–199, 233; role in public sphere, 117–135; Russian expansionism, 169–180; sensational news, 132–133; trade and, 122–123, 131–132; War of American Independence and, 195–203
Preston, 51
Price, William, 145
Priestley riots, 140–141
Prince Edward Island, 86–87
Prince-Bishopric of Salzburg, 156
Princeton, 200
Principal Navigations, Voyages, Traffiques, and Discoveries of the English Nation (Hakluyt), 43
print, culture of, 272
Private Acts, 240
private spaces, 145–146
privateers, 27, 69, 83
probate records, 256
progressivism, 117–118
proprietary libraries, 133–134
proselytizing, 208
Protestant Intelligence, 157
Protestant Interest, 155
Protestantism, 48–50, 56, 57, 155–157, 175–176, 205, 208, 209
proto-Romanticism, 165
Providence, 37, 99
providentialism, 56, 205–206
provincial newspapers/press, 120, 137–141, 193, 195, 198–199, 233
Prussia, 30, 66, 156, 157, 172, 176, 180
Pryse family, 117

Psalmanazar, George, 35
Public Advertiser, 111, 240
public spaces, 145–146
public sphere: aspects of analysis, 272; in Britain, rethinking, 136–146; depictions, 135–136; electoral spaces, 114–117; empiricism and, 6; existential geographies, 99–102; geography and, 5, 6; power, forms of, 103–110; the press and, 117–135; tourism, religion, and culture, debate over, 152–166; transformations, 110–114
Publick Occurrences Foreign and Domestic, 192
publishing: books, 133–134; British county maps, 93–94; chart copyrights and, 216–217; national culture and, 142–143; politics and, 266; printing revolution, 118–119; provincial opinion, 90–91; territorialization and, 77, 79–80
Puritanism, 153

Québec, 66, 87, 218
Queen Anne, 109, 121
Queen Charlotte, 134
Queen Charlotte Island, 87
Queen Mary, 102
questionnaires, 95
Quiberon Bay, 13

racism, 226
radicalism, 61
Radnor, 2nd Earl of, 92
Ralph, James, 23
rambler/wanderer theme, 164
Rape of the Lock, The (Pope), 60
Rape upon Rape or the Coffee-House Politician (Fielding), 26
Raper, George, 18
Raphael, 162
Reading, 120
reconnaissance, 64, 184–185, 186
Red Sea, 17, 22, 27, 215, 219
reductionism, 258, 265
Reflections and Resolutions proper for the Gentlemen of Ireland (Madden), 55

Reflections on the Revolution (Burke), 181
regional dynamics, 57–58, 112, 115, 137–141, 231, 234, 249–250, 266
regionalism, 137
Reich, Emil, 246
Reise um die Welt (Forster), 16
relative command, 186
religion: confessional geopolitics, 48–50; expansionism and, 208–209; geological knowledge and, 37; morality themes, 99–102; national culture and, 152–166; nationalism and, 49; pilgrimages, 102; political geography and, 155–157; political stability and, 159–160; reductionism, 266; religious geography, 213; religious surveys, 253–254; transoceanic world, 208–209
Remarks on the Importance of the Study of Political Pamphlets, 131–132
Renaissance, 162
Rennell, James, 83–84, 211
Repton, Humphry, 106
Repulse Bay, 13
reshaping, 105–106
Restoration of 1660, 115
retrospect, geographies and, 245–249
Revolution Settlement, 49, 50, 57, 115, 123, 201–202
revolutionary ideology, 181–182
Reynolds, Joshua, 162, 210
Rhineland, 81, 180
Richardson, Samuel, 112
Richelieu, Cardinal, 174
Richmond, Dukes of, 29, 89, 116
Ringrose, Basil, 68
Ripon, 233
River Dee, 235
road maps, 52
roads, 106, 112, 165, 231–237
Robertson, C. Grant, 246–247
Robertson, William, 6, 206
Robinson Crusoe (Defoe), 11
Rockingham, Marquesses of, 116
rococo, 161–162
Rocque, John, 92, 107–108, 143–144
Rodger, Nicholas, 259
Rogers, Woodes, 11

Rolt, Richard, 23
Roma, Spiridion, 211
Romantic era, 146, 164
Romanticism, 165, 213
Rome, 158
Rome, classical, 162–163, 179, 271
Rome, imperial, 271
Rooke Island, 87
Roque, Jean de la, 22
Rosen, Adrienne, 255
Rothwell, Thomas, 94
route maps, 64
route surveys, 84
Roy, William, 52
Royal Academy of Arts, 142
Royal Academy, 162
Royal African Company, 7
Royal Astronomical Society, 218
Royal Botanical Gardens at Kew, 34
Royal Engineers, 52, 67, 68, 186
Royal Essequebo and Demerary Gazette, 194
Royal Exchange, 239
Royal Geographical Society, 218
Royal Institution, 34
Royal Military College, 72
royal names, 87–88
Royal Navy. *See* navy, British
Royal Primer, The, 142
Royal Society, 2, 14, 16, 20, 34
Royal United Services Institute, 219
"Rule Britannia," 161
rural, urban vs. *See* urban, rural vs.
Russia: Britain and, 72; expansionism, 169–180; explorations of, 9, 13; France and, 176, 177; political geography, 156–157; in the press, 127, 169–180; Prussia and, 66; Sweden and, 178; Turkey and, 134
Russo-Swedish War of 1741-43, 81
Russo-Turkish War of 1768-74, 134
Ryder, Dudley, 125–126

Sabbatarianism, 241
Sacheverell disturbances, 123
Sackville, George, 64
Sackville family, 107

Safavid Empire, 26
"Safety and Tranquillity—An Excellent New Ballad," 171
Saint Lucia, 130
Saint-Domingue, 204–205
Salamanca, 183
Sale, George, 209
Salisbury and Winchester Journal, 236
Salisbury Journal, 139
Salisbury, 53, 111, 120, 236
Salmon, Thomas, 2, 133
Samarang, 220
San Marino, 158
Sandby, Paul, 94–95
Sandwich Island, 87
Sanskrit, 212–213
Sapperton Tunnel, 237
Sardinia, 128–130
satire, 26–28, 60, 154, 274
Savanna-la-Mer, 194
Savannah, 144–145
Savannah River, 83
Savery, Thomas, 228
Savoy-Piedmont, 29, 49, 156
Sawyer, Robert, 217
Sayers, Robert, 199
scared sites, 102
Scheldt River, 182
science: empire and, 22; geography and, 5; popularization of, 34
Scotland: agriculture in, 113; Britain and, 44, 214–215; Britishness and, 50, 54–58; Calvinism in, 49; census of, 254; coal industry, 227, 229; electoral politics, 114–117; England and, 227; France and, 80; home fortification, 104; maps of, 38; maps of, 81; migration patterns, 255; national culture, 143; press in, 124; Revolution Settlement, 201–202; Spanish invasion of, 55; statistical records, 268–269
Scottish Highlands, 52, 53, 54, 81, 113, 165, 207
Scottish Lowlands, 54
Scottish Missionary Society, 209
Scottish Privy Council, 54
sea charts, 70

Sea of Marmora, 176
Secret Commonwealth, The, 100
sectionalism, 203
security/defense: mapping and, 69; personal, 104; politics and, 58
seeds, 32–34
Selby, 233
Selkirk, Alexander, 11
Senegal River, 20
Senex, John, 3
sensibility, 110
Serbia, 27
Series of Adventures in the Course of a Voyage Up the Red Sea, A (Irwin), 22
sermons, 192, 193
Seven Years' War, 13, 14, 16, 49, 81, 83, 130, 131, 153, 160, 161–162, 182, 186, 187, 199
Severn, 232
Severn River, 240
sexuality, 210
Shah, Nadir, 26
Shakespeare, William, 77
Shakespeare cult, 163–164
Sharp, Bartholomew, 68–69
Sharp, James, 233
Shaw, William, 142
Sheffield, 134, 236
Sheffield Advertiser, 19, 239
Shelburne, 2nd Earl of, 231
Shelley, Percy, 152
Sheraton, Thomas, 142
Sherborn, 90
Sherborne Mercury, 137
Sherlock, Thomas, 53
ships, advances in, 17–18, 71, 219
Showers, Samuel, 84
Shrewsbury, 144
Shrewsbury Chronicle, 240
Shropshire, 274
Sicily, 28, 64, 130
Simpson's Island, 87
Sinclair, John, 268–269
Sirius, 18
Skull, Nicholas, 145
slave narratives, 114
slave trade/slavery: abolitionism, 205; Britain, 20, 113–114, 194, 197, 205; classical models and, 271; debate over, 21, 114; France and, 20, 66, 131, 205; racism and, 226
Smith, Adam, 163, 206, 245
Smith, William, 38, 234
Smith, William Sidney, 176
Smollett, Tobias, 9, 28–29
Smyth, William, 218
Snares, 18
Snowdonia, 164
social class: data sets and, 255; elite, 91, 95–96, 103–110, 153–154; national culture and, 142–143; power and, 258–259; public sphere and, 103–110
Social Darwinism, 174
social exclusion, 61
social status, 24–25, 31, 37
Society for the Encouragement of Arts, Manufactures, and Commerce, 93
Society for the Promotion of Christian Knowledge, 208–209
Society for the Propagation of the Gospel in Foreign Parts, 208–209
Society of Antiquaries, 2
soft power, 142
Somerset Levels, 232
South America, 19, 22–23, 71, 194
South Atlantic, 204
South Carolina, 200
South Essex, 232
South Sea Bubble, 170
South Sea Company, 126
South Seas, 210, 226, 264
South Staffordshire, 228, 230
South Wales, 113, 229, 230
South Yorkshire, 228
South-East England, 229, 234
Southern Continent, 14–15
Southwark, 61
Southwest Pacific, 18
Spain: Britain and, 43, 130, 156, 160–161, 187; in Caribbean, 191; expansionism, 81; explorations of, 9, 11, 12, 14, 18; Florida and, 130, 202; France and, 180, 183; Gibraltar and, 200; Ireland and, 156; knowledge hoarding, 68–69; maps of, 186; navy, 46, 71; New World,

58; political geography, 156; political stability of, 159; Sardinia and, 128–130; Scotland and, 55; Seven Years' War, 161; Sicily and, 28, 130; Spanish Atlantic, 204
spatial matrix. *See* power, spatial matrix
Spaulding Gentlemen's Society, 233
specialization, 237, 238, 240
Spence, Thomas, 108
Spilman, James, 178
Spitalfields, 109
Spithead, 61
Sri Lanka, 19, 83, 214
St. Augustine, 81
St. Christopher Gazette, 194
St. George's Channel, 87
St. George's Chronicle and New Grenada Gazette, 194
St. Helena, 204
St. Ives, 94
St. Jago Intelligencer, 194
St. James, 109
St. James's Chronicle, 32, 48, 132, 164, 237
St. James's Evening Post, 125, 173
St. James's Post, 128
St. James's Street, 160
St. James's Weekly Journal, 128
St. John, Henry, 25
St. John Bullen, Henry, 73
St. Lawrence, 218
St. Lucia Gazette, 194
St. Mary's River, 83
St. Patrick's Purgatory, 102
St. Petersburg, 172, 175, 178
St. Quentin, Dominique de, 25
St. Winefride's well, 102
Staffordshire, 94
Stamp Act, 131, 187, 195, 197
standardization, 64, 70, 120, 142, 240
Stars and Planets the Best Barometers and Truest Interpreters of All Airy Vicissitudes, 35
State of the Poor, The (Eden), 269
statecraft, 6, 136
Statistical Account of Scotland (Sinclair), 268–269
statistical accounts, 268–269
Statistical Breviary (Playfair), 268

steam power, 71, 119, 219, 228–229, 230
Sterne, Laurence, 9
Stockport, 142, 230–231, 239
Stoke-on-Trent, 236
Stourton, 92
Stow, John, 270
Stowe Atlas, 92
Straits of Gibraltar, 200
Straits of Sunda, 217
strategic culture, 256–257
strategy: geopolitics, 45–50; terminology, 44–45
Stratford-on-Avon, 164
Strathclyde, 112
Strict Settlement, 91
Stuart, Charles Edward, 51
subscription libraries, 133–134
succession, civilizational, 163
Suez Canal, 219
Suffolk, 230
Sumatra, 214
Summary of Geography and History, Both Ancient and Modern, A (Adam), 2
Surrey, 94
Survey of Cornwall (Carew), 93
Survey of London, Westminster, and Southwark, 144
Survey of the High Roads from London to Hampton Court (Cary)
surveys/surveying: agricultural, 111; in Britain, 78, 91–95; canal construction, 236; estate mapping, 91–93; in India, 83–85; in Jamaica, 85; in London, 143–144; landownership disputes and, 88–89; military 52–53, 64; naval charting, 215–220; in North America, 82–83; religious, 253–254; route surveys, 84
Sussex, 58, 89, 116, 230
Swaledale, 88
Swansea, 94, 198
Sweden: Baltic provinces, 177; Finland and, 170; France and, 176; Jacobite support, 127, 128, 172; Norway and, 28; Russia and, 169, 170, 171, 178
Swift, Jonathan, 11, 55, 273
Swiss Confederation, 158
Symes, Michael, 21

System of Geography, A (Moll), 3
System of Universal Geography (Bankes), 274
systematization, 6

Table of Cases Calling for Relief (Bentham), 269
Tacitus, 163
Taff Valley, 229
Tahiti Revisited (Hodges), 210
Tahiti, 14, 210
Taiwan, 220
Tasmania, 19
Taunton, 57, 90, 235
Tavistock, 109
tax policy, 191
taxation, newspapers and, 118, 119
Taylor, Alexander, 68
Taylor, Isaac, 144
tea, 34
technology, advances in, 118–119, 228–229, 230
Teesdale, 164
teleological approaches, 117–118
territorialization: landownership and agriculture, 88–91; mapping/maps, 77–85; naming and appropriation, 85–88; overview, 95–96; surveying, 91–95
textile manufacturing, 112
Thames River, 235
Thames-Severn canal, 237
thermometers, 36
Thetford, 112
Thorn massacre, 175–176
Tibet, 21
Ticonderoga, 66
Tierra del Fuego, 71, 220
timekeeping, 70–71
Times, 119, 183
Tiresom, Thomas, 126
Tithe Commission, 254
Tithe Commutation Act, 254
tithe maps, 92
Titley, Walter, 30
topography, 186
Tories, 58–59, 60, 116–117, 121–122, 130, 155, 265

Tour in Wales (Pennant), 165
Tour of Doctor Syntax, The, 274
Tour of Scotland (Pennant), 165
Tour through Ireland, 10
Tour through the Whole Island of Great Britain, A (Defoe), 10
Tour to the North of Devon, A (Williams), 273
tourism, 37, 38, 152–166
town maps, 94–95
Townshend, Viscount, 89
trade: in American colonies, 197; American Revolution and, 196–197; Anglo-Russian trade treaty of 1734, 175; charts and dangerous waters, 219; consumerism and, 237–239; Egypt and, 215; India and, 215; Irish Sea and, 227; mental geographies, 175; press and, 122–123, 131–132; routes, 4, 20
trade winds, 8
transformations, 110–114
Translations of the Royal Society, 8
transnationalism, 266–267
transoceanic world: British press and empire, 192–195; consumerism and, 237–239; developmental stages, 205–208; geography and deep history, 191–192; India, 211–214; naval world power, 215–220; new Atlantics, 203–205; overview, 190, 220–221; Pacific Islanders, 209–211; political geographies, changing, 214–215; politics and, 58–59; religion, 208–209; War of American Independence, 195–203
transportation, 231–237, 251
travel, 4, 23–24, 152–166, 231–237
travel narratives, 9–12, 34–35, 273–274
Travels in Africa, Egypt and Syria (Browne), 20
Travels in India (Hodges), 210
Travels in the Interior Districts of Africa (Park), 21
Travels into Abyssinia (Bruce), 19
Travels into Siberia and Tartary (Pallas), 35
Travels through Arabia (Niebuhr), 22
Treatise of Ancient and Present Geography (Wells), 3

Treatise of Fortification, A (Ozanam), 81
Treaty of Nystad, 170
Treaty of Utrecht, 73
Tredegar, 117
Trelawny, Edward, 85
Trent River, 235
Trenton, 200
Trevor, John, 108
Trevor, Robert, 32
Triennial Act, 136
Trigonometrical Survey, 185
Trinder, Barrie, 255
Trinidad Weekly Courant, 194
triumphalism, 56
True and Exact Map of the Seat of War in Brabant and Flanders, A, 80
Trusler, John, 34–35
Tuathail, Gearóid Ó., 258
Tunbridge Wells, 251
Turkey, 26–27, 72, 134, 175, 177
Turkish Empire, 174
Turner, Cholmley
Turner, Samuel, 21
Turnip Townshend, 90
turnpikes, 112, 233, 237, 240
Tuscany, 81
Twelfth Night (Shakespeare), 77
Tyne River, 51, 227
Tyrawly, 2nd Lord, 32

Ukraine, 169
underworld, 100, 102
Union Journal: or, Halifax Advertiser, The, 49, 99, 131, 236, 238
Union of the Crown, 54
United Provinces, 115, 156, 158, 271
United States, 202. *See also* American colonies; North America
Universal British Directory (Barfoot and Wilke), 238
Universal Geographical Dictionary, A, 66
Universal Geographical Dictionary; or, Grand Gazetteer, A, 66
Universal Journal, 25
Uranus, 14
urban, rural vs.: existential geographies, 101, 136–137; industrialization and, 231;

London and, 59–61, 142–143, 146; politics and, 158–159; power dynamics, 103–110; transformations, 111–112, 113
urban planning, 84
urbanization. *See* industrialization
utilitarian, geographical information as, 25, 38, 69, 85 136–137, 257, 268

Vale of Berkeley, 232
Vale of Glamorgan, 113
Valmy, 30
Vancouver Island, 18
Vancouver, George, 18–19
Vansittart, Henry, 212
vegetables, 32–33
Venice, 27, 158
Verden, 48
Vidal, Alexander, 219
Vienna, 177, 184
View of Edinburgh (Barker), 136
View of the Coasts, Countries, and Islands (Moll), 4
View taken in the bay of Oaite Peha, Otaheite, A (Hodges), 210
Vinegar Hill, 68
Virgil, 14
Virginia, 82, 113
Viterbo, 102
Vitruvius Britannicus (Rocque), 108
Voyage Round the World, A (Funnell), 11
Voyage to Arabia the Happy, A (Roque), 22
Voyage to New Holland (Dampier), 33
Voyage to New Holland (Dampier), 8
Voyage to the South Sea and Round the World, A (Cooke), 11
Voyages and Travels in the Levant, 35
Vyse, Charles, 142

Wadham College, 91
Wafer, Lionel, 11
Wager Bay, 13
waggoners, 68
Wake, Archbishop, 253
Wake, William, 49
Waldegrave, 1st Earl of, 110
Wales: Britishness and, 54, 56–58; coal industry, 227; coal industry, 229, 230;

electoral politics, 117; home fortification, 104; language in, 57; maps of, 94; population, 38, 230; press in, 124; routes to London, 111; sacred sites, 102
Wallis, Samuel, 14
Wallis's Island, 87
Walpole, Horace, 110
Walpole, Robert, 53, 89, 160, 190
Walpole ministry, 123
Walter, John, 27, 119
War Boats of the Island of Otaheite, The (Hodges), 210
War of 1812, 202, 203
War of American Independence, 14, 64, 72, 182, 186–187, 195–203, 266, 267
War of Jenkins' Ear, 12, 43
War of Spanish Succession, 8
War of the Austrian Succession, 81, 12
War of the Bavarian Succession, 180
War of the Polish Succession, 154 175
War of the Spanish Succession, 29, 58, 80, 81
War Office, 251
war(s)/wartime: battle panoramas, 136; charts and, 219–220; explorations during, 8–9; food production during, 89; geographical knowledge and, 187; map popularity and, 79–82; maps/mapping, 199–201; nationhood and, 202; press in, 120, 125–126, 131, 182–183, 198
Warminster, 111
Warrington, 134
Warwick, 143
Washington, George, 200
Waterloo, 177
Watling Street, 251
Watson, John, 49, 131, 226
Wealth of Nations, The (Smith), 206
weather, 35–37, 100, 220
Webber, John, 210
Webster, Alexander, 254
Wedgwood, Josiah, 152, 236
Weekly Jamaica Courant, 194
Weekly Journal: or, The British Gazetteer, 26, 128, 171
Weekly Medley, 28, 126
Weekly Mercury, 192
Weekly Register, 193
Wellington, Duke of, 183, 186
Wells, Edward, 1, 3
Wentworth Wodehouse, 116
Wesley, Charles, 208
Wesley, John, 208
Wessex, 161
West Africa, 66, 131, 218–219
West Country, 58, 90
West-Country Farmer, The, 90
West End, 109, 110
West Florida, 32, 199, 202
West Indies, 194, 201, 208
West Midlands, 229
West Riding, 199, 230
West Sussex, 116
Western and Midland Directory (Bailey), 238
Western Europe, 174–175, 179, 180–184
Western Territory, 113
Westminster, 55
Westminster Journal, 101
Westmorland, 251–252
Wexford County, 68
Wharton, 1st Marquis of, 88
Whately, Thomas, 105
Whigs, 58–59, 60, 116–117, 121–122, 123, 154, 170, 173–174, 181, 190, 265
Whitaker, Jeffrey, 93
Whitefield, George, 208
Whitehall Evening, 135
Whitley, James, 99
Whitworth, Charles, 178
Wide Streets Commission, 144
Wigan, 227
Wilkes, John, 124
Wilkinson, John, 229
Wilkinson, Robert
William III, 51, 54, 80, 115, 155, 156
Williams, Reeve, 135
Williams, Thomas Hewitt, 273
Wilson, Henry, 210
Wilton, 101
Wiltshire, 101, 232
Winchester House, 109
witchcraft, 100–101
Wolfe, James 15
Wolverhampton, 144

Wood, Mark, 85
Woolmer's Exeter and Plymouth Gazette, 140
Wootton, John, 107
Worcester, 51
Worcester Journal, 127, 128, 139, 142
Worcester Post-Man, 135
World Described, The (Moll), 3, 55, 81, 111
Wrigley, E. A., 250
Wye Valley, 164
Wynn family, 117
Wynnstay, 117

xenophobia, 152, 155, 157

Yaghan, 220

Yemen, 22
York Courant, 59
York, 144, 233
York, Archbishop Blackburne of, 143
York, Archbishop Drummond of, 253
York, Archbishop Markham of, 254
York Place, 109
Yorkshire, 88, 107, 111, 116, 230, 233
Yorktown, 212
Young Lady's Geography, The, 134

Zinzendorf, Karl von, 229
zodiac iconography, 102
Zoffany, Johann, 210
Zorndorf, Battle of, 66
Zoroastrianism, 213

JEREMY BLACK is Professor of History at the University of Exeter. He is author of many books, including *A History of Britain: 1945 to Brexit* (IUP), *Other Pasts, Different Presents, Alternative Futures* (IUP), *War and Technology* (IUP), and *Fighting for America: The Struggle for Mastery in North America, 1519–1871* (IUP). Black is a recipient of the Samuel Eliot Morison Prize from the Society for Military History.

www.ingramcontent.com/pod-product-compliance
Lightning Source LLC
Chambersburg PA
CBHW030744230426
43667CB00007B/832